Scar Tissue

HYPERION   New York

ANTHONY KIEDIS
with Larry Sloman

Scar Tissue

Dedicated to Bill and Bob

Contents

Acknowledgments

AK would like to thank:

Larry Ratso Sloman for his constant and heartfelt thought-fulness toward those he engaged to compile this story. Ratso's wily investigative knack was invaluable for the construction of this project, but his consideration for the well-being of others was paramount to the bigger picture. God bless this talented man and his badass style.

Thanks also to bandmates, family members, friends, enemies, lovers, detractors, teachers, troublemakers, and God for making this story come true. I love all of you.

LS would like to thank:

Anthony for his incredible candor, sincerity, memory, and open-heartedness.

Michelle Dupont for the tea, sympathy, and everything else.

David Vigliano, Superagent.

Bob Miller, Leslie Wells, Muriel Tebid, and Elisa Lee at Hyperion.

Antonia Hodgson and Maddie Mogford in England.

Bo Gardner and Vanessa Hadibrata for all their help above and beyond the call.

Blackie Dammett and Peggy Idema for their gracious Midwestern hospitality.

Harry and Sandy Zimmerman and Hope Howard for the L.A. hospitality.

Michael Simmons for the EMS call.

All of AK's friends and colleagues who gave so much of their time to reminisce, especially Flea, John Frusciante, Rick Rubin, Guy O, Louie Mathieu, Sherry Rogers, Pete Weiss, Bob Forrest, Kim Jones, Ione Skye, Carmen Hawk, Jaime Rishar, Yohanna Logan, Heidi Klum, Lindy Goetz, Eric Greenspan, Jack Sherman, Jack Irons, Cliff Martinez, D.H. Peligro, Mark Johnson, Dick Rude, Gage, Brendan Mullen, John Pochna, Keith Barry, Keith Morris, Alan Bashara, Gary Allen, Dave Jerden, Dave Rat, Trip Brown, Tequila Mockingbird, Grandpa Ted, Julie Simmons, Jennifer Korman, Nate Oliver, Donde Bastone, Chris Hoy, Pleasant Gehman, Iris Berry, Sat Hari, and Ava Stander.

Cliff Bernstein, Peter Mensch and Gail Fine at Q-Prime.

Jill Matheson, Akasha Jelani, and Bernadette Fiorella for their amazing transcribing skills.

Langer's for the best pastrami west of Second Ave.

Mitch Blank and Jeff Friedman for the emergency tape repair.

Lucy and Buster for the canine companionship.

And, most of all, my wonderful wife Christy, who kept the home fires burning.

Scar Tissue

Introduction

I'm sitting on the couch in the living room of my house in the Hollywood Hills. It's a clear, crisp January day, and from my vantage point, I can see the beautiful expanse known as the San Fernando Valley. When I was younger, I subscribed to the conventional wisdom, shared by everyone who lived on the Hollywood side of the hills, that the Valley was a place where the losers who couldn't make it in Hollywood went to disappear. But the longer I've lived here, the more I've come to appreciate the Valley as a soulful and quieter side of the Los Angeles experience. Now I can't wait to wake up and look out on those majestic mountain ranges topped with snow.

But the doorbell interrupts my reverie. A few minutes later, a beautiful young woman enters the living room, carrying an exquisite leather case. She opens it and begins to set up her equipment.

Her preparations complete, she dons sterile rubber gloves and then sits next to me on the couch.

Her elegant large glass syringe is handcrafted in Italy. It's attached to a spaghetti-shaped piece of plastic that contains a small micro-filter so no impurities will pass into my bloodstream. The needle is a brand-new, completely sterilized microfine butterfly variant.

Today my friend has misplaced her normal medical tourniquet, so she pulls off her pink fishnet stocking and uses it to tie off my right arm. She dabs at my exposed vein with an alcohol swab, then hits the vein with the needle. My blood comes oozing up into the spaghetti-shaped tube, and then she slowly pushes the contents of the syringe into my bloodstream.

I immediately feel the familiar weight in the center of my chest, so I just lie back and relax. I used to let her inject me four times in one sitting, but now I'm down to two syringes full. After she's refilled the syringe and given me my second shot, she withdraws the needle, opens a sterile cotton swab, and applies pressure to my puncture wound for at least a minute to avoid bruising or marking on my arms. I've never had any tracks from her ministrations. Finally, she takes a little piece of medical tape and attaches the cotton to my arm.

Then we sit and talk about sobriety.

Three years ago, there might have been China White heroin in that syringe. For years and years, I filled syringes and injected myself with cocaine, speed, Black Tar heroin, Persian heroin, and once even LSD. But today I get my injections from my beautiful nurse, whose name is Sat Hari. And the substance that she injects into my bloodstream is ozone, a wonderful-smelling gas that has been used legally in Europe for years to treat everything from strokes to cancer.

I'm taking ozone intravenously because somewhere along the line, I contracted hepatitis C from my drug experimentation. When I found out that I had it, sometime in the early '90s, I immediately researched the topic and found a herbal regimen that would cleanse my liver and eradicate the hepatitis. And it worked. My doctor was shocked when my second blood test came up negative. So the ozone is a preventative step to make sure that pesky hep C virus stays away.

It took years and years of experience and introspection and insight to get to the point where I could stick a needle into my arm to remove toxins from my system as opposed to introducing them. But I don't regret any of my youthful indiscretions. I spent most of my life looking for the quick fix and the deep kick. I shot drugs under freeway off-ramps with Mexican gangbangers and in thousand-dollar-a-day hotel suites. Now I sip vitamin-infused water and seek out wild, as opposed to farm-raised, salmon.

For twenty years now, I've been able to channel my love for music and writing, and tap into the universal slipstream of creativity and spirituality, while writing and performing our own unique sonic stew with my brothers, both present and departed, in the Red Hot Chili Peppers. This is my account of those times, as well as the story of how a kid who was born in Grand Rapids, Michigan, migrated to Hollywood and found more than he could handle at the end of the rainbow. This is my story, scar tissue and all.

1.

"Me, I'm from Michigan"

I'd been shooting coke for three days straight with my Mexican drug dealer, Mario, when I remembered the Arizona show. By then, my band, the Red Hot Chili Peppers, had one album out, and we were about to go to Michigan to record our second album, but first, Lindy, our manager, had booked us a gig in a steakhouse disco in Arizona. The promoter was a fan of ours and he was going to pay us more than we were worth and we all needed the money, so we agreed to play.

Except I was a wreck. I usually was whenever I went downtown and hooked up with Mario. Mario was an amazing character. He was a slender, wiry, and wily Mexican who looked like a slightly larger, stronger version of Gandhi. He wore big glasses, so he didn't look vicious or imposing, but whenever we shot coke or heroin, he'd make his confessions: "I had to hurt somebody. I'm an enforcer for the Mexican mafia. I get these calls and don't even want to know the details, I just do my job, put the person out of commission and get paid." You never knew if anything he said was true.

Mario lived in an old, eight-story brick tenement downtown, sharing his squalid apartment with his ancient mother, who would sit in the corner of this itty-bitty living room, silently watching Mexican soap operas. Every now and then, there'd be outbursts of bickering in Spanish, and I'd ask him if we should be doing drugs there—he had a giant pile of drugs and syringes and spoons and tourniquets right on the kitchen table. "Don't worry. She can't see or hear, she doesn't know what we're doing," he'd reassure me. So I'd shoot speedballs with granny in the next room.

Mario wasn't actually a retail drug dealer, he was a conduit to the wholesalers, so you'd get incredible bang for your buck, but then you'd have to share your drugs with him. Which we were doing that day in his tiny kitchen. Mario's brother had just gotten out of prison and he was right there with us, sitting on the floor and screaming each time that he tried and failed to find a working vein in his leg. It was the first time that I'd ever seen someone who had run out of useful real estate in his arms and was reduced to poking a leg to fix.

We kept this up for days, even panhandling at one point to get some more money for coke. But now it was four-thirty in the morning and I realized we had to play that night. "Okay, time to buy some dope, because I need to drive to Arizona today and I don't feel so good," I decided.

So Mario and I got into my cheesy little hunk-of-junk green Studebaker Lark and drove to a scarier, deeper, darker, less friendly part of the downtown ghetto than we were already in, a street that you just didn't even want to be on, except the prices here were the best. We parked and then walked a few blocks until we got to a run-down old building.

"Trust me, you don't want to go in," Mario told me. "Anything can happen inside there and it's not going to be good, so just give me the money and I'll get the stuff."

Part of me was going, "Jesus Christ, I don't want to get ripped off right now. He hasn't done it before, but I wouldn't put anything past him." But the other, larger part of me just wanted that heroin, so I pulled out the last $40 that I had stashed away and gave it to him and he disappeared into the building.

I'd been up shooting coke for so many days straight that I was hallucinating, in a strange limbo between consciousness and sleep. All I could think was that I really needed him to come out of that building with my drugs. I took off my prized possession, my vintage leather jacket. Years earlier, Flea and I had spent all our money on these matching leather jackets, and this jacket had become like a house to me. It stored my money and my keys and, in a little nifty secret pocket, my syringes.

Now I was so wasted and chilly that I just sat down on the curb and draped my jacket over my chest and shoulders as if it were a blanket.

"Come on, Mario. Come on. You've got to come down now," I chanted my mantra. I envisioned him leaving that building with a dramatically different pep in his step, going from the slumping, downtrodden guy to the skipping, whistle-while-you-work, let's-go-shoot-up guy.

I had just closed my eyes for an instant when I sensed a shadow coming over me. I looked over my shoulder and saw a hulking, big, dirty, crazy-looking Mexican Indian coming at me with a huge, industrial-sized pair of cut-your-head-off giant scissors. He was in mid-stab, so I arched my back as forward as I could to get away from his thrust. But suddenly a skinny, little jack-o'-lantern Mexican bastard jumped in front of me, holding a menacing-looking switchblade.

I made an instantaneous decision that I wasn't going to take it in the back from the big guy; I'd rather take my chances with the scarecrow killer in front of me. This was all happening so fast, but when you're faced with your own death, you go into that slow motion mode where you get the courtesy of the universe expanding time for you. So I jumped up and, with my leather jacket in front of me, charged the skinny guy. I pushed the jacket onto him and smothered his stab, then dropped it and ran out of there like a Roman candle.

I ran and I ran and I didn't stop until I got to where my car was parked, but then I realized that I didn't have the keys. I had no keys, no jacket, no money, no syringes, and worst of all, no drugs. And Mario was not the kind of guy to come looking for me. So I walked back to his house, but nada. Now the sun had come up and we were supposed to leave for Arizona in an hour. I went to a pay phone and found some change and called Lindy.

"Lindy, I'm down on Seventh and Alvarado and I haven't been asleep for a while and my car is here but I have no keys. Can you pick me up on the way to Arizona?"

He was used to these Anthony distress calls, so an hour later, there was our blue van pulling up to the corner, packed with our equipment and the other guys. And one deranged, sad, torn-up, filthy passenger climbed aboard. I immediately got the cold shoulder from the rest of the band, so I just lay down lengthwise under the bench seats, rested my head in the center column between the two front seats, and passed out. Hours later, I woke up drenched in sweat because I was lying on top of the engine and it was at least 115 degrees out. But I felt great. And Flea and I split a tab of LSD and we rocked out that steakhouse.

Most people probably view the act of conception as merely a biological function. But it seems clear to me that on some level, spirits choose their parents, because these potential parents possess certain traits and values that the soon-to-be child needs to assimilate during his or her lifetime. So twenty-three years before I'd wind up on the corner of Seventh and Alvarado, I recognized John Michael Kiedis and Peggy Nobel as two beautiful but troubled people who would be the perfect parents for me. My father's eccentricity and creativity and anti-establishment attitude, coupled with my mother's all-encompassing love and warmth and hardworking consistency, were the optimal balance of traits for me. So, whether through my own volition or not, I was conceived on February 3, 1962, on a horribly cold and snowy night in a tiny house on top of a hill in Grand Rapids, Michigan.

Actually, both of my parents were rebels, each in his or her own way. My dad's family had migrated to Michigan from Lithuania in the early 1900s. Anton Kiedis, my great-grandfather, was a short, stocky, gruff guy who ruled his household with an iron fist. In 1914, my granddad John Alden Kiedis was born, the last of five children. The family then relocated to Grand Rapids, where John went to high school and excelled in track. As a teen, he was an aspiring Bing Crosby–like crooner, and an excellent amateur short story writer. Growing up in the Kiedis household meant that my granddad couldn't drink, smoke cigarettes, or swear. He never had a problem conforming to that strict lifestyle.

Eventually, he met a beautiful woman named Molly Vandenveen, whose heritage was a pastiche of English, Irish, French, and Dutch (and, as we've recently discovered, some Mohican blood, which explains my interest in Native American culture and my identification with Mother Earth). My dad, John Michael Kiedis, was born in Grand Rapids in 1939. Four years later, my grandparents divorced, and my dad went to live with his father, who worked in a factory that produced tanks for the war effort.

After a few years, my granddad remarried, and my dad and his sister had a more conventional home life. But John Alden's tyranny was too much for my dad to bear. Dad had to work in the family businesses (a gas station and then a drive-in burger joint), he couldn't play with his friends, he couldn't stay up late, he couldn't even think of drinking or smoking cigarettes. On top of that, his stepmom, Eileen, was a devout Dutch Reform Christian who made him go to church five times during the week and three times on Sunday, experiences that later embittered him toward organized religion.

By the time he was fourteen, he had run away from home, jumping a bus to Milwaukee, where he spent most of his time sneaking into movies and drinking free beer in the breweries. After a while, he returned to Grand Rapids and entered high school, where he met Scott St. John, a handsome, rakish, ne'er-do-well who introduced my father to a life of petty crime. Hearing the stories of their exploits was always depressing to me, because they were so unsuccessful. One time they went to a nearby beach, stripped down to their boxer shorts in an attempt to blend in, and then stole someone's unattended wallet. But there was at least one witness to the crime, so there was an immediate APB on the beach for two guys in boxer shorts. They got nabbed and had to spend the whole summer in jail.

At the same time that Jack, as he was known then, and Scott were raising hell in Grand Rapids and beyond, Peggy Nobel was leading what looked like a life of conventional propriety. The youngest of a family of five, my mom was the embodiment of a midwestern sweetheart—petite, brunette, and cuter than the dickens. She was very close to her dad, who worked for Michigan Bell. She always described him as a sweetheart of a man—wonderful, loving, kind, and fun. Peggy wasn't as close to her mom, who, although brilliant and independent, followed the conventions of the day and eschewed college for life as an executive secretary, which probably made her a little bitter. And, as the rigid disciplinarian of the family, she often clashed with my mom, whose rebellious attitude took some unconventional routes. My mom was enthralled with black music, listening almost exclusively to James Brown and then Motown. She was also enthralled with the star athlete of her high school class, who just happened to be black—a pretty taboo romance for the Midwest in 1958.

Enter Jack Kiedis, freshly back in Grand Rapids from a jailhouse stay for a burglary in Ohio. His sidekick Scott was stewing in the Kent County jail for a solo caper, so my dad was on his own when he went to a party in East Grand Rapids one night in May of 1960. He was reconnoitering the talent when he looked down a hallway and caught a glimpse of a small, dark-haired angel wearing white-fringed Indian moccasins. Smitten, he jostled people and rushed to the spot where he'd seen her, but she was gone. He spent the rest of the night trying to find her, but was content just to learn her name. A few nights later, Jack showed up on Peggy's porch, dressed up in a sport jacket and pressed jeans, holding a huge bouquet of flowers. She agreed to a date to see a movie. Two months later, after obtaining permission from her parents, the still–seventeen-year-old Peggy married Jack, who was twenty, on the day before her parents' thirty-fifth anniversary. Scott St. John was the best man. Six weeks later, Peggy's dad died from complications of diabetes. A few weeks after that, my dad started cheating on my mom.

By the end of that year, somehow Jack convinced Peggy to let him take their brand-new blue Austin Healy and, along with his friend John Reaser, drive to Hollywood. Reaser wanted to meet Annette Funicello, my dad wanted to be discovered and become a movie star. But most of all, he didn't want to be tied down to my mom. After a few months of misadventures, the two friends settled in San Diego until Jack got word that Peggy was seeing a man who had a monkey back in Grand Rapids. Insanely jealous, he drove 100 mph without stopping and moved back in with my mom, who was just innocent friends with the primate owner. A few weeks later, convinced that he'd made a huge mistake, Jack moved back to California, and for the next year, my parents alternated between being married and being separated and between being in California and being in Michigan. One of those reconciliations led to an arduous bus ride from sunny California to freezing Michigan. The next day, I was conceived.

I was born in St. Mary's Hospital in Grand Rapids, five hours into November 1, 1962, just shy of seven and a half pounds, twenty-one inches long. I was nearly a Halloween baby, but being born on November 1 is even more special to me. In numerology, the number one is such a potent number that to have three ones all in a row is a pretty good place to start your life. My mom wanted to name me after my dad, which would have made me John Kiedis III, but my dad was leaning toward Clark Gable Kiedis or Courage Kiedis. In the end, they settled on Anthony Kiedis, which was an homage to my great-grandfather. But from the start, I was known as Tony.

I left the hospital and joined my dad, my mom, and their dog, Panzer, in their tiny new government-funded home in the country outside of Grand Rapids. But within weeks, my dad started getting wanderlust and cabin fever. In January 1963, my granddad John Kiedis decided to uproot the entire family and move to the warmer climes of Palm Beach, Florida. So he sold his business and packed up the U-Haul and took his wife and six children, plus my mom and me. I don't remember living in Florida, but my mom said it was a pleasant time, once we got out from under the yoke of the abusive patriarch of the Kiedis family. After working at a Laundromat and saving some money, my mom found a little apartment over a liquor store in West Palm Beach, and we moved in. When she got a bill for two months' rent from Grandpa Kiedis, she promptly wrote to him, "I forwarded your bill to your son. I hope you hear from him soon." Mom was working for Honeywell by then, pulling in sixty-five dollars a week, one week's worth of that going toward our rent. For another ten dollars a week, I was in day care. According to my mom, I was a very happy baby.

Meanwhile, my dad was alone in his empty house in the country. Coincidentally, the wife of one of his best friends had left him, so the two buddies decided to move to Europe. Dad just left the house with his car still in the garage, packed up his golf clubs, his typewriter, and the rest of his meager possessions, and took off for Europe on the S.S. *France*. After a wonderful five-day trip that included the conquest of a young French woman married to a Jersey cop, my dad and his friend Tom settled in Paris. By then, Jack had grown his hair long, and he felt simpatico with the beatniks on the Left Bank. They had a pleasant few months, writing poetry and sipping wine in smoke-filled cafés, but they ran out of money. They hitchhiked up to Germany, where they were inducted into the army to get free passage back to the States on a troopship.

They were packed in like sardines, tossed around on turbulent seas, and dodging vomit along with insults like "Hey, Jesus, get a haircut." That ride home was the worst experience of my father's life. Somehow he convinced my mother to let him move in with her again. After her mother died in a tragic car crash, we all moved back to Michigan in late 1963. By now my father was determined to follow the lead of his friend John Reaser and enroll in junior college, ace all his courses, and get a scholarship to a good university and ultimately get a good job and be in a better position to raise a family.

For the next two years, that was exactly what he did. He finished junior college and got many scholarship offers but decided to accept a scholarship from UCLA, go to film school, and realize his dream of living in Los Angeles. In July 1965, when I was three years old, we moved to California. I have some vague recollections of the first apartment that the three of us shared, but in under a year, my parents had once again split up, once again over other women. My mom and I moved into an apartment on Ohio Street, and she found a job as a secretary at a law firm. Even though she was in the straight world, she always maintained that she was a closet hippie. I do remember her taking me to Griffith Park on the weekends to a new form of social expression called Love-Ins. The verdant rolling hills were filled with little groups of people picnicking and stringing love beads and dancing. It was all very festive.

Every few weeks, my routine would be interrupted by a special treat, when my dad came to pick me up and take me on outings. We'd go to the beach and climb down on the rocks, and my dad would put his pocket comb out, and all these crabs would grab it. Then we'd catch starfish. I'd take them home and try to keep them alive in a bucket of water at my house, but they'd soon die and stink up the entire apartment.

In each of our ways, we were all prospering in California,

especially my dad. He was having a creative explosion at UCLA and using me as the focal point of all of his student films. Because he was my father, he had a special way of directing me, and the films all wound up winning competitions. The first film, *A Boy's Expedition,* was a beautiful meditation on a two-and-a-half-year-old who rides his tricycle down the street, does a big slow-motion wipeout, and lands on a dollar bill. For the rest of the film, I go on a wild ride through downtown L.A. going to the movies, buying comic books, taking bus rides, and meeting people, thanks to that buck I found. In the end, it all turns out to be a fantasy sequence, as I pocket the bill and ride off on my tricycle.

My dad's budding career as a director got derailed in 1966, when he ran into a cute young roller-skating carhop who introduced him to pot. When I was about four, my dad and I were on one of our outings, walking down Sunset Strip, when he suddenly stopped and gently blew some pot smoke into my face. We walked a few more blocks, and I was getting more and more excited. Then I stopped and asked, "Dad, am I dreaming?"

"No, you're awake," he said.

"Okay." I shrugged and proceeded to scamper up a traffic light post like a little monkey, feeling slightly altered.

Once my dad got into pot, he started hanging out at the music clubs that were part of the new scene on Sunset Strip. Correspondingly, we saw less and less of him. Each summer my mom and I returned to Grand Rapids to see our relatives. Grandma Molly and her husband, Ted, would take me to Grand Haven Beach, and we'd have a great time. During that stay in the summer of 1967, my mom ran into Scott St. John at Grand Haven. After they spent some time together, he talked her into returning to Michigan with him, in December 1967.

The move wasn't all that traumatic, but Scott coming into the picture was definitely disturbing. There was nothing calming or soothing or comforting about this chaotic character. He was big and tough and swarthy and mean, with black greasy hair. I knew that he worked at a bar and that he got in a lot of fights. One time

I woke up early in the morning and went into my mom's room, and he was lying on the bed. His face was just obliterated, with black eyes and a bloody nose and a split lip and cuts. Blood was everywhere. My mom was putting ice on one part of his head and cleaning up the blood off another part of his face and telling him he should probably go to the hospital. He was just being gruff and gnarly and mean. It was unsettling, knowing that my mom was in love with this guy. I knew he had been a friend to someone in the family, but I didn't realize that he was my dad's best friend.

Scott had a short fuse and a big temper, and he was physically volatile. It was the first time in my life that I had received pretty hard-core spankings. One time I decided that I didn't like the tag in the back of my favorite blue jacket because it was itchy. It was pitch black in my room, but I knew where the scissors were, so I went to cut the tag out, and I ended up cutting a huge hole in the coat. The next day Scott saw the hole, pulled down my pants, and spanked me with the back of a brush.

So it was a rough little patch there. We were living on a very poor side of Grand Rapids, and I entered a new school to finish kindergarten. Suddenly, I stopped caring about learning, and I became a little rogue. I remember walking across the schoolyard and just cursing wildly at age five, stringing together forty curse words in a row, trying to impress my new friends. A teacher overheard me and called a parent/teacher conference, and I started developing the mentality that authority figures were against me.

Another manifestation of my emotional discombobulation was the Slim Jim episode. I was with a friend of mine, and we had no money, so I stole some Slim Jims from a candy store. The owner called my mom. I can't remember my punishment, but shoplifting Slim Jims wasn't the average thing for a six-year-old boy to do in Grand Rapids.

In June 1968, my mom married Scott St. John. I was the ring bearer, and at the reception, I got a purple Stingray bicycle as a gift, which elated me. Now I equated their marriage with a great bicycle that had training wheels.

There was a stretch around this time when I didn't see much of my father, because he had gone to London and become a hippie. But every now and then I'd get packages from England stuffed with T-shirts and love beads. He'd write me long letters and tell me about Jimi Hendrix and Led Zeppelin, and all these different bands he was seeing, and how great the English girls were. It was like my dad was on some kind of psychedelic Disneyland ride off in the world, and I was stuck in Snowy Ass, Nowheresville, U.S.A. I knew that there was this magic out there in the world, and that my father was somehow the key to it. But I also, especially in retrospect, enjoyed growing up in a calmer clime.

That summer I went out to California for a few weeks to see my dad, who had returned from London. He had an apartment on Hildale in West Hollywood, but we spent a lot of time in Topanga Canyon, where his girlfriend Connie had a house. Connie was a fantastic character with a huge shock of flowing red hair, alabaster skin, really beautiful and crazy as could be. Besides Connie, my dad's friends were all these quintessential drug-saturated hippie cowboys. There was David Weaver, a nonstop-talking huge man with shoulder-length hair, a handlebar mustache, and basic California hippie attire (not quite as stylish as my dad). He was a brutal brawler who fought like a wolverine. The last corner of my dad's triangle was Alan Bashara, a former Vietnam vet who sported a huge Afro and a big, bushy mustache. Bashara wasn't a macho, tough-guy hippie; he was more the Georgie Jessel of the group, spewing a mile-a-minute comic shtick. So with David, the cool, tough, fighting guy; my dad, the creative, intellectual, romantic guy; and Alan, the comedian, it was working for all of them, and there was no shortage of women, money, drugs, and fun. It was round-the-clock partying with these guys.

Weaver and Bashara had a house near Connie's, and they ran a rather enormous marijuana business out of Topanga Canyon. When I first got there, I didn't realize all this; all I saw was a lot of people constantly smoking pot. But then I walked into a room, and Weaver was sitting there counting stacks of money. I could tell that the vibe was very serious. I thought, "Okay, I don't even know if I want to be in this room, because they're doing math," so I went into the next room, where there was a small mountain of marijuana on top of huge tarps. Connie would constantly have to come get me and take me out to play in the canyon. It was "Don't go in that room! Don't go in this room! Keep an eye out, make sure no one's coming!" There was always the element of suspense that we were doing something we might get caught for, which would give a kid some worry, but at the same time, it's like, "Hmm, what's going on in there? Why do you guys have so much money? What are all these pretty girls doing everywhere?"

I do remember having a sense of concern for my dad. At one point some friends of his were moving from one house to another, and they filled this big open truck with all their possessions. My dad jumped up and rode on top of the mattress, which was precariously balanced on top of all of the other belongings. We started moving, and we were careening down these canyon roads, and I was looking at my dad barely holding on to the mattress, going, "Dad, don't fall off."

"Oh, don't you worry," he said, but I did. That was the beginning of a theme, because for many years to come, I'd be scared to death for my dad's life.

But I remember having a lot of fun, too. My dad and Connie and Weaver and Bashara would all go to the Corral, a little shit-kicker bar in the middle of Topanga Canyon where Linda Ronstadt and the Eagles and Neil Young played regularly. I'd go with the adults, and I'd be the only kid in the crowd. Everyone would be wasted, drinking and drugging, but I'd be out on the floor, dancing away.

When I got back to Michigan, things hadn't changed much. First grade was pretty uneventful. My mom worked days as a secretary at a law firm, and after school I'd stay with a babysitter. But my life took a decided turn for the better in the fall of 1969, when we moved to Paris Street. We'd been living in a real poor white-trash section of the city, with lots of quadruplexes and shantytowns, but

Paris Street was like something out of a Norman Rockwell painting. Single-family houses and manicured lawns and neat, clean garages. By now Scott was mostly out of the picture, but he had stayed around long enough to impregnate my mother.

Suddenly, I had a trio of beautiful young teenage girls watching me after school. At age seven, I was a little too young to be having crushes, but I adored these girls in a sisterly way, in awe of their beauty and their budding womanhood. I couldn't have been happier to spend time with them, whether it was watching TV or swimming in the local pool or going for walks in the small wildlands in the area. They introduced me to Plaster Creek, which would become my secret stomping grounds for the next five years, a sanctuary from the adult world where my friends and I could disappear into the woods and make boats and catch crawfish and jump off bridges into the water. So it was definitely a huge relief to move to that neighborhood where everything seemed nicer and where flowers grew.

I even liked school. Whereas my previous school seemed dark and dismal and dreary, Brookside Elementary was a pleasant-looking building that had beautiful grounds and athletic fields that ran beside Plaster Creek. I wasn't as JC Penney as the rest of my classmates, because we were on welfare after my mom gave birth to my sister, Julie. So I was wearing whatever hand-me-downs we'd get from the local charitable institutions, with the occasional "Liverpool Rules" T-shirt I'd get from my dad. It didn't really register that we were on welfare until about a year later, when we were at the grocery store and everyone else was paying in cash, but my mom broke out this Monopoly money for the groceries.

Being on welfare bothered her, but I was never fazed by that so-called stigma. Living with a single parent and seeing that all of my friends had mothers and fathers in the same house didn't make me envious. My mom and I were actually having a blast, and when Julie came into the picture, I couldn't have been happier to have a baby sister. I was really protective of her until a few years later, when she became the subject of many of my experiments in torture.

By the third grade, I'd developed real resentment toward the school administration, because if anything went wrong, if anything was stolen, if anything was broken, if a kid was beaten up, they would routinely pull me out of class. I *was* probably responsible for 90 percent of the mayhem, but I quickly became a proficient liar and cheat and scam artist to get out of the majority of the trouble. So I was bitter, and I'd get these ludicrous ideas, such as: "What if we detached the metal gymnastic rings that hang next to the swings, use them like a lasso, and put them right through the picture window of the school?" My best friend, Joe Walters, and I snuck out of the house late one night and did it. And when the authorities came, we scampered like foxes down to Plaster Creek and never got caught. (Many, many years later, I sent Brookside an anonymous money order for the damages.)

My problem with authority figures increased as I got older. I couldn't stand the principals, and they couldn't stand me. I had loved my teachers up until fifth grade. They were all women and kind and gentle, and I think they recognized my interest in learning and my capacity to go beyond the call of scholastic duty at that stage. But by fifth grade, I'd turned on all the teachers, even if they were great.

By now there was no male figure in my life to rein in any of this antisocial behavior. (As if any of the males in my life would have.) When my sister, Julie, was three months old, the police started staking out our house looking for Scott, because he had used some stolen credit cards. One night they came to the door, and my mom sent me to the neighbors while they interrogated her. Weeks later, Scott showed up and came storming into the house in a complete violent rage. He'd found out that someone had called my mom and told her he'd been cheating on her, so he rushed over to the phone in the living room and pulled it out of the wall.

I started shadowing him every inch, because my mom was terrified, and I wasn't having any of that. He started to go into my room to get my phone, but I threw myself in front of him. I don't think I was too successful, but I was prepared to fight him, using all the techniques that he had taught me a few years earlier. My mom finally sent me next door to get the neighbors, but that was clearly the end of his welcome in that house.

Still, about a year later, he attempted to reconcile with my mother. She flew to Chicago with little Julie, but he never showed up at their rendezvous spot—the cops had busted him. She had no money to get back home, but the airlines were nice enough to fly her back free. We went to visit him at a hard-core maximum-security prison, and I found it fascinating but a little disconcerting. On the way home, my mom said, "That's a first, and that's a last," and shortly after that, she divorced him. Lucky for her, she worked for lawyers, so it didn't cost her anything.

Meanwhile, my admiration for my dad was growing exponentially. I couldn't wait for those two weeks every summer when I'd fly to California and be reunited with him. He was still living on the top floor of a duplex house on Hildale. Every morning I'd get up early, but my dad would sleep until about two P.M. after a late night of partying, so I had to find a way to entertain myself for the first half of the day. I'd go around the apartment to see what there was to read, and on one of my searches, I came across his huge collection of *Penthouse* and *Playboy* magazines. I just devoured them. I even read the articles. I had no sense that these were "dirty" magazines or in any way taboo, because he wouldn't come out and say, "Oh God, what are you doing with those?" He'd be more likely to come over, check out what I was looking at, and say, "Isn't that girl incredibly sexy?" He was always willing to treat me like an adult, so he talked openly and freely about the female genitalia and what to expect when I ended up going there.

His bedroom was in the back of the house, next to a tree, and I remember him explaining his early-warning system and escape plan. If the cops ever came for him, he wanted me to stall them at the front door so he could jump out the bedroom window, shimmy down the tree to the top of the garage, go down the house behind the garage to the apartment building, then on to the next street. That was confusing to me at eight years old. "How about if we just don't have cops at the front door?" But he told me that he had been busted for possession of pot a few years earlier, and he'd also been beaten up by cops just for having long hair. All that scared the pants off of me. I certainly didn't want my dad beaten up. All this only reinforced my distaste for authority.

Even though I had concerns about my dad's well-being, those trips to California were the happiest, most carefree, the-world-is-a-beautiful-oyster times I'd ever experienced. I went to my first live music concerts and saw artists like Deep Purple and Rod Stewart. We'd go to see Woody Allen movies and even an R-rated movie or two. And then we'd sit around the house watching all those great psychedelic TV shows like *The Monkees* and *The Banana Splits Adventure Hour,* a show that featured these guys dressed up like big dogs, driving little cars and going on adventures. That's how I looked at life at that time, psychedelic, fun, full of sunshine, everything's good.

Every so often, my dad would make an unscheduled visit to us in Michigan. He'd show up with a lot of heavy suitcases, which he stored in the basement. I realized from my trips to California that he was involved in moving huge truckloads of marijuana, but it never registered that when he came to visit, that was what he was up to. I was just euphoric that he was there. And he couldn't have been more different from every other person in the state of Michigan. Everyone on my block, everyone I'd ever come into contact with there, wore short hair and short-sleeved button-down shirts. My dad would show up in six-inch silver platform snakeskin shoes with rainbows on them, bell-bottom jeans with crazy velvet patchwork all over them, giant belts covered in turquoise, skintight, almost midriff T-shirts with some great emblem on them, and tight little velvet rocker jackets from London. His slightly receding hair was down to his waist, and he had a bushy handlebar mustache and huge sideburns.

My mom didn't exactly embrace my dad as a good friend,

but she recognized how important he was to me, so she was always pleasant and facilitated our communication. He would stay in my room, and when he left, she would sit down with me, and I would write him thank-you notes for whatever presents he'd brought me, and tell him how much fun it was to see him.

By the fifth grade, I had begun to show some entrepreneurial talent. I'd organize the neighborhood kids, and we'd put on shows in my basement. I'd pick out a record, usually by the Partridge Family, and we'd all act out the songs using makeshift instruments like brooms and upside-down laundry tubs. I was always Keith Partridge, and we'd lip-synch and dance around and entertain the other kids who weren't quite capable of partaking in the performance.

Of course, I was always looking to make a buck or two, so one time when we had the use of a friend's basement, I decided that I would charge whatever these kids could come up with, a dime, a nickel, a quarter, to come down to my friend's basement and attend a Partridge Family concert. I set up a big curtain and put a stereo behind it. Then I addressed the crowd: "The Partridge Family are basically shy, and besides, they're much too famous to be in Grand Rapids, so they're going to play a song for you from behind this curtain."

I went behind the curtain and pretended to have a conversation with them. Then I played the record. All the kids in the audience were going, "Are they really back there?"

"Oh, they're there. And they've got someplace else to be, so you guys get running now," I said. I actually got a handful of change out of the deal.

During fifth grade, I also devised a plan to get back at the principals and the school administrators I despised, especially since they had just suspended me for getting my ear pierced. In a school government class one day, the teacher asked, "Who wants to run for class president?"

My hand shot up. "I'll do it!" I said. Then another kid raised his hand. I shot him a look of intimidation, but he kept insisting he wanted to run, so we had a little talk about it after class. I told him that I was going to be the next class president, and if he didn't bow out immediately, he just might get hurt. So I became the president. The principal was dismayed beyond belief. I was now in charge of assemblies, and whenever we had special dignitaries come to the school, I was the one who showed them around.

Sometimes I'd rule by intimidation, and often I'd get into fights in school, but I also had a tender side. Brookside was an experimental school with a special program that integrated blind and deaf and mildly retarded older kids into the regular classes. As much of a hooligan and an intimidator as I was, all of these kids became my friends. And since kids can be evil and torment anyone who's in any way different, these special students took a beating at every recess and lunchtime, so I became their self-imposed protector. I was keeping an eye on the blind girl while the deaf guy was stuttering. And if any of the jerk-offs teased them, I'd sneak up behind the offender with a branch and brain them. I definitely had my own set of morals.

In sixth grade, I started coming home for lunch, and my friends would congregate there. We'd play spin the bottle, and even though we had our own girlfriends, swapping was never a problem. Mostly we just French-kissed; sometimes we'd designate the time that the kiss had to last. I tried to get my girlfriend to take off her training bra and let me feel her up, but she wouldn't give in.

Somewhere late in the sixth grade, I decided that it was time to go live with my dad. My mom was at her wits' end with me, clearly losing all control. When I wasn't given the green light to go live with him, I started to really resent her. One night she sent me to my room, probably for talking back to her. I don't think I even grabbed anything—I went straight out my bedroom window to make my way to the airport, call my father, and figure out a way to get on a plane and go straight to L.A. (None of the flights went straight to L.A., but I didn't know that.) I never even made it as far as the airport. I ended up at the house of one of my mom's friends, a few miles away, and she called up my mom and took me home.

That was the point at which my mother started considering letting me go. A big factor in the final decision was the entrance into her life of Steve Idema. Since Scott St. John had gone to jail, my mother decided that maybe her idea of reforming bad boys wasn't such a good one. Steve was a lawyer who provided legal aid for the impoverished. He had been a VISTA volunteer working with poor people in the Virgin Islands. He was a totally honest, hardworking, compassionate, stand-up fellow with a heart of gold, and my mom was crazy about him. As soon as I realized that he was a good guy and that they loved each other, I began lobbying harder to go to California and live with my dad.

2.

Spider and Son

When I left Michigan at twelve years old in 1974, I told all my friends that I was moving to California to be a movie star. But as soon as I started driving around with my dad in his Healy, singing along to the pop songs on the radio (which I wasn't particularly good at), I announced, "I'm going to be a singer. That's really what I'm going to do." Even though I verbalized it, I didn't think about the vow for years.

I was too busy falling in love with California. For the first time in my life, I felt like this was where I was supposed to be. It was palm trees and Santa Ana winds, and people I liked looking at and talking to, and hours I liked keeping. I was forging a friendship with my dad that was growing by leaps and bounds every day. He thought it was great because he had this young guy who could handle himself, whom all of his friends and girlfriends loved.

I wasn't slowing him down in the slightest; if anything, I was giving him a new prop. So it was working out to our mutual benefit. And I was going through the roof with new experiences.

Some of the most memorable of those new experiences happened right in my dad's little bungalow on Palm Avenue. He lived in one half of a house that had been split into two units. It had a quaint kitchen and wallpaper that was probably from the '30s. There were no bedrooms per se, but my father converted a small add-on storage room into a bedroom for me. It was all the way at the back of the house, and you had to go through a bathroom to get to it. My dad's bedroom was the den, a room that was enclosed by three swinging doors that led to the living room, the kitchen, and the bathroom. It had nice black wallpaper with big flowers, and a window that looked into the side yard, which was teeming with morning glories.

I had been there only a few days when my dad called me into the kitchen. He was sitting at the table with a pretty eighteen-year-old girl he'd been hanging out with that week. "Do you want to smoke a joint?" he asked me.

Back in Michigan, I automatically would have answered no. But being in this new environment made me adventurous. So my dad got out a thick black *American Heritage Dictionary* box. He opened the box, and it was full of weed. Using the lid as a preparation area, he broke off some of the pot, letting the seeds roll down to the bottom of the lid. Then he took out some rolling papers and showed me exactly how to roll a perfectly formed joint. I found the whole ritual fascinating.

Then he lit up the joint and passed it to me. "Be careful, don't take too much. You don't want to cough your lungs out," he counseled.

I took a little drag and then passed the joint back to him. It went around the table a few times, and soon we were all smiling and laughing and feeling really mellow. And then I realized I was high. I loved the sensation. It felt like medicine to soothe the soul and awaken the senses. There was nothing awkward or scary—I didn't feel like I had lost control—in fact, I felt like I was *in* control.

Then my dad handed me an Instamatic camera and said, "I think she wants you to take some pictures of her." I instinctively knew that some form of skin was about to be exposed, so I said to her, "What if we pull up your shirt and I'll take a picture of you?"

"That's a good idea, but I think it might be more artistic if you just had her expose one of her breasts," my dad said. We all concurred. I took some pictures, and no one felt uncomfortable about it.

So my entry into the world of pot smoking was as smooth as silk. The next time I smoked, I was already a pro, rolling the joint with an almost anal precision. But I didn't become fixated on it, even though my father was a daily pot smoker. For me, it was just another unique California experience.

My first priority that fall was to get into a good junior high school. I was supposed to enroll in Bancroft, but when we went to check it out, we saw that the building was in a shady neighborhood and scarred with all sorts of gang graffiti. The place just didn't scream out, "Let's go to school and have fun here." So my dad drove us to Emerson, which was in Westwood. It was a classic California Mediterranean building, with lush lawns and flowering trees and an American flag waving proudly in the breeze. Plus, everywhere I looked, there were these hot little thirteen-year-olds walking around in their tight Ditto jeans.

"Whatever it takes, I want to go here," I said.

What it took was using Sonny Bono's Bel Air address as my home address. Connie had left my dad for Sonny, who had recently split with Cher. But everyone stayed friendly, and I'd met Sonny on my previous visit and he was fine with the deception, so I enrolled.

Now I had to find a way to get to school. If I took a city bus, it was a straight shot, 4.2 miles down Santa Monica Boulevard. The problem was the RTA was on strike. My dad was established in his routine of staying up late, getting up late, being high most of the time, and entertaining women all the time, so he wasn't exactly going to be a soccer mom and drive me to and from school. His solution was to leave a five-dollar bill on the kitchen table for a cab. Getting home would be my project. To facilitate that, he bought me a Black Knight skateboard, which had a wooden deck and clay wheels. So I'd skateboard and hitchhike or walk the four miles home, all the time discovering Westwood and Beverly Hills and West Hollywood.

I went through almost all my first day at Emerson without making a friend. I started getting worried. Everything seemed new and daunting. Coming from a small midwestern school, I wasn't exactly an academic. But at the end of the day, I had a creative arts class, and there was a friend waiting to happen—Shawn, a black kid with bright eyes and the biggest smile. It was one of those times when you march up to somebody and say, "Do you want to be my friend?" "Yeah, I'll be your friend." Boom, you're friends.

Going to Shawn's house was an adventure. His dad was a musician, which was a new one for me, a dad who went out to the garage and practiced music with friends. Shawn's mom was as warm and loving as could be, always welcoming me into the house and offering me some exotic food as an after-school snack. I had come from the most clueless area of the world when it came to cuisine. My culinary world consisted of things like white bread and Velveeta and ground beef. Here they were eating yogurt and drinking a strange substance called kefir. Where I came from, it was Tang and Kool-Aid.

But the education was a two-way street. I taught Shawn a new pickpocketing technique I invented that semester, something I called "The Bump." I would target a victim and walk up to him and bump into him, making certain I bumped him right on the object that I had coveted. It might be a wallet or a comb, whatever, it usually wasn't anything over a few dollars' value, because that was what most kids had.

My antisocial behavior at school continued unabated at

Emerson. The minute someone would confront me in any way, even just telling me to get out of the way, I would pop him. I was a tiny fellow, but I was a quick draw, so I soon became known as the guy you didn't want to fuck with. And I'd always come up with a good story to avoid being suspended after a fight.

Perhaps one of the reasons I didn't want to get suspended was that I would have let down one of the few conventional positive role models in my life at that time—Sonny Bono. Sonny and Connie had become surrogate parental figures to me. *The Sonny and Cher Show* was probably the biggest thing on television then, and Sonny was always generous about ensuring that I'd get whatever extra care I needed. There was always a room for me in his mansion in Holmby Hills, and an attentive around-the-clock staff to cook whatever I desired. He lavished gifts on me, including a brand-new set of skis and ski boots and poles and a jacket so I could go skiing that winter with him and Connie and Chastity, Sonny's daughter with Cher. We would sit on the chairlift, and Sonny would give me his version of life, which was different from my father's or even Connie's version of life. He definitely was on the straight and narrow. I remember him teaching me that the only unacceptable thing was to tell a lie. It didn't matter if I'd made mistakes or fucked up along the way, I just had to be straight with him.

One time I was at his Bel Air mansion during a star-studded Hollywood party. I didn't care about the Tony Curtises of the world at that point, so I started going up and down in the mansion's old carved-wood elevator. Suddenly, I got stuck between floors, and they had to use a giant fireman's ax to free me. I knew I was in big trouble, but Sonny never screamed at me or demeaned me in front of all the adults who were watching this rescue. He just calmly taught me a lesson to respect other people's property and not play in things that weren't made to be played in.

I never liked that there might be some expectation of how I should behave in order to be in that world. I was a twelve-year-old kid, destined to be misbehaving and out of line.

One time later that year, we were hanging around the house, and Sonny and Connie asked me to get them coffee. "How about if you guys got your own coffee?" I answered somewhat flippantly. I had no problem getting the coffee, but it seemed to me that they were bossing me around.

Connie took me aside. "That's curbside behavior," she told me. "If you act that way, I'm just going to say 'Curbside,' and you'll know that you have to go and rethink what you just did." Forget that. Where I was coming from, I could act however I wanted. My dad and I were getting along famously precisely because there were no rules and no regulations. He wasn't asking me to get him any coffee, and I wasn't asking him to get me coffee. It was "take care of yourself" where I came from.

I was growing up quickly, and in a way that definitely wasn't Sonny-friendly. More and more, I was getting high and partying with my friends and skateboarding and committing petty crimes. All the stuff I wasn't supposed to do was the stuff I wanted to do immediately. I had my eye on the prize, and it wasn't really hanging out with Sonny. So we grew apart, and I was okay with that.

Correspondingly, my bond with my dad got stronger and stronger. As soon as I had moved in with him, he instantly became my role model and my hero, so everything I could do to bolster the solidarity between us was my mission. It was also his. We were a team. Naturally, one of our bonding experiences was to go together on his pot-smuggling escapades. I became his cover for these trips. We'd take seven giant Samsonite suitcases and fill them up with pot. At the airport, we'd go from one airline to another, checking in these bags, because at that time they didn't even look to see if you were on that flight. We'd land at a major airport, collect all the suitcases, and drive to someplace like Kenosha, Wisconsin.

On our Kenosha trip, we checked into a motel, because my dad's transactions were going to take a couple of days. I was adamant that I wanted to go with him when the deal went down, but he was dealing with badass biker types, so he sent me to a movie, which turned out to be the new James Bond flick, *Live and Let Die*. The transactions took place over a three-day weekend, so I wound up going to that movie every day we were there, which was fine with me.

We had to return to L.A. with thirty grand in cash. My dad told me I'd be carrying the money, because if they caught someone who looked like him with all that money, he'd be busted for sure. That was fine with me. I'd much prefer to be part of the action than be sitting on the sidelines. So we rigged a belt piece, stuffed it with the cash, and taped it to my abdomen. "If they try to arrest me, you just fade away," he instructed me. "Just pretend you're not with me and keep on going."

We made it back to L.A., and I later found out that my dad was only getting two hundred dollars a trip to mule that pot for his friends Weaver and Bashara. I also discovered that he was supplementing that meager income with a nice steady cash inflow from a growing coke-dealing business. In 1974 cocaine had become a huge scene, especially in L.A. My dad had developed a connection with an old American expatriate who brought up cocaine from Mexico. Dad bought the coke and then cut it and sold it to his clients. He wasn't selling ounces or kilos, just grams and half grams and quarter grams. But over the course of a day or two, it started to add up. He'd also move quaaludes. He gave a doctor a sob story about never being able to sleep, and the doc wrote a prescription for a thousand quaaludes, which cost maybe a quarter apiece and had a market value of four or five dollars. So between the coke and the ludes, it was a pretty lucrative business.

Pops never tried to hide his drug dealing from me. He didn't go out of his way to tell me about it, but I was such a shadow to him that I'd observe all his preparations and transactions. There was a small add-on room, similar to my bedroom, off the kitchen. It even had a door that led to the backyard, and my dad set up shop there.

The centerpiece of his drug paraphernalia in that back room was his triple beam scale, which was put to more use in our household than the toaster or the blender. His work plate and snorting tray of choice was a beautiful green-and-blue Mexican tile, perfectly square and flat. I'd watch him cut up the coke and strain it and then take a brick of Italian laxative called mannitol and strain it through the same strainer so it would have the same consistency as the coke. It was important to the bottom line to make sure the coke had been cut with the proper amount of laxative.

There were a lot of people coming by, but not as many as you would think. My dad was fairly surreptitious about his dealings, and he knew the risk would increase with a lot of activity. But what his clientele lacked in quantity, it sure made up for in quality. There were plenty of movie stars and TV stars and writers and rock stars, and tons of girls. One time we even got a visit from two famous Oakland Raiders on the eve of the Super Bowl. They came over pretty early, about eight or nine P.M., and they looked a lot straighter than the usual clientele, sitting on my dad's homemade furniture and looking sheepish and unnerved by the fact that there was a kid hanging around. But it all worked out. They got their stuff, and they went out and won the Super Bowl the next day.

What was kind of annoying about the whole experience was the late-night traffic. It was then that I saw the real desperation this drug could induce. I wasn't being judgmental about it; it was more like "Wow, this guy really wants that damn coke." One guy who was an insatiable garbage disposal for the cocaine was the brother of a famous actor. He'd come by every hour on the hour until six in the morning, wheeling and dealing and shucking and jiving and talking long promises. Each time he knocked, my dad would get out of bed, and I'd hear him sigh, "Oh, no, not again" to himself.

Sometimes my dad wouldn't even open the door, he'd just talk to people through the window screen. I'd be lying there in bed listening to "It's too late. Get the hell out of here. You owe me too much money, anyway. You're into me for two hundred and twenty dollars." My dad had a list of what people owed him. I'd look over that list and hear him say, "If I could just get everyone to pay me what they owe me, I'd have all this money."

It was hard to convince me that we weren't living large, especially on the weekends, when my dad took me out nightclubbing, where he was known as the Lord of the Sunset Strip. (He was also known as Spider, a nickname he had picked up in the late '60s when he scaled a building to get into the apartment of a girl he was fixated on.)

Sunset Strip in the early '70s was the artery of life that flowed through West Hollywood. People constantly jammed the street, shuttling between the best clubs in town. There was the Whisky a Go Go and Filthy McNasty's. Two blocks from the Whisky was the Roxy, another live music club. Across the parking lot from the Roxy was the Rainbow Bar and Grill. The Rainbow was Spider's domain. Every night he'd get there around nine and meet up with his posse—Weaver and Connie and Bashara and a rotating cast of characters.

Getting ready for the night out was a ritualistic experience for my father, since he was so meticulous about his appearance. I'd sit there and watch him preen in front of the mirror. Every hair had to be just so, the right cologne applied in the right quantity. Then the donning of the tight T-shirt and the velvet jacket and the platforms. Eventually, we'd go to custom tailors to replicate his outfits for me. It was all about mimicking my dad.

Part of that ritual was getting the right high to start the night. He was obviously saving the grand finale of chemical cocktail for much later in the evening, but he didn't want to leave the house without the appropriate beginnings of that buzz, which usually revolved around alcohol and pills. He had quaaludes and Placidyls, which were downers that stopped you from having motor skills. When you mixed them with alcohol, they stopped the guy next to you from having motor skills. But my dad's pills of choice were Tuinals.

When I went out with him, he'd pour me a small glass of beer. Then he'd break open a Tuinal capsule. Because the powder from the Tuinals was so horrible-tasting, he'd slice up a banana and shove the broken-up Tuinal in the banana. He'd take the part that contained more powder and give me the smaller portion. Then we were ready to go out.

Our royal reception would start as soon as we walked up to the Rainbow's door. Tony, the maître d' of the club, would greet my dad as if he were the most valued customer on the Strip. Of course, the hundred-dollar bill that my dad handed him as we walked in didn't hurt. Tony would lead us to my dad's table—the power table, right in front of a huge fireplace. From that vantage point, you could see anyone who was coming in the club or walking down from Over the Rainbow, a nightclub within the club. My dad was incredibly territorial. If a person who didn't pass his muster sat down at the table, Spider would confront him: "What do you think you're doing?"

"Ah, I just want to sit down and hang out," the guy would say.

"Sorry, pal. Out of here. You've got to go."

But if someone came in who was of interest to my father, he'd jump up and arrange seating. His policing of the table made me uncomfortable. I didn't necessarily want interlopers to sit down, but I thought my dad could have been kinder and gentler. Especially when the booze and the downers were flowing at the same time, he could be an asshole. But he was a great catalyst for getting interesting people together. If Keith Moon or the guys from Led Zeppelin or Alice Cooper was in town, they'd be sitting with Spider, because he was the coolest guy in the house.

We'd be at the Rainbow most of the night. He didn't stay put at the table the whole time, just long enough for his anchors to arrive to hold down the table, and then they'd all take turns making the rounds within the restaurant bar area, or going upstairs. I always loved the upstairs club. Whenever one of my dad's girlfriends would want to dance, she'd ask me, because Spider was not a dancer.

The night wouldn't be complete without cocaine, and it became a great sport to see how clandestinely you could consume your blow. The experienced coke hounds were easy to spot, because they all had the right-pinkie coke fingernail. They'd grow that pinkie at least a good half inch past the finger and shape it perfectly, and that was the ultimate coke spoon of the time. My dad took great pride in his elaborately manicured coke nail. But I also noticed that one of his nails was decidedly shorter than the rest.

"What's up with that one?" I asked.

"That's so I don't hurt the ladies down below when I'm using my finger on them," he said. Boy, that stuck in my mind. He actually had a finger that was pussy-friendly.

I was the only child present for all this insanity. For the most part, the adults who didn't know me just ignored me. But Keith Moon, the legendary drummer for the Who, always tried to make me feel at ease. In the midst of this chaotic, riotous, party-life atmosphere where everyone was screaming and shouting and sniffing and snorting and drinking and humping, Moon would take the time to be still and take me under his arm and say, "How you doing, kid? Are you having a good time? Shouldn't you be in school or something? Well, I'm glad you're here, anyway." That always stuck with me.

We'd usually stay until closing time, which was two A.M. Then it was time to congregate in the parking lot, which had filled up with girls and boys in their outlandish glam-rock clothing. The parking-lot scene was all about getting phone numbers and bird-dogging and finding the afterparty. But sometimes it was the scene of an altercation that oftentimes involved my dad. He'd take on biker gangs in front of me, and I'd be the little guy jumping into the middle of these scraps, going, "This is my dad. He's really wasted right now. Whatever he said, just go ahead and forgive him. He didn't mean it. And please, don't hit him in the face, because it really hurts a kid like me to see his dad get hit in the face."

I did have a horrible feeling that my dad would end up hurting himself badly in a fight or in a car accident. At that point in the night, he'd be so high that walking across the room was a vaudevillian routine of a guy stumbling, falling down, and somehow managing to stay up on his feet. He'd be bouncing off furniture, holding on to anything that was stable, slurring every word, but still he'd try to get into the car to drive to the party. I'd be, "Oh, shit, my dad can't talk. This is not good." When he'd had too much, I become responsible for his security, which was a difficult place to find myself.

All of this was taking an emotional toll on me, in ways that I couldn't even articulate. Even though I had friends at Emerson, and I was going to the Rainbow on weekends as my dad's sidekick, I was alone a lot and starting to create my own world. I had to get up in the morning and go to school and be a guy in his own private bubble. I didn't mind it, since I had this space to pretend in and create in and think in and observe in. Sometime that year, one of the neighbor's cats had kittens, and I used to take one of the fluffy white kittens up on the roof of the garage apartment behind us to hang out with. He was my little friend, but at times, I would scold that kitten, for no reason other than to exert power over him. During one of these scolding sessions, I started thumping the kitty in the face with my fingers. It wasn't anything deadly, but it was an act of aggression, which was strange, because I'd always been an animal lover.

One time I thumped the kitty too hard, and his little tooth punctured his little kitty lip, and a drop of blood was drawn. I completely freaked out. I started feeling intense self-loathing for bringing harm to this tiny animal that still stayed affectionate toward me even after that incident. I was fearful that my inability to stop myself from engaging in that behavior was a sign of an incipient psychosis.

But on the whole, I wouldn't have traded my lifestyle for anything else, especially some of the mundane realities of my friends at Emerson. I'd go to their houses and see their dads come home from their office buildings and not have any time or energy or compassion for their kids. They just sat there and drank their whiskey and smoked their cigar and read their paper and went to bed. That didn't seem like a much better option.

Trying to get some sleep so I'd be rested for school the next day while people were having sex on the couch and shooting cocaine and cranking the stereo was definitely not a mundane reality. But it was mine. On school nights, I'd stay home, but Spider would be right at his power table at the Rainbow. And half the time the afterparty was at our house. I'd be at home asleep, and all of a sudden I'd hear that door open and a stream of maniacs would flood into the house. Then the music would begin, and the laughter and the cutting of the lines and the general mayhem would ensue. I'd be trying to sleep in my back room, which was connected to the one and only bathroom, and people would be in and out of there, pissing and screaming and doing drugs.

Thank God I had my '70s alarm clock radio. Every morning at six-forty-five, it would wake me up with the popular music of the day. I'd usually be dead to the world, but I'd stumble to my closet, put on a T-shirt, go to the bathroom, and get ready to go to school. Then I'd walk through the house and survey the damage. It always looked like a battlefield. Sometimes there were people passed out on the couch or on the chairs. My dad's doors were always shut. He was usually asleep with some girl, but sometimes he would still be awake, closed off in his module.

One of the reasons I cherished that alarm clock was that I really was that anxious to get to school every day. I loved almost all of my classes. As crazy and as high and as full of the nightlife as his routine was, my dad was backing me 100 percent in all of my classes. He had come from an academic background himself, and I think he knew the importance of studying and of learning and exposing yourself to new ideas, particularly the creative avenues that were offered. Every day he'd use some crazy-ass esoteric word to get me to increase my vocabulary. He also expanded my tastes in literature from the Hardy Boys to Ernest Hemingway and other great writers.

At school, the class that I looked forward to most was English. Jill Vernon was my teacher, and she was by far the most profoundly inspirational one I'd ever come across. She was a diminutive lady with short black hair, about fifty years old. She really knew how to communicate with kids and turned everything she talked about, writing, reading, whatever, into something interesting and appealing and fun.

Every day we'd spend the first fifteen minutes of class writing in a journal. She'd put a trigger sentence up on the board, and we were supposed to riff on the sentence to any other subject that we felt like. Some of the other students would write for five minutes and stop, but I could have written away the whole class time.

Mrs. Vernon would regularly keep me after school and talk to me about writing, because she could see how I poured my heart into those essays.

"I read all these journals, and I have to say that you have a special gift for writing, and I think you should be aware and do something with it," she told me. "You should continue to write."

When you're in seventh grade and this really wonderful woman whom you look up to takes the time to express an idea like that to you—that was a bell that wouldn't stop ringing for the rest of my life.

Another bell started ringing around that time. My dad had told me about his first attempted sexual experience, and it wasn't a pleasant one. He went to a whorehouse in downtown Grand Rapids. The prostitutes were all black. My dad was sent up to a room, and a few minutes later, a middle-aged lady with a little potbelly came in. She asked him if he was ready, but he was so scared that he blurted out, "I'm sorry, but I can't do this." How could anyone have performed under those circumstances? Going to a weird place and ending up with a weird person with absolutely no connection to you and having to pay for it? I think that experience had a lot to do with him wanting my first sexual experience to be nicer. I just don't know if he envisioned that my first time would be with one of his girlfriends.

As soon as I moved in with my dad, the idea of having sex became a priority for me. Actually, the anticipation and the desire and the infatuation with the inevitable act had been rolling long before I got to California. But now I was eleven on the cusp of twelve, and it was time to act. Girls my age at Emerson wanted nothing to do with me. My father had a succession of beautiful young teenage girlfriends whom I couldn't help fantasizing about, but I couldn't quite get up the nerve to approach them. Then he started seeing a girl named Kimberly.

Kimberly was a beautiful, soft-spoken eighteen-year-old redhead with snow-white skin and huge, perfectly formed breasts. She had an ethereal, dreamy personality that was typified by her adamant refusal to wear her glasses despite terrible nearsightedness. I once asked her if she could see without them, and she said that things were very fuzzy. So why didn't she wear the glasses? "I really do prefer the world unclear," she said.

One night shortly before my twelfth birthday, we were all at the Rainbow. I was high as a little kite on a quaalude, and I got up the courage to write my father a note: "I know this is your girlfriend, but I'm pretty sure she's up for the task so if it's okay with you, can we arrange a situation where I end up having sex with Kimberly tonight?"

He brokered the deal in a flash. She was game, so we went back to the house, and he said, "Okay, there's the bed, there's the girl, do what you will." My father's bed was bizarre to begin with, because he had piled four mattresses on top of one another to create an almost thronelike effect. He was a little too present for my taste, and I was nervous enough as it was, but Kimberly did everything. She guided me the whole way, and she was very loving and gentle, and it was all pretty natural. I can't remember if it lasted five minutes or an hour. It was just a blurry, hazy, sexy moment.

It was a fun thing to do, and I never felt traumatized then, but I think subconsciously it was probably something that always stuck with me in a weird way. I didn't wake up the next morning going, "Geez, what the hell was that?" I woke up wanting to go brag about it to my friends and find out how I could get the arrangement happening again. But that was the last time my dad ever let me do that. Whenever he'd have a new beautiful girlfriend, I'd say, "Remember that night with Kimberly? How about if—"

He'd always cut me off. "Oh, no, no, no. That was a onetime deal. Don't even bring that up. It's not going to happen."

The summer of 1975 was my first trip back to Michigan since I moved out to live with my dad. Spider gave me a big fat ounce of Colombian Gold, which was at the time the top of the food chain when it came to weed, and some Thai sticks, and a giant finger brick of Lebanese hash. That was my supply for the summer. Naturally, I turned my friends Joe and Nate on for the first time. We went to Plaster Creek, smoked a fattie, and emerged doing somersaults and cartwheels and laughing.

All summer I told people about the wonders of living in Hollywood, and about the different, interesting people I had met and the music I was listening to, which was everything in my father's collection from Roxy Music to Led Zeppelin to David Bowie, Alice Cooper, and the Who.

In July of that summer, my mom married Steve. They had a beautiful wedding under a willow tree in the backyard of their farmhouse out in Lowell. So I felt that things were okay for her and my sister, Julie. I went back to West Hollywood at the end of the summer, anxious to resume my California lifestyle, and to get back to someone who would become my new best friend and partner in crime for the next two years.

I first met John M at the end of seventh grade. There was a Catholic boys' school immediately adjacent to Emerson, and we used to razz each other through the fence. One day I went over there and got into a verbal put-down match with some kid who claimed to know karate. He was probably learning his forms and had no idea about street fighting, because I whomped on his ass in front of the whole school.

Somewhere in that melee, I made a connection with John. He lived at the top of Roscomar Road in Bel Air. Even though it was in the city, there were mountains and a reservoir behind his house that had a giant waterfall that drained into another reservoir. It was the perfect playground. John's dad worked for an aerospace company and was a heavy drinker, so nothing was discussed, feelings were not talked about, you just pretended like everything was okay. John's mom was super sweet, and he had a sister who was confined to a wheelchair with some degenerative disease.

When I started eighth grade, John became my best friend. It was all about skateboarding and smoking pot. Some days we could get pot, and some days we couldn't. But we could always skateboard. Up to that point, all of my skateboarding had just been street skating for transportation, and jumping off curbs, basically getting where I had to go with a modicum of style in the way I rode; really, it was as functional as it was anything else. In the early '70s, the sport started to elevate, and people were riding in drainage ditches and along banks and in emptied-out swimming pools. It was about the same time that the Dog Pound skaters in Santa Monica were taking skateboarding to a new, higher semiprofessional level. John and I were doing it for fun and challenge.

John looked like an all-American kid. He had a real taste for beer, and we'd go and hang out in front of the local country market and talk adults into buying beer for us. Getting drunk wasn't my preferred high, but it was kind of exciting to get out of control in that way, to feel you didn't know what was going to happen.

We graduated from asking people to buy us six-packs to pulling off heists for our booze. One day we were walking through Westwood and saw workers at a restaurant loading cases of beer into a third-floor storage area. When they left for a second, we climbed up on a Dumpster, grabbed the fire-escape ladder, pulled ourselves up, opened the window, and took a case of Heineken that lasted us for the next couple of days.

We graduated from beer heists to stealing whiskey from the supermarkets of Westwood. We'd go to the supermarket and take a bottle of whiskey and slip it up a pant leg, pull the sock up over it, and walk out with a bit of a peg leg. It was terrible-tasting, but we'd force ourselves to get it down. Before we knew it, we were out of our minds on the firewater. Then we'd skate around and crash into things and get in mock fights.

At a certain point, John decided to grow his own marijuana garden, which I thought was very inventive of him. Then we realized it would be easier to search out other people's gardens and steal their weed. One day after we'd searched fruitlessly for weeks, we found a patch that was guarded by dogs. I diverted the dogs, John stole the weed, and we brought all these huge plants back to his mom's house. We knew we had to dry them out in the oven first, but John was worried that his mother would come home, so I suggested since most people were still at work, we should use somebody else's oven.

We walked a few houses down from John's, broke in, cranked the oven, and shoved this mound of weed in. We stayed there for an hour, and though the weed never became smokable, now we knew how easy it was to break into people's houses, and we started doing that with some regularity. We weren't out to take people's televisions or go through their jewelry; we just wanted money, or stuff that looked fun to have, or drugs. We went through people's medicine cabinets, because by now I'd seen a lot of pills and I knew what to look for. One day we found a huge jar of pills that said "Percodan." I'd never taken one, but I knew they were considered the crème de la crème of painkillers. So I took the jar and we went back to John's.

"How many should we take?" he asked.

"Let's start with three and see what happens," I guessed. We both took three and sat around for a few minutes, but nothing happened. So we took a couple more. The next thing we knew, we were out of our minds on an opium high and loving it. But that was a onetime thing. We didn't take the Percodans again.

Our small successes with pulling off heists emboldened John. He lived across the street from his old elementary school, and he knew that all the day's receipts from the cafeteria were kept in a strongbox and stored in the freezer every night. It turned out that during his last month as a sixth-grader, John had stolen a set of the janitor's keys to the school.

We plotted out a strategy. We got some masks, wore gloves, and waited until after midnight one night. The keys worked. We got into the cafeteria, went to the freezer, and there was the strongbox. We grabbed it and ran out, right across the street to John's house. In his bedroom, we opened that box and counted out four hundred and fifty dollars. This was by far the most successful take we had ever had. Now what?

"Let's get a pound of pot, sell some, and make a profit and have all the weed that we ever wanted to smoke," I suggested. I was sick of running out of pot to the point where we would have to clean pipes to try to find some THC resin. I knew that Alan Bashara would have a pound of pot lying around, and he did. Unfortunately, it was shite pot. I had the idea to sell it out of my locker at Emerson, but that was too nerve-racking, so I ended up taking the pot home and selling it out of my bedroom, all the time dipping into the brick and smoking the better pieces. At one point, I was trying to sell this shitty pot to a couple of junkies who lived across the street, but even they were critics. When they saw my bottle of Percodans, they offered me five dollars a pill. I sold the whole jar in one fell swoop.

The pinnacle of my eighth-grade drug experimentation with John was our two acid trips. I didn't know anyone who took LSD; it seemed like a different generation's drug. Still, it sounded like a more adventurous experience that wasn't about getting high and chatting up the ladies but about going on a psychedelic journey to an altered state. That was exactly how I saw my life then, going on these journeys to the unknown, to places in the mind and in the physical realm that other people just didn't. We asked all around, but none of our stoner friends knew how to score acid. When I went to Bashara's house to score the weed, it just so happened that he had a few strips with twenty little pyramid gelatin blotches, ten bright green and ten bright purple. I took two hits of each color and ran home to John. We immediately planned the two trips. The first would be that upcoming weekend. We'd save the second for when John and his family went to their beach house in Ensenada, Mexico.

We went with the purple acid first. Because it was so pure and strong, we immediately got incredibly high. It was as if we were looking at the world through a new pair of glasses. Everything was vivid and brilliant, and we became steam engines of energy, running through the woods and jumping off trees, feeling totally impervious to any danger. Then the spiritual aspect of the acid kicked in, and we started to get introspective. We decided to observe families in their homes, so we broke into different backyards and started spying on the residents through the windows; as far as we were concerned, we were invisible. We bellied up to the windows and watched families eat dinner and listened to their conversations.

The sun began to set, and John remembered that his father was coming home from a business trip that day and he was due for a family dinner.

"I don't think that's a great idea. They're going to know that we're crazy out of our minds on acid," I said.

"We know we're crazy high on acid, but I don't think they'll be able to tell," John said.

I was still dubious, but we went to his house and sat down and had a full formal dinner with John's straight-laced dad and his sweet mom and his sister in the wheelchair. I took one look at the food and began to hallucinate and couldn't even think of eating. Then I started watching with fascination as John's dad's mouth opened and these big words came floating out of it. By the time John's parents started turning into beasts, both of us were laughing uncontrollably.

Needless to say, we both absolutely loved it. It was as beautiful and remarkable and hallucinogenic as we ever could have imagined. We'd had mild hallucinations from smoking pot, when we might see colors, but nothing where we felt like we were traveling to a distant galaxy and suddenly understood all the secrets of life. So we could hardly wait for our next acid trip in Mexico.

John's folks had a beautiful house on a white sandy beach that went on forever. We dropped that green acid in the morning, walked out to a sandbar, and stayed out in the ocean for seven hours, just tripping on the shimmer and sparkle of the water, and the dolphins, and the waves. Those two times were the best acid trips I ever had. It seemed later like they stopped making really good LSD, and acid became much more speedy and toxic-feeling. I'd still hallucinate wildly, but it was never again as peaceful and pure a feeling.

I don't want to imply that John was my only friend at Emerson, because that wasn't true. But again, most of my friends were outsiders in the social scheme of things. Sometimes I'd have the occasional feeling of less-than. I was less than because I wasn't as rich as most of these kids. I also felt left out when it came to girls. Like every good boy going through puberty, I started fixating on every hot girl who came into my line of vision. And Emerson was full of them. They were rich little prima donna debutante girls with names like Jennifer and Michele. Their skintight Ditto jeans came in a myriad of pastel colors and did something truly wonderful to the young adolescent female body. Just framed it, formed it, cupped it, shaped it, packaged it perfectly. So I couldn't take my eyes off them.

But whenever I approached a girl and asked her to hang out with me, she'd go, "You're joking, right?" They were beautiful, they were hot, but they were snobs. All those girls wanted a guy who was a couple of years older, or one who had some game or a car. To them I was a freak to be avoided, and I hated it. The same sense of confidence and self-assuredness that I took into my other life, my club life and my party life, and my father's friends' life—where I felt at ease and in control and capable of communicating—I just didn't have that with the girls in my junior high school. They didn't give me anything in terms of confidence-building—with the exception of Grace.

Before I talk about the anomaly that was Grace, I should backtrack and pick up the thread of my sexual history. After my liaison with Kimberly, I had no sexual involvement with women for about a year. But around the same time as my Kimberly experience, I discovered the art and joy of masturbation, thanks to *National Lampoon*'s Photo Funnies. For some reason, masturbation was not a subject that my dad broached. He taught me every minuscule part of the female anatomy, but he never told me that if I needed sexual satisfaction, I could do it myself. *National Lampoon* inspired me to figure it out.

All this experimentation took place one afternoon in my add-on bedroom. I wasn't a horribly late physical bloomer, but I was by no means early. Around the first month that I was even capable of having an orgasm and ejaculation, it dawned on me that I could use photos to achieve that end. Surprisingly, I didn't use my dad's vast collection of *Penthouse* and *Playboy* magazines. I was attracted to the realism of the girls in those *Lampoons,* the fact that the girls weren't in the conventional postures of what was supposed to be sexy. They were just real naked girls. Shortly thereafter, I would abuse every magazine I could in my quest, especially in high school, when it would become almost a contest to see how many times you could jack off in one day, and what stimuli you were jacking off to, and what implements you were incorporating into the process. But that was much later.

Around the time my hormones started raging, I had the wonderful experience of being babysat one night by Cher. I was in the eighth grade and still hanging with Sonny and Connie from time to time, and for some reason, they got jammed up, so Cher volunteered to watch me for the night. We camped out in her bedroom, having a heart-to-heart talk for hours on end, really getting to be friends for the first time.

After a while, it was time for bed. Because it was a large house and I might get spooked being alone, Cher let me crash on her bed until Sonny and Connie came to pick me up. In my mind, there was a bit of tension—not that I was going to make any moves on this woman, just the idea that I'd be in bed with such a gorgeous creature. But I thought it was okay because we were friends.

Then Cher got up to go to the bathroom and get ready for bed. It was dark in the bedroom, but it was light in the bathroom, so I watched her take off her clothes, all the while feigning to be on my way to sleep. There was a woman's naked body, and it was long and slender and special and just thrilling. Not that I had the wherewithal to want some physical relationship with her, but in my mind, it was a stimulating and semi-innocent moment. After she put on her nightgown, she walked back into the room and got into bed. I remember thinking, "This is not bad, lying next to this beautiful lady."

The next woman who would advance my sexual education was also older than I was. Becky was an ex-girlfriend of Alan Bashara. She was about twenty-four at the time and small and beautiful, with adorable curly hair. She was also into quaaludes. I would go on errands with her, and she'd break up some ludes, and then we'd pile into her Fiat and drive around town. The days would always end up with us both getting high, coming home, and fooling around. Our sessions turned into great instructional lessons for me, because she showed me exactly how to go down on a girl. One time she even told me to massage her buttocks. "Wow, I never would have thought of that!" I marveled.

Sex was still pretty sporadic for me in the eighth grade. But even then there wasn't a kid I knew who was getting laid. Every one of my friends was destined to stay a virgin for the next few years, so part of the joy for me was going to school the next day and telling my friends, "Hey, I spent the night with a girl." They were like, "Whoa, that's beyond comprehension." They were even more amazed after my experience with Grace at Emerson.

It started, like a lot of my sexual encounters at that time, with a quaalude. Or half a lude, to be precise. I brought a lude to school and split it with John. We planned to meet up at lunch and share our experience of what it was like to be high during school. By the fourth period, I was totally loaded. I was in my journalism class with a beautiful girl named Grace, who was very physically developed for a fourteen-year-old, especially for a Japanese girl. I knew that she had always had a crush on me. Suddenly, I had a brainstorm. I asked the teacher if I could take Grace on a campus assignment and wander around and see if we could generate some stories for the class newspaper. I was assertive because I was high and feeling the gregarious coercion of quaalude running through me. The teacher said, "Okay, just make sure you're back before the end of class."

Grace and I left the classroom and walked down the hallway, right into the men's bathroom, which was this big old beautiful bathroom built in the '30s, with lots of stalls and a tall ceiling and huge windows. I started to play with her breasts and kiss her, and she loved it. I was high and she wasn't, but she was just as horny as I was and equally willing to have this experience. Just as I began to finger her, a little kid came into the bathroom, saw us in the stall, and screamed and ran out. Instead of panicking and aborting the mission, I was determined to find a safer place. So we walked around the campus and found a janitor's utility shed behind one of the bungalows. We immediately stripped down and started going for it. Much to my surprise, she seemed to know exactly what she was doing. As soon as I came, I stood up, and since I was a teenager, my dick stayed hard. Instantaneously, she went right down on her knees and started giving me a blow job, and I came again. I was amazed. How did she even know to do that? We got dressed and ran back to class, giggling the whole way. As soon as I got to lunch, I told my friends the whole story, and they were dumbfounded and envious. That was just another day at the office for me, because I was pretty willing to do whatever came my way.

In July, I went back and spent a typical summer in Michigan, a relaxing domain of forest and lakes and peach orchards, shooting my BB gun and hanging with Joe and Nate. But when the summer ended, my mom and I decided that I should stay on in Michigan for the first semester of ninth grade. My mom was pregnant with her third child, and she wanted me around for the birth so I could bond with my new sibling. Because she and Steve lived in Lowell, which was in the country, I wound up going to school in a town with a population of under two thousand people.

Most of the kids ostracized me. All the popular guys, the meatheads who were sons of farmers, were calling me "girly boy" and "Hollywood" and "faggot" because I had long hair. When school started, I showed up wearing different clothes and a different haircut and a different attitude, and these hay-baling hillbillies wanted to kill me. My only solace was my relationships with girls, who seemed to appreciate me a little more. That semester I hooked up with a hot Hispanic girl and a blonde named Mary, who was the winner of L'Oreal's Long and Silky hair contest in the Midwest. She was beautiful and a year older, but our relationship never developed into the full-blown romance that I had envisioned. We spent most of our time together holding hands and making out, and she let me touch various parts of her body, but she never gave up the whole enchilada. I couldn't tell if she was humoring me because I was younger and two heads shorter than her.

On October 3, 1976, my mom gave birth to my second sister, Jennifer Lee Idema. It was a joyful time in the family, and we had a real nice little unit going on with Steve and Julie and my mom and the new baby and Ashley, the dog. As well as bonding with Jenny, I spent some quality time with Steve. He was always so supportive of whatever I did.

When I returned to Emerson for the second half of ninth grade, a sea change had taken place. When I left, I was the king of the campus in the misfit-outcast realm. But when I came back, it was Tony Who? There were new kids who were in charge now, and some of them had whiskers. (I was miles away from having a single whisker.) So I developed a new identity. I was going to become an actor, mainly because that was what my dad was doing.

Spider had always had an interest in acting. By now he was getting tired of life as the Lord of the Sunset Strip. He was fed up with selling drugs and the constant barrage of people invading the house at all hours of the night. So when Lee Strasberg opened a branch of his institute in Los Angeles, Pops decided to enroll. He'd come home after class all excited about Method acting and sense memory recall and all these new concepts. It all seemed quite a craft to get your head around.

As part of his decision to start in a new direction, my dad cut off his long hair. Overnight, he reinvented himself with a distinctive, slicked-back film noir '30s gangster look. Within days, I was sitting in a barber chair asking for a '30s gangster haircut. By this time, all of the other kids were starting to catch up to me, and long hair was no longer a real sign of rebellion and individuality, so I got the haircut and baffled all my schoolmates with this new look. When my dad started wearing double-breasted pin-striped suits with black-and-white spectator shoes and nice white button-down shirts with fancy ties, the first thing I did was go out and get an identical outfit made up. Now it was time for me to enroll in acting school. I took children's classes with a woman named Diane Hull, and they were wonderful. We were taught that there was more to acting than merely pretending: You really had to get yourself into the headspace of the character you were playing.

After a few months of studying, my dad dropped a bombshell on me. He was going to legally change his name from John Kiedis to Blackie Dammett. For his new last name, he had combined the first and last names of one of his favorite authors, Dashiell Hammett. "What do you want your stage name to be?" he asked me. In one more gesture of solidarity with my dad, I said, "Well, it's got to be something Dammett, because I'm your son." So Cole Dammett was born. Get it? Cole, son of Blackie.

From that day on, he was known only as Blackie, both professionally and personally. No John, no Jack, no Spider. But I had the two separate identities going. There was no way I was shaking Tony at school. And my family wasn't about to start calling me Cole. But Blackie did. He called me Cole more often than not, because he always stayed in character.

With our stage names set, it was time to get agents. He found an agent to represent him, and then he got a recommendation for a child actor's agent for me. Her name was Toni Kelman, and she was the hottest child agent in all of Hollywood. By the time I signed, I had already been cast in a movie. Roger Corman was doing a triple-R-rated version of *Love American Style* called *Jokes My Folks Never Told Me*. It was the quintessential '70s flick with beautiful naked women throughout. The director had gone to UCLA with my dad, and he came over to visit one day. I answered the door.

"I'm here to see your dad," he said cordially.

I didn't know this guy, and I certainly didn't know his relationship to Blackie, so I summoned myself up to my five-foot-something height and hissed, "Well, who are you?"

What I was saying with my body language was "I'll kick your ass if you try to come in my house, even though I'm just a kid." He was so impressed with my confidence that he cast me in two vignettes as this badass kid who tells dirty jokes in a classroom.

Right off the bat, I got hired to do an after-school special and a public-network children's show. Of course, I was cast as the bad kid in both shows. But it was work. And it was piling up. I started an account at my dad's bank, and soon I opened that bankbook up and saw a couple of grand in there, a shocking amount of money for me.

I was getting spoiled, cast for every part auditioned for. One afternoon I was at John's house when Blackie called to tell me that I had just been cast as Sylvester Stallone's son in *F.I.S.T.*, his next movie after *Rocky*. I was so excited I ran out of the house, whooping and singing the theme song to *Rocky* with my arms up in the air. I was convinced that I would be the Next Big Thing because I was co-starring with Sly Stallone, even though I had only one scene with him at the dinner table.

When I got to the set, I went to Stallone's trailer and knocked on the door, figuring we should bond before we shot our big scene.

"Who's that?" said a gruff voice from the trailer.

"It's Cole. I'm playing your son in the scene we're about to do," I answered.

He cautiously opened the door. "*Why* are you here?" he said.

"I'm playing your son, so I thought that we should get some hang time in so I could develop—"

Stallone interrupted me. "No, I don't think so," he said and looked around for a PA. "Somebody come and get this kid. Get him out of here," he screamed.

We did the scene, and when I delivered my big line, "Can you pass the milk?," the camera wasn't exactly in tight for a close-up. It turned out to be a don't-blink-or-you'll-miss-it role, but still, it was another credit.

Having been in *F.I.S.T.* helped when I went to Paramount to audition for a film called *American Hot Wax,* which was the story of Buddy Holly and the DJ Alan Freed. It was a big movie, and I was auditioning for a key role in the film, the president of Buddy Holly's fan club. After cattle calls and innumerable callbacks and even a screen test, it narrowed down to two candidates—me and the hottest child actor around, Moosie Drier. I was confident that I'd get the role because Blackie had gone all out to help me prepare for the role, learning all of Buddy Holly's songs and buying the big horn-rimmed glasses. So when Toni called me to tell me that I hadn't gotten the part, I was shattered.

That night Connie took me to a friend's house, and we went on a total drug binge—snorting coke, smoking pot, sipping booze, and chatting about how I was going to get them next time and end up being the biggest movie star this town ever saw and yadda, yadda, yadda, an endless stream of nonsensical cocaine gabbing between the boy who had just lost the role of a lifetime, the lady who wanted to help him out but really was kind of lost herself, and the guy who just wanted to get in the lady's pants. It went on until the wee hours of the morning, when the coke finally ran out, at which point the reality ran in, and it was not so nice. The chemical depression of the drugs wearing off, combined with the reality of the loss, made for a brutalizing twenty-four hours for me.

Despite my other early success, I wasn't the most disciplined or diligent of acting students. I dug it and I participated in it and I learned from it, but I wasn't committed to putting all of my energy into that world. Having fun with my friends and running around town and skateboarding were still high on my list. Getting high was high on my list.

I had already discovered the pleasures of cocaine before that night Connie tried to cheer me up. When I was thirteen, Alan Bashara had come over to our house on Palm in the middle of the day and told my dad that he had some incredible cocaine. Back in the '70s, cocaine was very strong and very pure; it wasn't so chemical-heavy as it is these days. I'd been seeing the adults do it for the last year and a half in the house, so I told them I wanted in.

Bashara made me a line, and I snorted it. Twenty seconds later, my face went numb and I started feeling like Superman. It was such an unabashedly euphoric rush that I felt like I was seeing God. I didn't think that feeling would ever go away. But then, boom, it started to wear off.

"Whoa, whoa, can we get some more of that?" I was frantic. But Alan had to leave, and my dad went about his business, and I was bummed out. Fortunately, the young boy's chemistry doesn't take that long to recover. An hour later, I was fine and moving on to the next thing.

So I fell in love at first sight with cocaine. I would always check the house to see if there was anything left behind from the night before. There frequently was. I'd scrape the plates with a razor blade and scour the empty glass vials and cobble the residue together, then take it to school and share it with John. But we always waited for school to let out. Except for that half quaalude, I never did drugs in school.

Cocaine inadvertently led me to heroin. I was fourteen and with Connie one day when she took me for a ride to Malibu. We wound up at a coke dealer's house where all these adults were doing massive amounts of the white powder from a huge pile on the drawing table. I was right in there with them, monkey see, monkey do, and we were all as high as can be. At one point they decided to go out somewhere. By now there was only one small solitary line on the mirror. "You can stay here, but whatever you do, don't do that little line," they said. I just smiled and said okay.

The minute they closed that front door, WHOOSH, I snorted up that line. When they came back in, they saw that the line had been Hoovered.

"Where's that line?" someone said.

"Well, I got confused . . ." I started an alibi.

"We better rush him to the hospital. He's going to OD." Everyone was getting frantic. Unbeknownst to me, that little line was China White heroin.

But I was fine. Really, really fine. I realized that I liked the heroin even better than the cocaine. I was high on the coke, but I didn't feel jittery or nervous. My jaw wasn't grinding. I wasn't at all worried about where my next line of coke was going to come from. I was in a dream, and I loved it. Of course, on the ride home I threw up, but that was no biggie. I just asked Connie to stop the car real quick, and blupp, right out the window. They were keeping a keen eye on me, sure I would go into cardiac arrest, but nothing ever happened. I loved it, but I didn't pursue it.

By the end of ninth grade, on the surface, things seemed to be looking up. Blackie was studying acting and really getting into his roles, sometimes to a frightening extent. He became a regular at the Hollywood Actors Theatre, which was a nonequity ninety-nine-seat theater off Hollywood Boulevard. Whether he was playing a bit role or the lead, he'd completely immerse himself in the character. A lot of it had to do with finding the look of a person. He became a great master of disguise, changing his wardrobe, his hair, his glasses, his posture, and his demeanor. He'd decorate his scripts with pictures and writing and artifacts that were representative of the character.

The problems began when he started to *become* his characters. And they reached a boiling point when he got cast as a transvestite in a Hollywood Actors Theatre production. Blackie was so completely unafraid of what people would think of him, and so completely enraptured with the idea of becoming this character, that he lived as a transvestite for months. He had taken all these pictures of himself in drag and mounted them above the fireplace, along with charts and graphs and diagrams and posters pertaining to transvestitism.

Then my brawling, voraciously hetero dad started wearing cutoff hot pants with his whole package encased over to one side in nylon pantyhose. He'd put on a tube top and wear gloves with rings over them. His makeup would be immaculate, down to the hot-pink lipstick. He'd prance around the house in high heels, sucking on a lollipop, talking all crazy gay. It got worse when he started to go outside like that. He'd just walk up and down Hollywood Boulevard, talking to strangers in character.

I started off supportive and proud of his great commitment to his art. But in the end, I broke down. All of my masculinity was being challenged. So when he started yelling at me one day for some school problem, I called him a faggot. The second that word came out of my mouth, he took a swing at me. And my dad was fast. Somehow I managed to catch his right jab before it could connect. I was about to counter with a punch of my own, but I got only halfway before I thought it wouldn't be a good idea to get violent with my own father. By now he had shoved me up against the bookshelf, and there was this fist-holding standoff between us. Ultimately, there was no bloodshed, but the energy was violent and ugly. And something would never be the same between us for decades to come.

3.

Fairfax High

I'll never forget my first day of high school. I arrived at Uni High and checked in with my counselor to get my class assignment. Then she dropped the bombshell.

"Tony, I know you've been going to Emerson for three years under a false address. Because you don't live in the district, you can't go to school here."

I didn't know it then, but that was one of the most eventful twists of fate I'd ever experience.

I went home to figure out which high school was in my district. It turned out to be Fairfax High, a sprawling school on the corner of Fairfax and Melrose. I went there the next day and felt like an alien in a sea of people who already knew one another. Because I was a day late, a lot of the classes I wanted were full. I didn't know any students, I didn't know any teachers, I didn't even know where the cafeteria was.

I started filling out my class forms, and when they asked for my name, I impulsively wrote "Anthony" instead of "Tony." When roll was called, the teachers all called out "Anthony Kiedis," and I didn't correct them. I just became Anthony—this slightly different guy who was more mature, more in control, more adult.

Fairfax was a true melting pot. There were Chinese immigrants, Korean immigrants, Russian immigrants, Jewish kids, and tons of black kids, along with the white kids. Once again, I started befriending all of the loneliest and the most unwanted kids in school. My first friends were Ben Tang, a scrawny, uncoordinated, huge-bespectacled Chinese kid, and Tony Shurr, a pasty-faced ninety-eight-pound weakling. About a month into the school year, Tony and I were talking in the quad at lunchtime when a tiny, crazy-looking, gap-toothed, big-haired kid came waltzing up to Tony, put him in a headlock, and started roughing him up. I couldn't tell at first if this was friendly fooling around or if the guy was bullying my best friend at Fairfax, so I erred on the side of friendship. I stepped in, grabbed him off Tony, and hissed, "If you touch him again like that, you're going to regret it for the rest of your life."

"What are you talking about? He's my friend," the kid protested.

It's weird. Even though we were starting off on this "I'll kick your ass" aggressiveness, I felt an instant connection to the remarkable little weirdo. Tony told me his name was Michael Balzary, soon to be known beyond the confines of Fairfax High as Flea.

Mike and I became inseparable. He lived about five blocks from me on Laurel Avenue. Every day we'd walk home from school, scrape together our meager assets, and buy a plate of taquitos to share at this hamburger/taco grease shack. Then we'd play football in the street. In a strange way, I was going from this very adult life with my father, partying and nightclubbing and hanging out with primarily his friends, to having a second, genuine no-worries childhood.

Mike was another outsider at Fairfax. He had been born in Australia. His father was a customs agent who had moved his family to New York and enjoyed a pretty conservative, stable lifestyle until Mike's mom took up with a jazz musician. Mike's parents split up, and he and his sister and his mom and his new stepdad moved to L.A.

Mike was painfully shy and insecure, and much more sheltered than I had been, so I assumed the alpha role in the relationship. This would be the dynamic that would continue for a long time, and it would be a beautiful thing, because we shared so much together. However, it would also carry an aspect of resentment for him, because I was kind of a bastard and a mean-spirited bully at times along the way.

Mike would never go anywhere without his trumpet. He was first trumpet in the school band, which meant that we'd work together—I was in play production that year. I was impressed by his musical skill and the fact that his lip was always swollen from playing the trumpet. His trumpet playing also opened me up to a whole other world—the world of jazz. One day Mike played me a Miles Davis record, and I realized that there was this type of music that was spontaneous and improvisational.

Even though Mike was living in a more or less traditional family unit, his situation at home seemed as chaotic as mine. He would regale me with stories of his out-of-control stepfather, Walter. For years Walter had dealt with an alcohol problem. He had gotten sober, a concept that I was unfamiliar with then, but now he was a real hermit. I hardly ever saw him, and the few times that I did, he'd be real gruff, screaming because Mike could not remember once to take out the trash on the right day. Every single time it was "Oooh, oooh, I forgot it's Thursday. I'll be in so much trouble."

Mike's mom was a real sweetheart, even if she had a bizarre Australian accent. But for the first few months I knew him, Mike kept talking to me about his older sister, Karen, who was back in Australia. "She's a wildcat," he'd tell me. "She's really hot. She's got a million boyfriends, and she's the best gymnast at Hollywood High. She went streaking in the middle of a citywide competition." I had to meet this Balzary sister.

Later that school year, Karen finally showed up. She was young and foxy and incredibly forward. By then it was common for Mike and me to sleep over at each other's houses. In fact, Mike's room had two tiny cot beds, one for him and one for me. His family had a hot tub in the backyard, and one night Mike, Karen, and I were in the tub drinking some wine. Karen's hand was continually wandering over to me under those bubbles, and when Mike called it a night and I was about to do the same, Karen grabbed me. "You stay," she implored. Time to meet the sister.

Karen immediately took charge. She started making out with me, then took me back to her bedroom, where she spent the next three hours introducing me to a variety of sexual experiences I hadn't even known were possible. She was on her game, doing things like going to the sink and coming back with a mouthful of hot water and giving me a blow job. What in heaven's name had I done to deserve this beautiful experience?

The next day Mike asked, "How was my sister?" I spared him the details because, after all, she *was* his sister, but I did thank him profusely for introducing us. Years and years later, he came to me and said, "We're really good friends, but this is something that's been bothering me for years. While you were in the room with my sister, I went outside the house and was peeping through the window for a few seconds." By then I couldn't have cared less, but it was probably a good thing that he waited as long as he did to tell me.

Mike was into pot when I first met him, so I began to dip more and more into my dad's stash to satisfy our needs. I knew the hiding places on top of the bookshelves where he kept his half-smoked joints. But he locked his main stash in the same closet where he kept his scale. One day I was hanging out with Mike in his stepdad's cellar workshop, and I came across a huge cache of skeleton keys. It was a one-in-a-million chance, but I asked Mike if I could try these keys on Blackie's closet, and sure enough, I found one that worked. So I started to carefully skim off my dad's stash of grass, quaaludes, and coke. Mike was impressed that I could grab a bud and leave everything so intact that Blackie never realized anything was missing.

My first real bonding trip with Mike happened that semester, when we went skiing on Mammoth Mountain. The Greyhound bus ride up was full of your classic mixed-nut variety of derelicts and forlorn people—a girl with a black eye, a speed freak who'd just been fired from his job, the whole bus culture of weirdos, and us two green kids.

Immediately, I went to the back bathroom, smoked half a joint, then passed it to Mike, and he repeated the ritual. By the time we got to Mammoth, a blizzard had started, and it was pitch black. Our plan was to spend the night in the laundry room of the condos there, a tip that one of my Emerson friends had given me, but the Greyhound left us in the middle of nowhere. We set out in the general direction of the condos, and suddenly Mike got a horrible stomachache. We walked and walked, and we were freezing, and Mike was nearly in tears from the pain. Just as frostbite was about to set in, we made an arbitrary turn and found the condos. We walked into the laundry room, got out our sleeping bags, and rolled one out beneath a rickety plywood shelf for folding clothes and the other on top of the shelf. I popped a few quarters in the dryer and curled up on the floor while Mike slept on the rickety shelf that was meant to hold a few pounds of clothes.

The next morning we went to rent skis. We picked out all our equipment, and Mike tried to pay with the credit card his mom had given us, but the seventeen-year-old girl behind the counter wouldn't take it. She insisted Mike's mom had to be there in person to authorize the charge.

Mike tried to explain that his mom was already on the

slopes, but she wouldn't budge. I had to salvage this trip, so I went outside and approached a lady who was getting ready to ski with her kids and asked to borrow her jacket and her ski hat and her glasses. Somehow I convinced her, and I put on her parka and her hat and her big square sunglasses. I took our mittens and hats and stuffed them in the parka to make tits, and I channeled Mike's mom's voice in my head, and then I went back into the ski shop and marched up to the girl behind the counter.

"I can't believe you pulled me off the slopes for this. This is my card, and I gave it to my son. What is your problem?" I said.

The girl was scared out of her mind, hearing this crazy woman's voice coming from behind this ski mask, and we got the stuff. We had the time of our lives, getting stoned on the chairlift and cutting in line and being the little bastards that we were. Mike had no idea at all how to ski; the first time down the mountain, he fell about fifty times. By the third time, he was keeping up with me. He just willed himself to learn to ski within an hour.

That night we went back to the laundry room and quartered our way through another night. We got in a second day of skiing, and it was time to go home. For some reason, I decided that the ski shop really didn't have a good inventory system, so these skis were now ours. We walked to the Greyhound station and loaded the rentals onto the bus with everyone else's skis. We were just about to board when a sheriff's car drove up. The sheriff got out and said, "You two. Over here now."

"What's the problem?" I said innocently.

"Those skis are stolen property. I need some ID," he said.

"Oh, no, no, no, no, we're not taking these. Did you think we were taking these skis? No, no, we rented these, and we were actually going to bring them back. In fact, we could probably just leave them here and go now," I desperately riffed.

We finally convinced the guy to just ticket us, and we promised to come back up and resolve the issue. We made it back down to Hollywood. The trip had been a monstrous success, even with a bad taste left in the mouth from the sheriff thing at the end. Some time passed and no calls, no summonses, no bad news coming from up north. And then one day it happened. Both Mike and I had been keeping an eye on the mail, but on the same day, while we were in school, both Blackie and Walter got letters.

Now we were in serious trouble. Walter was strict, and my dad wasn't having any kind of extra inconvenience in his life, especially because minors had to bring their parents to court in Mammoth. Now these guys had to deal with our problem. We were thinking it was going to be the end of the world as we knew it, but oddly enough, both our dads used that trip as a bonding session with their sons. Ultimately, we got off with a slap on the wrist, and all we had to do was write a letter every couple of months for six months, telling them how we were doing.

But my ski escapade with the authorities was minor compared to what would happen to Blackie that fall.

It was the perfect fall California day—sunny and beautiful. I came home from school about three-thirty P.M., like any other day, but my dad seemed a little aggravated over something. We were in our living room, which had a nice picture window that looked out over our front yard, when Blackie froze in his tracks. I looked out and I saw these Grizzly Adams–looking guys, big, burly lumberjack types, lurking in our front yard. My dad put his hand on my shoulder and said, "I think these guys might be undercover—"

As soon as that word came out of his mouth, the solid oak front door was kicked in. Simultaneously, the back door was flattened, and a phalanx of guys with shotguns and bulletproof vests and pistols poured in. Their shotguns were loaded and cocked and aimed right at my dad and me. They were all screaming, "Freeze! Freeze! Get on the floor!" like we were some huge operation. One false move of the finger and we would have been full of lead. They handcuffed us to each other on the couch and set about the business of systematically destroying our house.

It turned out that my dad had called a prostitute to come

over a few nights earlier, but when she got there, she wasn't my dad's cup of tea. To be a good sport, he offered her some cocaine. She stormed out and called the cops and told them that Blackie might be the Hillside Strangler, who was terrorizing L.A. at that time.

The cops spent the next two hours shredding mattresses and going through every article of clothing in the closet and stealing all these nice switchblades that I'd bought in Tijuana, so they could go home and give them to their kids. Thankfully, they weren't finding any drugs. Just when I was thinking that they might not discover my dad's treasure trove, one of the anal knuckleheads burrowed a hole up into the ceiling of the back closet and found everything. At that point my father and I knew the gig was up. They took out the big rocks of coke, the bags of weed, and the huge quaalude jar.

They started deliberating what to do with me. They were talking about taking me to juvie, but I knew I had to stay out of jail so I could help Blackie get bail. I convinced them that I had nothing to do with any of this and I needed to be in school in the morning. They finally agreed that I could stay in the ransacked apartment, and then they took Blackie away.

We were both crushed. I had visions of my dad going away for years. So I called up Connie, and she got her new boyfriend to put up his house as collateral. The next day, Blackie was out of jail. He had saved up around seven grand, which he had to immediately put down for a good lawyer; this put even more of a strain on our finances, because he had really cut down on his dealing and was more into his acting.

Luckily for us, a few months earlier I had been cast in a Coca-Cola commercial, and that was pretty good bank for a fifteen-year-old kid. But it generated more friction with my dad, because I was making more money than he was. He even tried to get me to pay some rent, which became a bone of contention between us, as did the 20 percent he was already taking out of my acting income as my manager. All of this was creating a schism in the Kiedis partnership.

Meanwhile, I was totally preoccupied with my budding social life at Fairfax. A few months after I met Mike, I met another person who would become one of the closest friends I'd ever have. Every so often, we'd have weird local high school rock bands that would play on the outdoor stage on the quad at Fairfax. Sometime that first semester, I saw a silly group called Anthym play. When I say "silly," don't get me wrong; all these guys were really talented, but they were a little behind the times as far as I was concerned. They were doing covers of Queen and Led Zeppelin, all these bands whose times had come to an end, and they all had these big, poodly-looking, long curly hairdos.

At the gig, some people were passing out these homemade rectangular Anthym buttons, so I took one. I was wearing the pin one day when I ran into one of the guitar players from Anthym. His name was Hillel Slovak. We started talking, and he invited me over to his house for a snack.

Within a few minutes of hanging out with Hillel, I sensed that he was absolutely different from most of the people I'd spent time with. I usually felt like the leader in most relationships with kids my age, because of all the crazy experiences that I'd had as a kid, but I immediately knew that Hillel was at least my equal, and in fact knew a lot of things that I didn't. He understood a lot about music, and he was a great visual artist, and he had a sense of self and a calm about him that were just riveting. Hillel was Jewish, he looked Jewish and talked about Jewish stuff, and the food in that kitchen was Jewish. He made us egg-salad sandwiches on rye bread that day, which was totally exotic food to me then.

After the sandwiches, we had a meaningful heart-to-heart chat. By the time I left his house, I was thinking, "Well, that's my new best friend for life right there." It had been like that when I met Mike and Joe Walters. Sometimes you just know. Hillel had a Datsun B10 station wagon, and we spent many, many nights driving up to the top of the Hollywood Hills, pulling into a rest stop, looking out over the city, putting in some crazy progressive-rock tapes, smoking weed, and discussing the girls at Fairfax.

It was one thing to meet Mike and Hillel, who would both become such important people in my life, but what were the odds that I'd meet three soul mates that first year at Fairfax? I had actually met Haya Handel before Mike or Hillel. During the first week of school, I was in Spanish class, and my eyes were riveted by this amazingly beautiful girl with long brown wavy hair, perfect pale skin, and big brown eyes that radiated with a mad twinkle. She was Jewish, and she was also by far the smartest person in the class, but she was amazingly down-to-earth and surprisingly flirtatious.

Of course, I immediately developed a major crush on her. Whenever I saw her, I'd chat her up. But she soon made it known to me that she was not available as a girlfriend. At first I thought she was seeing this blond guy named Johnny Karson, who would later play a major role in my life, but she told me that he was just her old friend from junior high. It turned out that she was going out with a guy named Kevin, a tall, strapping, handsome black kid who was the star of the gymnastics team. I knew Haya was from a conservative Jewish family, and they felt it would be taboo for her to date anybody but a Jew, so her relationship with the black gymnast was a big secret from her family. We'd talk, and she'd confide in me, "I really want to go out with my boyfriend, but I can't—it's too risky, and my parents might find out." It was all tragic information because it wasn't me, but I definitely didn't lose interest and move on.

We sat side by side in another class that semester. It was right after lunch, so I'd always see her boyfriend walk her to class, where they'd do their little good-byes. One day I just decided, "Fuck it, I'm bringing flowers." I bought a bouquet and wrote a poem, but by the time I got back to school, class had already started. I rushed into the classroom, and the teacher said, "Is there a good reason why you're late?"

"Well, not really," I said and handed Haya the flowers and the poem. Everyone oohed and ahhed, and the teacher instantly cut me some slack. Haya was embarrassed, but she realized that this guy must be pretty crazy about her. That signaled the beginning of my getting in with her, but it was a rocky beginning that would stretch out into the next year at school.

By the second half of tenth grade, I had somehow burned through all the money I had saved from my acting career, which was mostly dormant, since I just wanted to concentrate on being a regular high school kid. Since Blackie's cash flow was so meager, I got a part-time job as a delivery boy for an upscale liquor store called John and Pete's. I loved that job. I'd drive recklessly, breaking all the laws, speeding and going on the wrong side of the street and cutting around traffic to make my deliveries so I could take my time getting back to the store. After a few weeks, I realized that if I hid a bottle of booze or a six-pack in the store trash, I could go back to the Dumpster later, retrieve it, and be good for the night. Combined with the thirty bucks in tips I'd pull in a shift, if I worked a few days a week, I'd have my spending money.

But my first year at Fairfax was mostly an oasis from responsibility. I had all of this beautiful free time to roam and play and walk aimlessly and discover, to talk and get into mischief and steal and vandalize and go visit some friend and try to find some pot to smoke and maybe play some basketball. There really was no pressure, no anxiety. I might have homework, but I did it after dinner.

Mike was my constant companion. On those long walks, we'd pass all of these one-, two-, three-, and sometimes four- and five-story apartment buildings that were built around a central pool. One day an amazing idea was triggered. I looked at the building and said, "That's a diving board, my friend."

I had gotten some experience in Michigan with jumping off of railroad trestles into bodies of water. Sometimes we would wait until right before the train came, and it was an amazing rush. Mike was game for anything, so we started out by jumping off second-story buildings into the pools. It didn't matter if people were sitting around the pool sunbathing; that made it all the more fun, to be that guy who flew out of the sky and landed next to an unsuspecting sunbather.

If there was any chance of getting caught, we'd make the jump and then take off like bats out of hell and cut through some backyards and get away. But there were other times where we'd come out of the water and recognize that we weren't in any danger of getting busted, so it was yet another opportunity to freak somebody out by yelling or dancing around or mooning.

We finally worked our way up to five-story buildings. Our favorite was on King's Road. We'd get up on the roof and look down and see a postage stamp of water, and we would go for it. Then I started experimenting with different styles of jumping. I wasn't about to dive into a pool, but I started jumping off the building backward, doing superman things. I would run out, and instead of jumping far ahead, I'd jump straight up and go into an arch and lie down and then go back straight into the pool.

It didn't matter how deep the pools were. You don't need much water to land in. If it's a shallow pool, as you hit the water, you let your body go sideways, so you're using the width of the water as well as the depth.

My dad knew about the jumping, and he wasn't a fan. He didn't try to put a stop to it, but he'd lecture me from time to time: "Don't you go jumping. I know you're smoking pot all the time. It's not a good combination." At that point we didn't communicate about a lot of things. He'd complain, and I'd ignore him and say, "Whatever. Fuck you."

One day in June of that year, Mike and I had been eyeing this apartment building just down the block from my house. The pool was small and teardrop-shaped, and the deep end was the smallest section of the teardrop. To get to the top of the building, we had to climb over railings, and we made enough of a commotion climbing up that somebody started yelling at us to get down.

We never even thought of aborting. I told Mike to go, and he jumped, and I heard the splash. Then I got up on the railing. I didn't even look down to see my angle: I was more concerned with the people who were yelling.

I jumped, and as I was in the air, I realized that I had put too much into the leap and I was going to overshoot the pool, but there was nothing I could do about it. The concrete was coming up at me, and I landed smack on my heels and missed the pool by about ten inches. I was dazed and fell back into the pool and started to sink. Somehow, despite being in paralytic shock, I managed to push myself up out of the pool, roll over onto the lip of the concrete, and emit this inhuman sound that sounded like it came from the depths of Hades.

I looked over and saw Mike, but I couldn't move. Somebody called an ambulance, and the paramedics clumsily rolled me onto a gurney, almost dropping me in the process. They didn't stabilize the stretcher in the back of the ambulance, so I was bumping around in agony the whole ride to the hospital. It was pain and shock and horror, and I knew something was seriously wrong, because I still couldn't move.

They took me to Cedars Sinai and did an X ray, and after a while, the doctor came into the room and said, "You broke your back, and it doesn't look so good." I had been keeping a pretty optimistic stiff-upper-lip outlook on the whole thing, but when he gave me the prognosis, I started weeping. "There goes my summer. There goes my athleticism. There goes my life."

I started hitting on every nurse who came by, desperate for painkillers, but they wouldn't give me anything until the doctor had okayed it. Then Blackie came rushing in, screaming, "What did I tell you? Now who's right? Did I not tell you this would happen? You smoke pot. You jump off the thing. This was bound to happen." I just looked at the nurse and said, "Somebody take him away from here. He's not allowed in here." At last they got me medicated, and rigged up a pulley system with a harness and a medical bustier girdle. I was told that my vertebrae were flattened like pancakes and that a month in traction would help stretch them back.

During the first week in the hospital, I got visits from Mike and Hillel and a few other friends. By now I had won Haya over, and she was kind of my girlfriend. Once she came to visit and lay down on the bed with me and let me feel her up, which was a real treat. "Okay, broke the back, but at least I've got my hands on the breasts of the girl I've been in love with since the first day of Spanish class."

After two weeks of traction, I started getting stir-crazy. One day Hillel came to visit, and I told him, "I can't stay here for a day longer. You have to get me out of here." He went downstairs to get the car ready, and I unstrapped the girdle, rolled over, and tilted myself up on my two feeble legs. With my bare ass flashing out of my hospital gown, I started lurching like Frankenstein down that hallway. All the nurses went crazy, screaming that I couldn't go anywhere for two more weeks, but I didn't care. Somehow I made it down the steps, and Hillel helped me into the car. Before I went home, I made him drive me to the building where I had messed up so I could try to figure out what I'd done wrong.

I spent the next few weeks horizontal in my own bed. I got some lovely visitations from a friend of my father's named Lark, who was a beautiful, relatively successful twenty-something actress. She came by at all hours, during the day, late at night, whenever, just to fix me up sexually. I had gotten my girdle back, and I had to keep telling her to be real careful, but I was getting absolutely ridden by a wild nymphomaniac banshee. That made the convalescing time a little more pleasant.

That summer I went back to Michigan, but I was still struggling with my back. Every time I'd get an X ray, the doctors always said it didn't look right—it was crooked, the vertebrae were still smushed. It was never good news. But over time, my back progressively got better. At some point Mike took a Greyhound out to visit me. He showed up at my house after this torturous journey, looking totally haggard and sleep-deprived, since he had been squeezed the whole way out between a giant snoring Indian and someone who kept constantly throwing up. He had a *Penthouse* with him, and I remember opening it up and all the pages were stuck together. "Uh, that was the way it was when I got it," he lied.

But he was as happy as a bunny rabbit once we got settled in. My mom treated him like her own son, and Steve let us take his car and explore Michigan. We took a camping trip to the Upper Peninsula, we visited my aunt and my cousins, and we went water-skiing. We were two kids, grown up in some ways but children in other ways, but certainly not thinking of ourselves as children— thinking of ourselves as Masters of the Universe over all other life forms, including adults. We were hipper, cooler, smarter, we knew more about pretty much everything there was to know more about, and we were fine with that. Adolescence is such a fun time in your life, because you think you know it all, and you haven't gotten to the point where you realize that you know almost nothing. So we had our summer fun, and when Mike was ready to go back, I remember my mom going to town with bags and bags of food for this poor kid who had to go on the Greyhound. She baked him a pecan pie and gave him a huge industrial-sized bag of Pepperidge Farm Goldfish and treated him like a little prince.

I went back for my second year at Fairfax, but things were getting increasingly troubled at home. After the bust, while my dad was waiting to be sentenced, he became a lot more careful. He stopped selling drugs completely and became the prototypical starving actor. We'd fight over the most mundane things. One time he was outraged that I ate a can of his soup; another time I infuriated him when I ate a sandwich out of the refrigerator that he had been coveting all day.

Around this time Blackie also tried to impose a curfew on me. He arbitrarily decided that I had to be in by midnight. If I broke curfew, I'd be locked out. One night I went out skateboarding and got home a few minutes after midnight, and the door was locked. I knocked and I knocked and knocked, but there was no answer. Finally, he came to the door, totally incensed. "What did I tell you? There's no getting in here after twelve." He complained that he had to get up early to go to acting classes, and I was interrupting his sleep. This from the same guy who kept me up till six in the morning throughout my junior high years.

The next time it happened, my neighbor came out and offered to let me crash on his couch, but I declined. I had tried to leave my window open a crack so I could sneak back in, but my dad was so security-conscious that he'd make sure the house was airtight before he went to bed. So I had to wake Blackie again, and he was even madder this time. We had a shoving match in the kitchen, and he told me that I had to either follow his rules or get out.

It was a no-brainer. I called Donde Bastone, this friend of mine, and asked if he wanted a roommate. I had met Donde during my first year at Fairfax, but by the eleventh grade, he had dropped out and was dealing weed out of his own house on Wilcox. He was the only sixteen-year-old I knew who had it together enough to have his own pad and a great little car. He agreed to let me move in, but he laid out exactly how much rent I had to pay and what my responsibilities would be around the house.

In the middle of the day, Haya came over in her huge car, and we started loading my stuff. It consisted of some clothes, my stereo, and a large neon Shamrock Billiards sign that my dad had given me. Unfortunately, as I was pulling out of the driveway, Blackie came home.

"Whoa, whoa, whoa! Where do you think you're going?" he said.

"I'm out. I'm leaving. You're seeing the end of me."

"What's all this stuff in the car?" he asked.

"That's my stuff," I maintained.

"That's not your stuff, that's my stuff."

"You gave me this stuff," I reminded him.

"I gave it to you as long as you're living under my roof. If you're not in the house, it's not your stuff." We had this big argument over the belongings, which I lost, but I didn't even care at that point. I just wanted out.

I moved in with Donde and immediately concluded that he was way ahead of his time in many different ways. For one, he had an extraordinary record collection (complete with special shelving units built to house it) and a really nice sound system. Part of his deal, along with being a knucklehead and smoking pot, was to play music all day and all night. Every waking hour in that house, there was a record spinning. Thankfully, he had incredible taste in music. He wasn't one of those guys who was exclusively into ska or punk rock or vintage blues; he was into everything. And because he had friends who worked at record companies, he was always getting advance copies of albums by David Bowie or Talking Heads.

Our house also became the party house, and we'd throw these rather gala affairs every couple of weekends. It was one of those periods when the drugs and alcohol were working to perfection and not interfering with getting work done, and no one was strung out on anything. Donde always seemed to come up with some cocaine for these parties, and cocaine then was a treat, not something that we had all the time, so we weren't carried away with it.

Around this time my relationship with Hillel intensified. I was taking a health class that was two doors down from Hillel's art class. His art teacher was very liberal, so I'd get passes from my health class to go to the bathroom, and I'd go and have some intense conversations while Hillel was doing his anatomical drawings. Mike and Hillel were also becoming friends and developing an interesting musical bond. Anthym was about to play a series of shows at other high schools, and out of nowhere, Hillel began to secretly teach Mike how to play the bass guitar. Todd, the current bass player in Anthym, wasn't a very good musician, though he did provide the band's PA system. But Hillel and Alan Mishulsky, the other guitarist, and Jack Irons, the drummer, were authentic musical talents, so Hillel was looking to replicate that on the bass.

When Todd walked in on a rehearsal one day and saw little Mike playing Anthym songs on Todd's bass through Todd's bass amp, he took his equipment and quit the band. So Mike was in.

Right before they started playing around, I approached Hillel and asked if I could introduce the band. Actually, I got the idea from Blackie, who had long been introducing his friends' bands with comic ironic Vegas-type speeches. Hillel agreed, and for my first introduction, I reworked one of Blackie's classic vamps. I used Cal Worthington, who had become famous in L.A. for his tacky late-night used-auto ads.

"Ladies and gentlemen, Cal Worthington calls them the hottest rockers in L.A. Their parents call them crazy, and the girls call them all the time, but I call 'em like I see 'em, and I call them Anthym," I screamed. Then I flew off the stage into the audience and danced for the entire show. It didn't matter one bit if I was the only person dancing, I was so into supporting my friends' art.

But as much as I was a fan of the whole band, it really became about me and Mike and Hillel. Hillel had known Jack and Alan much longer, but when he found us, he felt that we were his guys. For one, Hillel was really into weed, and those other guys weren't. We were into insanity and pushing the envelope, and Alan and Jack were much more mama's boys. So me and Mike and Hillel became the real Three Musketeers for the next two years in high school. For our own amusement, we created alternate identities, three Mexicans who spoke in stylized Cheech and Chong accents. I was Fuerte (strong), Mike was Poco (small), and Hillel was Flaco (slender). Together, we were Los Faces. We were a gang, but not a ruffian gang; we were a comedy gang. We spent hours and hours playing these characters, and it helped us develop a sense of camaraderie that would last for years.

Meanwhile, my friendship with Haya was progressing, but not as smoothly as my bond with Mike and Hillel. We still had one major problem—I wasn't the nice Jewish boy her family had envisioned. I'll never forget the way she explained the situation to me: "This is how it is. I love you. You're my man. But my parents can never know, because they don't want me to date someone who isn't Jewish. So as far as they're concerned, you and I are best friends, and we work on school stuff together, and that's it. Don't be affectionate toward me when you come over. Just act like my friend."

It was hard. Her father barely spoke a word to me. Her mother was more cordial, but they both smelled something uncomfortable in their lives, and it was me. I could always see how their repression manifested itself in her psyche. As much as she tried to not limit herself to her parents' confined world, they still exerted a strong hold on her, a bond that she'd fight against, but when push came to shove, she'd never break it. She was their daughter.

I knew she loved me, but she was afraid to go too far with that love. During eleventh grade, I was crazy about the idea of making love to her. I'd had all of these different sexual experiences, but never one based in true love. I knew how much fun fucking could be, but here was a chance to do it for real. I was trying to get her to sleep with me, but she wouldn't commit. "No. Give me time. I'm not ready. There's a birth-control issue." She kept putting it off, and it became this ongoing "Are you ready yet?" In the meantime, she'd give me hand jobs, which she was great at, but I wanted this girl in my arms while I was inside her.

It was maddening. She was my world. I adored her. I would have done anything for her. But she wasn't giving it up. Seven months into the relationship we went on a date, and I was wearing my best clothes, and I'd done my hair the best I could. We went back to my room with no intention of anything happening, and started to kiss. We took off our clothes, and we were basically in a sphere of love and light and warmth, and the rest of the world disappeared. It was better than I ever could have dreamed, it was that thing I had been looking for, that love mixed with the rapture of sex.

Once Haya and I started having a regular sexual relationship, I couldn't have been happier. I wanted to have sex with her all day and all night, every day and every night. If I didn't see her for a while, all I could think about was being with her. When I'd go on a trip to Michigan, I couldn't wait to see her again. Every song I listened to was about her. We had our special songs, David Bowie's "Heroes" and the Beatles' "Here, There and Everywhere."

My senior year at Fairfax was rife with contradictions. Me and my friends were definitely outsiders, living by our own moral code, one tenet of which was Thou Shalt Steal Your Meals. Mike and I refined a method of food thievery that was unbeatable for about two years, until the supermarkets finally caught on to it. I would go into the market and fill up a little red plastic basket with the finest provisions they offered—filet mignon, lobsters, cognac, you name it. Then I'd take my basket over to the magazine rack, which was directly adjacent to the entrance. I'd pick up a magazine and set my basket on the floor and, while I was perusing the magazine, I'd surreptitiously slide the basket under the chrome railing. Then Mike, who had been waiting outside, would dash in, grab the basket, and go right out the exit door. Soon we had an eight-foot-tall stack of empty red baskets behind my house, a testament to our continuing ability to feed ourselves in style.

We still used our old tried-and-true bottle-up-the-pants method to steal booze. Once I even upped the ante and stole a pair of skis. I went to the back of the sporting-goods store and asked, "What's the best pair of skis that you have in here in my size?" The salesman said, "Well, these racing skis." I waited for him to leave, and I picked up the skis and walked right out the front door. I had decided that if I walked boldly right past the cashier, they would think, "He's picking up something that he's already paid for, because he's not stopping."

In some respects, our antisocial impulses were getting reinforced by the music that we were listening to. When I first started Fairfax in 1977, punk rock had just begun to make itself felt in Los Angeles. But it was a tiny subculture. Blackie, to his credit, was on the cutting edge of the new music scene. He was one of the first people to frequent a punk-rock club called the Masque, which was on Hollywood Boulevard. Whenever punk-rock groups from New York would come to town, they'd play the Whisky, and Blackie and I would always wind up at the Tropicana Motel, a seedy old classic paradise on Santa Monica Boulevard, which was where the bands stayed and where the afterparties were. At that time, my favorite record was Blondie's first. Every one of those songs was indelibly etched on my soul, and I was totally in love with Deborah Harry.

So when Blondie came to town, we headed to the Tropicana for the party. They had a suite, and Debbie was in the front room. We started talking, and I was smitten, totally melting. In my delusional state, I thought, "This is a once-in-a-lifetime opportunity. You might never see this woman again. You better make your move." With complete earnestness, I said, "I know I haven't known you that long, but will you marry me?"

She smiled and said, "That's so kind of you to ask. I think you're a great guy, but I don't know if you know this—that guitar player I was playing with tonight, who's back there in the bedroom . . . well, that's my husband. We're very happily married, and I really don't have any room in my life for another man." I was crushed.

Mike and I began hanging out in the punk scene by necessity. Shortly after we started Fairfax, I had brought Mike to the Rainbow one night. Before we got there, we drank a lot of Michelob beer. I had a tolerance for alcohol, but apparently he didn't. We were sitting at Blackie's power table, and the girls were there, and the music was going, and Mike looked at me and said, "I'm not feeling so good." He started to rush outside, but before he could go two feet, he began projectile-vomiting all over the Rainbow. Not what they wanted from two underage kids in their establishment. He threw up all the way into the parking lot, where they gave him the boot. Then they came in for me and said, "Get out there with him. You're never coming back here again." I kept trying to get back in for a year, but they had really eighty-sixed me. It was time to find my own scene.

My first punk concert was a daytime show at the Palladium. Devo was playing, along with the Germs. I was standing in the back, just fascinated. The music was cool as shit, these people looked incredible, almost too cool for me—there was no way I could ever be accepted by this crowd, because they were light-years ahead of me in terms of style. I remember walking over to the side of the stage, where people were going in and out of the backstage area, and there was this girl with some fucked-up punk-rock haircut, and she was taking giant safety pins and piercing her cheek with them, one after the other. That was new to me.

Mike and I began trying to worm our way into this new scene, where, unlike at the Rainbow, I had no clout. There was an explosion of amazing bands in L.A. at that time, X and the Circle Jerks and Black Flag and China White, the list could go on and on. The energy was unbridled, more creative and exciting and bombastic than anything anybody had ever seen. Fashion-wise, energy-wise, dance-wise, music-wise, it was like the dawning of the Renaissance in my own town. Rock had become this boring old beast, ready to die, and now there was fresh crazy-ass blood flowing through the streets of Hollywood. The first wave of punk rock had already crested, but there was a second coming. It wasn't a violent hard-core scene, like the bands from Orange County. In Hollywood it was more about creativity and originality. The Screamers and the Weirdos were two of Hollywood's first punk-rock bands, but they sounded nothing alike.

What all these bands did share was an element of anarchy and nonconformity. That first X record, or all the Black Flag records from that time, were masterpieces. Darby Crash's lyrics for the Germs were as good as it ever got in the world of punk rock. He was on to a whole other level of intelligence.

So Mike and I hung out in the parking lot of the Starwood, probably the best punk-rock venue around then, and we started to poke our noses through the door of this world. The Starwood was a tough club to sneak into, but there was a side door near the parking lot, guarded by a huge bouncer. If a fight broke out and his attention got diverted, we'd slip in as fast as we could. Sometimes, if a bunch of people were going in, we tried the crawling thing and used them as cover. When we couldn't sneak into the show, we'd linger in the parking lot, but neither of us had a lot of mojo or game, so we'd have to watch the goings-on. Nobody was inviting us to hang out.

One time Mike and I sneaked into the Starwood for a Black Flag show. We were fish out of water. We loved these bands, but we dressed all wrong and we had the wrong haircuts and the wrong shoes and we didn't even dance like all the punks. Those guys had the really cool boots with the chains wrapped around them and the right combination of ripped-up plaid clothes and spiked haircuts. Mike and I were lucky to have one leather jacket between the two of us.

Black Flag put on an amazing show. They had a guy onstage called Mugger who was in charge of security. Every time someone tried to jump up onstage and dance around a bit and then jump back off, Mugger would just attack the person and get into a brutal fistfight. During all this, the band did not miss a beat. One guy managed to get past Mugger and stage-dive. He flew right by me, and I got kicked in the head with his heavy steel-toed boot. I almost passed out.

One of the reasons we didn't plunge feet-first into this scene was that in some ways, we were still model students at Fairfax. At least I was. It was a strange dichotomy. I smoked tons of pot, took pills, and drank on the weekends. But it never got out of control. I never missed school. It was important to me to be the straight-A student. In a way, I was a rebel by getting good grades, because most of the stoners and the druggies were getting no grades. I didn't want to be like them. When I was a junior, I got my report card, and it was A's all the way down the line, which I loved. I wanted to be the best at whatever it was that was in front of me.

On my terms. I didn't necessarily want to study for hours to get there, but I wanted to do enough at the last minute.

By this time we were all thinking about college. At the end of my senior year, my grades were starting to slip, and I had to go to Mrs. Lopez, my Spanish teacher, and beg, borrow, and steal to get a B. Mike was having his own problems with grades. He always vacillated between being an absolutely brilliant student and an absolute flunk-out. Our last semester he was in Don Platt's honors history class with Haya. Platt was a no-nonsense general who was in total command of his class. He was bald but in great physical shape, with a perfect tan, a suave Gavin MacLeod type.

Mike and I had been running around like maniacs the week before his big final, and he didn't study for it, so he cheated. The last guy on Planet Earth you'd want to get busted by for cheating was Don Platt. He was not afraid to call you out in front of the class and humiliate you. That's what he did to Mike, who came out of class that day white as a ghost. Getting a D in Platt's class would put a pretty major dent in Mike's chances for getting a good grade-point average.

But it wasn't my worry. I was already a shoo-in to college with my grades. In fact, I planned to go to Don Platt for one of my recommendations so I could go to UCLA. I had been Platt's student for three years, and I had aced every one of his classes, so I knew he'd give me the crown jewel of all recommendations. A few days later, I went to see him after school, and he had a very unwelcoming look on his face. I asked him for a recommendation, and it was as if he already had a speech prepared. "Anyone who associates with Michael Balzary is not a friend of mine, nor is he getting a recommendation from me. For all I know, you and Michael were cheating the whole time you were in my classes."

This was absurd. I was probably the best student he'd had in ten years. The only time I'd even come close to crossing him was in my first semester. I had chosen to do an oral report on Uriah P. Levy, who was a great American naval officer. During the course of my research, I discovered the derivation of the word "fuck." It came from the early naval logs that the captain would keep. If a crew member was punished for having sexual intercourse, it was noted in the log as "FUCK" (for unlawful carnal knowledge). That was too good a factoid not to share with the class.

So I was up there spieling on Uriah P. Levy and the navy, and it was all Monty Pythonesque to me. I got to the punishable offenses, and I walked up to the chalkboard and wrote "F, U, C, K" in huge letters. I looked over at Mr. Platt, and the blood was rushing to the top of his bald head, but I never cracked a smile and continued to explain the concept. Meanwhile, Mike and the rest of the class came unglued, but there was nothing Platt could do. I had him.

Now he thought he had me. I tried to make my case for the recommendation, but he wasn't having any of it. "There's the door," he said. I walked out of there shell-shocked. Ultimately, I wound up going to the geometry teacher, and he was nice enough to write me a great recommendation. But I still had to get even with Platt.

Somewhere along the line that semester, I had stumbled upon some cardboard boxes of beautiful big black and red plastic marquee letters. Thinking they might be useful for an art project, I kept them. At the end of that Memorial Day weekend, the night before we were supposed to return to classes, Mike and I were driving around, stoned on pot, listening to music, when a brilliant idea came to me.

We drove up to the marquee in front of Fairfax High and started climbing up the pole, armed with the appropriate letters. Then we spelled out DANDY DON PLATT SUCKS ANUS, and motor-oiled the pole and the platform to inhibit the progress of anyone who would try to take our message down.

We looked up at the sign, congratulated each other, and went home and fell asleep. The next day we went to school, and there was a whole hubbub of activity around the marquee, people taking pictures and workmen trying to circumvent the motor oil and get those letters off.

Nobody ever came to Mike or me for questioning. We weren't even suspects. Maybe Platt had screwed over enough kids that there was an abundance of people with a motive. But that wasn't the end of it. At the end of that summer, we decided to leave a message for the incoming class at Fairfax. So we went back to the box of letters, climbed back up that pole, and left DANDY DON CONTINUES TO SUCK ANUS.

4.

Under the Zero One Sun

I was thrilled to find out I'd been accepted to UCLA. Not only was I going to the same university my father had, but Haya, who could have gotten into any school in the country, had chosen to stay home and go to college with me. It was like the planets had aligned.

But I came back down to earth pretty fast. I never felt at home at UCLA. The student body was filled with Poindexters and Asian kids who weren't there to socialize or yuk it up at all. Everyone there was all business, all the time. I didn't make one friend the entire time I was there. Besides, club-going and partying at Donde's house and running around with Hillel and Mike was way more important to me than studying Chinese history, which was, don't ask me why, one of the classes I signed up for.

On top of these general woes, my finances were completely on the skids. I had no income except for the twenty dollars a month my mom was sending me. So I reverted to my old practices. When it came to getting textbooks, which were incredibly expensive, I went to the campus bookstore, filled up my basket, walked over by the exit, nudged it past the sensors, then bought a pack of gum and picked up my free books on the way out. When it came to food, I'd go to the school cafeteria, which had a great selection of hot and cold meals, and fill up a tray. Before I got to the register, I'd start going backward in line, as if picking up things I had missed, until I got to the end of the line. Then I'd walk out with the food. I never got caught. Hillel would often come and join me, because he was on a budget, too. Those meals with him were probably the most joyous moments of my college career.

That year, Hillel, Mike, and I perfected something we called dining and dashing. We'd pick restaurants that had a lot of traffic and a lot of waitresses, like Canter's on Fairfax. We'd eat our food, then individually slip out the door. The sad thing was, we didn't stop to think that these poor waitresses were getting stuck with the check, and even if the restaurant didn't make them pay for our meal, they weren't getting their tips. It wasn't until years later, when I had to examine the consequences of some of my earlier behavior, that I began to make amends by going back to these places and putting some money in their tills.

Hillel had a lot of free time on his hands that first semester, because he didn't go on to college after Fairfax. I'd meet him after school and hang out with him on the weekends and get high on pot. He was a late bloomer to drug use, but he loved his weed.

I relished the time I spent with him, since I sure wasn't looking forward to school. I hated all my classes except one: an expository composition class taught by a young female professor. Each week we had to write a composition that she'd critique. Even though I was the great procrastinator and would wait until the night before the paper was due to even think about it, I loved that class. I got an A on every paper, and like Jill Vernon, the teacher would keep me after class and encourage me to write more.

If some of my other classes had been Recreational Drugtaking

101 or, better yet, Advanced Coke Shooting, I might have fared better at UCLA. I was fourteen the first time I shot coke. I was at one of my dad's parties back on Palm Street, watching all the adults shooting up, and I badgered them into making up a small load and shooting me up. At the end of my senior year at Fairfax, I started shooting up again. One of the first times, I was alone at home and felt so ecstatic that I called Haya. I told her, "This is the greatest feeling ever. We have to do this together." I didn't see it as a road to death and insanity, I just saw it as a beautiful, beautiful feeling.

As euphoric as that feeling is, the comedown from shooting coke is horrific. Dante's *Inferno* times ten. You fall into a dark and demonic, depressing place, in an agonizing state of discomfort, because all of these chemicals that you normally have to release ever so slowly to keep yourself comfortable in your skin are now gone, and you have nothing inside to make you feel okay. That's one of the reasons I took heroin a few years later. It became the eighty-foot pillow to break that cocaine fall.

I never had any qualms about using needles to ingest drugs. Once I even made shooting up into a weird art project. I was still at Fairfax, and I'd had a fight with Haya. She had been ignoring me for a couple of days, so I drove over to her dad's store, where she worked. I pulled up in front of her car and, in broad daylight, stuck an empty syringe in my arm and drew out a couple cc's of fresh blood. Then I walked up to her car, squirted the blood back into the palm of my hand, smeared it on my mouth, and made blood kisses all over her windshield and the driver's-side window. My romantic little blood project worked. I went home and got a call later that day: "I got your message. That was so nice. I love you so much." Unfortunately, the blood stained the glass, and despite repeated washings, we never could erase all the traces of those blood kisses.

I was comfortable with syringes, but my dilemma was how to get them. I figured it out one day when I was walking through

Wearing a shirt that I wish I still had. It probably came from my faraway dad. I seem to be honing and sharpening my strategic powers over a game of Don't Break the Ice. 2247 Paris Street S.E., Grand Rapids, Michigan. Approximately 1971.

May 1, 1969
Dear Dad
how are you Dad

Please work hard So I can
go to California.
My Dog had puppies

Tony Kiedis.

Mom used to sit me down for the occasional correspondence with my renegade pops. Little did I know I was encouraging the sale of weed by the kilo. Either way, I was California dreaming at the tender age of six.

At the age of twenty-one, I was already an angel away from killing myself behind the wheel of my mother's Subaru. Nobody told me that dope-sick junkies shouldn't drink three buckets of beer and try to drive home. I played a show with the Red Hots in New York City less than a week later. 1984.

Like father, like son. I've got to tell you, little boys love their dads. It's a fact. Doesn't matter what the scenario is, we love our dads. And need 'em. This is one of the rare but sacred visits my father made to my house on Paris Street. Early 1970s.

I've never met a girl that had more style or spunk than Jennifer Bruce. I don't think anyone has. We used to drag ourselves out of bed and grab a simple breakfast at Joseph's Café in the heart of Hollywood. I wasn't doing too well and she was right behind me. Bless her heart, we loved and needed each other in the worst way. 1985.

This is Christmas. Right out of a fairy tale! It would have been the second or third Christmas that Jennifer had come back to Michigan with me. We were still in love and still perpetrating classic '80s California fashion. 1986.

This is from the "I love my mama" series of photos. There were dozens, but I could use only a couple. There is no stronger or more reliable creature on Earth than the Mother. This is mine at her backyard wedding to Steve Idema. Lowell, Michigan. Summer of 1973.

To this day, Mom's house in Michigan is still my greatest sanctuary for peace and relaxation. Here we are in the yard sometime in the mid '90s. As you can see from her shirt, she is forever my number one fan, and like my dad, she has been from day one.

When I was fourteen, I moved back to Michigan to be with the family for the birth of my youngest sister, Jenny (the baby in the picture). I stayed for the first semester of ninth grade and attended Lowell High. By this time, I was a pretty regular pot smoker, and I'm probably stoned in this photo.

This must be our first U.S. tour
when we played Top of the Rock in
my hometown of Grand Rapids,
Michigan. The next day the paper
wrote, "If I had a son like that, I'd
shoot him." My mom wrote a letter
to the editor putting them all in
their places. Flea and I were having
fun. 1985.

Hard to say where the hell I got my sense of style from. This was taken a mere
few months after the Red Hot conception, and I had no real performance role
models. I think I wore whatever I could find nearby. Back then we would often
end up wearing each other's clothes. 1984.

My book publishers tried to kick this photo out of the lot, but I thought it was way too picturesque. Notice the flowers, my favorite hat, and the buttons on my jacket. 1972.

Childhood portrait of my mom. She reminds me of my amazing nephew Jackson in this picture. Funny how a family thread keeps on weaving its way through the generations. What a cutie. 1940-something.

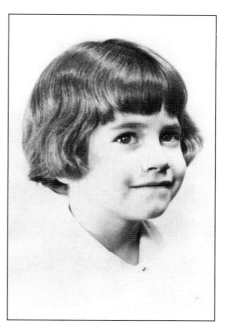

In 1974, the single most important possession in my life was my fiberglass Bane skateboard with Cadillac trucks and fan urethane wheels. The second most important was my li'l sis, Julie. This is us sharing a bit of love for the camera on summer vacation.

My mom took pictures of me after I had been crying over a tricycle wipeout. I think it shows her skill as a photographer. It was just the two of us living together at the time in West Los Angeles, and we made the most of our togetherness.

a supermarket that had a pharmacy. I saw an advertisement for insulin, and a lightbulb went off in my head. I realized that if I went up to the counter and acted like a diabetic and ordered my insulin first, when I asked for syringes, they wouldn't even question it. I marched up and ordered the Lente U 100 insulin. The pharmacist went to the refrigerator and got out a box of insulin vials, and as he was walking back, I offhandedly said, "Oh, you'd better throw in a pack of micro-fine threes, too." Without missing a beat, he grabbed some syringes. That scam worked for me for years and years.

My drug use increased exponentially during that first year at UCLA. I knew that just down the road, life was in session, and that was where I would go for my education, which included going to every concert I could afford. I saw the Talking Heads and the Police. I even went to New York with Donde to visit his family and see some shows. It was Donde's birthday, so we dropped some acid and went to Tracks to see John Lurie and the Lounge Lizards, then to the Bottom Line to take in Arthur Blythe. To our amazement, Blythe had Kelvyn Bell, the great guitar player from Defunkt, playing with him. The show was incredible, and after it was over, I went to the bar and talked to Kelvyn about music and about his guitar playing and the records that I knew he'd played on. He was very happy to engage about music with this eighteen-year-old boy from Hollywood who was blazing on acid.

I was excited because Kelvyn was one of the people who had gotten me seriously into music. Donde had his Defunkt album, and when we'd have people over to the house, he'd put it on and say, "Everyone get around. Anthony's going to dance," and I'd bust some moves. Dancing became this playful competition for us, and at one point we all started going to dance contests. We'd show up at Osco's, a hip punk-rock disco on La Cienega, and Hillel and Mike and I would enter the contest. We were off the map. Most people would break out conventional dance moves that you'd seen before, but we'd go out and invent steps.

Besides constantly playing records, Donde also had an inexpensive electric guitar and an amplifier. On the weekends when he wasn't working at his dad's telephone answering service, he would sit there and bang away on this electric guitar. He knew a few chords, but he had a really harsh tone, so when he'd start noodling around, I usually got out of the house. Still, one day Donde suggested that he and I and Mike should form a band. He'd play guitar, I'd sing, and Mike would play bass. Though it was more of a joke than anything else, we rehearsed a few times at his dad's theater in Hollywood. The biggest contribution to this project was the name. Our friend Patrick English used to refer to his dick as a "spigot," and I thought it was such a fantastic nickname that I became Spigot Blister. Donde named himself Skid Mark. I forget Mike's name. We called ourselves Spigot Blister and the Chest Pimps, the chest pimps being the pimples that resided on Mike's pubescent chest. Our rehearsals consisted mostly of making noise. In retrospect, it was more of an exercise in coming up with personas than coming up with music. We didn't write any songs or even any lyrics, we just made some bad noise and screamed and banged on things. Eventually, we lost interest in the whole project.

But seeing Kelvyn Bell was inspirational for me, and I had a distinct feeling, even though I didn't have a concrete means of achieving it, that whatever I ended up doing with my life, I wanted to make people feel the way this music was making me feel. The only problem was that I wasn't a guitar player and I wasn't a bass player and I wasn't a drummer and I wasn't a singer, I was a dancer and a party maniac, and I didn't quite know how to parlay that into a job.

Every attempt that I'd made to even keep a job had turned into a dismal failure. Back at Fairfax, I went through a succession of shitty little jobs that highlighted how incapable I was of fitting into society. I worked at a collections agency, I worked for a country store, I even worked as an underage waiter at the Improv, but I got canned from each of these gigs. At UCLA, I was so desperate for money that I read a notice on the crappy-jobs-where-we-can-exploit-the-students-and-get-them-to-work-for-nothing board that a rich family in Hancock Park needed a dog walker for their two German shepherds. I didn't mind taking the daily walk, and I didn't mind hanging out with the dogs, but it was a pathetic situation to have to walk these dogs for all of twenty-five dollars a week.

Sometime during that first year, I couldn't pay Donde rent anymore, so I had to leave. I went back to that same job board and found a notice that said, "Room and board for young male student, willing to participate in the caretaking of a nine-year-old boy. Single mother needs help taking the boy to and from school." The woman lived in a small, quaint house in Beverlywood. She was a young mom who'd been jilted by some dude and was now alone with a so-called hyperactive, attention-deficit kid who was being dosed with Ritalin. She liked me right away. My responsibilities weren't that great, basically making sure that the kid got to school in the morning and was picked up in the afternoon and served a snack.

For me it was ideal. I had a roof over my head, some food in my stomach, and a nice room where Haya would regularly visit and we would engage in some noisy lovemaking sessions. After a while, I bonded with the little guy. He might have been a touch mentally challenged, but he wasn't hyperactive or suffering from a shortened attention span. When we were together, he wasn't spastic or out of control. I had read that when adults took Ritalin, instead of having a calming effect, it would stimulate the postadolescent chemical balance. One night Hillel and Mike came over, and we decided to test those theories. Sure enough, in combination with a nice stolen bottle of Finnish vodka, we were off to the races. We ate handfuls of the Ritalin and became three drunk comets running around the house. The kid had a great time, and when his mom and her date came home a bit tipsy, she partied with us, never realizing that we were high on her son's meds. Eventually, though, she fired me from the job.

I was almost history at school, too. From the first few weeks,

I had felt totally alienated from campus life, so much of an outsider that I memorialized the feeling with a harsh, bizarre haircut. I decided to cut all of my hair really short except for the back, which was long, down to my shoulders. I wasn't mimicking hockey players or people from Canada, it was just my idea of a punk-rock haircut. It was probably inspired by David Bowie and his Pinups era, but it wasn't flaming red, and I didn't have the standing-up thing in the front, I had bangs. To people at UCLA, it was abominable. Even my friends were freaked out by it. But Mike approved. He always said that one of my greatest accomplishments was that I had invented the mullet.

The height of my alienation from UCLA came later that year. Mike and Hillel and I had just finished one of our Canter's dine-and-dashes. We were tripping on acid, wandering the streets. We passed an alleyway, and I stumbled on all these clothes that had been discarded by a bum. I immediately had an acidic moment of clarity and stripped naked and donned this oversize, strange, mismatched set of clothes. In a way, they were beautiful and regal; the pants even had some kind of silk iridescent pattern streaking down. Combined with the Spigot Blister haircut, I was quite a sight. I stayed up all night, and in the morning, I went to my classes wearing this mystical bum outfit. But I was still hungover from the acid, so I went out and lay down on the lawn.

Haya spotted me. "What's wrong with you?" she asked.

"I've been up all night on acid, and I can't hack my astronomy class right now," I said.

"You look terrible," she said. She was right. I looked terrible and I felt terrible, and that was the moment when I realized that I wasn't going to cut it in this environment. What I didn't realize then was that Haya and I were not going to make it, either.

I'd had two regrettable instances of infidelity during that year at UCLA. The first was with a well-endowed party girl. She kept coming by my house and wouldn't leave me alone. Before we went out dancing one night, I made it clear to her that I was in a committed relationship. But I have a sneaking suspicion that we split a quaalude at some point that night and went back to her apartment. She started to make sexual advances, and I remember thinking, "I'm going to do this. I'm gonna sleep with this girl, and I'm going to regret it forever, but I can't stop myself."

She disrobed, I lost all control, and I slept with her. I had a great time and then felt just crushed, demoralized, and disgusted with myself afterward. You instinctively know that nothing will ever be the same, and you have to carry that knowledge around with you like a huge weight. The next time you see your girl, you can't look at her straight in the eyes the same way you did for all those years.

The second infidelity was even worse. I was writing a paper for one of my classes and needed some help, and it turned out that Karen, Mike's sister, had some expertise in that area. I'm sick to my stomach just thinking about this. Karen had a little house in Laurel Canyon, and Haya dropped me off there. Once again I was putting myself in a dangerous situation, because Karen was a wildcat. By the time I got there, she was already drunk on a bottle of wine, and she'd just eaten garlic soup, which didn't exactly turn me on. But she was looped and insistent, and when you're eighteen years old, it doesn't take that much provoking to get you to a place where you can't stop yourself. So we ended up having a very—for me—tormented sexual romp. A huge amount of guilt and shame and self-disappointment immediately followed.

I don't mean to say that these episodes destroyed my relationship with Haya. I was able to encapsulate them in a protective wrapping of gray matter and understand that they meant nothing as far as the way I felt about Haya. But there was enough other baggage in our relationship that seemed to ultimately doom it. The major problem still was the conflict between her loyalty to her parents and her feelings toward me. Her parents' disapproving voices were always in the back of her mind. And if anything, her parents' attitudes got more inflexible as our relationship progressed. One night when I was still living in Donde's house, Haya and I spent a few glorious hours together. We were under the impression that her parents thought she was somewhere else, so she was so happy. We were lying in bed, talking and laughing, and it started getting late, and then the phone rang.

I picked up the phone, hoping it was a call for Donde, but the male voice at the other end was as cold as ice and as serious as stone. It could have been an executioner.

"Anthony, put Haya on the phone."

I looked at her, and she knew she had to take the call. She started listening to his tirade about how she was no good and how he would disown her, and she started crying. I tried to tell her that I loved her and that they didn't have her best interests in mind, but she just sighed and said, "No, this is my family. I can't turn my back on them." And she went home to the people who were doing that to her.

By the end of that first year at UCLA, Haya and I had begun to have talks about what we were going to do. At one point, Hillel had even given me a chai, the Hebrew letter that signifies life, and I wore it on a chain around my neck. I guess this baffled Haya's dad enough for him to call me into his house and ask about my background. I explained that I was mostly Lithuanian, and he liked that.

"Did you know that before World War Two, ten percent of the population of Lithuania was Jewish?" he said.

Then he went to his library and got some Lithuanian genealogy books out and desperately tried to find out what the chances were that I had some connection to a Jewish bloodline. I humored him, but I knew it was a lost cause.

So Haya and I were having these talks, and they were getting serious and sad, because she was driven in school and under the domination of her family, but we were madly in love with each other. The stress of college and her unique family dynamic was taking a toll on our sex life.

I was terribly hurt and confused, and my ego and sexual confidence started ebbing.

Little by little, our relationship was disintegrating, not in an immature way but in a profound way, when we both quietly understood that our worlds might be too disparate and there might not be a future for us. We wound up having our final talk at Hillel's house, which had become a sanctuary for me during that unmanageable year. Hillel gave us his room, and Haya and I looked at each other and said, "You know, this really isn't going to work." Then we lay there in Hillel's bed, holding each other tight and crying for what seemed like hours because we both knew that this great love was coming to an end.

I never made the decision to quit UCLA at the end of my first year. My classes were over, and once again I went to that job board, but this time I found something really interesting. It was a job as a jack-of-all-trades for a graphic arts film company, and they were paying ten dollars an hour, which was way over the minimum wage. The company had compact office space on La Brea. The offices were modern and high-tech, and the owner of the company, David, was very manicured, very pristine-looking, and clearly gay. Just by observing, I could tell that he ran a tight, efficient ship. My interview went well (I'm sure it didn't hurt that I was an eighteen-year-old male), and I started work the next day.

My job consisted mostly of running film to the developers, being in charge of the petty cash, and doing whatever else David wanted. This was one of the first companies to specialize in graphic animations for commercials and network logos. David had gotten in on the ground floor of computer animation and was making a fortune. Even though I was just a runner, he took a shine to me and began to explain these complex graphic applications. It wasn't a sexual thing; from day one we had open hetero-homo discussions about the desirability of men versus women. Even though I was the embodiment of the type of boy he was constantly searching for, he never sexually harassed me or made me feel uncomfortable in the workplace.

It didn't take me long to apply my lifelong skill of taking advantage of situations, so when he sent me out to buy personal things for his house, such as a new quilt, I'd usually order two of the same item and keep one for myself. No one ever seemed to notice, and since he had a house in the hills and a Ferrari and a Porsche Carrera, I didn't think he'd miss it. He must have seen me much more for what I was and much less for what I thought I was getting away with, because he was no dummy, but he let me slide.

To me it was summer vacation, and I was making money faster than I could spend it. Mike was working at an animal hospital, and our friend Johnny Karson, who used to hang out with Haya in junior high school, had a job at Warner Bros. For years Mike and I had dreamed of getting our own place in Hollywood, so the three of us decided to pool our resources and rent a nice little house right near the Formosa Café. We settled into the house, but three weeks later, an even nicer house down the block went up for rent. It had a larger yard, and it was a couple of hundred dollars a month cheaper. So we jumped ship, battled to get our security deposit back, and moved down the road.

Pretty soon it was evident that JK was the odd man out, since he had a nine-to-five life working at Warner's. Mike and I didn't let our jobs get in the way of our partying, which, even at the first house, consisted of shooting a lot of cocaine. We'd blast a B-side song by the Police called "Fall Out," and then Mike and I would shoot the coke and run around the house in a temporary state of euphoric mega-bliss. We'd raise our arm high in the air to stop the bleeding and start rhapsodizing, "Oh my God, oh my God, oh my God, this is a good one, this is the big one, this might be too much, oh no, it's not too much, I'm good, I'm good, oh this is incredible," and then we'd sing along with the song. One rather normal, non-coke-shooting citizen would have to deal with these two madmen who were paying more attention to their own world than the outside world.

When JK planned to go away skiing at Mammoth for a few days, Mike and Hillel and I decided to have the party to end all parties. Mike and I went on a booze-stealing binge and stocked the house. Then we emptied all the furniture out of the house so there'd be more room for dancing. Hillel helped us distribute flyers, and I duct-taped huge letters to the living room floor that spelled out DANCE.

Mike had been squirreling away these colorful pills from the animal hospital, not to consume them but as souvenirs. We had a chest-high shallow mantel that went all the way around the house, so we alternated patterns of blue and yellow and red pills along the mantel, creating a kind of Japanese rock-garden effect.

Then the hordes arrived. The booze started flowing, and the music was pumping and people were dancing and disappearing into bedrooms and going off in the bushes, and it became the best party we'd ever gone to, let alone thrown. As the night wore on, everyone started consuming the pills, not realizing that they were for doggie constipation or feline psychosis or whatever.

At some point, the house took on a life of its own, as if its energy was pulsating out of the windows into the world. We passed out sometime early the next morning, and when we came to, Mike and I looked around the place. It was a war zone. The floors were covered in an inch of goop; there were food and crushed pills and vomit and empty beer bottles and cigarette butts and general debris everywhere. I knew JK was coming home that night, so I got out some mops, a bucket, water, and soap and went around that house the entire day and cleaned every nook and cranny. By the time I was done, it looked like no one had ever come over.

Even though I was able to hold down my job at the graphics company, I had definitely become a cocaine addict. We had a fairly constant supply, because both Mike and I were making money, and he was able to supplement what we bought by trading bass lessons for coke from some dealer in Topanga Canyon. I'd look forward to the days he taught, because as soon as that lesson was finished, we'd be shooting the cocaine. There was never enough to go on for more than an hour or so, but I had a real need to get those drugs in me.

The psychological addiction was in full effect. I wasn't physically weak, but psychologically, I wanted cocaine constantly.

My burgeoning use wound up exploding into some episodes of full-blown cocaine psychosis. One time I got ahold of a lot of coke and shot it by myself all through the night and into the next day. I was alone in my bedroom and became convinced that someone had broken into the house in broad daylight. Then I started having visual hallucinations of this intruder going through the house. I'd rush into room after room, convinced that he had jumped out of the window right before I got into that room. So I thought, "Okay, I know how to deal with this." I climbed up onto the roof of the house, holding an old car tire, thinking that I'd lure the guy out and then throw the tire at him so that it would perfectly donut him and immobilize him, like in a cartoon. Luckily, Mike came home and talked me into coming down.

It wasn't only coke that I was abusing. Around this time, I met a punk-rock girl who asked me why I would shoot cocaine when, for twenty dollars, I could shoot speed and be high for two days. I ended up spending a night with her, shooting speed and getting crazy high. Every time I took speed or coke or even a speedball, something would flip inside my head, and no matter what I was doing or who I was with, I'd grab a pencil or a marker or some paint and I'd start drawing on paper or cardboard or people's walls, whatever. I just had to draw the minute those drugs hit me. And if I wasn't drawing, I was having sex.

During that summer of 1981, heroin hadn't become prominent on the drug scene. I remember being at Al's Bar downtown with Mike and seeing a whole table of young punk rockers who were nodding out, and thinking that didn't look like too much fun. But there was another voice in the back of my mind that had been speaking to me every now and then. It said, "You've gotta find some of that heroin again. That's the drug that people are afraid of, so it's got to be the best drug." I wasn't looking back fondly on my fourteen-year-old's experience with that one line of

China White; I was more into the idea of taking a truly subversive drug.

One day a new guy came to work. He looked like a rockabilly singer, with a black pompadour, big black Roy Orbison shades, super-pale skin, and a bizarre demeanor. I asked my coworker Bill what was up with that guy.

"That's the way you look when you do heroin," he said.

Bingo. Here was my connection to the world of heroin.

After a few days, I approached the guy and said, "Can you get me some of that damn heroin?" He said, "Absolutely, absolutely." Junkies always want to get new guys drugs because they can rip them off. So we made plans to do the heroin that night at my house. I was so excited that I rushed home and told Mike and JK that I was going to shoot heroin that night.

"What? You can't shoot heroin. You'll die," they cautioned. I told them that this guy had shot it for a while, and they were so intrigued that we decided they should watch me shoot up.

That night the guy came over and was taken aback to see an audience sitting on chairs around the kitchen table. But he set up the spoons and went through the whole ritual of cooking up this Persian dope, which I'd never seen before. Because it was oil-based, he needed a lemon to cook it up with. First he fixed himself and got a little stoned, and then he said, "It's your turn." He fixed up the rig, and it was brown. I'd never shot up anything that was brown before. Everyone was on pins and needles, wondering if I was going to die. I shot up but didn't feel much. I asked him for some more, and he said okay, but this would be the end of the dope. He gave me another shot, and still there was no great dreamy go-sink-into-the-couch-and-sleep-for-twelve-hours opium rush. Later I found out that the dope he scored was pretty weak. It was a decidedly underwhelming high, and it didn't light my fire or inspire me to go searching out a heroin connection. It was a waste of money, and the grand spectacle of doing it in front of my friends fizzled out, and everyone left.

By the fall of 1981, even though I hadn't made a conscious decision, I was not a UCLA student anymore. School didn't fit into this raging, drugging-clubbing lifestyle I was leading. I certainly didn't look like a student. I had traded in my already weird Spigot Blister haircut for a flattop. I had been seeing flattops around the club scene, and I thought they looked cool, so I went down to Bulgarian Bud's Flattops on Melrose Avenue, and for four bucks they shaved off all the hair on the sides and back of my head and left a half inch of hair standing straight up on top of my head. When I did that, it was like I had totally erased all my ties to my past. Now I was a crazy, out-of-control punk rocker. When I showed up for work the next day, David was amazed. "Oh my God, you've cut off all your hair," he said.

Just then a Devo song came on the radio, and I turned it all the way up and started dancing all over the office.

"That's a very violent style of dancing," he fretted. But I was off and running into my new identity.

The whole time I was working, I was dipping into the petty-cash box, getting more and more into shooting cocaine, and drinking lots of alcohol and taking lots of pills. I didn't see it happening, but the wheels were falling off of me. I didn't care about work, I didn't care about my health, I didn't care about responsibilities like paying rent, I was just on a runaway train ride. The horribly ironic cosmic trick of drug addiction is that drugs are a lot of fun when you first start using them, but by the time the consequences manifest themselves, you're no longer in a position to say, "Whoa, gotta stop that." You've lost that ability, and you've created this pattern of conditioning and reinforcement. It's never something for nothing when drugs are involved.

After I called in sick one too many times, David fired me. I felt really sad that I had let him down. I was also sad that the goose laying the golden eggs was gone. Then I got more bad news. It seemed that JK had brought a copy of the party flyer we had printed up to our landlord. He told him that we had distributed the flyers in record stores on Melrose and had a wild party that endangered the house. Meanwhile, JK had lined up two other friends to move in. By the time his eviction procedure worked, we were ready to go. Our lives had begun to self-destruct to the point where we couldn't have paid rent regularly.

Before we left the house, I did manage to scrape together some money and buy myself a used car. I had been using a Capri that Steve and Peggy gave me as a high school graduation present. I never maintained it, so for the last year, it had no muffler and zero brakes. I'd routinely hit the curb with my wheels when I wanted to stop. One morning the car just ceased, and when I checked the oil, it was bone dry. The whole engine had turned to stone, so I said good-bye to my car, thanked it for a couple of years of faithful, accident-free service, and left it on the street. I picked up a copy of *The Recycler* and found a beautiful '62 T-Bird for six hundred dollars. It was big and bad and, soon enough, would become a mobile bedroom for me.

For some reason, it didn't faze us when Mike and I found ourselves out on the street. The whole concept of sleeping didn't make much sense to us then. There were all these new clubs opening and a whole post-punk scene developing in Hollywood. There was the Lasa Club and the Zero One after-hours bar and the CASH Club, which stood for Creative Artist Space of Hollywood. We'd end up at these places because we were out all night, every night, going with this invisible flow, following the party.

Mike was in a little better shape than I was. He wasn't hitting the drugs as hard, and he still had income from his animal-hospital job. When we left the Formosa house, he ended up crashing at the CASH Club. CASH was run by a woman named Janet Cunningham, who had a legit job as an extras casting director for the film industry. If you were an actor or a painter or a musician, Janet would let you crash at this loft space for free. During the day it would be a hangout spot, and at night there would be performances. At the time Mike moved in, Larry Fishburn lived there, along with a great

Guadalupian drummer named Joelle, a French painter named Fabrice, and an authentic punk rocker named Animal Boner. Not only did this guy have some of the first tattoos I'd ever seen other than on old sailors, his were on his kneecaps, and they read METAL KNEECAP FACTORY.

Because Mike was staying there, I'd wind up crashing there, too, from time to time. That was when we started doing heroin. Fab, in addition to being an artist, began to get a steady source of China White heroin. It was so pure that you could sniff one line and be loaded. Mike started sniffing it, too, but he always remained a lightweight around heroin. The joke was that all you had to do was show him a bindle of H, and he'd start vomiting.

By now my flattop was growing out, so one night when we were out in the Valley at a party, I asked Hillel to give me a Mohawk. I knew he was good with shapes and dimensions, so we went into the bathroom and he hawked me up. Because my flattop had already been trained to stand up, I didn't have to use eggs or gel or whatever the other punks used to straighten their Mohawks. Mine just stood up on its own, like the horsehair that stuck out of the top of those old fighting helmets.

The Mohawk gave me a new persona and new energy. Even though I didn't have a place to live or a job, it didn't matter, because I had this new set of armor and a good feeling about myself. I would dress up in a white frock dress with no underwear and black combat boots and go out dancing. One of the great new places that I discovered was Radio Club, L.A.'s first hip-hop club. I'd go there with Mike and Gary Allen, our crazy black, gay fashion-designer friend who was from Arkansas and was the lead singer in a band called Neighbor's Voices. We'd dance for five hours straight and get completely wasted.

When it was time to sleep, I wasn't picky. I'd go with the flow. If I was with Mike, I might crash where he was. Hillel's was a favorite spot on my couch tour. His family always made me welcome and never made me feel like the loser that I was, even though one time I overstayed my welcome and Hillel came to me and said,

"I think if you stay on the couch tonight, my mom's going to have a little more than she can handle. She's been through a rough time of her own." I ended up sleeping in my T-Bird, parked right in front of Hillel's house. Between the bucket seats and the metal trim, I couldn't get comfortable, so I got out and crashed on their front lawn. In the morning, the neighbor's kids came out to play and saw this Mohawked freak in thrift-store clothing passed out on the grass. Eventually, Hillel invited me in for coffee and toast.

When I wasn't at Hillel's, I'd stay with my friend Keith Barry. He lived with his hip dad in a small two-bedroom back house in Hollywood. His pops was a daily weed smoker, so that became another pit stop to get high. Keith had always been an outcast, so he got behind my Mohawk persona. He was also a great musician, and he turned me on to some stellar old jazz. He let me crash on his bedroom floor, and that was fine with me. I'd roll up a towel and put it under my head and be set. But like at Hillel's place, Keith's dad began to feel a little put off by my presence, so I wound up sleeping in their tiny backyard. It was barely big enough to contain a couple of lawn chairs, but that was all I needed to curl up in.

Whenever I got any money, I'd go on a drug binge. The problem was, I didn't have a home to do the drugs in. So I'd start off using in somebody's house, and when they got finished, I'd go off to get more. I began to do a roaming drug-shooting thing where I'd get the drugs, go into underground parking garages, hide out in a corner behind someone's trunk, set up, and then shoot up. I'd get all crazy high and go walking the streets, and then I'd find an alley or a school yard, or go behind a bush and do some more.

Sometime that spring, my homeless period came to an end. I ran into Bill Stobaugh, a friend of mine from my old graphics job. He was a white guy, but he had a shock of huge Eraserhead hair jutting up from his head. Bill's beautiful psychedelic artwork earned him the nickname "The Hallucinogenius." He was a Renaissance man of sorts, a filmmaker, a guitar player, a collector of beautiful old twelve-string guitars. He had gone on to a few other graphic-design houses, and he was helpful in finding me part-time work that put some coin in my pocket.

One of these places was called Mid-Ocean. It was owned by a giant six-foot-five overachieving Irishman named Ray. He was capable of doing twenty tasks at once and getting them all done. His petite blond wife ran the financial side of the business. They were doing cutting-edge animation work, including all the animation for *Blade Runner*.

Ray and his wife sort of adopted me, and once again I got a job as a runner. But once again I started doing heroin. I'd stay up all night doing smack, and then I'd go to work and have to shuttle some film down to Orange County to get processed. I'd be driving their little red pickup truck, nodding out on the freeway. It's amazing I didn't get killed in a car crash.

While I was at Mid-Ocean, Bill realized that I didn't have a home, so he asked if I wanted to move in with him. He had this great huge dark basement with many windows that looked up to the sidewalk. It was in a classic old Hollywood apartment building that had mostly Mexican tenants. The space was raw, with no walls, but he offered me one corner if I would help him build security bars on the windows to keep the riffraff out.

One night shortly after I moved in, I decided to go on one of my infamous coke binges. I had one of those weird walking nights when I walked up and down Hollywood Boulevard, popping into the porno shops, doing weird shit. I came home during the night maybe once, quietly, to get either money or warmer clothes, but I ended up staying out all night.

The next day I walked into Mid-Ocean, and Bill charged me with a look in his eyes that I'd never seen before. "I'll kill you, you motherfucker." He had always been such a mellow, trippy fellow, so I asked him what was wrong. He stopped in his tracks, maybe because he saw something in my eyes that he wasn't expecting, but he told me that he had gotten robbed the night before and every single one of his precious guitars was gone, and that I was the only person who could have done it.

"Bill, I know I'm crazy, I know that I'm shooting drugs and doing weird shit and disappearing, and I can see where you would blame me for something like this happening, but you'd better take another route, because I didn't do it. If you don't focus on whoever did do it, they're going to get off scott-free," I said. He couldn't get his head around the fact that anyone else could have done it. I was the only one with keys. But I was sure it was an inside job and that the maintenance people in the building had robbed him.

That was the end of my rooming with Bill. There was no way I was going to live with a guy who thought I'd robbed him. Now I had to find another place to stay. At Mid-Ocean they had set up a little loft space above the primary artwork room that was accessed by a ladder and had a couple of futons. I started crashing there and getting up early enough that nobody knew I wasn't just the first person to work that morning.

By now Mike (who had been dubbed "Flea" on a trip he took to Mammoth with Keith Barry and JK) had moved into an apartment in what we called the Wilton Hilton, a great old classic brick building on Wilton and Franklin. The place was filled with artists and musicians, and it was managed by a super-kooky seventy-year-old fireplug of a landlady. Flea was living with Joel and Fabrice, his buddies from CASH. At some point Hillel became a semi-resident, too. So when my tenure with Bill ended, I wound up staying over there a lot. All during this time, What Is This (which was Anthym's new, more mature name) continued to play live shows and develop a cult following. I was still introducing them, but by now I was writing my own poetry for the intros. One time I even rhymed "metropolis" with "acidophilus." The more they played, the more Flea became the acknowledged star of the band. Whenever they'd give him a bass solo, that would be the climax of the whole evening.

At that time, Fear was the most famous punk-rock band in

L.A. They had gotten national attention when John Belushi took them under his wing and featured them on *Saturday Night Live*. So when their bass player left the group, it was natural that they'd try to get Flea to replace him. One day Flea came to me and dropped the bombshell that he had been asked to audition for Fear. This was a dicey situation, because Flea and Hillel were my two best friends in the world. But we talked, and it turned out if Flea had to choose between the two different styles of music, he would end up in the Fear camp. So I advised him to go and audition.

He came back from the audition with the job, but now he had to face Hillel, the guy who had taught him how to play bass in the first place. Flea got so nervous before their meeting that he threw up. And Hillel did not take the news well. "I have no words for you," he said, and left the room. What Is This replaced Flea with a series of mediocre bass players; meanwhile, Flea vaulted into punk-rock mini-stardom. After several months of noncommunication, Hillel had to forgive Flea. Something in him knew that even though he'd been wronged, it was Flea's destiny, and he had to swallow his ego a bit and allow Flea to flower. It was hard, because none of us had any father figures to consult with on these heavy issues. Eventually, they became friends again and resumed jamming.

I was still working at Mid-Ocean, driving that pickup truck all throughout the summer of 1982. An amazing song kept blasting out of the radio that I had on the center console. It was called "The Message," and it was by a rap group from New York called Grandmaster Flash and the Furious Five. I went out and bought the cassette and played it over and over and over. A few weeks later, they came out to L.A. and played at a place called the Country Club, and they were incredible. Their theatrics were inspired, and each had his individual persona, and their rapping was fantastic. Grandmaster Flash was the man behind the turntable; the sounds and the rhythms and the funkiness and the coolness that this guy emanated from the stage were really impressive.

But more than anything else, "The Message" started to get me thinking. These guys were all writing rhymes, something that

Hillel and I had been in love with for a long time. He and I would break into the top floor of the Continental Hyatt House on Sunset, which was a private club, and we'd have it to ourselves and look out at this spectacular view of the city, and we'd smoke a joint and invent these crazy characters and spontaneously erupt into these rhyming sessions. It was the first time I had ever attempted rapping.

So when "The Message" became the hottest song that summer, it started dawning on me that you don't have to be Al Green or have an incredible Freddie Mercury voice to have a place in the world of music. Rhyming and developing a character were another way to do it.

5.

Deep Kicking

In some ways, I owe my career to my friend Gary Allen. In February 1983, Gary and Neighbor's Voices were scheduled to play the Rhythm Lounge at the Grandea Room on Melrose. A few days before the gig, he suggested that Flea, Hillel, and I open for his band and do one number, with me fronting this band.

Although Hillel and Flea were initially skeptical, since I wasn't a singer, Gary had recognized my potential as a performer, mainly from my maniacal cavorting on the dance floor at various clubs around town. We decided to put together something, and it instantly became clear to me, thanks to Grandmaster Flash, that I didn't have to sing a song, I could go out there and rap a poem. All of us had latched on to the energy of Defunkt and the raw edginess of the Gang of Four and, of course, the cosmic freedom implicit in Jimi Hendrix's guitar playing, so we would channel all those influences. But mainly, we wanted to do something based in funk, because What Is This had absolutely nothing to do with the funk.

We didn't have a space to rehearse, and we weren't taking this gig that seriously, so we decided all we really needed to do was get together in Flea's living room at the Wilton Hilton and have an a cappella rehearsal. Flea and Hillel had such exquisite telepathy going on that they could just look at each other and know what to play. So Flea came up with his bass line, and Hillel invented a funky guitar riff, and Jack Irons, the drummer in What Is This, laid down a beat. Then I went off to write some lyrics.

I got lucky. I decided to write something I knew about—my very colorful friends and our wild nightlife scene. I called the song "Out in L.A.," and there were references to Flea and Tree (Keith Barry's nickname) and Slim, who was Hillel. In the great tradition of rap, I wrote a verse about my sexual prowess, and I called myself "Antoine the Swan," for no other reason than it rhymed. For years and years, people would come up to me and ask, "What's the real thing behind the swan? You got a curve in your dick?" In a way, it was an ironic reference, because my dancing style was so ungraceful and unswanlike. I would attempt the physical maneuvers of a prima ballerina, and I'd wind up crashing or knocking over a table or pulling the curtains down.

It was a pretty ambitious first song. I wrote in places for a bass solo, a guitar solo, and an a cappella vocal breakdown. After we rehearsed it to the point where we felt like we had it, I came up with a name for us. We weren't looking for a permanent band name, because this was just going to be a one-off, so I called us Tony Flow and the Miraculous Masters of Mayhem—that was how we wanted to play, majestic and chaotic.

We showed up to the Rhythm Lounge, and there were about thirty people in the club, all there to see Neighbor's Voices. I was wearing a paisley corduroy three-quarter-length robe and a fluorescent orange hunting cap. Oddly enough, I was totally sober. I had no idea how performing was going to make me feel; all I knew was that as we got up onstage, there was this weird sense of a force field traveling among us. I had seen Flea and Hillel and Jack play a million times, but I'd never seen so much intensity in their faces or purpose in their body language. Flea looked like a cylinder of glowing energy. Unbeknownst to me, he'd been snorting heroin before the show.

The stage was microscopic. I could have reached out in either direction and touched Hillel or Flea. We didn't even get a proper introduction, but people started to take notice as we were plugging in. All the anticipation of the moment hit me, and I instinctively knew that the miracle of manipulating energy and tapping into an infinite source of power and harnessing it in a small space with your friends was what I had been put on this earth to do.

And then Jack Irons, bless his heart, cocked his neck back and hit his sticks together and counted off "One, two, three, four." When the music started, I didn't know what I was going to do, but I had so much juice flowing through me that I did a flip in that tight space and nailed it. And we all just erupted. We had no idea what we were about until that moment, but right into the song, we realized that we were about exploding and killing it with everything we had. As we performed, everybody who was in that room who hadn't been paying attention zombied all the way up to the stage. When we finished, the audience was completely stunned and speechless, frozen in their tracks.

Solomon, the French guy who was promoting that show, rushed out of his DJ booth and, with typically passionate French body language, touched me and said, "Can you please come back and play next week at my club? Maybe you could have two songs by then?" Although we hadn't planned on playing again, I said, "Of course, we'll be here next week, and we'll have another song for you." We were so high off of that show that the idea of playing the next week seemed totally natural.

We got together during the week and wrote a song called "Get Up and Jump." Flea had been working for a long time on a bass part that was syncopated and intertwined and complicated, combining picking and slapping in a strange and beautifully funky way. I had to write lyrics, so I came up with some more that were character-based. I took the theme of jumping and wrote verses about different cartoony versions of jumping—jumping rope, Mexican jumping beans. But the most memorable line in that song was about Rona Frumpkin, a girl Hillel had a crush on.

One of Hillel's more outstanding characteristics was his big red nut sack, which he was very proud of and which he would put on display with hardly any urging. We used to joke about Hillel's package, because when he would put his dick and nut sack together, he'd form a pumpkin shape in his trousers, which would become a lot more pronounced when he was around Rona. So I wrote a verse that included "Hillel be jumping on that little baby Frumpkin / Say what, you got a pumpkin in your pants?"

We decided we were going to get theatrical for show number two, so we choreographed a funny dance to the popular song "Pac Jam." The night of the show, the club was packed to the rafters, so we began our performance by marching in the front door and pushing our way through the crowd with "Pac Jam" blasting out of a boom box. When we got to the stage, we started in on this retarded robotic dance. Jack couldn't get the synchronized moves together, so we abandoned the dance halfway through and went right into "Out in L.A." and then "Get Up and Jump."

I guess my Frumpkin lyrics worked, because she was in the audience, and later that night, Hillel finally was able to hook up with her. So whenever anybody in the band was having trouble scoring with a certain girl, I'd insert her name, and boom, it was like clockwork, twenty-four hours would not pass without that girl falling under the spell.

After the second show, we realized this was too much fun to give up. At last, I had something to do that had meaning and purpose. I felt I could put every idea and stupid little philosophy that I had into a song. One indication that we were getting serious was that we felt we had to come up with a name for the group. We started going through these huge laundry lists of idiotic, meaningless, boring names. To this day, both Tree and Flea claim they came up with the Red Hot Chili Peppers. It's a derivation of a classic old-school Americana blues or jazz name. There was Louis Armstrong with his Hot Five, and also other bands that had "Red Hot" this or "Chili" that. There was even an English band that was called Chilli Willi and the Red Hot Peppers, who later thought we had stolen their name. But no one had ever been the Red Hot Chili Peppers, a name that would forever be a blessing and curse. If you think of Red Hot Chili Peppers in terms of a feeling, a sensation, or an energy, it makes perfect sense for our band, but if you think of it in terms of a vegetable, it takes on all these hokey connotations. There's a restaurant chain named after the vegetable, and chili peppers have been merchandised in everything from home-decoration hangings to Christmas-tree ornaments. Suffice to say that we were weirded out when people started bringing chili peppers to our shows as some kind of offering.

Around this time, Hillel, Flea, and I combined resources and found an incredibly inexpensive three-bedroom house on an infamous street called Leland Way, which was a one-block street that was also known as Pot Alley because the Mexican mafia dealt pot on that street. It was a dangerous, unsavory neighborhood filled with drug dealers and bums, but we didn't care. In fact, it gave me material for our songs. Every night I'd stare outside my bedroom window and watch the LAPD helicopters circling and hovering over our block, shining their lights down onto this maelstrom of pot-dealing activity.

From "Police Helicopter"

Police Helicopter sharking through the sky
Police Helicopter landin' on my eye
Police Helicopter takes a nosedive
Police Helicopter no he ain't shy

That house became a beehive of musical activity. Hillel would always be playing his guitar. I'd come home, and Flea would be out on the porch playing. He probably should have been practicing his downstrokes with a pick, for Fear, but instead he'd be coming up with these soulful and emotional funk grooves. I'd sit there and listen and interject, "Yeah, that's the one! I can work with that," and I'd run into my room and get my pad of paper and we'd write a song. It's the same formula that we use today to write songs, which is no formula. We just show up and start improvising, and I start collecting notes. That's what separates us from a lot of other bands, because with us, all things are born from the jam. We go in and start wailing and see what works.

Our third show was pretty memorable. It was at the Cathay de Grande, which, unlike the Rhythm Lounge, was a real-live music venue. The night was promoted by a scenester named Wayzata Camerone, who had offered us two hundred dollars, which was more than double what we had received from our last show. Unfortunately, the place was sparsely populated that night, maybe thirty people, but we had a rooting section. I had been going out with a beautiful French girl named Patricia, who was there, along with Flea's girlfriend and Tree and my dad, who by then had reconciled with me. The show was as exciting and energetic and explosive and out of control as our first two. We did four songs—the two we already had and two new ones, "Police Helicopter" and "Never Mind." "Never Mind" was an audacious putdown of a variety of other bands (Gap Band, Duran Duran, Soft Cell, Men at Work, Hall and Oates), telling the world to forget about them, because we were what they were going to be into now.

At some point during that set, I was drinking a beer onstage, and I vaulted onto the near-empty dance floor and started spinning around like a whirling dervish with my beer held out, so anyone who was within ten feet of me got showered. Between songs that night, we performed a few a cappella chants that were derived from school-yard and camp songs. Hillel had introduced us to one named "Stranded," and we did some simpleton choreography to go with the song: We put our hands in the air as we sang, "Stranded, stranded, stranded on the toilet bowl/What do you do when you're stranded and there ain't nothing on the roll?/To prove you're a man, you must wipe with your hand/Stranded, stranded, stranded on the toilet bowl."

Even though there weren't too many people there, everybody loved the show. But at the end of the night, Wayzata was strangely making himself scarce. I located him and attempted to collect our money, but he started hemming and hawing about the small crowd.

"That's really too bad, but there was a guarantee involved, and as the promoter of a club, that's the risk you take," I said.

He reached into his pocket and fished out some money. "Well, here's forty. Maybe next time we do a show together, we can fix the balance," he said and ducked into the men's room to avoid me.

I rushed right in after him and ended up picking him up and plopping him down into the urinal and shaking him down for whatever other cash he had, which didn't amount to the right sum, but I couldn't conceive of someone breaking a deal and then trying to weasel out of it.

Another indication that we were making noise on the scene was that we began to get mentioned in the *L.A. Weekly* feature called "L.A. Dee Dah," which was a social column that chronicled the happenings of the L.A. music scene. Flea and I became stars of this gossip column, not because we were trying to but because we were crazy and high and out every single night until five A.M. at every underground club there was. When we started getting a lot of mentions, I was thrilled.

One of my first mentions was a blind item that linked me to a "certain avant-Germanic chanteuse," Nina Hagen. I didn't know that much about Nina when I met her at that Cathay show, but I knew she was an alluring German singer who had a local cult following in the Hollywood punk scene. We were still backstage after the show when Nina came into the tiny bathroom/dressing room area and started giving me the crazy eyes. She pulled me aside and started ranting in this thick East German accent about how much she loved our band. It escalated into Nostradamus-like predictions: "Now you are the most beautiful band in the world that I've seen, and in five years the rest of the world will know about you, and in seven years you will be the biggest band in the world." I was thinking, "All right lady, whatever."

But she had such style and grace and was so overwhelming and alluring that I remember looking over at Patricia, who was bumming that I was getting all this love from this German girl. Nina gave me her phone number, and I quickly jumped ship.

I called her the next day, and she invited me over for breakfast. She had a modest but pretty house with a pool. She also had a beautiful little girl named Cosma Shiva. We ate breakfast, and Nina was definitely into a healthier, more organic cuisine than mine. We talked a lot that day, and Nina told me about her life in East Germany and the different men who had been in her life—the crazy junkie who was the father of her child, and her new boyfriend who was out of town for the month. I found her absolutely intriguing, and she was so loving that we started a hot-and-heavy romance from that day forward. It lasted about a month, but we continued to be good friends, and she continued to be an avid supporter of our music. Right after our romance ended, she asked if Flea and I would write a song for the record she was working on, and we came up with "What It Is."

Meanwhile, we were continually expanding our own canon of songs. One of the early songs we wrote in the Leland Way house was "Green Heaven." I had been reading a lot of books about whales and dolphins, and I had always been acutely aware of social injustice. In L.A. in the early '80s, the police department was rife with corruption. So I started writing a song that would contrast life above the sea and life below the sea—chronicling the excesses of the Reagan years and comparing them to this idyllic Shangri-la that was happening below sea level, with animals that I considered to be of equal brain power.

FROM "Green Heaven"

Here above land man has laid his plan
And yes it does include the Ku Klux Klan
We got a government so twisted and bent
Bombs, tanks and guns is how our money is spent . . .

Time now to take you to a different place
Where peace-loving whales flow through liquid outer space
Groovin' and glidin' as graceful as lace
Never losing touch with the ocean's embrace . . .

Back to the land of the policeman
Where he does whatever he says he can
Including hating you because you're a Jew
Or beating black ass that's nothing new

We ended up spending twenty-four hours writing "Green Heaven," and it became the epic centerpiece of our shows. Hillel would do an amazing talk-box intro for the song: He'd run a big plastic tube out of a guitar box alongside a mike. Then he'd put the tube down his throat and play the guitar. The sounds from the guitar would go into his mouth, and by shaping his lips, he could form words from the guitar sound. It was painfully psychedelic, in the sincere use of that term, not pop psychedelic or misconstrued television-grade psychedelic, but the real heart-and-soul-of-the-cosmic-journey-to-outer-space psychedelic.

As political as these lyrics seemed to be, I never once considered the Red Hot Chili Peppers a sociopolitical outfit like, say, the Dead Kennedys. I just felt that we were there to create beauty, induce joy, and make people laugh, and if the lyrics happened to include political or social commentary, then so be it. But it was never our responsibility to go out and be the U2 of our generation.

Even though we were a band now, Flea would still go off to rehearse with Fear, and Hillel and Jack would go off to rehearse with What Is This, and there was never any conflict about any of that. We saw playing our songs as a fun thing to do, not as a career move. None of these guys was thinking of quitting their day jobs to do the Red Hot Chili Peppers, and I was fine with that. I was just happy to be planning for our next show, because each one was monumental to me. I couldn't sleep the night before. I'd lie there in bed and think about the performance. And if I did fall asleep, I'd instantly start dreaming about the show. When I got up, the first thing on my mind was "It's show night! There's a show tonight!" and the whole day would revolve around the buildup to the gig.

Soon after Flea and Hillel and I moved in together, Hillel fell in love with a new lady. When Hillel fell in love, he disappeared. He's your best friend, he's with you day and night, he falls in love, see you next year. So Flea and I were out running around to clubs, and we'd always wind up at the Zero, which had moved from Cahuenga to a great new location at Wilcox and Hollywood Boulevard. One particular night, Flea and I acquired a small quantity of China White and a quaalude. We did the drugs, and it was a unique combination. They let us into the Zero, and I started feeling really good and really confident. It was early in the evening, and not many people were in the club, but this redhead with alabaster skin and blue eyes kept walking back and forth in front of me. She was wearing an old pair of overalls with no shirt underneath, so her tits were visible from most angles. I couldn't take my eyes off her, and I stumbled right up to her with the assurance of those chemicals racing through my brain and said, "Hi!" And she said, "Hi" and started rubbing on me like a cat in heat. We immediately walked over to the stairs and made our way toward the roof, but we never even got that far.

She unsnapped her clothes, and they dropped to the floor, and we started making out. I didn't even know her name, but I knew she wanted to fuck, so I was all ready to launch into that when she turned around, took my dick, and went straight to the ass. It wasn't a porno situation, she was being very gentle about it, but that was where she wanted it. We were enjoying this for a few minutes when this huge moron of a bouncer came marching up the stairs and flipped out. I think she later told me that he was overreacting because he liked her and she never gave him the time of day, but whatever the reason, he threw us off the stairs.

She suggested we go to her house, which was two blocks away. By then she had told me her name was Germaine and that she lived in an old seven-story apartment building. When we got in the elevator, instead of going to her apartment, we went straight up to the roof, where we had sex all night long. I was still high on the heroin, so all this time I wasn't able to come. When the sun began to come up, she sat down on top of the archaic elevator machinery, and we started having another round of intercourse. I was going and going and got another rhythm up and the sun started shining and she started screaming and just then somebody hit the elevator button and electricity started arcing across this old machinery and gears started engaging and motors rumbled and I finally came. It was a dramatic ending to a surreal night. I said good night to her and ran through the dawn all the way home, convinced that life was good. And even though that asshole bouncer tried to eighty-six me from the club, the owner, John Pochna, set him straight and I spent many enjoyable nights there in the future, as I did with Germaine.

A couple of months after our band started performing, we decided to make a demo tape of our songs. We got Spit Stix, the drummer from Fear, to be our recording engineer, and we rented out three hours of time at a hole-in-the-wall recording studio on

Hollywood Boulevard. To give you an idea of the level of professionalism we're talking about here, the entire budget came to three hundred dollars, which included the studio time, the engineer, and the tape. For some reason, I was the only one with money that week, so I gladly gave it up for the cause.

Those demo sessions were by far the most productive and inspired recording that we've ever done. In the last twenty years, we've never once hit a moment when there was as much magic and oneness happening. We were in the zone. Everything was recorded in one take, and everything was perfect. We finished our six songs so fast that we had enough time left to record the a cappella ditties, something we hadn't planned on doing.

We walked out of there with a master tape and a few small cassette dubs. When we got home and listened to the music, we were in awe. People had always said that we were a live act that could never translate to record, but now we had the proof—that was bullshit. Flea and I took the cassettes, wrote our names on the plastic boxes, and began to hit the pavement to try and get bookings. We weren't even thinking of getting a record deal. For me, this whole process was a two-part thing. You wrote and practiced the songs, and then you played shows. And we wanted to play bigger and bigger shows.

We also wanted to spread Chili Pepperdom to New York. About a week after we made that tape, our friend Pete Weiss offered to take us there. Pete was a native Los Angelean who had met Flea on the movie set of *Suburbia,* a film about the punk-rock scene in L.A. that Flea had acted in. Pete was a boom-mike operator and a musician and an all-around Renaissance man who was about a year and half older than we were. He had a basement apartment in Hollywood that became a clubhouse for us. He also had a beautiful classic old American car that we'd drive down to the beach or cruise around in, smoking pot and chasing girls.

Pete worked for the screenwriter Paul Schrader, who was moving to New York and had enlisted Pete to drive a huge Ryder truck packed with his belongings to his new Fifth Avenue pad.

Flea and I jumped on the chance to go to New York. We had our secret weapon, our cassette, and we had visions of playing it for people in New York. When they heard its brilliance, doors were going to open, seas were going to part, and people would be dancing in the streets. There was no doubt in our minds that we'd be booked into every club in New York.

Our good friend Fab also climbed aboard for the journey, which was great for me, because somewhere out in the California desert, he came to me on the sly and told me that he had a small quantity of heroin. So we sniffed that China White and got really high. Except for a few run-ins with some crazy-assed truckers, the drive was pretty uneventful. Pete dropped us off in SoHo and then headed back up Fifth Avenue to unload Paul's stuff. Flea and I had the tape burning a hole in our pocket, but we also had the business of survival at hand. We didn't have a place to stay, but Fab knew two models who lived on Broome Street, so we went by their building. "I'm going to stay with these two models, but I can't exactly bring you guys," he said.

"Okay, but how about if we go in and maybe wash up or something?" I suggested.

We went up to their place and completely moved in. For four days these beautiful models were constantly kicking Flea and me out of their beds and bedrooms. We were leeches.

We set about the business of playing our demo tape for different club people. Of course, we had no contacts or tactics. We'd go to a club and ask for the manager. They'd point out his office, and we'd go back there, pop in our cassette tape, and do a wild dance to our own music, trying to sell ourselves. Only problem was, nobody was buying it. We got the warmest reception from this cigar-smoking Italian stallion who ran the Peppermint Lounge. He gave us a few minutes. Most people showed us the door and said, "Get the fuck out of here with your cassette tape." After a few rejections, I could tell that this wasn't the way to go about getting booked into a club.

So Flea and I spent a day sightseeing. We went up to Central

Park and sat down on a bench, put our tape in the boom box, and blasted our music. We wanted someone to know that we had made this fucking tape. We got a lot of scornful looks from people who thought we were obnoxious to play such loud music, but amazingly, every kid who came within earshot completely rocked out to it. That was interesting. When we got back to L.A., we wrote a song called "Baby Appeal," and that became a staple of our early act.

Shortly after we got back from New York, Hillel moved out to live with his girlfriend. Rent was due, and Flea and I had about two hundred bucks each. We had the option of scraping together enough money to pay another month's rent, or going out and buying some high-quality leather jackets, the absolutely de rigueur possession of every self-respecting punk. So we headed to Melrose Avenue, which was becoming a center for cool vintage clothing. There was a guy from New York named Danny who had recently opened up a small shop with a bunch of great vintage James Dean leather jackets.

Flea and I picked out the perfect leathers, but when we went to buy them, Danny's prices were astronomical, at least a hundred dollars more than what we each had.

"Listen, I've got a hundred and fifty, and my friend here has a hundred and seventy, so why don't you just give us the jackets for that?" I suggested.

"Are you crazy? Get out of my shop," he yelled.

But having seen these jackets, we couldn't conceive of not owning them, so I came up with the idea of picketing the store. We made up some signs that said UNFAIR BUSINESS PRACTICES. DANNY IS A GREEDY MONSTER. I figured he'd be amused by the lengths we'd go to get these jackets. We started marching around in front of his store with our signs, and Danny came running out.

"What the fuck are you little punks doing? Get out of here before I break these signs over your head," he screamed.

I thought I detected a modicum of amusement in his voice, so I came up with another plan. We would stage a hunger strike in front of his store until he agreed to sell us our jackets. We went back and plunked down on the sidewalk.

Danny ran out to confront us. "What now?"

"It's a hunger strike. We're not moving or eating or drinking until you give us those jackets," I said.

"Jesus Christ, you guys. How much money do you have?" he said.

We finally had him. He took us inside and tried to steer us to some lower-priced leathers, but we held out and gave him all our money for the two fine jackets.

Later that same day, we were parading down Hollywood Boulevard in our brand-new vintage jackets, not realizing the irony that we were in the hottest punk-funk band in L.A. with no place to live and no money, when this kooky mop-topped, bespectacled, bookwormy-looking punker in a funny jacket came up to us. "Hey, you guys are in the Red Hot Chili Peppers," he said. He had met Flea one night when he was a DJ at a club and spinning a Defunkt record. Flea had vaulted over into his booth and turned the record over, because he thought this guy was playing the wrong side.

His name was Bob Forrest, and besides the occasional DJ job, he also ran the Sunday Club, which was one of the hottest live venues around. Bob asked us what was up, and we told him our woeful tale of new jackets but no home.

"That's so crazy. A half an hour ago my wife left me for good," he said. "If you guys want, you can crash at my place."

Forrest lived on the third floor of a classic apartment building called La Leyenda, which had seen better times, especially before the influx of punk rockers. He had a one-bedroom apartment filled to the brim with tons of books and records. Flea set up shop in the living room, and I took over the breakfast nook.

Bob had gone to college for a few years before he dropped out. He was working at a bookstore when we met him, probably for minimum wage, but his job became a great source of income for us because they bought used books. Flea and I would go out and heist books from personal collections or libraries. A stack of books meant ten dollars, and ten dollars meant we could buy drugs and shoot them and get high. We'd usually buy coke, which was a bad drug to be doing when you didn't have a lot of money, because the minute it's gone, you want more. But we'd get it and run back to Bob's house and dump it into a martini glass, put in the right amount of water, and stick our syringes in there and shoot the liquefied coke. We'd do that a couple of times until it was gone, then we'd bum out and feel raw and violated and run down to the Zero to drink off the pain, find a girl to take away the pain, or find more coke.

That summer we made a reliable speed connection, a Middle Eastern guy who ran a rehearsal studio. So we started shooting speed, which is a lot different than shooting coke. Cocaine is a clean ultra-euphoric too-good-to-be-true feeling that lasts for about three minutes. Your ears ring and your jaw opens up and for those three minutes you feel totally at one with the universe. Speed is a lot dirtier and less euphoric and a bit more physical. Every inch of your skin starts to tingle and turns into chicken skin.

We started going on these three-man speed binges and we'd stay up for days on end, playing cribbage. We even started a band together, the La Leyenda Tweakers. Unfortunately, we decided to perform outside of our apartment, and we did a show so stoned on speed that we resembled three mental patients. The *L.A. Weekly* gave us our first bad review. We knew that we were wreaking havoc with our bodies, but we were so delusional that we thought that if we just ate watermelon, it would cleanse both our bodies and our souls of this heinous chemical torture that we were incapable of stopping. We'd buy the watermelons in vast quantities and go back to the house and cut up each one into three parts. Once we'd finished the watermelon, we'd march up to the roof of La Leyenda and have the ceremonial throw-offs of these big watermelon rinds and watch them explode in the parking lot below. That would be the end of a vicious speed run. Then we'd go and try to get some sleep before we woke up and started the cycle all over again.

Sometime in the middle of July, we were able to get it together to play what would become a legendary Chili Pepper gig. We got a job to headline the Kit Kat Club, which was a classic strip club that had been putting on rock shows. All four of us worked real hard to prepare for the show. At Hillel's request, we even learned to cover Jimi Hendrix's "Fire." We got to the club that night, and they gave us a huge dressing room that must have normally been used by the strippers. I made sure the lyrics were together, and then I wrote out the set list, which was a responsibility that I'd taken on early in the band's life. We had an extra-special surprise that night. Since we were playing at a strip club and the girls would be dancing onstage with us, we decided that the appropriate encore would be for us to come out naked, except for long athletic socks that we'd wear over our stuff. We had already been playing shirtless, and we realized the power and beauty of nudity onstage.

I'd come up with the idea of using socks, because back when I was living with Donde Bastone, he had a pot customer who developed a serious crush on me. She was cute, but I kept resisting her advances, which included sending me gag greeting cards with foldout rulers to measure the size of your dick, and even photos of herself blowing some sailor. One day she showed up to the house, and I decided to answer the door buck naked except for a sock wrapped around my dick and balls.

We were jazzed to play. Our interaction had gotten better and better. Before, our shows were one big finale of fireworks from beginning to end; now we had started to develop differing dynamics onstage. About ten minutes before we were scheduled to play, someone broke out a joint. We had never smoked weed before a show, but we all passed it around and took a hit, even Jack. As soon as the weed hit me, I become paranoid and terrified that all of this hard work and this perfect feeling were about to be ruined by being stoned on pot. Hillel and Flea started feeling the same way. I went for a run around the block to clear my head, and it worked.

We had to follow a fantastic performance by an anarchistic outfit of eccentric masterminds called Roid Rogers and the Whirling Butt Cherries. But that only served to pump me up higher, because I wanted to show everyone that we were stronger. So we hit the stage that night and we just wailed. Jack and Flea were incredibly tight, and Hillel was in another dimension. I had a great vocal monitor, so I heard myself fine, which wasn't always the case at our shows. We finished the set and ran backstage, and we were all in a frizzle tizzy. Jack was cackling, because when he gets nervous, he just starts laughing.

When we walked back onstage wearing only the socks, the crowd audibly gasped. We weren't deterred for one moment by the collective state of shock that the audience was experiencing. We started rocking "Fire," and our friend Alison Po Po had shoved her way to the front row and she started taking swoops at my sock. I was focused on the song and my performance, but another part of my brain started telling me how many inches I had between my sock and her farthest reach. As I watched a bunch of our friends who had all rushed the stage and were grabbing for the socks, I had a totally liberating and empowering feeling. You're young and you're not jaded yet and so the idea of being naked and playing this beautiful music with your best friends and generating so much energy and color and love in a moment of being nude is great. But you're not only nude, you've also got this giant image of a phallus going for you. These were long socks. Usually, when you're playing, your dick goes into protection mode, so you're not loose and relaxed and elongated, you're more compact, like you're in a boxing match. So to have this added appendage was a great feeling. But we never figured that the socks were going to become an iconic image associated with us. We never thought that down the line, we'd do it again and promoters would want to add riders to our contracts to ensure that we'd do it on their stage. It left a more lasting impression than we ever intended for it.

One person in the audience who was really impressed was a thirtyish talent manager named Lindy Goetz. Lindy used to work as a promotion guy for MCA Records, and he had managed the Ohio Players, one of our favorite groups. Flea and I scraped up enough money to get out to the Valley, where Lindy's offices were. Lindy was a five-foot-six redheaded, mustachioed Jewish guy from Brooklyn who had somehow found his way to L.A. in the late '60s. That afternoon we smoked some pot and did a line or two of coke and swapped stories. I don't think we realized it at the time, but Lindy was on his way down from his high-rolling payola-paying days. He had managed the Ohio Players, but that was when their career was on the downswing.

He were trying to keep face and maintain a facade of having a business, but the bills weren't getting paid, and the money wasn't coming in. Lindy seemed like a likable guy, even if he was dishing out some pretty lame one-liners. After our long conversation, Flea and I asked for a minute to confer.

"Let's ask him if he'll take us out to lunch," Flea said. "If he will, he's got the job."

We went back in. "Okay, if you take us for Chinese food right now, you can be our manager," I said.

We got moo shu pork and a new manager. And a meal ticket. For the next few months, we'd wake up and go, "What's for lunch? Nothing? Let's go see Lindy." He lived in a deluxe apartment building in West Hollywood and was married to a girl named Patty, who was from Atlanta. We'd go over to Lindy's, and she'd cook up the fried chicken, and we'd eat every last bit. On a good night, we'd do a little cocaine and smoke some weed and talk about the future. Lindy told us that his first task was to get us a record deal, which I wasn't even that concerned with. It seemed like a cool and exciting thing, and I guess that's what bands do, but I didn't know anything about making a record.

If we were going to try and get a record deal, we'd need a lawyer. Someone gave us a recommendation for a guy named Eric Greenspan. We went to his law firm, which was in an opulent building on Wilshire Boulevard. When Flea and I walked into the lobby, we thought we were in the Mormon Cathedral. This firm represented the countries of both Israel and Egypt. We took the elevator up to Eric's floor and then went up to the lady at the reception desk.

"We're the Red Hot Chili Peppers, and we're here to see Eric Greenspan," I said.

"Well, I don't know, let me . . ." She seemed taken aback.

For some unknown reason, we decided to moon her. We turned around, exclaimed, "We're the Red Hot Chili Peppers, goddammit, and we want to see Eric," and we dropped trousers. Just then Eric came running out and took us into his office. He had some great Gary Panter artwork on his wall. He told us that he represented Gary as well as some reggae acts like Burning Spear.

I cut to the chase. "We don't have a record deal, and we don't have any money. We just got a manager and we need a lawyer."

Eric didn't flinch. "Okay, I'll be your lawyer, and you don't have to pay me until you make some real money, and then we can do a standard five percent deal." So he became our lawyer and never made a penny until we started making real money. He's still our lawyer today. It's a pretty rare guy in this business who does that. We didn't look like a cash cow to anybody at that point. The popular money-making bands at that time were hair bands like Poison, Warrant, and RATT, that's what was at the cash registers. We were just anti-everything. We were probably anti–making money at that point.

In the space of five months, we had made a dent in the L.A. music scene. We'd gotten written up in the *L.A. Times,* and we were playing some respectable venues, like the Club Lingerie. The more prominent we became, the more Lee Ving started to sweat Flea about being in two bands. I remember he actually called once and said, "Are you going to be in my band, or are you going to be in that other band?" Flea said, "Well, I was going to be in both, but if you put it that way, I'll just be in my band."

Sometime that August, Flea and I went to a party for an arty magazine at a house in the Hollywood Hills. I had taken to wearing a ripped-up flannel pajama top, and my Mohawk had grown out and fallen over to one side. We were having a decent time hanging out in the backyard when I looked into the house and saw this cosmic creature of a young girl. She was walking like some kind of a princess, in slow motion, with her hands out to the sides. She had on a giant white discus of a hat with these big opalescent jewels going around the crown. She was wearing an ill-fitting futuristic-looking baggy dress made out of paper. She was a little bit chubby, but beautiful.

And she had this absolutely bizarre magnetism, walking around and talking purposefully, but slowly, like she was Alice in Wonderland and the rest of the world wasn't. But she also had the feel of a punk-rock version of Mae West, giving off that flamboyance and a brassy, sassy, untouchable vibe. Just the kind of girl I liked—the weirdo in the bunch.

I walked into the house and pulled on her ponytail or whatever boys do when they see a girl they like and don't know how to talk to.

"Oh my, who are you?" she said. We started talking, and she was speaking in riddles, not giving me straight answers. It turned out that her name was Jennifer Bruce, and she was a fashion designer and had designed her Mark of the Zorro hat. Within minutes, I was blown away by her presence, her aura, and her fashion statement. In a city that was rife with people trying to look different and act different and be all this and all that, here was a person who was accomplishing it with ease, because she was a natural-born superfreak whose tendency in life was to look like the inside of an oyster shell.

She wasn't exactly melting in my arms; she was keeping me at a distance. I don't think she gave me her phone number, but I kept pressing. "Come on, you don't have a choice. You're going to be my girlfriend whether you like it or not," I said.

She must have felt something, because she was giving me enough to continue the process, but then she disappeared and

I went off in a new direction. However, she was thoroughly etched into my consciousness.

I had other things to attend to, one of which was opening up for Oingo Boingo at the Universal Amphitheater. Oingo Boingo had come up from the same club scene we were in, and they'd just kept going. They weren't our favorite band in the world, but they had some interesting instrumentation. We knew their trumpet player, and he offered us the opening slot for their big show. Here we were with no record deal, a ten-song repertoire, and we were going from playing in a club before two hundred people to playing to an audience of four thousand.

We went out onstage that night wearing our weirdest clothes. Right in the middle of the first song, Flea broke a bass string. Suddenly, it was crickets time, and I had to talk to the audience while Flea changed his string. Within seconds, the crowd was booing and throwing stuff at us, chanting, "We want Oingo Boingo." But it was combustible material for getting the energy going. We started in again, and Flea was so wound up that he broke another string. At this point, Danny Elfman, who was the lead singer of Oingo Boingo and also a fan of ours, strolled out onstage wearing a bathrobe and with a face full of shaving cream, as if he was coming straight from his dressing room. He took the mike and told the crowd that he really liked us and they should be respectful, and then he left, but the few unruly guys in the crowd didn't heed his endorsement. We soldiered on and got cooking, and by the time we finished, I think we let them know that we were for real and that they had just been hit with something they wouldn't soon forget.

After the show, we were celebrating backstage when Blackie, who had been one of our earliest supporters, came up to Flea and me. He was wearing tight black gloves, and he fanned out a couple of envelopes with plane tickets in them.

"This is for you, Anthony, and I want you to take Flea," he said.

"Take him where?" I was baffled. I looked in the envelope

and saw two round-trip tickets to London, England. It was time for my rite of passage to Europe.

We had a few things to attend to before we left for Europe, one of which was the complications that arose from getting a record deal. We had an inkling that record companies had been snooping around us, especially after our shows at the Lingerie and the Universal Amphitheater and a triumphant return to the Kit Kat Club in September. One executive from EMI/Enigma, Jamie Cohen, was particularly aggressive in going after us. One night Flea and I were hanging out at La Leyenda when we got a call from Lindy. He told us that we had a record deal with EMI/Enigma. I was so excited, the last thing I thought was there might be problems. I remember celebrating and thinking that everything was going according to plan, that we just had to buckle down, be studious, and get to work.

I was still excited about our deal when the phone rang again. Flea answered it. In the background, I heard him say, "Are you sure? Wow, wow, that's really bad news." I was sitting there going, "What? What? What?" when Flea hung up the phone and looked at me.

"Jack and Hillel just quit the band. What Is This got their own record deal, and they're choosing to stay in that band," he said.

I was speechless and in shock, feeling like a piano had fallen on my heart. I stumbled off to the couch and started to cry. This couldn't be possible. We had invented something as a band, we had created this thing that the world must hear about, and all of a sudden it was like we were aborting a baby at six months. Flea was sitting there going, "This is fucked up, this is fucked up."

Our sound was based on the drumming of Jack Irons and the guitar playing of Hillel Slovak. It wasn't like these were incidental guys, they made up our vibe. We were kids from high school, we were a team, you can't go shopping for a new mom and dad, it doesn't happen. I was thinking, "Okay, my life is over, my cause is lost, there's nowhere to go," when Flea said to me, "We're going to have to get two other guys," and I went from a dead wilted flower to "Huh, other guys? Is that possible?"

"Yeah, I know some good musicians," he said.

Once I started thinking about it, I realized that we had the songs, we had a record contract, we had Flea, we had me, we still loved what we did. We just hadn't done it yet, so we needed to find a way to make it happen. Flea immediately suggested that we hire Cliff Martinez as our drummer. He'd played in the Dickies, Roid Rogers, the Weirdos, and Captain Beefheart. I didn't know much about Beefheart, but I knew he was legendary. Flea and I went over to talk to Cliff. He lived in a wacky one-room apartment that you accessed through an underground parking garage on Harper. It wasn't a proper apartment, just a storage room that had been converted. He had been in the Weirdos, so his band fashion sense was you get a washboard and you turn that into a shirt, then you find a teapot and you make a hat out of it. When he played with Roid Rogers, he performed with a tampon hanging out of his ass. He was far and away the most eccentric one of us all. I thought I knew some bizarre human personalities, but Cliff was on a new level, though in a very likable way.

When we asked him to join the band, he was goofy with joy, smiling and laughing and saying, "Let's do this. I hope I'm what you're looking for, because this can be an amazing journey." We had our first jam, and it was clear from the get-go that Cliff Martinez not only could play crazy funk beats and super-inventive one-of-a-kind avant-garde art beats, but he could do a variety of styles and do them all well.

Now we had to find a guitar player. When we were jamming with Cliff, we discussed guitarists, and he suggested Dix Denney, a guy he had played with in the Weirdos. Flea had previously jammed with Dix, and he was a lovable fellow whom I had partied with. We felt comfortable that we could go on with these two guys. And Flea and I could go on to Europe.

We had a great time in Europe, exploring London, Paris, and then Amsterdam. In Paris, I ditched Flea for a few days to hook up with a beautiful Danish girl. He gave me the silent treatment when I got back, but then I bought some beautiful painted powder-blue tin cups off a street vendor and put them in the epaulets of our leather jackets, and we instantly became the Brothers Cup. We went on to Amsterdam and spent a few more days in London before returning home, but I realized that during the whole trip, I was unable to get Jennifer out of my mind, despite my fling with the Danish girl and a short-lived crush I had developed on a French hooker.

We returned to an interesting situation in our apartment at La Leyenda. We had been battling with the landlord for months over the rent that we weren't paying, and she had sent many eviction notices, but we ignored them. A few months before we left for Europe, she had the door taken off the apartment. Even that didn't stop us. We proceeded to carry on living there like it was no big deal that our apartment didn't have a front door. We figured there was nothing worth stealing anyway. It got to the point where we couldn't walk into the place, because she would hear us from her nearby apartment and make a charge, so we started climbing up the fire escape and entering through a window. Then she'd rush in through the front door and see Flea sleeping naked, and she'd be furious. When we returned from Europe, she'd finally persuaded the marshals to show up, and they posted notices that we were going straight to jail if we occupied the premises again.

Flea moved in with his sister, who had a one-room apartment above a garage in a Mexican part of town on East Melrose. Before long, I found my way there, and the three of us would share her queen-size bed. I didn't stay there for a long time, but it was long enough for me to get back on my feet and find Jennifer.

Sure enough, I ran into her one night, and we connected. She lived out in the deep Valley in Encino with her dad, who was an ex-marine turned insurance salesman, and her little sister. They were in a classic giant megalopolis Valley apartment building with absolutely no character or charm. Jennifer's best friend was her cousin, both bleached-blond Valley girls with an extreme flair for personalized fashion statements, divas who would spend hours painting their faces with outrageous makeup and creating kooky costumes before they went out clubbing.

They loved their Kamikazes and they smoked their Sherms, which were Nat Sherman cigarettes that were soaked in PCP. They were a couple of nutters, but there was something about Jennifer that I found absolutely fascinating, not just aesthetically but spiritually— something in her eyes, something in her soul, something in her being that attracted me. I fell for her.

No sooner did we start hanging out than we became boyfriend and girlfriend. Now I had this new person in my life who started taking up a lot of my time and energy, but she counterbalanced that by being an overall muse and a great giver. Jennifer was only seventeen, but she was coming off a relationship with a well-known Hollywood punk rocker. I was a fan of his, so I was a little bit jealous to hear the stories, but I also gave her extra credit for having been this guy's girlfriend. She was a hard punk-rock flower who didn't take shit from anyone and was very certain about herself and very accomplished for a young person. She was going to the Fashion Institute in Los Angeles when we met. She even had her own car, a yellow hatchback MG.

Like me, Jennifer was a very sexual being, although she had very little sexual experience. I'd been going strong for a while and was very sexually attracted to her. When we first started making love, I asked her if she'd ever had an orgasm, and she said she hadn't. She'd get close when she was in the bathtub and using the showerhead, but she'd never had one during the act of sex. I promised that we'd work on that, and I started going down on her for what seemed like ages. She came closer and closer, and we finally cracked the code and she became this orgasmic being, which was a great accomplishment but also a great relief.

One time early in our relationship, she wanted to take acid with me. We dropped some and were driving around in her car, dying to have sex, so I took her to Flea's sister's place. I decided that instead of having sex in Karen's bed, which wouldn't have been a great idea, we'd go in the bathroom and have sex in the shower. We ended up in that shower for a long time, and we got pretty loud and it became a quasi-spiritual experience complete with hallucinations of rainbows. Then Karen came home. Karen was such a sexual person herself, and we were like sex friends who would share our various sexual escapades, so I didn't think she would mind that I was having sex in her shower. But I was wrong, boy I was wrong. When I emerged from that bathroom, Flea pulled me aside and told me that Karen was very upset and what I had done in there was just not cool. So that was the end of my crashing with Flea and his sister.

I started staying out in Encino, and Jennifer's father was not too pleased. But he did love his daughters, and if that meant he'd have to tolerate a hooligan, then so be it. To me the Encino house was yet another refrigerator and a source of food and a place where I could be taken care of, especially when I fell ill that fall. I had suddenly lost all my strength, and even getting out of the bed was an effort. When I finally went to the doctor, he told me that I had hepatitis. Ironically, it wasn't the type you get from needles, it was the hep you get from eating bad shellfish. After a week in bed, I was pretty good to go.

Now that I had captured the heart of the girl I'd been pining away for, it was time to get back to the business of being a band. One of our first problems was that Dix wasn't cutting it at guitar. Cliff had learned all our songs right away. He'd go home and practice all night long and make sure he knew exactly what to play. Dix was a great musician who couldn't apply himself to other people's parts. If you asked him to write a song, he was a wizard. But when it came time to learn Hillel's experimental funk riffs, that wasn't his thing. We didn't quite understand that; we thought anyone should be able to learn anything.

He would come to rehearsal, and we'd have monster jams, but then we'd say, "Let's play 'Get Up and Jump,'" and Dix would draw a blank. That was a major problem, because we planned on recording all of our early songs. So Flea and I decided to fire Dix.

But how do you fire this gentle, lovable, quiet man? We came up with a plan to invite him over for a game of croquet. We'd explain in a civil manner that his style and our style were not melding appropriately, and therefore we should both be free to go off and express ourselves in our own manners.

There was a small yard across the street from Flea's house, and we set up for a croquet game without even consulting his neighbors. We were hitting the balls around, and I said, "So, Dix, how's everything?"

"Good," he said.

"We've been doing some thinking, and what we were thinking—uh, Flea, why don't you tell him what we were thinking," I said.

"Well, we were thinking, strictly in musical terms—uh, Anthony, I think you could probably say it better," Flea hedged.

"Well, musically speaking, let's say that we're going in this direction, and Flea, why don't you go ahead and take over from there."

"You're a musical genius of your own variety, and you're kind of going in that direction . . ." Flea said.

"And your direction and our direction just don't seem meant to be together. We're sorry," we both said.

We kept on going on about how our musical directions were different, and Dix was listening, as usual, and not talking at all. After we thought we had told him that we had incompatible paths, Dix turned to us and said, "Okay. So rehearsal tomorrow is the same time?"

We had to spell it out that we couldn't play in the band with him anymore, and at last it dawned on him and he packed his bags and got in the car and left. That was the first of many heartbreaking firings that Flea and I would have to preside over. We thought we would always be four knuckleheads from Hollywood, but now we were learning that we would have to deal with the realities of life.

We had guitar auditions and saw a lot of people, but it came down to two guys: Mark Nine, this hip avant-garde art school refugee who had been in a band with Cliff called Two Balls and a Bat; and Jack Sherman. I had no idea of his background, no idea how he got to the rehearsal, but I knew he was a nerd the minute he walked into the audition. Now, that wasn't a bad thing, we were embracing of the nerd energy at that time. But this guy was a nerd without even realizing he was a nerd. He had this combed-back Jewfro hair that didn't have any kinks, and he was neat and tidy. He'd come in with a huge smile, and he didn't look very cool when he was jamming, but he locked right in with Flea and Cliff and it wasn't stagnant and it wasn't a struggle for them to find each other and there was an actual musical flow. Plus this guy had crazy chops, and the most complicated things came naturally to him. We played some of our songs, and though he didn't have a down-and-dirty nasty-dog element to his sound, he was techni-cally efficient, hitting all the notes in the right places. His playing didn't have the same spirit as Hillel's, but at least he was playing the parts.

So it was down to this hip dog and this average Joe. When we were leaving the rehearsal space that night, Jack was going, "Wow, that was really an amazing jam, and you guys are really cool. I haven't played funk like that since 1975, when I played in this Top Forty band . . ." We told him that our first step was to make this record and then go out on tour.

"Oh, wow, making a record, that'll be neat," Jack said. Then he stopped in his tracks. "But should you want me in your band, I have to check with my astrologer before I go on tour, because I can-not go on tour when there's a third moon in Venus that could be rising on the backside of Jupiter's astral projection toward the fifth universe."

We were waiting for him to go "Just kidding," but he went on about these conjunctions and retrogrades and whatever, so we fi-nally had to ask him if he was for real.

"No, I'm serious about this. It should be okay, but I do have to check with my astrologer," he said.

We told him that we'd get back to him, and he left. We

rehashed everything and somehow decided to go with the nerd. We thought that he had a lot of experience, and he was an amazing guitar player in his own way. He wasn't the raw, explosive hellcat of funk that we were looking for, but he'd definitely be capable of going into the studio and putting down these parts, so we hired him. That was another moment of celebration, because now all the pieces were there.

With the band set, I needed a place to live. Bob Forest and I had heard that these office spaces in a classic old Hollywood Boulevard two-story office building were for rent, and they were cheap. Back then the Hollywood Boulevard area was in a state of disrepair. The building was called the Outpost, and it had probably been there since the '20s, the kind of building that at one time would have housed private detectives. It was beautiful, with an elegant staircase and hallways with tall ceilings and old light fixtures and big tall windows and those old-school bathrooms with ten urinals, all nice old materials and tiles. I had saved up a few hundred dollars, and I told the landlord that I was a writer and I needed a place to work. We knew we couldn't tell them we wanted to live in an office building, even though there were a couple of other people living there; you don't say it, you just quietly go about it, and they don't know and it's okay. They showed me a few different places, and I took the biggest and nicest one. It had a tall ceiling and several huge windows looking out on Hollywood Boulevard. It was one big long room with no bathroom and a nice wooden door. Bob was on a tighter budget, so he took the cheapest space, which faced the back parking lot. My rent was $135 a month, and Bob's was probably $85, just dirt cheap. We couldn't have cared less that there were no bathrooms in the suites; we figured we'd wash up in the sinks.

Those Outpost rooms would become the scene of much decadence, debauchery, and the decline of young minds. Shortly after we moved in, Greg, an old kooky Orange County friend of Bob's, moved in down the hallway. He was a coke fiend, a coke dealer, and a wannabe guitar player. A designer moved in next to me who lived with her boyfriend, a huge ornery guitar player named Carlos Guitarlos, with whom I'd had run-ins in the past. I set about the business of decorating my new house. I put a bed in the corner, loft-style, and I moved in a desk. Carlos's girlfriend offered me this little round sofa that was covered in furry leopard skin, which was an absolute find.

Having Bob in such proximity was both a blessing and a curse. He would always be coming over, and we'd hustle up whatever meager amounts of money we could to go buy drugs. The heroin supply had eluded us, so we were doing coke and then trying to drink our way out of it. Of course, our new neighbor Greg had what seemed to be an endless supply. One night I got on a roll and was buying stuff from Greg, and I couldn't stop and he couldn't stop, so he started fronting me the drugs. I kept going back to his place and getting more and more. I even gave him some expensive skis I had as collateral until I could hock a guitar in the morning, which was a charade of lies to keep the white powder flowing, because I had no cash and no guitar. I thought that Greg would pass out and fall asleep for five days and not hassle me.

The party finally came to an end, and I passed out in a gnarly state of discomfort. After sleeping for a few hours, I heard loud banging on my door. It was Greg, and he wanted his money. I was thinking that if I didn't answer the door, he'd go away, I could out-patience him. Wrong. He kept coming back periodically, hitting the door harder each time. Eventually, I heard the cracking of wood. I peeked up from the bed and saw a big ax coming right through my beautiful thick wooden door. Hmm. Did not look good. I figured I could stay right there in bed and he'd rage in and chop me up with that ax because I had no money or guitar to hock, or I could charge him and try to turn the whole thing around and stand a chance of surviving.

I flew to the door, threw it open, and screamed, "You bastard! Look what you're doing to my door!"

The air seemed to deflate from this enraged coke fiend. He

looked at the door and then at me and said, "Oh my God, I'm so sorry. I am going to fix that door right now."

I decided to parlay my advantage. "What were you thinking?" I said. "Now you owe me money for this."

Greg looked confused. "No, you owe me money."

"Owe you money? Look at what you did to my door, my friend. I think we should just call it even."

"I don't know . . . I owe my guy all that money . . ."

"Look, keep the skis. Get out of here, you destroyed my door."

Greg turned around and walked off like a puppy dog with an ax in his hand. There was a big sliver that had been chopped out of my door, and you could see right into my place, so I got some cardboard and taped it up. Then I went back to sleep.

That wasn't an atypical day at the Outpost, I'm sad to say. A lot of my days revolved around hanging out with Bob, doing drugs at night, waking up the next day with no money, and scraping together ninety-nine cents to go downstairs and get a slice of pizza.

Flea was no longer a participant in our insanity. While we were still living at La Leyenda, he had read about this D.C. band called Minor Threat, who were promulgating an anti-drug philosophy in a song called "Straight Edge." Flea was so demoralized and depressed from all these drugs we had been doing that he tore their lyrics out of the magazine and shaved his head and tried to embrace this not-getting-high philosophy. It didn't stick, but it did stop him from going further down. He leveled off and did a lot less drugs, whereas Bob and I were out of control. One time while I was at the Outpost, I had been shooting coke and speed, and I ran out of everything. There comes a point when you want to keep shooting something, even if you're high, just to get a new rush. Someone had given me a hit of acid and I had a bottle of vodka, so I took the acid, put it in a spoon, poured some vodka in the spoon, dissolved that blotter acid as best I could, and shot the LSD mixed with vodka. It was the first time I ever peaked on acid in one second.

And instead of tasting heroin or cocaine or speed in the back of my mouth, I was tasting vodka.

Somewhere along the line, I ran into some China White heroin again. I can remember spending all my money on coke and lying in bed, not being able to sleep. I'd call Jennifer in the Valley and ask her to come and take care of me, which meant bringing by some money so I could get some heroin to come down. It would usually be about four in the morning, and Hollywood Boulevard was dead quiet, and I was an empty soul lying on the mattress, waiting to hear the sound of her MG. I was such a dope fiend that I could hear that distinctive sound of her car when she got off the freeway, ten minutes before she'd show up. And she'd give me twenty or forty or sixty dollars, whatever she had. She didn't have a drug problem at this point, so she would be there to rescue me. That was our pattern, me listening for the car to come up, and this sensation of absolute relief when I knew she was parking downstairs.

By now my drug-shooting escapades were starting to impinge on the band. I'd miss a rehearsal, then I'd go AWOL for a while, and I was starting to alienate myself from Flea. We had the record deal and we had work to do, and I would be lying on the floor of my Outpost space, rolled up in some blankets after a wretched night of abuse, trying to get some sleep. One day I was in that situation and there was a knock on the door. It was Flea. He came into the room, which was a squalid mess, and he looked at me. "Anthony, get up."

I sat up.

"I can't do this with you anymore. You're too fucked up. I gotta quit the band."

I woke up, because that wasn't what I was expecting him to say. I thought he'd say, "Dude, you're a mess, we gotta talk about you not getting quite so high anymore," but when he said he had to quit the band, all of my cells reverberated and I bolted up. That was the first taste of the fact that I could be destroying the dream we had created of this amazing funk band that was all about dancing and energy and sex. I wanted to be in that band with Flea more than anything. But how could I communicate that to him? Then it popped into my mind.

"Flea, you can't quit," I pleaded. "I'm going to be the James Brown of the eighties."

How could he argue with that?

6.

The Red Hots

After we signed our record deal, Flea and I made the EMI offices our home away from home. A few people there were friendly to us, but we got the distinct feeling that if there was a totem pole of bands on their label, we weren't on it, let alone at the bottom of it. We even had trouble getting past the security guards at the front door. Every time we'd go there, we'd walk past a giant Rolls-Royce parked by the entrance. We'd ask whose car that was, and they'd say, "Oh, that's Jim Mazza's. He runs the company." But whenever we asked to meet him, we were told that we didn't need to, he wasn't involved in the day-to-day decision-making of any band. I can guarantee you that he did not know there was a band on his label called Red Hot Chili Peppers.

One day Flea and I went there in the afternoon, and Jamie Cohen, who had signed us, was out. We demanded to see a higher-up, and his secretary came out. "He's not available. He's in a very important board meeting with the entire staff of EMI International. They've all flown in for this meeting," she said.

Flea and I ducked around the corner and conferred and decided to drastically increase our visibility at EMI. So we went into the little bathroom, took off our clothes, went straight for the door, ran in, jumped up on the table, and ran up and down, hooting and hollering. Then we looked down and realized that it wasn't just men at that meeting. It was the entire multicultural EMI team from around the world, and they all had their briefcases and papers and graphs and charts and pointers and pencils, and we had trashed everyone's stuff. When this sank in, we jumped off the table, ran out of the room, and struggled to put on our underwear while being chased by the security guards, who had been notified of our intrusion.

We took off like two pieces of mercury and outran the guards through the parking lot and up Hollywood Boulevard until we got to Waddle's Park. Then we sat down and lit up a big, fat joint of green Hawaiian weed to celebrate the act of letting EMI know who we were. Halfway through the joint, I started getting a little paranoid.

"That was a good idea, wasn't it?" I asked Flea. "But what if they kick us off the label? They looked pretty upset. Come to think of it, they were screaming at us. Oh, God, what if we don't have a deal anymore?" When we came down off the pot high, we called Lindy to find out if we'd been dropped yet.

But it all blew over, and we got ready to make our first album. Jamie and Lindy wanted to know who we wanted to produce the album, and Flea and I both, without hesitation, recommended Andy Gill, the guitar player from Gang of Four. Their first album, *Entertainment,* was what had inspired me to get into dancing back when I was living with Donde. The music was so angular and hard and edgy, the epitome of that English art school funk, and Gill's lyrics were great and sociopolitical, but in a way that didn't seem like they were taking themselves too seriously.

Lindy got in touch with Gill's manager, and he agreed to produce us, which we thought was a great victory. When we met with him and he made disparaging comments about his earlier work, we should have seen the writing on the wall. But we started doing preproduction on the album at the SIR Studios, which were on Santa Monica, right near Vine, just a few blocks from my new house with Jennifer. I had a little money from the record deal, and Jennifer sold her MG, and we scraped together enough to rent a small house on Lexington Avenue, in a pretty gnarly area of Hollywood that was home to all varieties of prostitutes, from transsexuals to young boys.

Andy Gill started to go about this business of preproduction with Cliff and Jack and Flea and me, but it made no sense to me. I didn't really know what the hell a producer even did. It was a weird, uncomfortable situation for me, and the pressure started affecting me. I went on horrible drug binges, disappearing for days on end. It usually involved shooting coke, because I had gotten a few good coke connections. Bob Forest had turned me on to a guy who was a band member in a prominent L.A. rock group. He lived in a huge high-rise in Hollywood. I was such a scammer and a weasel that he ultimately refused to even let me up to his apartment. Whenever I showed up, he'd drop a can that was attached to a string from his balcony, and I'd have to put my money in, and only then would he throw the coke down. But my most reliable source of coke was the valet parking operation at a nearby shopping plaza. Someone told me that when you pulled up to park your car, all you had to say was "I need a ticket" or "I need a half a ticket," and that was code for buying cocaine. I'd go there morning, noon, and night and score lots of tickets.

Heroin began entering the picture more, too. Jennifer hated me when I'd shoot cocaine, because I would disappear and act weird and not be the most warm and reachable person. She wasn't afraid to get in my face and scream and throw punches at me. But one night we had been at the Power Tools Club downtown, and

I ran into Fab, who had recently moved into a huge loft that was a block away from the club. We went over to his house and he sold me a little itty-bitty miniature micro-bindle of the strongest China White heroin that you'd ever want to find, so strong that you didn't even have to inject it.

We snorted some, and it was like sinking into heaven. Jennifer loved it, and we went home and had sex for twelve straight hours, the beginning of the never-ending heroin sex merry-go-round that she and I would partake in. But that initial high is the feeling that you're doomed to be chasing for the rest of your life, because the next time you do it, it's good but not quite like that. Even still, China White was so cheap, and seemed so harmless. It wasn't like I was on the streets doing weird shit or sticking needles in my arm and ending up with a hundred bruises and blood dripping all over the place. It seemed so much more elegant to hang out at this loft with the paintings and the French people and sniff a little stuff and feel euphoric, and it lasted and lasted, and when you woke up in the morning, you still had some money in your pocket. China White was such a deceiving organism. At first it showed you the heaven, it didn't show you the hell.

Jennifer and I started doing more heroin, but I would still go on these maniacal coke binges. When I could, I'd steal Jennifer's new car, an old taxicab that she called the Circus Peanut because it was the color of those marshmallow candies. When I couldn't, I'd be forced to walk to my new dealer, a writer who lived a few miles from me. He dealt both heroin and coke, which was pretty convenient for me. But I'd never get good deals, since he was using himself. Of course, I was my typical pain-in-the-ass client self, always waking him up or generally harassing him until he'd let me in.

One day I was shooting coke at his place, but I got all crazy and he kicked me out. I had been fastidious about using sterile rigs and sterile cotton when I first started shooting up, but by now I didn't care much. If I had to, I'd use a syringe that I found in the street. Instead of sterilized cotton, I'd use a section of my sock or, more commonly, the filter tip of a cigarette. At first I'd use only sterilized spring water to dissolve the stuff in, but now I'd just pull the back off a toilet or look for a lawn sprinkler or even a puddle.

This crazy behavior began to encroach on my professional life. I started missing rehearsals and writing sessions. Then I even began to miss some live shows, including a big punk-rock show at the Olympic Auditorium downtown, where we were playing with our friends the Circle Jerks and Suicidal Tendencies.

I had started a binge a couple of days before, and when the day of the show came, I just could not stop using. I kept telling myself, "Okay, this is the last gram of stuff I'm going to do, and then I'm going to make it to the show." Letting the band down like that was the most gut-wrenching feeling I ever had. But Keith Morris, my friend from the Circle Jerks, filled in for me. He just sang the same line, "What you see is what you get," over and over again for every song. It wasn't the only time I'd miss a gig because I was on a run. We played Long Beach early on, and I was a no-show, so kids from the audience were invited up to sing the lyrics. Another time Lindy's brother sang.

We decided to record the album at El Dorado Studios, which is right on Hollywood and Vine. El Dorado was a classic old Hollywood studio with nice vintage equipment. For our engineer, we hired Dave Jerden, a soft-spoken, experienced, and competent man behind the board. Andy Gill was much different than we had expected. He was approachable, but he was also very English, semi-aloof, clearly intelligent, but with no edge. We were these aggressive, volatile individuals, and then there was this soft, smarty-pants English guy. Even though we all liked him and he was interested in us, he wasn't becoming the fifth finger on our hand. He certainly didn't embrace our musical aesthetic or ideology. It was almost like it was beneath him. He had been there, done that, and that was fine, but let's move on, go somewhere else. And we were like "Somewhere else? This is who we are!" So there was a little tension.

One day I got a glimpse of Gill's notebook, and next to the

song "Police Helicopter," he'd written "Shit." I was demolished that he had dismissed that as shit. "Police Helicopter" was a jewel in our crown. It embodied the spirit of who we were, which was this kinetic, stabbing, angular, shocking assault force of sound and energy. Reading his notes probably sealed the deal in our minds that "Okay, now we're working with the enemy." It became very much him against us, especially Flea and me. It became a real battle to make the record.

Andy's thing was having a hit at all costs, but it was such a mistake to have an agenda. He should have just made us the best band that we were. We would come up with these really beautiful, rough, interesting sounds, and he'd go, "Oh, no, no, you could never get that sound on the radio." We'd say, "And your point is what? We're not making this to get on the radio." He'd say, "Well, I am, I'm shooting to get something on the radio here." Jack Sherman also wasn't coming from the same place that Flea and I were. He was new in the band, and he was being far more cooperative with Andy, going for these clean, supposedly "radio-viable" sounds.

If the two bonded, it was because Andy saw Jack as a patsy he could control in the studio. We would argue all the time about the tone of Jack's guitar. Andy was trying to soften it up, and we'd be outraged. "That's weak and soft and lame and this song is punk rock and it's got to be thrashing and hard," we'd scream.

Part of the frustration we had with Jack was that he was a polished guitar player who really didn't have a punk-rock pedigree. Plus he was so anal, so unlike Flea and me. One day Jack was getting ready to play in the studio, and I got there early. He had a little guitar cloth in his hand, gently cleaning the neck of his guitar. Then he went into his pristine doctor's bag of stuff and pulled out what looked like air freshener, and he started deftly spraying this along the neck of the guitar.

"What the hell is that? What are you doing to your guitar?" I said.

"Oh, this is Fingerease. It helps your fingers glide up and

down the neck easier," he said. I was used to Hillel, who played so hard that his fingers would start to come apart. He knew he had a good night if his guitar was covered with blood. And here was this guy doing this gay spray job of mist onto his fretboard so his fingers could glide easily. I would razz him about that. "Do you have your Fingerease? Don't leave home without the Fingerease." He'd come back with "Oh, you probably don't even know what a diminished seventh chord is."

For the first couple of days in the studio, everything seemed fine. But I soon realized that Andy was going for a sound that wasn't us. By the end of the sessions, Flea and I would literally stomp out of the studio into the control room, crawl over the console VU meters, and scream, "Fuck you! We hate you! This is shit!" Andy was completely calm the whole time. And Dave Jerden was like one of those dolls in the back of cars with the bouncing head, going, "We gotta listen to Andy. We gotta listen to Andy."

We did some lighthearted stuff, too. We were in the middle of a heated argument with Andy one night in the studio when Flea said, "Let's put this on hold. I'm going to take a big shiny shit."

"Oh yeah, be sure and bring that back for me, then, won't you," Andy said drolly.

"Okay," Flea said.

"I wouldn't put it past you," Andy said.

I followed Flea out of the room. All the way to the bathroom, we were saying, "Let's really bring him the shit."

So Flea defecated, and we put it in an empty pizza box that was in the studio, and we went running back down the hallway and delivered the shit pizza to Andy.

He just rolled his eyes and said, "How predictable."

To this day, Flea points to that incident to demonstrate why we're such a good band: because we brought shit to Andy Gill.

I do remember bursts of happiness during that period. The new songs like "Buckle Down," "True Men," "Mommy, Where's Daddy," and "Grand Pappy DuPlenty" all sounded exciting and great. But I was terribly disappointed when I heard the mixes of

"Get Up and Jump," "Out in L.A.," "Green Heaven," and "Police Helicopter." All those songs sounded like they had gone through a sterilizing Goody Two-shoes machine. When we used to play them, they were so vicious-sounding, and now they sounded like bubblegum pop.

The tension affected Dave Jerden, and he was treated for a stomach ulcer and missed a week of work. Then Andy had to go to the hospital and have a cancerous testicle removed. While he was in the hospital, Flea and I tried to get Dave Jerden to remake the album, but he wasn't having it.

The album was released, and it wasn't something to celebrate. I felt like we had landed between two peaks, in the valley of compromise. I wasn't ashamed of it, but it was nothing like our demo tape. Still, our take was "Okay, this is our record, and let's keep marching on," especially after I read the first review. I picked up *BAM*, a little Bay Area music magazine, and they simply assassinated the album. I was very hurt, but I realized that sometimes people got it, sometimes they didn't. I couldn't put too much stock in what writers had to say about our music. Then we got a rave review in one of the first issues of *Spin* magazine, so we had the yin and yang of record reviews. At any rate, we were being acknowledged by someplace other than the "L.A. Dee Dah" column.

Right before the record came, we posed for our first poster. We had done a photo session in our socks previously, and that went on to become infamous, but this was our first official promotional poster. Right before the session, I grabbed a Magic Marker and started drawing all over Flea's chest and stomach and shoulders. It was just lines and squiggles and dots, but it looked great. We were into wearing unflattering hats then, but Cliff showed up, and he was the most outside dresser of all of us. He was wearing a huge mask with a hat over it and some kind of gloves so that you couldn't see one inch of his skin. He looked like a cloth-covered robot. Then Flea put me in a headlock, and we shot the poster.

We would mug for the camera at all of our shoots. We had been born in an era when posing and posturing and pursing and

pretty-boyness had taken over the landscape. It was all about trying to look as handsome as possible while making thin and empty
music. And we were anti whatever was popular. So mugging and
distorting our faces seemed like the natural response to all of these
people trying to manicure themselves to perfection.

We also made our first video. Enigma/EMI came up with
some money, and we hired Graham Wiffler, who had done films for
this oddball San Francisco group called the Residents, which we
loved. He designed a video for "True Men," and we showed up and
put in an eighteen-hour day doing things like sprouting up from
under the stage through these sand holes, because some farmer was
watering his cornfield. We completely gave up the body. If we'd
had to dive onto a bed of nails ten times in a row, we would have
done it. I remember waking up the next day and feeling a hundred
years old. I loved the video, although it was still weird to look at
something and see Jack Sherman instead of Hillel.

Probably a week after our record came out, unbeknownst to
me, Flea got a call from Johnny Lydon, of Sex Pistols fame, to audition as the bass player for his new group, Public Image. Flea quietly went and did the audition, not unlike the time that he had
auditioned for Fear when he was playing in What Is This. It went
very well, and he was the first choice. Then he consulted with Hillel, like he had with me when he was approached by Fear. They listened to both groups, and Hillel asked Flea if he wanted to be a
supporting member of Lydon's trip or a creating member of something new. Flea made up his mind to stick with our band. Thank
God for that, because I was a torn-up rag doll of a human being at
that point. I'm sure Flea was constantly thinking, "Jesus Christ, I
can't rely on this freak. He's dying out there, covered with track
marks. Black and blue, up and down. Stealing cars, disappearing,
going to jail. Just a fucking nutcase. How can I tolerate that?"

One time around then, we were supposed to be rehearsing,
but I didn't show up. Jack Sherman was raring to go, but Flea was
sitting there with his bass on his lap and his head hanging down.

"C'mon, let's do something," Jack said.

"Shut up," Flea growled.

"What's wrong with you? Why are you so down? Why can't we just get some work done?" Jack complained.

"If your friend could die at any minute, you'd be down, too," Flea said.

I didn't hear about that exchange until this year. That early on, as far as I remember, Flea never expressed anything even close to that to me. Whenever we would talk about it, it was never "I'm worried about you. I think you might have a problem, or you might be setting yourself up to die young." It was always "I can't do this. You left me hanging. I need someone I can rely on." I assumed that he was more like Jack and didn't consider himself a brother's keeper, just a driven professional who needed a reliable partnership.

The album was released that summer, and to promote it, we were scheduled to go to New York and play the CMJ New Music Seminar, which was the most important venue for alternative acts to get themselves known. I almost didn't make it to New York, not because of cocaine and heroin, but because I abused another drug—alcohol. I was home in Michigan for my annual summer visitation. I brought Jennifer, who showed up with her typical tricolored canary-yellow, pink-feathers-coming-out-of-her-head hairdo. When I introduced her to my family, they didn't know what to make of her. She looked like a giant field of blossoming daffodils. And the first thing she did was march out to the peach field behind the house and build a tepee. I thought she was going to build a toy tepee, but she had this legitimate passion for Native American culture, so she spent all afternoon and well into the night out in the woods harvesting tepee poles. I don't know if she had brought material with her, because she always had bags full of clothes and raw materials, but she wound up building a fifteen-foot-tall bona fide tepee that withstood the next harsh Michigan winter.

Before I left L.A., I was using more heroin than I wanted to. I started off with these rules that I'd do it once a week, because if you do it more than once a week, you're in danger of getting strung out. Then it would be like "I'll do it twice this week, but I won't do it at all next week." Day three comes up, and you're like "I'm just going to put a day in between each time I use, because that way I can never get strung out." Then it was like "If I do it two days in a row, and then don't do it for two days, and then just do it one day, I won't get strung out." I was losing that battle.

Meanwhile, Jennifer was making great friends with my sisters. My mom didn't know what to think of this pretty, crazy bird. Of course, like all moms, she didn't realize that the craziest bird in the house was her own son. One night I was feeling ill because I had run out of the tiny amount of dope I had brought with me. I intuitively knew that I needed some medicine to take away the pain, so I left Jennifer at home with my mom and went to go meet my friend Nate, who was at a bar with a bunch of straight, sheltered midwesterners. They all dressed the same, they all drank the same, they all drove the same cars and had the same kind of jobs and lived in the same kind of houses. And they drank a lot. Alcohol was never my first or even second or third drug of choice. I drank regularly, I just never got the tolerance thing happening. But I was feeling sick and going with the flow of this bar scene in Grand Rapids, which was kooky and lame and without much spirit. So I started drinking beer out of what seemed like giant popcorn containers. I was matching bucket for bucket with everybody there, and we were getting drunk and this was working for me, taking the place of all that stuff I'd run out of. I thought I was fine, but I had no idea how high I was.

It was about a twenty-mile drive down a straight country road to get back to my mom's house. I never wear a seat belt, even to this day, but when I was saying good-bye to Nate, as a joke, I made a big deal out of strapping on the belt. So I put the pedal to the metal on my mom's Subaru station wagon, which probably put me between eighty and ninety miles an hour. I was getting really tired, and I'd start to nod off and then jerk up sharply. I did this a few times, and then I decided that I was just going to close my eyes for a second. There was so much booze in me that my lights went out.

I blacked out, and the car veered into the oncoming lane, jumped the edge of the road, and hit a bump, at which point I woke up and saw a huge clump of trees in front of me. "Trees? What the . . ." Boom—the car accordioned into an elm tree face-on, and the engine was now next to me in the driver's seat, and the steering wheel had broken on impact with my face. I would have stayed there, unconscious and bleeding, for who knows how long if not for the fact that off in the distance, a person had heard the crash. By luck, that person was a paramedic who happened to have his ambulance in the driveway.

Within a matter of minutes, he had called some firemen, and they came and got the jaws of life and pried me out of the car. The paramedics were hovering over me, asking me who the president was. I answered each question perfectly, though I couldn't understand why they were testing me for brain damage. I didn't realize that my entire head had split wide open and I resembled a plate of spaghetti and meatballs.

I was rushed to the nearest hospital, and my poor mom was notified. She was home helping her husband, Steve, recover from his recent quadruple bypass surgery. But within minutes, my mother and my sister, Jenny, came marching into the operating room. They looked at me like a ghost. I asked if I could use the bathroom, and the nurses reluctantly let me. I went straight for the mirror, and looking back at me was the Elephant Man. My upper lip was so fat that it actually covered my nose. My nose looked like a bowl of cauliflower splayed across my whole face. My left eye was completely shut, but it looked like it had swallowed a pool ball before it closed. And there was blood everywhere. I instantly thought, "Oh my God, I will never look like a human being again." I could see out of only one eye, but I saw enough to know that was the end of my face as I knew it.

I stayed in the hospital for a week, taking Percodans every day and filling the script up faster than I could down them, loving this new supply of heroin. The doctor finally saw through my game and cut me off cold. After a few days, the swelling went down, and they repaired the broken bones. I had a broken skull, a broken eye socket, and a shattered orbital floor, which is the wafer-thin bone that supports your eyeball. The plastic surgeon had to work from a photo that my mom supplied, but with a little titanium and a little Teflon, he got me back to a reasonable facsimile of myself.

I called Lindy and apologized and told him I didn't think I'd be able to make it to the CMJ show. But Flea asked if I could show up. By then I had been fitted with a face cast that looked kind of cool, so we decided that I'd play with it on. Jennifer had made me a purple atomic-age angular cowboy hat, so I got on a plane with my face cast and my purple cowboy hat and my leather jacket with the cups, and the band did our best job at playing this huge showcase. I remember being nervous and terrified and stricken and energized, and it was the first time I realized that, okay, I had to find a way to take this adrenaline and this fear and these butterflies and turn them into a performance. It was a feeling that stuck with me for life, because if I don't have some of those feelings before a show, the juice is not flowing.

After the show, Flea and I crashed the MTV media room. George Clinton, Madonna, Lou Reed, and James Brown were on a panel, but Flea and I took over in the interview area. That was the beginning of our two-headed-monster routine; unlike some bands, we didn't have a singular spokesperson. We were the Loudmouth Two from the beginning, sitting in the same chair and sharing the same mike. It's something that, unfortunately, dissipated over the years, because we used to be so at ease with supporting each other and setting each other up, and starting and/or finishing each other's sentences in the best possible way. The weird sense of competition that's always been present between us didn't interfere with our singular purpose at that time. We were just happy to have a spotlight and happy to share it. I guess symbiosis is something that fades in time for no good reason. It's sad. We'd go out to the Zero Club early on and introduce ourselves to people as In and Out, and go into an Abbott and Costello routine: "I'm Out? I thought I was In." "Oh, I'm back In again?" We used to sleep side by side in railway stations. Now you couldn't get us to share the same house.

We felt we were the greatest, most successful band in the world. We didn't ever look at bands who sold lots of records and played in arenas as being more successful. EMI was disappointed in our sales, and when they told us that our record hadn't sold, I responded, "Okay. And the problem is what?" I wasn't one of these kids who grew up dreaming of gold records. To me, my life was what was in front of me, and that was going on this tour of America in a blue Chevy van. Everywhere we showed up, there were people, and they cared, and we rocked them out, and we gave it everything.

Nothing can describe how unprepared I was for any of this. Lindy said, "We're going on tour," and we said, "Okay. Where do we go?" This was when we got hooked up with Trip Brown, our first music agent. I didn't even know what a music agent was, but it turned out that besides a manager, you had to have yet another industry dude/weasel—not that our guys were weasels, but generally speaking, these guys are a weasely ilk. So Trip booked us on this tour that was sixty dates in sixty-four days, covering all of America. It never even crossed our minds to say, "Hey, that's a lot of shows, and there are no days off."

Before we left, the band invested in a beautiful blue Chevy van with white stripes. Lindy got it from a church group, and it was a big, heavy V8 that hauled ass. The few times that Lindy would let me drive it, I'd be able to get it airborne. Bob Forest wound up driving the van to our first gig, which was in Detroit. Bob was a talented songwriter and performer, but he offered to be our roadie, so we hired him. Having Bob drive your van across country is not as simple as it sounds. This was a guy who couldn't manage five dollars, he'd accidentally spend whatever money you gave him on the most useless things possible, none of which had to do with gas or oil or accommodations. So by the time he got to Detroit, he was a drunken wreck. And he was bitter and angry. "How come you guys got to fly and I had to drive?" "Because we hired you to drive the equipment. That's your job," we told him. And we had to live with it constantly, that "I'm happy to be out here, but fuck you guys, I should be performing."

Our first show was at a gorgeous old venue called St. Andrews Hall. Back in those days, we would sound-check before almost every show if it was at all logistically feasible. So we started, and Jack was being as anal as a man could be. He fastidiously pointed out every conceivable problem. "This cord is only eight feet long, and it has to be twelve feet, because I have to stand here to get the correct mix off my monitors, and I have to find my Fingerease, because the travel has made the guitar strings dry." We were ready to go buck wild and destroy the place, and he was standing there fretting.

We went to sound-check "True Men," and even though there was no audience, I let everything go on the first note, just to get started. I must have done some dance move that unplugged Jack, or kicked his guitar or kicked him or knocked his pedal over. And it wasn't intentional, but he quit. He walked offstage and said, "I can't be in a band where that's the sound-checking procedure. I need my plane ticket home." Lindy smoothed it out, and he played that night.

Jack would accuse me of deliberately trying to pull his cord out of his pedal. But you can't steer the dance, you're spinning like a top. I never exhibited any physical belligerence against him. To Flea and me, part and parcel of the stage experience was getting hurt. In fact, if you got hurt, it was the sign of a meaningful performance. If you came off the stage bleeding from the head or the body, you'd done your job, you went out there and you gave it everything. The stage was the stage, and that wasn't the place for boundaries. At one point, Jack even put tape down on the stage and told me that his space was off-limits. Why would you want to cut yourself off from your bandmate, spiritually or physically?

Right at the beginning of the tour, I knew that our relationship with Jack wasn't meant to be. We were crammed in the blue van, going from town to town, making no money at all. Flea was breaking his bass strings every night, and bass strings are real expensive. So he said, "I'd like to bring something up for band discussion. I'm having to replace my bass strings every other show, and that's pretty much my per diem, and I think it should be a band expense." Jack chimed in, "That's not a band expense. You chose that instrument. I am not chipping in for bass strings." Flea almost lunged at him in the van.

We had a lot of strange things happen that tour. We played Grand Rapids, and my dad's old friend Alan Bashara was the promoter. He booked us into a place called the Thunder Chicken, out in the suburbs. It was a big hick shack that usually booked country music or REO Speedwagon cover bands. Even though all my family and relatives were there, that didn't stop us from doing our usual show. That night Flea had a few beers before we went on, and he didn't handle his liquor too well, so he pulled his dick out onstage. It wasn't even that obnoxious of a dick pull, more like an exclamation point at the end of a song. But parents covered their kids' eyes, and people stormed out.

We left town, and the next day the local paper ran an article with a huge headline: IF I HAD A SON LIKE THAT, I'D SHOOT HIM. All of the local Christian Reform residents of Grand Rapids were talking about how horrible we were, that we were the devil's seed. My mom did not take that lying down. She responded with the lion heart of a mother and wrote a letter to the editor saying, "You do not know my son. This is one of the greatest men on earth. His capacity for compassion and helping his fellow man is beyond anything that you'll ever do with your life. I insist that you take back every negative thing that you said about my boy."

A couple of weeks into the tour, it was clear that Bob wasn't the most responsible roadie in the world. So Lindy hired this guy named Ben, and now we had another body crammed into that blue van. Both Ben and Bob were getting something like twenty dollars per diem for food, so Bob cut a deal with Ben. He would give Ben half of his per diem if Ben did all the roadie work. Bob spent the rest of his money on beer.

And drugs. Every night that we could, we'd get high on something. I didn't have a heroin habit, but I did have a constant craving for cocaine, especially after I drank. After a while on the road, I'd developed dope-fiend radar. We'd play some hole-in-the-wall club, and I'd zero in on the one person I knew had to be a dealer or at least know a dealer. People who are into drugs can sniff them out in the desert if they have to. And they'll find the codeine cough syrup or the person who's got some prescription that most resembles the drug of choice. It's weird, I was such a survivor and so wanted to be a part of life while I was trying to snuff out the life that was inside of me. I had this duality of trying to kill myself with drugs, then eating really good food and exercising and going swimming and trying to be a part of life. I was always going back and forth on some level.

Sometimes we had the drugs but didn't have the rigs to shoot them. We were staying in a sketchy downtown area in Cleveland one night, and I didn't feel like leaving the motel to find some syringes, so I sent Bob. An hour went by. Two hours. No sign from Bob. I went out into that bitter-cold night and asked a stranger on the street where someone would go to find drugs in Cleveland. He directed me to an all-night coffee shop about three blocks away. Off in the distance, I saw the neon, which was a beacon of hope. I went in and scanned the room, and sure enough, at one of the back booths, there was Bob in his torn-up suit and dreadlocked hair, sitting with two crazy-looking big black chicks.

I walked up to them and saw that one of these huge chicks was sitting on the outside of the booth. She appeared to have Bob pinned in. I was thinking she looked like a wide receiver for the Cleveland Browns, but when I looked closer and saw that besides all the lipstick and eyelashes and wigs and fluorescent clothing, there were some serious muscles on this chick, I realized she probably *was* a wide receiver for the Cleveland Browns. Then I saw that she was all over Bob, with her hand on his dick, sexing him up. I started screaming, "Get off my friend! Get off my friend!" and I was ready to dive into this fray, but then I realized that he had a smile on his face and he was enjoying himself. They'd been sitting there for hours, buying him drinks. We never got the syringes that night.

But we did in Chicago. We played to a packed house, and I went onstage wearing the executioner's hood that I had worn for our "True Men" video. Then I pulled off the mask and dove into the audience while I was still singing. The band was in a great groove, and this hot little club girl, cute as can be, grabbed me, dropped to her knees, yanked off my stretchy fabric pants, and started giving me a blow job right on the spot. I appreciated the gesture, but I didn't have the time or the inclination to have sex right then, I wanted to rock the place out.

We finished the show, and somehow Bob had managed to come up with a goodly amount of coke. We were staying at a run-down inner-city Travelodge with barbed wire all around it, but we didn't care, because we had the coke and some syringes and a bunch of beers. We went into our room and started slamulating huge amounts of club-bought cocaine. Poor Bobby instantly went into this cocaine psychosis and started going on about how we had to stop because there were police helicopters landing outside. He was glued to the window, convinced he was seeing helicopters. I can't remember if there were any helicopters or not, but if there were, they certainly didn't care about a couple of guys at the Travelodge shooting coke.

Bob was so paranoid that he was ready to run into the parking lot and throw himself at the mercy of the police. I tried to calm him down. He'd collect himself and then he'd go off again: "They're coming. They're coming again." He cowered for hours until that coke disappeared, which it always does. Then we found ourselves wide awake at five in the morning with our brains screaming for more dopamine. We found some booze and tried to drink ourselves into that early-morning torture chamber of half sleep when Satan's birds are singing outside the window. It was not fun. Some of the most depressing sensations known to humankind come in that morning netherworld when you run out of coke and you're in some seedy hotel and the sun is coming up and you've got to go somewhere. A few times on that tour, I'd do the all-night-drug thing and then get in the van, sleep on the floor under the seats all the way to the show, and have to wake up and feel like a wax statue with a core of Styrofoam and somehow find the power to play.

By the time we got to New York, about a month into the tour, Bob had had enough. We were staying at the Iroquois Hotel in Times Square, which was one step up from a welfare hotel. Flea and I and Bob shared a room, and I went out onto the fire escape to practice the songs, because this was New York and I really wanted to get it right. I was going to unveil a new look for New York: a woman's swimming cap, really big sunglasses, my usual paisley smoking jacket, and, for this show at the Pyramid Club, an inflatable airline vest that I'd stolen on the flight to Detroit. At the opportune moment, I'd pull the CO_2 cartridges and inflate.

That night we had the most fantastic audience—a mixture of drag queens and hipsters and dope fiends, Goth people and punk rockers. We rocked out and accomplished our mission and then went on to the afterparties. The next day we assembled in front of our hotel with the van. We were off to play Maxwell's in Hoboken, New Jersey. Bob had been up all night, and he'd really come to the end of his rope. He was pulling a Rumpelstiltskin on the sidewalk, banging his feet into the pavement, screaming and yelling, "I won't be treated like this."

"Treated like what? You're getting three squares a day and a place to stay and you're getting paid. You got Ben to do all your work for you, so all you have to do is drink, and you never show up anyway. How are we treating you?" we asked.

"This is a mockery. Don't you know who I am? I can't do this if Ben is going to be here. I quit. I quit this fucking tour," he said.

"Great, okay, we've got to go, so we'll see you back in L.A."

"No, I mean it, I'm not coming with you anymore," he insisted.

We were pretty relieved when he quit. As much as we cared about him and enjoyed the anarchy of his company, by the time we got to New York, it had lost its amusement. So we drove away and left him there. He was screaming and yelling and hissing the whole time we drove away. We went on to finish our tour, and he stayed in New York and went to work for a needle-dealing ring to support himself until he managed to get back to L.A.

When you're doing a lot of alcohol or cocaine, your thinking becomes skewed and you're willing to do a lot of things you normally wouldn't. I don't know if sleeping with a different girl more than half the time on tour while the love of my life was back in L.A. was due to drug-impaired judgment, though. At that point in my life, I had no morals. Even though I never stopped loving Jennifer, and I'd think about her every day and call her whenever I could afford it, I had no problem cheating on her. It became a momentum thing. If you don't actively seek out women, you lose that momentum, and even if you change your mind and decide you want to get laid, it becomes tough. But when it's happening every night, you're in that zone, and it becomes effortless, especially when you're the center of attention. That's what I wanted at that point in my life.

It would change a few years later. The instant that energy shifted and there was no effort required to have sex with girls because I was in a known band was the instant I stopped wanting to have sex with them. When we were punk rockers no one had heard of, I wanted to grab people's attention and show them who I was. It was all fun, and it made sense and I didn't feel weird about it. Of course, I was telling Jennifer that I was faithful, so I was not only cheating but also lying. But I was an out-of-control, selfish egomaniac, out to get mine morning, noon, and night.

Sometimes it was tricky to get yours, especially when we were at least two to a room. You'd have to be creative. Sometimes you could use the bathroom backstage or a room at an aftershow party. When I was rooming with Lindy, which I did on occasion, it was no problem. One night I ran into this girl from Nebraska. It was ironic, because Nebraska is the corn state, and she had pubic hair that resembled the precise texture of corn silk. You meet a lot of different pubic hair along the way—the nappy, the long, the short, the shaved, whatever. This girl had black corn silk growing out of her pubic mound. And she was a sweetheart, mild-mannered, not a hussy, not a whore, not a trampy backstage girl of any kind. I brought her back to our room, and Lindy was unflappable. He just lay there in his bed, put on his earplugs and eye mask, and zoned out.

Sometimes I combined my passion for drugs and girls. We had just played in South Carolina, and I was a little drunk, so I went straight into a coke hunt. The bartender at the club found me half a gram, and I did it all too soon. So I was horny beyond control when this fat girl approached me. She was probably about five-three, with an unusual chunky shape. She had a fairly large girth, and her tits were like enormous missiles that projected out from her elbows to the end of her hands. She was kind of pretty, though not the type of girl I'd ever hit on before. But she had our album, and she told me I was her favorite poet of all time, and she gave me this letter that, among other things, suggested my dick was a dolphin and her pussy was the ocean and I had to go for a swim in that ocean. She also wrote that she worshiped the ground I walked on and that she was my servant and she'd do anything for me.

"Can you get me some coke?" I started.

Sure she could. We just had to drive to her uncle's trailer in the next county. We drove out there, and there were guns and beer bottles and cigarettes and poker, a real southern drug-dealing trailer-park community. She got the coke, and we went back to her little apartment and did it all. As soon as we finished that coke, all of the clothes came off right away, and I had some of the best road sex imaginable with the most unlikely candidate. Because she wasn't typically hot, there was no pressure, whatever happened

happened, and we went for it all night with her big, beautiful, pillowy breasts and her crazy extra-wide body shape. The whole time we were fucking, she was telling me this was her dream come true, but not in a way that made it unpleasant. Later, I found that she had put twenty hits of acid in that letter to me, so I was able to barter it in the next town for some coke.

By the time we got to New Orleans, the tour was winding down, but the excitement level was ramped up. We were playing at one of the old World's Fair buildings, and we had luxurious backstage accommodations, including showers and couches and wall-to-wall carpeting. We had finished the set when a lovely young woman wandered into our dressing room. She had bleached-blond hair and fire-engine-red lips and giant eyelashes that made her look like a reincarnated southern version of Marilyn Monroe. As I was prone to do at that time, I made my move before anyone else could even talk to her. I grabbed her hand and pulled her into the bathroom and asked her if she could keep me company while I took a shower.

Once I got into the shower, she went into an impeccable rendition of Marilyn singing "Happy Birthday" to JFK. I got out of that shower ready to go. She immediately threw off her clothes and we made love on the floor. I had known the girl for five minutes, but I was certain of my affection for her. We spent the night together, and I found out more about her, including the fact that she went to Catholic school. (She would be the inspiration for a later song, "Catholic School Girls Rule.")

The next day we drove to Baton Rouge, and of course, she came with us. After we got offstage, she came up to me and said, "I have something to tell you. My father's the chief of police and the entire state of Louisiana is looking for me because I've gone missing. Oh, and besides that, I'm only fourteen." I wasn't incredibly scared, because in my somewhat deluded mind, I knew that if she told the chief of police she was in love with me, he wasn't going to have me taken out to a field and shot, but I did want to get her the hell back home right away. So we had sex one more time, and she gave me an interesting compliment that I never forgot. She said, "When you make love to me, it's like you're a professional." I told her that she should give herself a little time and she'd realize that it was because she didn't have much to compare it to. And I put her on a bus and sent her back to New Orleans.

Things had come to a head with Jack Sherman the previous night in New Orleans. We had been through hell and high water with him all across the country, and he had nearly thrown in the towel a few times. By now, we were actually playing well, and the shows had been getting better and better. The between-song comedic banter was a huge part of our act. It was our natural flow of things to take time out for chatty breaks with the audience. Those interludes would send Sherman off. In New Orleans, Flea broke a string during the first song, so I started riffing. Jack was giving me dirty looks or telling me to get on with the show, or some kind of negativity, to which I responded by pouring some jugs of ice water on him while he was taking a solo. It wasn't a hateful act, it was more theatrical, this-is-what-you're-going-to-get-if-you-fuck-with-the-singer type of thing.

Jack looked at me in shock and grabbed his mike. "I want you all to know that this is a historic show, because this is the last night that I will be playing with the Chili Peppers."

Then I went up to my mike. "I want you all to know that this is a show of historical proportions, because this is the last night that we'll have to play with this asshole."

It was high theater. We had the audience in the palm of our hand. They were going, "Is this part of the show? Is this for real?" And everybody was silent. Jack and I stared at each other. And he stepped up to the mike and said, "I think you owe me an apology, dude."

Another pause, and then I went up to the microphone. "I think *you* owe me an apology, dude."

By then Flea had changed his string, and he came over and we continued playing and it all blew over. But it was one of the most spectacular blowups, because it was bringing out this inner turmoil and making show business out of it.

Jack was the ultimate straight man, since he really was a straight man. He wasn't even faking it. That was what people liked about us. When we got feedback from the shows, it was "The music is really interesting. We had a great time dancing. But you guys are the funniest thing we've ever seen."

God bless Jack, he did keep the band afloat for a year, and if he hadn't, the years to follow probably wouldn't have. As awkward and combative and ornery as our relationship was with him, it was an important time. Even on that out-of-control tour, every single time we'd come offstage, I'd feel like I was levitating. It was the greatest high ever. It didn't matter if it was freezing outside and our backstage was an outdoor patio. We'd all be back there in the cold, sweating, going, "Can you believe this? They loved it. Let's go out there and make up a new song and give them an encore."

We came back from that tour with maybe five hundred dollars apiece, so Jennifer and I had to give up the Lexington house. Jennifer went to live with her mom, but my primary purpose in life became the pursuit of getting loaded. More and more, shooting speedballs became my thing. The whole point of speedballs is that you're going in two directions at the same time, which is a pretty divine feeling. Instead of getting this pure white-light cocaine rush, you're also getting this soft heroin rush, so it's not just a super-ringy and crystal-like feeling, it's also a little of the dark opium-den feeling. You're getting the best of both worlds; your serotonin and your dopamine are releasing at the same time.

When we came back from the tour, we realized that we had to let Jack Sherman go, which was sad. As much as we weren't on the same page with the guy, we knew it was a heavy thing for someone to go through. But we also knew it was time to get back to something that was rawer, that was coming from a common ground.

So the three of us went to Jack's apartment in Santa Monica, where he was living with his new wife. Flea and I were outside arguing, "Okay, who's going to say it? I think you should do the talking." "Why should I do the talking? I did it the last time." I think in the end, Flea took on the job of delivering the message. But first we had to walk down a long driveway to Jack's house. And as we started marching with full intention, we started laughing hysterically out of sheer nervous excitement, and the thrill of the unknown and the dawning of a new era for us. The more we realized we had to be serious and cut it off clean and move on, the more we couldn't stop laughing.

We got to the door trying to suppress the laughter, but we couldn't. We walked in and told him, "It's over. We're firing you. You're not in the band anymore." He was stunned and angry. We turned around and left.

At some point after we fired Jack, Flea came to me and said, "What would you think if Hillel wanted to come back to the band?" I said, "What?" because I knew he wouldn't suggest that unless he'd had some contact with Hillel. I told him, "What would I think? I'd give my firstborn son to get him back in the band. No questions. Let's go."

7.

Groundhog Year

When Hillel rejoined the band in 1985, it was a monumental feeling, like we were back on track. We finally had a guitarist who knew which songs worked for us and which songs I was capable of singing. Plus, Hillel was our brother. And, like a brother, he was worried about the amount of drugs I was doing. I was in and out of rehearsals, sometimes showing up late, sometimes not showing up. By then I had shown up at Jennifer's mom's two-bedroom apartment on Cahuenga, right at the Hollywood Freeway. God bless her mom, she accepted me, but I was a mess. I was the horrible, leeching boyfriend who had no money, lived under her roof, ate the Corn Pops out of the kitchen, and never replaced anything because I was strapped.

I would disappear for days on end behind my coke runs, then come back like a beaten puppy and try to quietly sneak in the house to get some rest. But Jennifer wasn't having it. She answered the door once holding a giant pair of leather clipping shears that she used for her clothing designing. I knew when she was bluffing and when she was out for blood and bone damage, and that particular time she would have gladly stuck those through my skull if I had gotten close enough.

"Where were you? Who were you sleeping with?" she screamed at me.

"Are you kidding me? I didn't sleep with anybody. I was trying to get high. You know how I am," I pleaded. Eventually, I sweet-talked my way back into the house.

The more Jennifer got into heroin, the easier it became for me to get into the house, because she needed a coconspirator to cop with, and I needed her money. She didn't mind me doing the dope, because when I'd do that, I was calm and we could actually be together and melt in each other's arms and nod out watching old black-and-white movies at four in the morning, enmeshed in the blissful, deadly euphoria of the opium. But she absolutely hated it when I was shooting the cocaine. Then I'd turn into a freak and disappear. Of course, I never wanted to shoot just heroin. So when we were shooting heroin in her room, I'd sneak out to do a hit of coke. But she was the total eagle eye. "No, you're not. Give me the coke. Give me the syringe. You're not shooting coke!"

I came up with these horrible and deceptive ways of getting high on coke. By then my hair was so long and matted that I'd slide syringes up into the undercarriage of my hairdo and consent to a full-body pat-down. I'd previously hidden the coke in a cereal box in the kitchen, so I'd rush downstairs and shoot up before Jennifer or her sister or her mom came in. I can't imagine the emotional terrorism that I inflicted on these people. I was lost in that addiction. And it was going to get a lot worse before it got any better.

I didn't have any idea how dependent on heroin I was becoming. It seemed like there was an endless supply. All these weird-ass dealers were popping up all over Hollywood. You had the Russian dealer who lived in a shitty apartment with his Russian wife and spoke hardly any English but had a nonstop supply of China White. You had the white-trash mullet-wearing Hollywood dealer on the corner of Sunset Boulevard. You had five or six different Frenchmen, from my old friend Fabrice to Dominique to François, and then five other people they knew.

If I was copping from Fab, I could go over to his house with fifty bucks and get a bindle that would last me a day—probably a tenth of a gram. But if I had to go to the Russian guy, who was a shyster, I'd give him fifty bucks and it would be good for one poke. Of course, I didn't go there with fifty bucks, I went with twenty-two, begging for the fifty-dollar bindle and offering to leave my shoes. Russians don't appreciate a negotiation, but that didn't stop me from hounding and begging and bickering and sleazing. I would sit there and wear that bitch out, make him feel the misery before I would.

The other French guys were pompous, arrogant, heartless dealers. Not a lot of fronting going on there. They were all dope fiends, too, so they knew what it was to need a little something to get well, but if you weren't a girl and you didn't have a lot of money, good luck. So I had to work every angle imaginable. I wasn't beneath showing up with a copy of our first record.

"I don't know if you've seen this record here, but this is my band. That's me there. I've got a manager who's holding a couple thousand dollars of mine right now. I'm going to reach him later. I don't know if you feel like coming to the show that we're having next week. Of course, you and your girlfriend would be welcome to attend." Any scam, any lie, any bullshit tactic whatsoever. It was a humiliating, god-awful place in which to find myself.

Somehow I was maintaining and still writing music and showing up to rehearsal more often than not. But without me really knowing it, my life was starting to leave me. I became broom-handle thin. Then the cops busted the old Fabster, which kiboshed his business. He went from dealing and being to able to inhale monster lines of smack, to having no smack, no cash flow, no customers, and a huge habit. Next thing I knew, Fab had aligned himself with a young Mexican guy. I called him Johnny Devil, because he was, quite obviously, *the* devil incarnate on Planet Earth— charming enough for you to want to hang out with him, and clever and conniving enough for you to see other faces that weren't his. But I liked him. He never burned me, and he was fair and generous and kind in his evil, devilish ways.

My habit was getting worse, and my money was diminishing rapidly, so I had to do the pawnshop thing. Every day I woke up as late as possible, because I knew I was about to get sick. I'd ask Jennifer for twenty dollars. There would be no twenty dollars.

"Do we have anything that we can sell?" I'd plead.

"We've sold everything."

"Can we sell this picture? Can we sell the fire extinguisher? Can we sell this rug? Is there an old radio that no one uses around the house?"

I kept going down to the pawnshop with anything I could find to get twenty or thirty bucks. Then I'd go meet the man, whether it was the Russian, the Frenchman, or the white-trash guy; I'd cop the stuff and go to a little hill at Argyle and Franklin, overlooking the freeway, throw the dope into a spoon, hit it with water, and shoot up immediately. The minute that shit hit me, it was like pouring water on a withered sponge. I'd go from being sick and miserable and weak and devoid of life to frisky and conversational. As soon as I shot the dope, up came the leg of pork, and I'd want to have sex with Jennifer right away. But she'd be mad at me for this ordeal of getting and buying and selling and pawning and copping.

One day I woke up, and the cupboards were literally bare. I borrowed Jennifer's sister's bike. I had no intention of pawning it; I was just desperate to get something. I didn't have the time to take the conventional street route to downtown, where the Devil lived, so I hopped on this one-speed beach cruiser, rode it out of the apartment grounds, up the on-ramp to the Hollywood Freeway, into the right lane of traffic, and peddled my way from Hollywood to downtown Los Angeles.

I finally got to Johnny Devil's, but his cash was low, and he was down on his flow. First we tried melting some Tuinals in a spoon and shooting that, but the minute the powder inside the capsules hit the water, it foamed up. We tried to get the foam into the syringe just to get some relief, but it wasn't working.

"You and I are going to find something," he promised, and we jumped into his car and drove out to the San Bernardino Valley. We stopped in a neighborhood that looked like it could have been uprooted from the poorest section of Tijuana. The whole area was brimming with one-story shacks in dirt yards. On each plot there were fires burning in oil barrels. There were no windows or doors on the houses. It was like being in Beirut during wartime.

Johnny pulled up to the curb and got out of the car. "You wait here. Don't move," he said, and disappeared into this labyrinth of streets and houses. I was so weak that I couldn't move if I wanted to. I sat there certain somebody was going to walk up and fill me full of twenty-twos and take the car and leave. Finally, the Devil reappeared out of a shadow, far away from where he entered. He was walking that purposeful walk. He got back in the car.

"Did you get it? Did you get it? Did you get it?"

He shot me an agitated look. "Just chill. Everything's going to be okay. Don't ask me nothing." He was obviously in a bad mood. For all I knew, he went in there and killed a family for that shit, he was acting so weird. But as soon as we got out of the neighborhood, he pulled a huge baseball-sized object out of his coat. It was pure Black Tar heroin. He twisted off a Bazooka gum–sized piece of the stuff and handed it to me and pocketed the rest.

"Uh, are you going to keep all of that? That's a lot. Maybe I can hold on to some of that," I schemed.

"That's how much I need," he said. We drove to some girl's house in Hollywood, and he proceeded to melt that fucking baseball down, shot after shot, until most of it was gone, all the while never once passing out or OD'ing or even becoming incoherent. He just settled into his demonic wellness. A few days later, he disappeared, and I never saw him or heard about him again.

Despite all my drug use, the writing for the second album was going well. I would watch Hillel and Flea play together, and I'd realize that music was an act of telepathy, that if you were standing next to your soul mate with a guitar in your hand and he with a bass, you could know what the other guy was thinking and communicate that through playing. Hillel had definitely grown as a guitar player in his time away from us. He started off as a Kiss-influenced player with some progressive rock thrown in. Then he experimented with the early Red Hot Chili Peppers, and now he'd come back with a weird, sultry element to his style. It wasn't all syncopated manic funk, there was something smooth and fluid in his style also.

While we were in the EMI rehearsal space on Sunset, we got a call that the legendary impresario Malcolm McLaren wanted to talk to us. McLaren was the mystery man who had created the Sex Pistols and Bow Wow Wow. Now he was looking for the Next Big Thing, and if we were lucky, the Starmaker would sprinkle his dust on us. He came to a rehearsal with a few cronies, and we played him a couple of our crazy-assed, complicated songs—fast and chaotic and dense and layered, with no rhyme or reason but a lot of feeling and a lot of funk.

He clearly wasn't impressed. "All right, then, can we have a chat somewhere, mates?"

We walked to a tiny meeting room adjacent to the rehearsal space. Someone started passing around a spliff the size of a Havana cigar.

"Okay, all that stuff you're playing, that's great, but it makes no sense. No one's going to care about that type of music. What I'm envisioning . . ."

He started throwing out words like "cacophony" and

"epiphany," and we were getting higher and higher, going, "What does he mean by a cacophony of sounds?"

At last he got to the point. By way of demonstration, he took out some pictures of surfers who were wearing hot pink punk-rock colors.

"I want to take this band and simplify all of the music. Turn it into old fifties rock and roll, simple as can be, bass, rote notes, guitar, simple riffs, basic beats. And I want to make Anthony the star, the front man, so there's no confusion. The public can get their head around looking at one central character, and the rest of you will be in the background playing the most simple rock and roll known to man."

He paused to get our reaction, and I looked over at Flea.

Flea had passed out.

I guess Malcolm could tell that his message hadn't been well received. I was kind of flattered that he thought I had the potential to be this front man, but everything else he said disavowed everything that we held near and dear to our hearts. It was like the Wizard of Oz had spoken, and what he said was too ludicrous to take seriously.

Now it was time for us to make our second record. EMI asked us who we wanted to produce it. Without hesitating, we said, "George Clinton," because after our first record, people came up to us and said, "You must be students of the P Funk," which was George's legendary funk group. We were latecomers to the Parliament/Funkadelic experience, and didn't know as much about George as we should have or later would, but we knew that if James Brown was considered the Godfather, then George was the Great God-Uncle of Funk.

So EMI got George on the phone, and we said, "George, we're the Red Hot Chili Peppers, we're from Hollywood, California, we're really hard-rocking motherfuckers, and we think you should produce our record." We sent him our record and our demo tape, and he liked them, and after Flea and Lindy went out to

Detroit to meet him, he agreed to produce us. To this day, when people ask me how we got George Clinton, I tell them that we asked him on the phone, but Flea always says, "Twenty-five grand," which was the amount of money that EMI agreed to pay him. I don't believe he did it just for the money. I think he also saw something special and beautiful and remarkable about these four kids who were attempting to keep the spirit of hard-core funk music alive, not in a pretentious or a copycat way but by helping to invent a new genre of funk.

We went to Detroit with about 70 percent of the songs finished. We had "Jungle Man," my ode to Flea, this half-man, half-beast born in the belly of the volcano in Australia and coming to the world and using his thumb as the conductor of thunder on the bass. "American Ghost Dance," "Catholic School Girls Rule," and "Battleship" (whose chorus, "blow job park," was inspired by Cliff's true-life adventures fending off blow-job entreaties at Mulholland rest stops while he practiced his vocal lessons). "Nevermind" and "Sex Rap" were songs that we had on our original demo, and "30 Dirty Birds" was an old Hillel camp song. George's vision was that we would hang out in Detroit with him for about a month before we went into the studio, so there was always room to write more songs.

We would record in George's studio, called United Sound, which was a two-story brick building in the middle of the barren wasteland that inner-city Detroit had become in the mid-'80s. Sometime in the '70s, George had taken over the studio from Motown, and that was where he recorded all those classic Parliament/Funkadelic albums. It was a great studio, with big old analog boards, a beautiful drum room, and separate horn rooms.

First the plan was to move into George's house for about a week, until we rented a house for the band. (We found a house on Wabeek Lake, which was in the most affluent of all suburbs. So it was this whole triangle of opposites, staying with George in the country, rehearsing downtown, where the land couldn't have cost more than ten cents a square foot, and living with rich whiteys on a golf course.) George lived in a contemporary country house on fifty acres in a place called Brooklyn, which was about an hour outside of Detroit. Even though it wasn't the most attractive countryside around (you could hear the nearby Michigan 500 auto races from his property), it was his sanctuary. There were a fishing pond and nice hills, and his house was graced with the presence of George's beautiful wife. She was totally sweet and maternal, not the Vixen of the Funk Superfreak you might think George would be hooked up with, but instead an "Oh God, wish this was my mom" type of woman.

Hillel and I shared a room, Cliff and Flea did the same, Lindy got his own room, and George and his wife were in their master bedroom. The idea was to stay out of the city to get the ball rolling, because we didn't want the sessions to become drug-derailed right away. But as soon as I got there, I felt like I had a horrible case of food poisoning. I started throwing up, my skin turned a strange color, and I couldn't eat. I had no idea what was wrong with me, but Flea said, "You're fucking dope sick." I was so clueless that I didn't even realize I was going through a proper heroin withdrawal.

For some stupid reason, we sent out for five hundred dollars' worth of coke, and Lindy and Hillel and Flea and George and I hoofed it all up. That made me feel great for about a half an hour. Then it was back to no sleep and dope sickness. After a few days, it subsided, and we set up shop in George's living room. Drums, guitars, bass, amps—we started playing and getting to know George.

To know George is to love him. He's a huge man with huge hair, but there's this other thing about him that's the size of an elephant—his aura. George is a guy who loves to tell stories, and he's not ashamed to admit to all kinds of weird and kooky and questionable behavior. We became the campfire kids listening to the grand master of psychedelic funk experience. "George, tell us another story about Sly Stone," and he would be off and running. Besides being a great raconteur, George was teaching us the importance of being regular. He would walk around the house with a bottle of prune juice, going, "You all know how old I am. You know how I can go all day and all night. It's because of this, it's because I'm regular."

George also had a stuffed-animal collection. Where there wasn't furniture, per se, in the house, there were life-size stuffed animals everywhere, some very old. I guess he had been a collector, and his fans and friends and family constantly added pieces, so we were in the middle of this big circus of stuffed animals.

After about a week of living with George, we moved into our house on the golf course. Then it was time to start making demos in a studio in downtown Detroit that was owned by a guy called Navarro, who was a colorful but nefarious old-school pimp/drug dealer/studio owner. He was an older gentleman, with the lowest, grumbliest, deepest Isaac Hayes/Barry White voice. You couldn't understand a lot of what he said, but you sure could understand what he meant. When he walked into the room, no matter who was there—girls, the crew, George—he was the man to respect.

So we started doing the demos. And we also started doing the coke, which was everywhere. We'd order the Popeye's chicken, and we'd order the cocaine. And if you could eat the chicken before you got too high on the coke, you'd have dinner. If not, you didn't care about dinner. Unlike us, George never acted like a weirdo when he was high on coke. You wouldn't know whether he was on a ton of coke or not; he just had a really strong constitution.

I'd get all tweaked out and try to finish these songs that I had started, and sometimes it would work and sometimes I'd go in circles, coming up with these complex word combinations. So I was writing, and George was listening to these Hollywood kids playing eccentric hard-core funk music, and loving every minute of it. I'd show him some lyrics and ask his opinion, and he'd go, "Wow, that's some outside shit. I love it. Go write another one, we need another verse."

At one point during preproduction, Flea, who had been listening to a lot of Meters, suggested that we do a cover of their song

"Africa." George thought about it and said, "What if you did the song 'Africa' but had Anthony do a rewrite so it's no longer 'Africa,' but it's your 'Africa,' which is Hollywood?" So I did the rewrite, and George later fashioned one of his incredible vocal arrangements behind it. I think he even sang one or two of the lines in that song.

"Freaky Styley" was another interesting George innovation. That was originally an instrumental overture to lead into another piece, but George was so into that swelling, riding groove that he was adamant it had to be its own song, even if the vocal was simple chanting. When we recorded that music, we were all in the control room, listening to that groove, which is still one of the best pieces of music that we ever wrote. George just started chanting, "Fuck 'em, just to see the look on their face. Fuck 'em, just to see the look on their face." We all joined in, and it was a spontaneous bit of musical combustion. The other vocal in that song, "Say it out loud, I'm Freaky Styley and I'm proud," was one of those born-in-the-moment colloquialisms. At that time we called everything that was cool "Freaky Styley." A dance, a girl, a drumbeat, anything. When this whole process was finished and we were sitting around the kitchen table going, "What should we call this album?," Cliff looked up and said, "Why don't we just call it what we call everything else? *Freaky Styley.*"

After a little while in Navarro's studio, we finalized the arrangements, and I had some new lyrics ready to go. George had a unique style of producing. It wasn't a lot of super-refined high-tuning, reacting to every kick-drum pattern. It was more from-the-heart producing. George was a master at hearing backup vocal parts, especially for esoteric parts of the song, where you wouldn't normally hear vocals. If you listen to the Funkadelic records or the Parliament records, the vocal arrangements within the body of music are masterpieces unto themselves. So he started hearing that stuff in our songs, and we were open to anything. If he said, "I want to do a five-person vocal at this part in the song," we jumped for joy.

We shifted over to United Sound and started recording the basic tracks. We always put down a scratch vocal, because that was the era when you'd record a scratch and then try to beat it. We didn't have comping vocals, where you'd sing a song twenty times and cut and paste the best syllables. George put me in the middle of the room, not off in some other room, so I felt like a part of the band, which was a wise thing to do, since everyone had always said, "Oh, the Chili Peppers are great live, but you'll never capture their zany onstage chemistry in the studio."

During the recording process, we started getting an unusual visitor. His name was Louie, and he was a pale and bald Middle Easterner. Turned out he was George's personal coke-delivery guy. After a few visits, it was clear that George was into this guy for a lot of money, but George was unflappable. Louie began showing up with a couple of henchmen, and he'd say, in his slow thick accent, "George, I'm real serious, man, you're going to have to make good before I can give you anything else. I'm running a business here."

George would go, "Louie, look around. Do you think I'm strapped for cash? In this business, you get paid when you get paid. When I get paid, you're the first motherfucker who gets paid after me."

Louie would look pained. "George, I've heard that before. I didn't bring these guys for show, and if they have to hurt somebody . . ."

George never blinked an eye, because he had a plan. He knew Louie was fascinated by the music business, so he intuited that making Louie a part of the whole process would ensure a steady flow of coke. Finally, George promised Louie that he could make his vocal debut on the album.

I was thinking, "Okay, I trust George, I know that everything's happening for a reason here, but I'll be damned if I'm going to let this motherfucker on my record. This shit is sacred." George told me, "Don't worry, everyone will be happy. He'll be on the record, and you will not mind." George was right. At the very beginning of "Yertle the Turtle," you hear a weird, out-of-context voice come in and say, "Look at the turtle go, bro," and then the song goes into a syncopated funk beat. That was Louie's debut, and that was what made him happy enough not to hurt somebody. The longer the sessions went on, the more regularly he would show up with the blow, because he was wanting his fifteen minutes in the damn spotlight.

Right before it was time for me to go in and do the final vocals, I decided I wasn't going to do any cocaine for two weeks, which is like deciding to be celibate when you're living in a brothel. My decision had nothing to do with sobriety, because even though I was twenty-three, I was still an emotionally troubled youth. I just didn't want to get back to Hollywood and go, "What happened? I had my chance making a record with George Clinton, and I fucked up." The two-week period was the time that was allotted for my vocals. I guess I realized it was harder to sing when you've got coke dripping down the back of your throat.

One of the reasons I was so concerned about my vocals was that during the preproduction process, Flea started to play a Sly Stone song, "If You Want Me to Stay," on the bass. Hillel and Cliff got into it, and we decided to cover that song, which was daunting to me, because I can sing anything I write, but another man's tune is always a challenge—let alone one by Sly Stone, one of the most original vocalists in terms of phrasing.

George must have sensed my uneasiness. "You have this in the bag, don't even worry about it. I know what you're capable of," he reassured me. Then he invited me to his house for the weekend to work on the song. First I decided to visit my mom for a few days, and I took the tape of the song with me and practiced it over and over again. On the way back from Grand Rapids, I stopped at George's house. We talked about the song and we practiced it, then we took these long strolls through his property. I didn't even see it, but he was quietly schooling me. We'd be talking about anything under the sun, and he was subconsciously building my confidence and steering me toward getting comfortable and creating magic in the studio. I think he realized that Hillel was a tremendously talented guitar player, Flea knew exactly what he was doing on bass, and Cliff was an ace drummer, but I was this guy with a lyrical ability who wasn't so sure of his voice.

Early in the morning, we'd go out fishing in his pond. His whole demeanor changed when he fished. He was no longer the rabble-rousing toastmaster of the funk universe, but more of an introspective, quirky man who had some vast experience. Fishing was his meditation. And he didn't care what we caught, he was eating it. Bluegills, sunfish, catfish, whatever that lake was spitting out was going in the frying pan. We'd catch them and bring them back, and his wife would cook them for breakfast.

By the time I left his place, I felt good about the song. George mentored me even during the recording process. He had a mike set up inside his booth, and he'd send up shout-outs or sing along. We'd be out there recording the basic tracks and hear this great voice coming through the little transistorized speaker. When we set up the vocal booth and it was just me doing my vocals, George came into the studio, put on headphones, and sang and danced along with me while I was singing. He was like a big brother to me, thoughtful, totally sensitive, and understanding of the colorful and zany place where we were coming from. I wanted never to let him down.

We finished the record, and in our minds, it so far surpassed anything we thought we could have done that we were thinking we were on the road to enormity. Some EMI execs made a trip out to Detroit to hear some of the material. We played them a few tracks, and instead of them going, "You guys are going to be huge," they said nothing. I'm dancing and singing along, going nuts, and they're like "Well, we'll see what we can do with this." Of course, we're talking about a record company that did not have an inkling of the awareness necessary to take something different and original and recognize its worth and introduce it to the world. They were looking for another band like Roxette.

We went back to L.A. feeling absolutely accomplished and more experienced, and then everyone jumped back into his madness.

By this time, Jennifer's mother had moved from Cahuenga to an apartment complex in Pasadena. Right next door to that was an abandoned building, so Jennifer and I started squatting there. The hot and cold water still worked, and we ran an extension cord into the building so we could listen to music, and we set up a bed and some candles.

That's when I really started getting into heroin sex. I realized that if you were in love with somebody and you were sexually inspired to begin with, being high on heroin could amplify the experience tenfold, because you could have sex all night and not be able to come but still be interested. I remember having these marathon sex encounters with Jennifer on that bed, thinking, "Life doesn't get any better than this. I'm in a band, I've got a couple of dollars in my pocket. I've got a beautiful, sweet, hot, sexy, crazy little girlfriend, a roof over my head, and some dope."

Those feelings would disappear, and the next day I'd be off on a run. Jennifer would do her best to deal with my insanity, as she was slowly working on her own. Around the time I got back from Detroit, I intensified my relationship with a girl named Kim Jones. My friend Bob Forest had this monstrous crush on Kim, but she had jilted him (he promptly wrote a song about her with the chorus "Why don't you blow me and the rest of the band?"). He was still obsessed with her, and he used to take me to her apartment in Echo Park, and we'd knock on her door to see if she was around.

Bob would recite her many virtues—she was brilliant and beautiful, she studied in China, she wrote for the *L.A. Weekly,* she was from Tennessee, plus she was a lesbian, because she had left Bob for this really hot girl. Turns out she wasn't a lesbian, but all of her other virtues were true. As soon as I met her, I knew we'd be best friends. We were both Scorpios, and there was never any sexual tension between us.

In some ways, Kim was a female equivalent to Hillel, because there was no crime you could commit that she would not forgive you for, no heinous act of selfish behavior that she would not try to find the good side of you behind. Of course, she was also a complete mess. Intelligent but dizzy, a drug addict, codependent, an enabler and a caretaker, just a beautiful, warm kindred spirit to me. I started to become closer and closer to Kim, because she was a source of love and comfort and friendship and companionship and like-mindedness without any of the difficulties of a girlfriend. I never lost my sexual attraction to Jennifer; the longer I was with her, the better the sex got, but I was not a great boyfriend. If I said I'd be home in an hour, I might stroll in three days later. Today, if someone did that to me, I'd have a heart attack, but when you're a kid, you don't know any better.

Kim didn't care if I left for three days at a time, so there was no downside to hanging out with her. It was never like "You motherfucker, you looked at that girl, you didn't come home, you spent all the money." Kim *expected* me to spend all the money, look at all the other girls, and disappear. One time I went over to Kim's house, and she wasn't there. In a fit of desperation, I grabbed her toaster oven and traded it for a bag of dope. When she got home, she was unfazed. "That's okay, we'll get another one."

Before long, I moved in with Kim, and our daily mission became getting high. She was getting some cash inflow—disability checks because her dad had died, checks from the *L.A. Weekly*, or checks from her mom at home in Tennessee. We'd cash them and meet some French guy or some Russian guy on a corner in Hollywood and buy the heroin, and if we had any money left over, we'd score some coke. Soon we both had a habit. Hillel was also using, and he had a crazy girlfriend named Maggie who was a friend of Kim's, so we'd have a lot of small drug parties.

From time to time the band would go on tours to San Francisco. We were still young enough and not so damaged that we could play well, even though we had these drug habits. In September 1985 we played two shows with Run-DMC, one in San Francisco and one in L.A. The L.A. show was at the Palladium, and besides opening for Oingo Boingo, it was our biggest show to date. Sold out. Of course, the night before the show, I went on a drug binge, so I showed up for the gig hammered on coke and heroin. The band was furious at me, but somehow I managed to pull it together and made it onstage. That show was notable for two things. About halfway through the show, George Clinton came rocking onto the stage, and he and I started doing a full, funky ballroom dance to our jams. He injected a fat dose of color and love and energy and meaning into that show.

It was also memorable because, shortly before George came out, I decided to interrupt the set and give a heartfelt, ten-minute-long rambling discourse on the dangers of doing drugs. I certainly hadn't planned the speech, but something came over me as I was looking down at my black-and-blue arms, and I just started rapping.

"If you haven't ever put a needle in your arm, don't ever do it. Let me tell you from experience that you don't have to do this, that's where I am right now, and it's horrible, and I don't want anyone to ever have to feel like I'm feeling right now. Let me do the suffering for you, because this is something that no one needs to subject themselves to. If you're doing this, okay, just do it, but don't ever think that you're going to be the same once you've gone this far."

I proceeded to explain, in detail, why it was a big mistake to shoot drugs. I kept going, I couldn't hang up on it. Meanwhile, the band was shooting me looks like "Oh my God, this fucking idiot." After the show, I was afraid to face the guys. I thought they'd hate my guts for saying that stuff and being a hypocritical moron. In the middle of everyone giving me dirty looks, my friend Pete Weiss, the drummer from Thelonious Monster, came backstage.

"Swan, I've heard you say a lot of stuff from the stage, but that was the coolest shit you ever said," he gushed. "That was riveting, you had every single ear in the place. They knew you were a fucked-up bastard but also that you cared and you were just trying to share some love. Don't let that band of yours fool you, you did the right thing tonight."

A month later, when it was time to tour the U.S. for *Freaky*

Styley, my speechifying hadn't changed anything for us. Both Hillel and I were strung out, but for the first time, I noticed that he wasn't doing so well. He seemed weak, and while I was able to bounce right back from a run, he didn't seem to have that Israeli fire stoking like he always had in the past. It became evident when we started our usual on-tour wrestling diversion. Hillel and I had teamed up; I was his manager, and he was set to wrestle Flea. Even though Flea was real solid, Hillel was bigger, and he had massive tree-trunk legs, like a tall Pan. We had a two-week buildup to this match, and when they wrestled in a hotel room one night, Flea destroyed him in as long as it takes to grab somebody and hurl him to the ground and pin him mercilessly to his death—ten seconds. I could tell that Hillel had no inner core of strength; he had been robbed by his addiction of the life force that allows you to at least defend yourself. It was a sad moment.

Hillel and I didn't do heroin on the road, so we would drink bottles of Jägermeister, because that gave us the feeling closest to a heroin high. He'd always tease me that I was a sloppy drunk, because I'd get drunk and take off all my clothes in the motel and walk down the hall and knock on people's doors, whereas he'd get drunk and act suave.

Leaving to go on tour was an ordeal for me then, mainly because of my volatile relationship with Jennifer. Even though I was staying mainly at Kim's house, Jennifer was still my girlfriend. Jennifer became convinced that Kim and I were having sex. One day she came by Kim's house, and Kim and I were sound asleep, naked and cuddling up. I know it would look like a bad scene if you were the girlfriend of the boy in the bed, but we were just having a nice drug high. No romance, just friendship.

Jennifer didn't quite see it that way. Kim and I woke up to Jennifer shattering the bedroom window. She wouldn't come in with a good, old-fashioned baseball bat; she made her entrance with an elaborately carved and painted bird-head cane from the Mayan lands. After she broke through the window, she proceeded to try to kill me with the cane.

Hillel and I, sitting at the edge of some motel bed during an American tour for our record *Freaky Styley*. Both of us look a wee bit worse from wear. And both of us seem to be attempting to unsuccessfully produce looks of well-being for the camera. Oh well, we were livin' fast and hard! 1986.

Los Faces of Fairfax at age sixteen. Left to right—me, Hillel, and Flea on a cross-country tear through Michigan in the summer of '79. We liked to eat, drink, be merry, and play lots of tricks on each other. The cabin on Little Manistee River.

My father and I used to run into each other out on the town long after I had evacuated the nest. Here he is, upholding the spirit of Bela Lugosi with a scowl and a classic Kiedis chin tilt. The T-shirt I'm wearing was a gift from Flea. He bought it in Amsterdam. And it later became the lyrical inspiration for our song "Buckle Down". . . . Red star, black fist. 1984.

Note the ridiculous haircut. The preposterous facial expression. The ludicrous tilt of the chin. Why am I trying to seduce the lens? I think I stole these hilarious mannerisms from my dad. Did I mention my outfit? The visible knee posture would later become my trademark for meeting girls.

Backstage immediately before our first-ever headlining show at an arena. It was the Long Beach Arena where I had seen Deep Purple and Rod Stewart when I was seven years old. I am not sure who this girl is or why my hand was mysteriously finding its way down the back of her skirt, but I do know that I was a free man. And why do I look like I'm consoling her?

I know it's blurry, but to me this is a meaningful shot. It's of Flea and me listening to some music that George Clinton wanted very much to play for us. That's Jennifer Bruce sitting on the bed with her back to us. I think we were all high on the first batch of Ecstasy to ever come through L.A. Some hotel, 1985 or '86.

Two minutes after our fourth-ever show at the Cathay de Grand on Gower and Selma, Gary Leonard took our picture in the backstage hallway. I think our collective enthusiasm shows up strong in this moment. We weren't jaded or tired of anything. 1983. (Photo credit: Gary Leonard)

Here we are in the midst of an official photo session. That's D.H., our drummer at the time, rocking the mike. We pulled a switcheroo of instruments for the hell of it and I was the only one who couldn't actually play the instrument I had switched to for the picture. 1988-ish.

Only God knows what club we are playing in here. I do guesstimate that it is some-where in America on tour for the *Uplift* record. Hillel is wearing spats on his shoes. Flea is working the thumb. And I am flanked by two of the greatest of all time.

Something wonderful happening in a church on our first-ever U.S. tour. It was somewhere in Oklahoma, and we were feeling the magic of being a band in front of about twenty people. 1985.

When it was time to leave on a tour, I'd avoid Jennifer for days before, because I knew some kind of hatchet was going to be thrown at me. One time I was early to the breakout place, which was the EMI parking lot on Sunset. I was with Kim, and we were both completely high on heroin, sitting in the front seat of some car.

I guess in my half-awake drug reverie, I had somehow unbuttoned Kim's blouse because I wanted to see her milky-white chest. I may even have been sucking on her nipple or holding her tit when, BAM, BAM, BAM, there was the loud sound of something rapping against the window. I looked up and it was Jennifer.

"You motherfucker, you've been gone for days, and I knew that this was going on," she screamed.

"Jennifer, believe me, I may have had her shirt open, but I've never had sex with this girl, she's just my friend," I protested.

"You said you were coming home three days ago, and you're leaving for three weeks, and by the way, I'm pregnant," she screamed.

Meanwhile, the dispute had escalated to the sidewalk, and Jennifer was trying to kill me or at least scratch my eyeballs out.

"Jennifer, you see, this is why I don't come home for three days before I leave, because I don't want to get hit and you're too hard to deal with and I know you're not pregnant, because you just had your period and I haven't had sex with you since you had your period, so don't try to tell me you're fucking pregnant." I tried to reason with her, but she was a bull. Not that I can blame her.

There was no stopping her, and Kim was getting caught in the crossfire, so I ducked inside the EMI building. Jennifer followed me in and proceeded to pull my hair and scratch at my face. I was still high out of my mind and trying not to lose an eyeball or a tuft of hair, so I started running through the halls.

Jennifer chased me. For some reason, I had a bag of cookies, so I started throwing the cookies at her, to keep her far enough away that she couldn't connect with any of her punches. She grabbed some blunt instrument, so I put my foot out to keep her from hitting me with it, and she went further nuts, if that was possible.

"Don't you try to kick me in my stomach just because I'm pregnant. I know you want to get rid of the baby," she screamed.

Thankfully, Lindy came to my rescue. "Jennifer, we're only going away for a couple of weeks. I know how much this boy loves you. You're all he ever talks about." Somehow we made it out on tour in one piece.

Despite our touring, EMI never got behind the album, and they wouldn't give us any money for a video. That didn't stop us. Lindy had one of the first home-video cameras, and he shot footage on our tours and took that footage and cut it into a BBC documentary that had filmed us lip-synching "Jungle Man" at the Club Lingerie in Hollywood. He attached two VCRs in some back room at EMI, did an edit, and we had a video for a hundred dollars. Later, our good friend Dick Rude shot a video for "Catholic School Girls Rule" that featured a shot of me singing from the cross, among other blasphemous things, so that video got played only in clubs.

When we weren't touring, I was pretty much staying high. It was like Groundhog Day every single day, exactly the same. Kim and I would wake up and have to look out of her window to see which direction the freeway traffic was going to determine whether it was dusk or dawn. Then we'd hustle up some money, get the drugs, shoot up, and go for a walk around Echo Park Lake, holding hands, in a complete haze. If I was supposed to show up to rehearsal, I would probably miss it. If I did show up, I'd be too stoned to do anything, so I'd nod out in the corner of the room or pass out on the loading dock.

Every day Kim and I would get high, and right in the middle of the euphoria, we'd vow that tomorrow we were going to get off that stuff. The next day we'd start the whole process over again. By now a lot of our friends were strung out on dope, and often the only time we'd see each other was when we were in our cars waiting to cop. We were each scoring from the same French guy, so we'd page him, and he'd call back and say, "Meet at Beverly and

Sweetzer in ten minutes." We'd drive down there, and on one corner we'd see Hillel and Maggie in their car and on another corner we'd see Bob Forest and his girlfriend. The dealer would go from car to car, and Kim and I would always get served last, because we were the most likely either to not have the right amount of money or to owe money; but we were patient and willing to take whatever we could get. Then we'd go back, and I'd be in charge of splitting the bag and loading the syringes. Because I knew I had a much greater tolerance to heroin than Kim, unbeknownst to her, I would always take 75 percent of the bag and give her the rest. Ironically, that practice almost killed her.

It happened at Hillel's one night. He had moved into an infamous Hollywood haunt called the Milagro Castle, right off Gower. Marilyn Monroe had once lived there, but now it was populated with drug dealers and punk rockers. One night after we scored some China White, Kim and Hillel and I went to his place to do the drugs. Hillel had his bindle, and Kim had our bindle, and for some reason Hillel offered to share his with Kim, so I could have a whole bindle to myself. I was in such a frenzy over doing my stuff that it didn't dawn on me that Hillel would actually split his bag fifty-fifty with Kim.

The high was amazing, and I remember Hillel and I going into the kitchen and sharing some Lucky Charms, dancing and talking and generally exuberant about how potent the drugs were. Then I realized that we hadn't heard a peep out of Kim for a while. It dawned on me that she'd taken much more than she ever had before.

I rushed into the living room and saw Kim sitting upright in the chair, basically dead. She was cold and white, and her lips were blue, and she wasn't breathing. Suddenly, I remembered all the techniques for reviving someone from a heroin overdose that Blackie had taught me when I was thirteen years old. I picked her up, dragged her into the shower, turned the cold water on her, and began giving her major mouth-to-mouth resuscitation. I was frantically slapping her face and screaming, "Kim, don't fucking die on me. I don't want to have to call your mother and tell her that her daughter's gone. I don't want to have breakfast alone tomorrow."

She started going in and out of consciousness. I was shaking her like a rag doll, screaming, "Stay awake!" Hillel had called 911, and when the paramedics showed up, I jumped out the window and ran away because I had outstanding warrants out for my arrest for moving violations. Hillel went to the hospital with her, and they got her up and running. About twelve hours later, I called her room in the hospital.

"Come and get me. Those motherfuckers ruined my high," she said. "I'm sick. We need to go cop." Amazingly enough, it never occurred to me that there might have been a problem there.

From time to time, I'd make halfhearted attempts to get clean. One of them was at the urging of Flea, who suggested that I might want to get off the stuff for a while and reconnect with what we were doing as bandmates. He was living in this cute apartment on Carmen Street, and he proposed that I come and kick on his futon. I showed up with a couple of bottles of NyQuil and said, "Flea, this is going to be ugly. I'm not going to be able to sleep, and I'm going to be in serious pain. Are you sure you want me in your house?"

He was willing, so we listened to music and I kicked. After a while, Flea said I should get an apartment in the building, so I did. Of course, Jennifer promptly moved in with me. Unfortunately, a new dope dealer named Dominique, who had usurped all the other French dealers, lived only about a block away.

Then it was time to go out on another tour leg. The night before, Jennifer and I were having one of those marathon sex/heroin sessions. We'd have sex for a couple of hours, and then we'd fight for an hour about me leaving the next day, and she'd be screaming as loudly during the sex as she was when she was yelling at me for going on tour. It was hard to distinguish when we were fighting and when we were having sex. So a neighbor who hated me called the cops on what he thought was a domestic-violence thing.

I was in the house, surrounded by tons of syringes and spoons and heroin, when the cops came to the door.

"We got a domestic-violence call here," the one cop announced.

"What are you talking about, domestic violence? It's me and my girlfriend, and that's that," I said.

"Can we come in and take a look around?" the cop asked.

I was saying no when Jennifer came to the door. She was obviously not abused, but she was hotheaded and still screaming at me. One cop was trying to poke his head in the door and shine his flashlight on Jennifer. In the meantime, the other cop had run a check on me and found the outstanding warrants, so they arrested me on the spot and dragged me out in handcuffs, half naked. All the neighbors were watching, convinced I was getting arrested for beating up a girl. Jennifer and I were screaming at each other as they took me away. It was just a bad episode of *COPS*. Thankfully, Lindy bailed me out, and we left on tour the next day, but during that period of my life, you had to plan on something like that happening before a tour.

Or when we got back from a tour. We were returning from a *Freaky Styley* tour leg when I ran into Bob Forest, who was waiting for us at the EMI parking lot. Bob was the classic shit-stirrer of the city. If he could stir the pot, if he could drop a hint, if he could make drama and conflict, he would. He loved it because, God knows, he was falling apart at the seams, and I'm sure it took some of the attention away from him.

Bob knew about my indiscretions on the road, but I was surprised when he came up to me and said, "Okay, you're out there doing all that crazy stuff. Don't you ever worry about Jennifer?" That was the last thing I would have worried about. In my mind, she would never do anything to betray me, even though I was cheating on her right, left, and center.

He smirked. "I've got some bad news for you, buddy."

My heart started pounding in my chest.

"My friend, the unusual hour is upon us when I'm going to share with you information you might not be too keen on," he continued. "Maybe a certain someone wasn't so loyal to you while you were away, either."

"You're crazy," I stammered. "Jennifer would rather cut her own wrists than take interest in another man. She loves me with every cell in her body. She's physiologically and emotionally incapable of giving herself to another man."

"No, it's possible. Because I have proof."

I threatened to crack his skull open on the pavement if he didn't tell me all he knew. Finally, he spilled the beans. Jennifer had slept with Chris Fish, the keyboard player of Fishbone, one of our brother L.A. groups, while I was out on tour. But it still didn't compute to me. I could have seen if she'd slept with Angelo Moore, who was the good-looking lead singer. What girl didn't want to fuck Angelo? But Chris Fish—a guy with bad dreadlocks and worse fashion sense?

I was mortified. It hadn't mattered that I'd slept with a hundred girls on the road in the last year. This killed me. The reality of my friend and my girlfriend doing this while I was away was incomprehensible demoralization to the tenth degree. I felt paralyzed. I probably gave myself cancer at that moment. But what could I do?

For some reason, I went to my father's house and formulated a plan. First I picked up the phone and called Chris. "Chris, did you fuck my girlfriend?"

There was a giant pause, and then a slow and stunned voice said, "Oh man, Bob spilled the beans."

I took a deep breath.

"You're not going to come after me, are you?"

"I'm not going to come after you, but you are not my friend, and stay the fuck away from me," I warned. End of conversation. He wasn't my problem. Jennifer was.

I called her. "Jennifer, I know what happened."

"Nothing happened," she protested.

"Nope, I know exactly what happened. I've spoken to Chris, and we are finished."

She started protesting, claiming Chris was lying, but I was adamant. "We're finished. Don't ever come around me, I hate your guts. Good-bye forever."

I hung up, and I meant it. It was time to move on. This sense of excitement came over me, and I called up Flea, and he and I and Pete Weiss went out driving. I stood on the top of the car as it was rolling down the streets of Hollywood, screaming, "I'm a free man. I'm a free man."

We had toured on and off till the spring of '86, and now it was time to start thinking about our next album. One of the producers we were considering was Keith Levene, who had been in Public Image Ltd. I knew Keith and thought he was a great guy, but I also knew he was a heroin addict, so we were in for a convoluted experience. But that sounded great to me, since I was a mess. The more convoluted the landscape was, the less obvious I would seem as a fuckup.

EMI had given us a budget of five grand for the demo, and that seemed pretty high to me. There was no way a demo should cost that much. When I brought it up with Hillel and Keith, I found out that they'd earmarked two thousand dollars for drugs to make the tape. I don't think Flea agreed to it, and I know Cliff had no idea; he was just caught up in the maelstrom of insanity.

I was late for the session, and as I pulled up at the studio, I wondered if they had been serious about putting aside funds to get high. The first thing I saw when I walked in that room was a mountain of cocaine and a small molehill of heroin. Hillel was fucking gizacked. They told me that the first fifteen hundred dollars' worth of drugs had already been consumed, so I started scooping and grabbing and snatching and saturating and got so loaded I was in no shape to be part of a creative process.

Poor Cliff was off in the corner of the studio, tinkering with what was then a brand-new device, a drum machine. You would hit the pads to create a preprogrammed drum sound, and you could record your own sounds so you could play the drums with whatever sound you wanted. Cliff's favorite was a baby crying. It was a low-tech device, but Cliff was fiddling with it as obsessively as we were with the drugs, laughing in a strange, nervous fashion. He looked at me and said, "I could play with this thing for ten years. This is like a whole band within itself." I remember thinking, "That's what he wants to do. He's sick of this circus, and he's looking at this machine and seeing his future."

It was obvious that Cliff's heart was no longer in the band. He didn't quit, but we sensed that he didn't want to continue, so Flea visited him and gave him the bad news. He took it pretty hard and had bitter feelings for a couple of years. But then Jack Irons, our original drummer, decided to come back to the band, which was as much of a shocker to me as when Hillel came back. Something must have happened with What Is This to shake Jack's loyalty, because he was not the kind of person to leave something for a better career opportunity. Whatever; he missed us and he loved us and he wanted to play music with us. So he came back and we began to write music again as the original foursome.

Then someone else came back into my life. About a month had gone by since I split with Jennifer. I was still shooting a lot of heroin and cocaine, not learning anything. I wasn't growing as a person. I wasn't setting goals or working on my character defects. I was just a fucked-up drug addict.

One night about three in the morning, there was a knock at my door on Carmen Street. It was Jennifer. She was working as a go-go dancer at a club, and it was obvious that she had come right from work, because she was dressed up in a thousand different colors, with feathers and boots and chains and crazy makeup that must have taken her a few hours to apply.

"Please just let me in. I miss you. I miss you," she begged.

"No chance," I said. "Just go. Don't get me in trouble, don't start yelling. I don't need cops at my house."

I closed the door and went back to sleep. When I woke up, I saw Jennifer curled up on the welcome mat outside my door, sound asleep. This went on for the next few weeks: Every night she'd come up and either knock or curl up and go to sleep on my doorstep. I even started going out my kitchen window and climbing down a huge lemon tree that was right outside (and which came in handy when I scored some Persian heroin, which was oil-based and had to be cooked up in lemon juice).

One night I succumbed. I can't remember if I gave in to her love or if I was so bad off that I needed twenty bucks or if she came offering drugs or whatever sad, sick, and bizarre circumstance it was, but I let her in and we picked up where we left off. High as kites together, back into the mix of a totally dysfunctional but passionate relationship. So passionate that it would be documented on a video that became a cult classic in the underground club scene of L.A.

It happened one night at the Roxy. Some people had organized a benefit for Sea Shepherd, a hard-core version of Greenpeace, and the Chili Peppers were asked to play. The theme of the night was that every band would cover a Jimi Hendrix song. There was a great bill that included Mike Watt, our friend Tree, and Fishbone, so we were psyched to play.

When I showed up at the gig, Fishbone was about to go on. Earlier there had been some discussion of Jennifer singing backup with Fishbone, but I kiboshed it. "You are not going to go onstage with *that* guy." Fishbone took the stage, and I made my way to the balcony. When I looked down, there was Jennifer onstage. That was not good. Now I had to make her pay for disrespecting me like that in front of my friends. At the same time, I kept my focus, because what really mattered to me was that I sing "Foxy Lady" well. Right before we were scheduled to go onstage, this young hippie girl walked backstage. She had brown hair, was really pretty, and had these huge tits poking through her tank top that couldn't help but be in everybody's face.

A lightbulb went off in my head. I went over and whispered in her ear: "We're going to do 'Foxy Lady,' and when we get to the end of the song, when we're freaking out onstage, I want you to come out and dance with me naked." Two can play the same game. The hippie goddess agreed. We went out and killed "Foxy Lady." It was like our band could have levitated. The drums were happening. Flea was digging in. Hillel was orbiting. I was giving it everything I had.

I almost forgot there was supposed to be a surprise guest. We came to the end of the song, and this slinky young hippie walked onstage. She hadn't gotten completely naked, but she was topless, and her big tits were just to-ing and fro-ing across the stage. She came up to me and started to do her hippie shimmy next to me. Norwood, the bass player from Fishbone, came out to join us, and we sandwiched this semi-naked girl.

Suddenly, a figure flew onstage as if shot out of a cannon. It was Jennifer. She grabbed Norwood, who's a big man, and tosse°d him aside like a rag doll. Then she grabbed the girl and literally threw her off the stage. Meanwhile, the band kept going. I realized that I was about to become the recipient of some serious pain. By then I had wound up on the floor on my back, singing the outro. And there was Jennifer, coming at me with fists and feet, punching and connecting and going for my crotch with her boots. I was trying to block the punches, all the while not missing a note. She kicked my ass till I finished the song and somehow escaped and ran off into the night.

Between my dysfunctional girlfriend and my dysfunctional platonic friend and my dysfunctional self, my life continued on a downward spiral. We had settled on a producer for our third album, Michael Beinhorn. He was a very intelligent fellow from New York who was into all of the same music that we were and had produced a hit by Herbie Hancock called "Rockit." But I was stuck in my Groundhog year, waking up every morning to the same gray reality of copping to feel right. I went on another horrible heroin run with Kim and stopped being productive. I was withering away, mentally, spiritually, physically, creatively—everything was fading out. Sometimes doing heroin was nice and dreamy and euphoric and carefree, almost romantic-feeling. In reality, I was dying and couldn't quite see that from being so deep in my own forest.

The few times I showed up at rehearsal, I wasn't bringing anything to the table. I didn't have the same drive or desire to come up with ideas and lyrics. They were still in me, but the process was thwarted, numbed out. We'd written some music for the third album, maybe four or five songs, but we needed a lot more. The whole band was suffering from Hillel and me being on drugs, but I was the much more obvious candidate to put the onus on, because I was literally asleep at rehearsal.

One day I showed up to rehearsal, and Jack and Hillel and Flea, who probably loved me more than any three guys on earth, said, "Anthony, we're kicking you out of the band. We want to play music and you obviously don't, so you have to go. We're going to get a different singer and go on, so you're out of here."

I had a brief moment of clarity when I saw that they had every right in the world to fire me. It was an obvious move, like cutting off your damn foot because it was gangrened, so the rest of your body wouldn't die. I just wanted to be remembered and acknowledged for those two or three years that I had been in the Red Hot Chili Peppers as a founding member, a guy who started something, a guy who made two records; whatever else came after that was theirs. Part of me was genuine in letting go of the band. But what made it so easy for me to accept was that now I knew I had zero responsibilities, and I could go off with Kim and get loaded.

Much to their amazement, I shrugged and said, "You guys are right. I apologize for not contributing what I should have been contributing this whole time. It's a crying shame, but I understand completely, and I wish you guys the best of luck."

And I left.

Once I didn't have anywhere to report to, it went from worse to worse than worse. Kim and I went for it. We were getting more desperate, and we owed too much money to the drug dealers around Hollywood, so we started walking from her house, which was not far from downtown Los Angeles, to known drug neighborhoods, mainly Sixth and Union. We went down and started introducing ourselves to these different street characters. I met a pretty talented hustler right off the bat. He was this scurvy street urchin, an out-of-control white-trash drug addict who was moving deftly in the downtown Latino drug world. He became our liaison to all the other connections. He still lived with his parents in this little wooden house. The kid was covered with track marks and abscesses and disease from head to toe, but he was a master of the downtown corners. Kim and I were always such petty punkass low-budget buyers that he would always do us right. We trusted this guy. We'd buy bindles of cocaine and bindles of heroin and walk a couple of blocks into these residential neighborhoods and shoot up right there on the street. We still had an air of invincibility and invisibility, so we thought we couldn't be touched.

About a week after I was terminated from the band, I had a defining moment of sadness. I was talking to Bob Forest, and he told me that my ex-band had been nominated for L.A. band of the year at the first annual *L.A. Weekly* Music Awards. For our circle, that was similar to getting nominated for an Oscar, so it was pretty exciting. Bob asked me if I was going to go to the ceremony. I told him I wasn't talking to the guys, so I couldn't imagine showing up.

But the awards show happened to be at the Variety Arts Theatre, a classic old venue right smack downtown. Coincidentally, I was in the same neighborhood that night, trying to hustle more drugs for my money than anyone wanted to give me. I was down to my last ten dollars, which is not a good feeling, because on a night like that, you want to be inebriated, and instead I was barely high. I remember doing a speedball with some gang dealer guys when I realized the *L.A. Weekly* event was going on.

I stumbled into the lobby of the theater in a bit of a haze. It seemed unusually dark inside, and there was hardly anyone there, because the show was in progress. The doors that led down the aisles of the theater were open, so I leaned up against one of those doors and started scanning the audience for my old bandmates. Sure enough, they were in the front. I hadn't been there for more than a minute when I ran into someone I knew who said, "Man, you shouldn't be here. This is going to be really sad for you."

Just then they announced the winner of L.A. band of the year: "The Red Hot Chili Peppers." "We won! We won the damn award!" I cheered to myself. I looked over at the guys, and they all had big grins and a pep in their step as they marched up onstage in their fancy suits and hats. Each guy got his award and made a little speech like "Thank you, *L.A. Weekly*. Thank you, L.A. We rock. We'll see you next year." Not one of them mentioned our brother Anthony who did this with us and who deserved a part of this award. It was like I had never been there those last three years. Not a fucking peep about the guy they had kicked out two weeks before. No "Rest in peace," no "May God save his soul," no nothing.

It was a poetically tragic, bizarre, and surreal moment for me. I understood getting kicked out, but I could not understand why on earth they didn't have the heart to give me a shout from the podium. I was too numb to feel sorry for myself; I was just trying desperately not to think about how bad I had fucked up and trying to escape any responsibility or reckoning. So I just said, "Ah, fuck them," to myself and tried to borrow five dollars from someone in the lobby so I could go out and continue to get high.

Money for drugs was a real issue for us, but one day Kim got a big check, and we went out and got a ton of smack and went back to her place to do it. I got so high and felt so good that I said to Kim, "I got to get off this stuff." Sometimes when you get that high, you think you're going to feel that good for the rest of your life, and you actually believe you can get off dope; you can't imagine that euphoria ever going away.

"I'm going to call my mom, go back to Michigan, and get on methadone," I told Kim. As far as I knew, that was the cure for addiction.

We were drooling and way too high for anyone's good, but Kim thought it was a great idea, so I picked up the phone and dialed my mom. "You're not going to believe this, but I have a pretty bad heroin problem here, and I'd like to come back to Michigan and get on methadone, but I don't have a penny to my name," I said.

I'm sure my mom was in shock, but she immediately tried to act together and rational. She must have sensed that my life was on the line and that if she flipped out and got judgmental, I would never come home. Of course, if she could have seen the way we were living, she would have had to be committed to a mental asylum.

She made the arrangements, and the next day the ticket arrived, but we couldn't stop getting high. The day of the flight came, but we had been getting high all night, and when it was time to go to the airport, we were incapable of getting it together. I called up my mom and made up some stupid lie about why I couldn't leave that day, but I'd change the ticket to the next day. That went on and on, and each time it was "I'm coming tomorrow, I'm coming tomorrow," while Kim and I were up in her house getting plastered.

Finally, I made up my mind to leave, but I had to do one last run and get really good and loaded right before the flight so I could be high the whole way home. The morning of the latest flight came around, and we went downtown to buy a bunch of balloons of dope and some coke.

Kim was driving an old Falcon that she had borrowed, and I kept jumping in and out of the car, looking for good deals on the street, filling the pockets of my trench coat with heroin, cocaine, spoons, cotton, syringes, you name it. I was out on one of the downtown streets when I saw someone that could be useful to me on the other side of the street. I crossed in the middle of the block, and before I knew it, a cop barked out, "Hey, buddy, you in the trench coat. Why don't you come over here?"

Out of the corner of my eye, I saw Kim parked behind the wheel of the Falcon. She slumped down and started moaning.

I weighed 120 pounds if I was lucky, and my hair was one big helmet of matted hair, like an elephant ear. I was wearing this trench coat that was hanging off my body, and my skin was a strange shade of yellow and green. I also had on canvas high-top sneakers, which were black and red and filled with marker drawings that I'd done. On the top of one of the shoes, I had drawn a pretty nice Star of David about the size of a silver dollar. Oh, and I had dark glasses on.

I was so busted.

By now the cop had backup.

"We saw you jaywalking back there, and you look a little suspicious," the first cop said. "Why don't you go ahead and show us your ID?"

"Uh, I don't have an ID, but my name is Anthony Kiedis, and I'm actually late getting to the airport to get on a plane and go to see my mom . . ." I stammered.

While this interrogation was going on, the other cop was systematically searching me inch by inch, starting with my sneakers and socks.

I was telling the first cop my date of birth and place of birth and address, and he was writing it all down, keeping me distracted while his partner searched me. The partner was up to my pants, going through the pockets, pulling out whatever scraps of paper and junk I had with me. He even went into the mini pocket, and I was getting more and more nervous because he was getting closer to my side pockets, which were packed with bad news.

"Does that jacket have any inside pockets?" the second cop asked. I started stalling and showed them my plane ticket and whatever else I had in the inside pockets.

Just as he had exhausted all the other pockets and was about to start in on the ones that were loaded, his partner looked down at my sneakers and said, "Are you Jewish? Why do you have the Star of David on your sneaker?"

I looked up and saw his name tag. It read COHEN.

"No, but my best friend in the world is Jewish, and we both have a thing for the Star of David," I said.

Cohen looked at his partner, who was about to find my stash, and said, "Kowalski, let him go."

"What?" Kowalski said.

"Let me talk to him for a second," Cohen said, and pulled me aside. "Look, you shouldn't be down here," he whispered to me. "Whatever you're up to, it's not working for you, so why don't you go get on that plane and get out of here. I don't ever want see you down here again."

I nodded and, as soon as the light changed, ran across the street, and that was the morning I made it to the airport.

By the time the flight arrived in Michigan I was still loaded on the drugs. I saw my mother in the waiting area and walked up to her, but she looked right past me because I looked like I had stepped out of a grave.

"Hi, Mom," I said meekly. The look of shock and horror and fear and sadness and disbelief on her face was unbearable. "Let's go straight to the clinic," I said.

We drove to the building and asked a worker where the methadone clinic was. They told us that the state of Michigan had discontinued the use of methadone six months prior to my arrival. That was really, really bad news for me, because normally, I would go hustle something somewhere. But I had no game left. I didn't have a penny in my pocket, and I could barely walk.

The counselor offered to admit me to a long-term treatment center, but that was a year's commitment. I would have rather gone out on the curb and died than check in for a year.

"The only other alternative is the Salvation Army," the guy said, "but there's no detox there."

We drove to a seedy part of Grand Rapids, and I checked in to the Salvation Army. "Thank you, we'll have your son back to you in twenty days," they said, and my mom left. I was at a loss. They took me to a big room and gave me a cot. I looked around and saw white kids, black kids, Hispanic kids, alcoholic kids, dope-fiend kids, crack kids, and a smattering of older guys. I fit right in.

I was facing cold turkey. I knew what to expect, because I'd been through it already. I knew I was going to be sick to my stomach, that every single bone in my body was going to hurt. When you're kicking, your eyelashes hurt, your eyebrows hurt, your elbows hurt, your knees hurt, your ankles hurt, your neck hurts, your head hurts, your back hurts, it all hurts. Parts of your body you didn't know could experience pain, experience it. There's a bad taste in your mouth. For a week your nose is running uncontrollably. I didn't throw up that much, but the worst agony was not being able to sleep. I couldn't get a wink the whole twenty days. I'd stay up all night and wander the hallways and go sit in the lounge and watch late-night TV. For the first few days I couldn't eat, but I got my appetite back and started to put some meat on my bones.

After a few days, a staff member came up to me and said, "You have to go to a meeting every day you're here." It was cold and snowing outside, and I was feeling pretty miserable, so I accepted my fate and marched along with all the other kids into this little room. I was not in a great state of comprehension, because I was in physical pain and emotionally agonized, but I sat down in the meeting and saw the twelve steps up on the wall. I was trying to read them, but I couldn't focus my eyes. I was trying to listen to these people, but I couldn't focus my ears.

I had mocked anything that had to do with sobriety or recovery for my whole life. I'd see stickers that said ONE DAY AT A TIME and I'd be like "Fuck that." I was a hustler, and a con artist, and a scammer, and a fiend, and a liar, and a cheat, and a thief, all these things, so naturally, I started looking for the scam. Was it a money thing? A God thing? A religion thing? What the fuck was going on here?

But as I sat in that meeting, I felt something in the room that made sense to me. It was nothing but a bunch of guys like me, helping one another get off drugs and find a new way of life. I was keen on discovering the loophole, but there wasn't one. I thought, "Oh my God, these people are coming from the same place as me, but they don't get high anymore, and they don't look desperate, and they're joking about shit that most people would send you to jail for talking about." One girl got up and started talking about not being able to stop smoking crack even though she had a kid. She'd had to give her kid to her mother. I was thinking, "Yeah, I'd do the same. I'd be leaving the kid with the mom and disappearing. I did the same thing with my band."

This was not a cult, not a scam, not a fad, not a trick, not an out-to-get-your-buck type of thing; this was just dope fiends helping dope fiends. Some of them were clean and some of them were getting clean because they were talking to the ones who got clean, and they were being honest about it and unafraid to say how fucked up they were. It flashed on me that if I did this, I could be clean.

I stayed there for the twenty days, not sleeping but going to meetings every day and listening and reading the books and gleaning a few of the basic principles.

After twenty days, I went back to my mom's house in Lowell, feeling a hell of a lot different than when I came. At age twenty-four, I was totally clean for the first time since I was eleven years old. I was able to sleep through the night, and my mom and I celebrated the next day. My stepdad, Steve, was real supportive, and so were my sisters. I was feeling pretty good, oddly in acceptance of the damage that I had created. There's a whole lot of optimism in those meetings, with people being freed from self-imposed prisons, so everything seemed fresh and new.

Steve had some old weights lying around the house, and I rebuilt them and did some weight lifting. I took long walks and played with the dog. It had been so long since I'd felt normal, and wasn't chasing something or calling someone or meeting someone in the middle of the night to talk him out of a bag of something. Amazingly, none of that was on my mind at all.

During my stay at the Salvation Army, I realized that if I didn't want to keep doing what I had been doing that I'd have to let go of Jennifer. I really wanted to stay sober, and I wasn't blaming her for my problem, but I knew that if I was with her, my odds of staying clean would be diminished.

I kept going to meetings while I was at my mom's house,

and I learned that alcoholism/drug addiction is a bona fide illness. When you recognize that there's a name and a description for this condition that you thought was insanity, you've identified the problem, and now you can do something about it.

There's a real psychological relief that comes from discovering what's wrong with you and why you've been trying to medicate the hell out of yourself since you were old enough to find medicine. I wasn't too clear on the concepts in the beginning, and I still wanted to cut corners and do things my way and take some short cuts and not do all of the work that was asked of me, but I did like the feeling and I did identify hugely. I also felt waves of compassion for all of these other poor motherfuckers who were destroying their lives. I looked at the people in the meetings and saw beautiful young women who had become skeletons because they couldn't stop using. I saw other people who loved their families but couldn't stop. That was what attracted me. I decided that I wanted to be part of something where these people had a chance of getting well, of getting their lives back.

After being in Michigan a month, I decided to give Flea a call to check in. We exchanged greetings, and then I told him about the cold turkey and the meetings and the fact that I didn't get high anymore.

"What do you mean, you don't get high?" Flea said. "You're not doing anything? Not even pot?"

"Nope. I don't even want to. It's called sobriety, and I'm loving it," I said.

"That's insane. I'm so happy for you," he said.

I asked him how it was going with the band, and he told me that they'd hired a new singer who had a bunch of tattoos, but I could tell in his voice that they weren't happy with him. I didn't really care. In no way or shape or form was I trying to get back in the band.

Flea must have heard something in my voice that first call, something that he hadn't heard since we were in high school. It's amazing to me, because it wasn't like me not to be angling my way back into the band as soon as I felt good. But I honestly didn't care then if I went back to the band or not. It was a real take-it-or-leave-it feeling, which is really not me, because I'm a control freak, and I want what I want and I want it immediately. However, at that moment I was relieved of all of the self-obsessed, driven behavior.

A few days later, Flea called me. "Do you think you'd want to come back here and maybe play a couple of songs and see how it feels to be back in the band?" he asked.

That was the first time I had even considered that as a possibility. I blurted out, "Wow, hmmm. Yeah, I would. There's really nothing else that I'd want to do."

"Okay, come back, and let's get to work," Flea said.

I got on the plane to go home, riding a whole new wave of enthusiasm for my new life. I decided to write a song about my monthlong experience of going to meetings, getting clean, and winning this battle of addiction. I look back on it, and it seems naive, but it's exactly where I was at that point of my life. I took out a pad of paper, looked out the window at the clouds, and started channeling this river of wordology that was cascading toward me.

From "Fight Like a Brave"

If you're sick-a-sick 'n' tired of being sick and tired
If you're sick of all the bullshit and you're sick of all the lies
It's better late than never to set-a-set it straight
You know the lie is dead so give yourself a break
Get it through your head, get it off your chest
Get it out your arm because it's time to start fresh
You want to stop dying, the life you could be livin'
I'm here to tell a story but I'm also here to listen

No, I'm not your preacher and I'm not your physician
I'm just trying to reach you, I'm a rebel with a mission

Fight like a brave—don't be a slave
No one can tell you you've got to be afraid

When I got back to L.A., within two months I was shooting heroin and cocaine again. My sobriety hadn't stuck for a long time, but now I knew there was a way out of the madness if I wanted it and if I was willing to do the work to get it. I had been given the tools; I just didn't want to use them yet.

8.

The Organic Anti-Beat Box Band

Rejoining the band wasn't the only thing that I talked to Flea about when he called me in Michigan. While I was away, Flea had a part in a science-fiction movie called *Stranded,* and he'd met a beautiful young actress named Ione Skye who he was certain was my type. We made plans for an introduction when I came home.

When I got back to L.A., I moved in with Lindy, who was nice enough to let me stay in the spare room of his two-bedroom apartment in Studio City. Of course, that meant he had to fend off all the calls from Jennifer. I had no desire to talk to her, especially after I met Ione. From the moment I laid eyes on Ione, I knew that goddess was going to be my girlfriend. It was a few days before her sixteenth birthday, and she looked like she'd come out of a fairy-tale book. Whereas Jennifer was this exquisitely manicured, modern, self-created sculpture of a punk-rock superstar, Ione was more of an au naturel, soft, soulful forest nymph. She had long, flowing curly brunette hair, a beautiful large flirtatious rack, and an overbite. I was always a sucker for an overbite.

Ione came from an alternative-lifestyle Hollywood family. Her dad was the folksinger Donovan, but he wasn't really in the picture. Her mother, Enid, was a beautiful hippie with blond ringlet hair. Ione had a brother named after her dad. They all lived in this great old Craftsman house on North Wilton, which was suffused with a warm, rustic, loving family vibe. Ione dressed like a hippie child and had an ethereal sixth sense about her, an extra gift. She was also way too sexually curious about everything. It was an energy that she didn't verbalize, but it worked for me at that age. She was probably the most beautiful, smart, sexy, caring, and nurturing young girl in all of Hollywood, and our attraction was mutual, thank God. A few days after we met, she was introducing me at her birthday party as her boyfriend. It was mind-blowing, how quickly I fell completely and deeply in love.

Now I was ready to go back to work. I sat down with our producer, Michael Beinhorn, and we went over the status of the songs. We were supposed to go into the studio and cut basic tracks in ten days, so I planned to write throughout the recording process. It wasn't an overwhelming amount of work; back then you needed only twelve songs for a record. We worked on "Fight Like a Brave," and Beinhorn put a football-rally chanting chorus on it. "Me and My Friends," a song that I'd written while driving home from San Francisco with my old friend Joe Walters, came together nicely. "Funky Crime" was basically a lyrical description of a conversation that we'd had with George Clinton, in which he maintained that music itself was color-blind but the media and the radio stations segregate it based on their perceptions of the artists. "Backwoods" was a song about the roots of rock and roll, and "Skinny Sweaty Man" was my ode to Hillel. I wrote another song, "No Chump Love Sucker," that was also in Hillel's honor. He had just been left high and dry and shattered by a girlfriend who dumped him for a guy who had more money and more drugs. So it was a revenge song against that type of evil, materialistic woman.

"Behind the Sun" was a definite branching out for us. Hillel had this unusual, melodic riff, and Beinhorn felt it was a song that could be a hit. He worked a lot with me on the melody, knowing that it wasn't my forte to get wrapped up in a pretty song. I guess my reputation at that time was for songs like "Party on Your Pussy," which EMI refused to put on the record until we changed the title to "Special Secret Song Inside." But it wasn't entirely accurate to think that all of our songs were raunchy. "Love Trilogy" became one of our all-time favorite songs. The music started off like a reggae thing, then it went into hard-core funk and ended up in speed metal. For years, whenever someone would question our lyrics, Flea would say, "Read 'Love Trilogy' and you'll know what real lyrics are all about." It's about loving the things that aren't necessarily perfect or always lovable.

From "Love Trilogy"

My love is death to apartheid rule
My love is deepest death, the ocean blues
My love is the Zulu groove
My love is coop-a-loop move
My love is lightning's blues
My love is the pussy juice
My love can't be refused

After fifty days of being sober, I thought, "That's a nice number. I think I should honor that number." I decided it was a good time to do drugs. My plan was to get high for a day or two and then go back to work. What I found was that once I started, I couldn't stop, and it really made a mess of the beginning of the recording process. The songs were amazing; Hillel was on fire; we were all in love with recording in the basement of Capitol Studios, another incredibly historical monument of Hollywood recording;

Beinhorn was working his ass off; and I went and got high and couldn't stop. Finally, I decided to do a bunch of heroin, get some sleep, and face yet another mess I'd made.

I went downtown and found an El Salvadoran who hooked me up, and I was in that opiate haze one more time. But all I could think about was the fact that I was supposed to be in the studio. I started hearing Jackie Irons's beat in my head for a song we were working on called "The Organic Anti–Beat Box Band." I sat in a downtown park, surrounded by an odd mixture of park people, and wrote the lyrics. I felt excruciating pain and guilt and shame behind not being there for the beginning of the record, but I thought if I showed up with something good to offer, the heat would diminish. And it did. I crashed at Lindy's, then got up and apologized and pulled it together for the rest of the session.

Part of the reason I relapsed was because I didn't have a support system. I didn't know anybody who was sober. I had ventured out to a couple of meetings on my own, but I had a lifetime of the mind-set "I can take care of whatever is wrong all by myself, and I don't need any of you yokels to guide me, because I don't, at this moment in time, want what you have." I went back into a self-imposed abstinence, which equaled what they call a "dry drunk." It's an accident waiting to happen. You're not putting the stuff into you that makes you bonkers, but you're not dealing with any of the shit that's been in there your whole life and makes you want to get high in the first place.

We had a great time making the record. It was inspiring to see Jack Irons back in the mix. He added such an important and different element to our chemistry. Hillel, Flea, and I were all pretty self-obsessed maniacs. Jack was the one wholesome fellow. He turned out to be messed up but in a different way. He was a nice element, really hardworking and joyful and supportive.

When it came time to record the vocals, I used Hillel as my bandmate/vocal producer. Every time I did a vocal, we both felt like I was going to a new place and that these were the best vocal expressions I'd ever put down on tape. Hillel was ecstatic, running in between takes, going, "I'm telling you, this is the most beautiful thing we've ever done. I can't wait to release this record."

Of course, on the last day, when the last note was done and in the can and our jobs were finished, Hillel and I found a French dealer and got loaded on some China White, reveling in our accomplishment. That opened up the floodgates. While I was still staying at Lindy's house, I orchestrated an absolutely gory scenario of speedballing. I didn't have a lot of money and I didn't have an automobile, so I'd wake up in the middle of the night, grab some spoons from the kitchen, and clean out Lindy's bucket of change. Then I'd take a fishing pole out of his closet, crack his bedroom door open, and fish his car keys off his dresser, feeling miserable that I was such a freak that I could be doing this to the poor bastard who was trying to help me out.

Once you've seen a solution to the disease that's tearing you apart, relapsing is never fun. You know there's an alternative to the way you're living and that you're going against something you've been given for free by the universe, this key to the kingdom. Drug addiction is a progressive disease, so every time you go out, it gets a little uglier than it was before; it's not like you go back to the early days of using, when there was less of a price to pay. It isn't fun anymore, but it's still desperately exciting. Once you put that first drug or drink in your body, you don't have to worry about the girlfriend or the career or the family or the bills. All those mundane aspects of life disappear. Now you have one job, and that's to keep chucking the coal in the engine, because you don't want this train to stop. If it stops, then you're going to have to feel all that other shit.

That chase is always exciting. There are cops and bad guys and freaks and hookers. You're diving into a big insidious video game, but again, you're being tricked into thinking that you're doing something cool, since the price is always bigger than the payoff. You immediately give up your love and your light and your beauty, and you become a dark black hole in the universe, sucking up bad energy and not walking around putting a smile on someone's face or helping someone out or teaching someone something that's going to help his or her life. You're not creating the ripple of love; you're creating the vacuum of shit. I want to describe both sides of how I felt, but it's important to know that in the end all the romantic glorification of dope fiendery amounts to nothing but a hole of shit. It has to appear enticing, because that's why God or the universe, creative intelligence or whatever you want to call it, put that energy here. It's a learning tool, and you can either kill yourself with it or you can turn yourself into a free person with it. I don't think drug addiction is inherently useless, but it's a rough row to hoe.

In my deluded mind, I thought that if I chipped away at a little bit of dope every now and again, I wouldn't go on these insane speedball binges and my life wouldn't spiral out of control. I moved into Ione's house, and a couple of times a week, I'd go out and buy forty dollars' worth of China White, smoke it, get high all night long, and then go to sleep and feel all right. About a month into living with Ione, she convinced me that I shouldn't go off and do that, so the compromise was I'd get the dope and bring it back and smoke it in bed with her. We used to have these all-night sessions when I'd smoke the dope and then we'd cuddle up in bed and read books like *Interview with the Vampire* and *Catcher in the Rye* to each other, all night long, until the sun came up.

Despite the occasional heroin smoking, I was keeping it relatively together while I was at Ione's house. We had lots of glorious days together. I'd wake up next to her in bed and think, "Jesus Christ, she is such an angel, and I'm so in love with her." Then we'd lie in bed and sing along to Bob Marley's record *Kaya* every morning, holding each other tight. We'd drive around in her little Toyota and have lunch and smoke pot together and make love all over the city. I was still carrying around that "one foot on a banana peel, one foot in the grave" energy, but I was trying to be respectful of this new place in my life. On one of those days, we had just smoked some pot, and I was thanking my lucky stars that this was where my life was at that moment, when the Stevie Wonder song

"I Believe (When I Fall in Love It Will Be Forever)" came on the radio. We pulled over and cranked up the radio and started weeping profusely because we were so in love and this song was describing our feelings.

A week later, I'd disappear into the downtown maze of ghetto dope hell. I'd borrow her car in the middle of the night and always mean to get it right back, but sometimes I'd be gone for days. That was when I started partnering up with this Mexican mafia drug dealer named Mario. I knew Mario from my downtown runs with Kim Jones. Mario always gave me a great deal, charging me the least amount of money for the most amount of drugs. I could have stayed in Hollywood, it was full of hookers who would deliver heroin to your house. But I didn't want to have a lot of dealers in my life and I'd convinced myself that if I went downtown it would only be for that one time, I wasn't really going back to that forlorn life.

When we weren't shooting up in his drug-infested apartment, Mario knew this safety zone beneath a freeway bridge, some weird hideaway that the LAPD never patrolled. He explained to me that no non-Mexican gang members were allowed there, so in order for me to get in, we had to lie and tell them that I was engaged to his sister. We walked up to the big guys guarding the gate, told them Mario was my future brother-in-law, and they let us in. Sheltered beneath that overpass right in the middle of the city, I spent countless days lying on a bunch of dirty mattresses and shooting up with a bunch of killers.

About the only thing that could tear me away from this endless cycle of abuse was to go out on tour. When it was time to start the touring for *Uplift,* a damn limousine came to pick me up for the trip to the airport. I figured if we were going out on tour in a limo, something must be working, and it was. We played some of the greatest shows of our lives on that tour, mainly because Hillel and I weren't obsessed with getting high. We drank a lot and did coke whenever we could, smoked a lot of pot, and maybe had one shipment of dope sent out. But we crisscrossed the country, charging these small stages for hundreds of willing and beautiful customers. Kids would come out of the woodwork to rock out with this different outfit from Hollywood. We weren't part of the punk-rock movement, or the post-punk movement, we were a different animal. I had no idea how these kids even knew about us, but they were the best audiences you could ever ask for—so much heart, so much spirit, so much enthusiasm, they'd just show up and give everything they had.

We did a lot of crazy things to while away the time while we were on tour. When we got to Texas, I decided to shave off all my pubic hair. I collected it and put it in a Ziploc bag and gave it to our roadie Nickie Beat as the "merch" for that night. He went out to the concession booth and tacked it up on the wall, next to the T-shirts, and started hawking "Anthony's pubic hair, only twenty-five dollars." At the end of the night, he reported that he couldn't get the money, but he did get panties from three different girls, with the promise that they'd bring their entire families to the next show.

On that tour, we came up with a new touring pastime called Tongue in the Dirt. In the past, a lot of our games and challenges revolved around food. On the *Freaky Styley* tour, we had something called the Truck Stop Vomiting Club. We'd typically eat horrible, greasy, disgusting food, and we knew it was no good for us, so we'd go on to the truck stop and upchuck it by whatever means necessary. Whether it was fingers down the throat, or thinking about something disgusting, your manhood was defined by your ability to make yourself vomit. Flea was always the hair trigger of these events. All he had to do was look at an egg and he was vomiting all over the place.

Then Hillel came up with something called the Grizzlers. Every day, when we'd hit a greasy spoon, to perk up the atmosphere of our experience, we'd turn our order into a rhyme. So we'd be in Utah, and the waitress would be hovering over us, waiting for the order, and we'd say something like "I don't know any Chinese, but I've worked with blacks, so give me scrambled eggs with a side of flapjacks." Then we'd end it with "Because we're the Grizzlers." We'd go around the table, and everyone would have a minute or two to compose a Grizzler verse.

Tongue in the Dirt evolved out of challenges Flea and I gave each other back in high school. I remember one time I was on a city bus with Flea when we were about fifteen, and I was a little under the weather and coughed up a hideous cookie of congealed phlegm into my hand. We were both looking at this fucked-up loogie with awe when I challenged Flea: "If you've got any balls at all, you'll eat this right out of my hand, because you're the only motherfucker crazy enough to do that." And he did! Tongue in the Dirt was born without our even knowing it.

In our newest refinement of the challenge, we'd get a few roadies and some of the girls who were traveling or visiting with us and form an irregular circle. If we were throwing a football around, we'd line up forty feet apart. If it was some awkward chunk of metal we'd found on the side of the road, we'd be closer together. The object of the game was to catch the object without dropping it. It was a group decision whether a particular throw was catchable or not. If a throw was not catchable, the person who threw would lose. But if someone fumbled a catchable throw, then he or she would lose. The loser would, as the name of the game implied, have to get down on hands and knees and lay his or her tongue flat down in the dirt and then come up and show the other players.

As the game developed, the more dirt you took in, the greater your honor. The losers began eating bugs off the grilles of cars or licking the entire circumference of a trash can, anything that would entertain their brethren with an audacious display of absurd bravado. It was a terrific game, because you could play it with a hockey puck or a football, and it was all about psyching out your opponents and making the unexpected throw and putting a spin on it. It was a great way to spend time with friends and de-stress. Tongue in the Dirt maintained its presence in the camp for a very long time.

It was during the *Uplift* tour that I had the first inklings that we were becoming a tiny bit famous. Girls would show up backstage and offer themselves to us. Suddenly, I became disinterested. Even under the influence, I couldn't be persuaded to sleep with these girls, because they would come up to me and go, "You're Anthony Kiedis. I want to fuck you. Let's go." I'd be like "Hmm. No. I'm going somewhere, and I think your friends are waiting for you." It was like when Groucho said he'd never join a club that would have him as a member. That was me. I wanted something that I couldn't have. I'd rather have a challenge or even failure than something that was too freely given. Most of the time.

The longer we were on that tour, the more our popularity increased. In the South, we had been booked into theaters instead of clubs. By the time we hit Denver, Lindy was ecstatic, because we had to move our show to a huge theater thanks to the ticket demand. That night, after the show, Hillel and I were sitting backstage, congratulating each other on our newfound success, when a girl came storming backstage.

"Anthony, I have to show you something," she screamed. "I'm so in love with you. Look what I did!" She pulled down her pants, and there was my name tattooed right over the old pubic mound. There was a guy standing a few paces behind her. "This is my boyfriend, but he doesn't care. I'm all yours if you want me," she said.

"Yeah, thumbs up, dude. Take her, she loves you," this guy said.

I didn't take him up on his offer, but Hillel and I looked at each other and realized that maybe all that touring for the last three albums had finally amounted to something. We still weren't getting radio airplay, but we were definitely infiltrating the psyche of American youth.

Touring was usually not a lucrative endeavor for us. After *Freaky Styley,* we each got three grand. But following this tour, Lindy announced that after expenses and including T-shirt sales, we were getting twenty-two thousand.

"To split?" I asked.

"No, we each get twenty-two thousand," Lindy said.

That was a quantum leap in finances for us, so my first order of business was to get a nice place to live for my angel girlfriend and me. But every time I'd go look at a place, they'd hand me a long application. I thought I could just fork over some dough and the house would be mine, but every landlord was asking for me to list my last five residences, along with my last five places of employment. Okay: The last place I lived was with my girlfriend's mother, before that was my manager's couch, before that a squat in Pasadena, before that I was homeless, before that it was another girlfriend's mother, before that it was Flea's sister's bed, before that a house that didn't have a door. My references weren't looking too good. They'd ask for bank-account numbers and credit cards, but I didn't even own a checkbook then. All I had was twenty-two thousand dollars in cash.

Eventually, I went to see a two-bedroom house on Orange Drive. It was a '30s triplex, very art deco, with wood floors and an old tiled bathroom. It was paradise. And it was a thousand dollars a month. After I inspected the place, the Russian landlord handed me an application, but I gave it right back to him.

"I can't fill this out. It doesn't work for me," I told him.

"Then you can't have the house." He shrugged. "Get out of here."

I pulled out a shoe box with five thousand dollars in cash. "This is the first five months' rent. If you don't like me after five months, then kick me the hell out," I offered.

He looked at the five grand. "The house is yours," he said.

So I had our dream house, and I still had a lot of money. I decided to celebrate my new acquisition with the yin/yang of drug use—a nice pile of heroin and cocaine. Once again, I started speedballing like a maniac. There was no furniture in the house, and I didn't even know how to get the electricity turned on in my name, so I went out and bought five watermelons and dozens of candles. I cut the watermelons in half the long way, and set them all over the floor of the house and shoved candles into their cores. So now the entire house was a sea of halved watermelons and candlelight. I inaugurated the bathroom by shooting up a ton of coke and dope.

I picked up Ione and brought her back to our dream house. She looked a little skeptical, especially because there were mad streaks of blood down both of my arms, and my eyeballs were spinning around in my head.

"I'm with you, we're in this together, it's going to be okay, but my mom is not having this," she said. "In fact, she's on her way down here right now."

"Baby, don't you worry about a thing. I'll handle the mom. This is my forte," I said. "They always told me I should have been a lawyer. Watch me work."

Enid pulled up in front of the house, and I marched out into the street, my shirt covered in blood, with crazy eyes and matted hair. She got out of her car and stood under the streetlight with her arms crossed, just beside herself.

"Enid, it's going to be okay," I reassured her. "I love your daughter with all of my heart. I would die for your girl. She's my baby, and I'll take care of her as good as you did."

She looked at the blood and then at me. "But you have a problem. You're not well."

"Enid, trust me. This is a passing phase," I said.

Enid was peeking past me into the house and staring at the watermelons and candles, probably convinced this was some sort of Satanic ritual sacrifice of the virgin. But somehow, in the midst of this debauched debacle, I was able to come to some state of clarity and convince Enid that things were going to be okay. I sent her home and kept her daughter, and we started our life together in that house.

The band's suspicions that we were moving to another level of popularity were confirmed when KROC asked us to play a daytime promotional show at the Palamino in the Valley, a classic old-school, beer-drinking, barroom-brawling cowboy venue where people like Linda Ronstadt and the Eagles had played on their way up. The day of the show, we drove to the gig and were within a half a mile of the venue when we got caught in a massive traffic jam. It was like the Rose Bowl Parade. Traffic was stopped, and there were cops on horseback, and we were indignant because we had to get to our show. Then we realized that all the traffic was from people converging on the Palomino for *our* show. Between the power of KROC and the celebrated sons of the moment returning from their tour, we had stopped traffic.

I must have gone on a pretty serious dope bender around this time, because in pictures of me from that show, I was frighteningly thin. Mario had reentered my life, and I was back to borrowing Ione's car and going on runs with him. One day, in the midst of an outing, we were running out of money, so he suggested that we go deeper into the jungle of downtown, where the drugs were stronger and less expensive. We piled into Ione's Toyota and drove down to skid row, where 90 percent of the people on the street looked like extras from *The Night of the Living Dead*. Even though it was broad daylight, Mario and I looked like an unlikely duo to be rolling through those streets. I had taken all of my drugs and syringes and spoons and put them up under the driver's-side visor of the car. Mario was in the passenger seat, scanning the streets like a computer for the right guy. I was driving cautiously, but all of a sudden, I saw a cop car in the rearview mirror. I alerted Mario, and he told me to make a left, so I dutifully put on the signal, got in the proper lane, and made the turn. The cops kept following us.

"Pull over by this alley," Mario said. As soon as I got near the curb, he opened the door and bizalted right out of the car. Now the cops were coming out of their car toward me.

"Who's your friend there?" the first cop said.

I tried to stay calm. "Uh, that's Flaco. Just a guy I know."

"Well, do you know your friend Flaco there is an escaped convict and on the most-wanted list?" the other cop said.

Next thing I knew, I was under arrest for being in the company of an escaped felon. Luckily, they didn't search the car, but they did put me in the back of their patrol car, and we started canvassing the neighborhood for "Flaco." Sure enough, they drove down some alleyway, and there he was. He looked at me like I had ratted him out, but when he got in the car with me, I made it clear that I hadn't said nothing to nobody. They took us to jail and separated us. They interrogated me, but I told them nothing, so they returned me to this glass-enclosed cell that was about as big as a large couch and stuffed with other prisoners. I was sitting there bemoaning my fate when I got a visit from the FBI.

"FBI? I don't even know this guy. I was just giving him a ride and—"

"Don't talk so much," the fed cut me off. "We're here to take pictures of your teeth."

Apparently, I fit the description of the Ponytail Bandit, a white kid who had successfully knocked off dozens of Southern California banks. Finally, a forensic dentist arrived and stuck his damn fingers in my mouth and turned to the agent and said, "This is not the guy."

They transferred me to the Glass House, the downtown L.A. County jail. It was a hellhole. By now my drugs were wearing off, and I hadn't slept in days and was feeling raw and empty and nervous. On arrival, they told me I'd have to undergo the old strip-down and bend over, spread my butt cheeks, lift up my nut sack, peel my foreskin back, full-body check, because they didn't know how long I was going to be in there and they didn't want me keestering in goods. The only problem was that they had just passed a new law that stipulated if you had track marks on you, you'd have to do a ninety-day mandatory sentence. And I had some track marks. So on my way to the full strip search, I started talking to the cop about to search me. I began to empathize with him, telling him I understood how rough it was being a cop, and he told me about his family, and we related as two humans for a minute. He asked me what I was doing downtown, and I told him that I was trying to get back in college and get my life together, just lying my ass off, trying to make friends with him. As soon as I took off my shirt, he looked amazed.

"Holy Toledo, look at your arms! You know that's a ninety-day mandatory," he said. I just laid on the bullshit about how I'd be fired from my job and I couldn't get back in college and I had to support my mom, who was disabled.

"Put your shirt on and keep your arms covered the whole time you're in here," he said.

After I'd spent the next few harrowing hours in a big dormitory room with fifty other inmates, a guard came into the cell and told me I could leave. Waiting for me in the corridor was Lindy.

"You motherfucker, I called you at nine this morning. It's nine at night! What took you so long to get me out of here?" I screamed.

"Well, Swanster, I got some advice from some of the other guys, and everyone seemed to think maybe it was a good idea if you chilled out in here for a minute and got some idea of where your life was going," he said. "It really wasn't my thinking. My thinking was if I was in there, I'd want to get out, but they said, 'Maybe if we let him sit in there for a little while, it'll help.'"

"Look, motherfucker, you better give me forty dollars, because that's not brotherly, leaving me in there like that," I said.

"Whoa, forty dollars? Swanster, I don't know if I should do that," Lindy said.

"That's the least you could do. If you don't give me the forty, I'm going to be sick," I warned. He gave me the money and drove me to a place where I could cop.

While my drug use remained blatant enough to send me to the Glass House, Hillel was battling his own demons in private. Whereas before, we'd be together or there'd be girls involved, a whole party atmosphere, now it was more reclusive and isolated. There was a dark feeling to it. He was going off into a more constant and necessary use of heroin and cocaine, while I was becoming more of a periodic binger. I'd go ballistic for a week, and people always murmured and rumored and gossiped and spoke behind my back about how I'd be the first person they knew who'd die of drugs. Every now and then, even Hillel would come to me and say, "Dude, don't kill yourself. Look at you, you're close to death." Ione was terrified, telling me, "Please don't die. I can't handle it."

That winter the band embarked on our first proper European tour. London was our first stop. Come the night of the show, Hillel was too sick to leave his room. Flea and I went to his room, and it was incredibly sad to see him losing the battle with this darkness. He didn't have that look in his eye that said, "Yeah, I'm losing, but I'm going to fight this thing through." Instead, he was wailing, "I can't do this. I'm dying here."

We convinced him to come to the club, and we took the stage and went into our trademark sizzling beginning, but Hillel was not part of what was happening. We tried playing another song, and Hillel stopped and mumbled to me, "I can't do this," and left the stage. I looked over at Flea and Jack and said, "Do something," and then I ran backstage, where Hillel was slumped over, crying into his hands.

"Hillel, you can do this. Get your fucking guitar and come back."

"No, I can't," he moaned. "Cancel it. It's over."

I ran back onstage, and we proceeded to play an entire set of a very rhythmic bass-and-drums-and-vocal thing. We started breaking out the jokes and the banter and the one-liners, and no one left, no one booed, people just went back to dancing and jumping around, but it was obviously the weirdest show we'd ever played, because there was no guitar. A couple of days after that, Hillel was fine, and he and I were back to joking about keeping an eye out for suspicious-looking characters who might be able to hook us up with a little of the downtown.

Somewhere in Europe, a car full of Dutch weirdos showed up. They were there to document our tour. They had a lot of great behind-the-scenes tumult to capture, especially when Jack entered a totally manic phase of his life. He had been an extremist when it came to love, maybe because he was a late bloomer in that arena. Once he latched on to a girl, she meant everything to him. He had been in this tight union with a woman, and while we were in Europe, she left him for a guy we knew. Jack got the horrible news while we were in Berlin. After the show, I scored a bunch of coke and went to a club and wound up making out in a bathroom stall with this beautiful German girl who didn't speak a word of English. After a while, Flea and Lindy had left, and I was all alone there with this girl, gacked out of my mind. I was willing to go at it right in that stall, but she wanted to take me home, and I wanted to get some coke, so we met a dealer who fronted me a bunch of drugs.

The next morning everyone was boarding the bus to go to the next venue when I pulled up in a big black Mercedes limo, accompanied by the drug dealer, a big, burly guy. He grabbed me, held me like a toddler, and marched me over to Lindy and told him that he was in possession of my passport and wouldn't give it back until Lindy paid for the blow I'd done the night before. No one was too happy that Lindy had to spend band money to bail me out.

During all of this tumult, poor Jack was out in the middle of the lawn surrounding the hotel, literally banging his head repeatedly on a tree.

"What's wrong with Jack?" I asked Flea.

"His girlfriend's left him, and he doesn't know what to do," Flea said.

We were still at a level where we were intimately connected to the audience. People would come backstage to meet us after the show, and we'd hang with them and even go back to their houses and check out their record collections. They were loving us and appreciating us and willing to give us the shirts off their backs, though we were still like one of them. It becomes so much different when you pull up in a tour bus, go through a back door of a giant building, go backstage, take the stage, go back off, and get back in the bus. There's no connection with the street or the local culture. We used to invite the whole audience back to our hotel. That was one of our ongoing jokes. I'd say, "There's a party in room

206 at the Finkelstein Hotel on Rotterwheel Avenue." That would be Flea's room. And he'd grab the mike and go, "No, no, the party's in 409. 409," which was my room.

Despite Hillel's meltdown and poor Jack starting a long and arduous section of his life, that tour did have many, many happy and magical moments. It's always at the end of a tour that you become this organic vessel. You're tight and it's effortless and you become one heart beating together. But then we flew to New York and played a big college show at NYU. I made a deal with Hillel not to get high before the show, because New York was dope town, but I lost sight of him before the show and when I got backstage, he was high on smack. Flea and I were furious.

"Dude, this is not happening. If you want to do this, do it after," we cajoled him. "Let's play the show and then go party. But you're not capable of doing that." And he wasn't. Hillel was pulling the exact routine that I had been before I got kicked out of the band. And when we got back to L.A., we fired him. Hillel started to miss rehearsals, and Flea was like "Fuck this. Hillel, you're out of the band." We began rehearsing with an ex-Funkadelic guitarist named Blackbird McKnight, whom Cliff had introduced to Flea. Hillel was bummed and sulking but accepting of his fate. We tried it with Blackbird for a few days, but then we decided to give Hillel another chance.

Then we went back to Europe to play a few festivals. We did a huge outdoor show in Finland on the same bill as the Ramones. It was a great show, one big massive orgy of eighty thousand drunken half-naked Finnish people. We rocked this enormous audience, but they weren't there to see us, they were there to see the Ramones. After our show, we all assembled to watch the Ramones, who weren't the most engaging fellows if they didn't know you. They kept to themselves in the backstage area. Before they went on, they went through their entire set in the dressing room with unamplified instruments.

When they went out, we huddled at the side of the stage, and someone came up with the idea of taking off our clothes and running onstage and doing a little dance in homage to the Ramones. Hillel was dead set against it, but Flea and Jack and I stripped down and skanked naked across the stage during "Blitzkrieg Bop." Later that night, I ran into Johnny Ramone and their manager in the lobby of the hotel.

Johnny bitched me out: "Who the fuck do you think you are to get on our stage during our show without your fucking clothes on? That was not cool."

"I'm sorry. We did it because we love you. We didn't mean to interfere with your aesthetic," I apologized. Johnny stormed away, but Joey Ramone, who'd been lingering in the shadows, came up and whispered to me, "Personally, I thought it was kind of cool," and then walked away.

Our next stop was Norway, and on the way to Oslo, we had to take a long train ride. Hillel and I wound up sharing a berth. I always had a deep connection with Hillel. He had that capacity to allow people to go past the barriers of their comfort zone with how much they wanted to reveal to people. I set up those cutoff barriers all the time with my close friends, always reserving 25 percent in a mystery zone. But with Hillel, you were comfortable showing that hidden 25 percent. I bonded with him closer than I ever did to any other male. Maybe part of it was that we shared the sickness of drug addiction. You can't understand the experience of addiction unless you're an addict, too. Hillel and I had that in common, but he also had a capacity for forgiveness that was beyond most mortals'. No matter what you did or what your flaws or failures or weaknesses were, he would never hold them against you. Unlike Flea, who had a real scrapping-brother-type relationship with me, Hillel wasn't competitive. He was paternal in a way. He wasn't a braggart, he wasn't a macho guy. He prided himself on being a man, but not in a macho way.

Hillel and I sat in that train berth, looking out at the scenery whizzing by, and talked about everything. A lot of what we talked about was drugs and heroin, and where we were with our addiction, and what we wanted to do about it. We were still pretty clueless as to the nature of the disease. I had a little more experience with meetings than Hillel. That spring Kim Jones had gotten clean, and I started to go to meetings with her. I had seen these transformations, people who had lost their will to live, coming back from their zombie states and radiating a new life force from their eyes. I took Hillel to a meeting once, but he hated to admit that he had a problem, he hated to admit that somebody could help him, and he was generally shy of crowds. After that I could never get him to a meeting again.

On the train, we agreed that the band was going really well, and we vowed to make a concerted effort to stop the drugging. In the next breath, we joked about Oslo being the heroin capital of Scandinavia. That was an ongoing thing with us. Whatever town we were in, it would become the heroin capital of the world.

I could see that neither of us was committing to anything positive. It was more like "Let me get high first, and then we'll see." I think we were sitting in the midst of a dark spirit, and we had to take the power away from that darkness and carry on as friends and bandmates. We both realized that we were at a point in our life when it was do or die.

We played Oslo and then flew back to L.A. We landed at the airport, gave one another a hug, and it was "Great tour, great being with you." "Call me in a few." "I'll be good. You going to be good?" "Yeah, I'll be good, too." We said good-bye. And then both Hillel and I made a beeline for our individual dealers. You probably could have set a stopwatch to see who copped first. I went home, checked in with Ione, and was off and running on a terrible, painful speedballing binge.

I was downtown and realized that all this time had melted off the clock, way more than I had planned. So I decided to come home and at least be with Ione, because unlike Jennifer, she would rather I use with her than away from her. She was like a little Mother Teresa. I'd come back from these long, terrible binges, and instead of her wanting to kill me or make me feel worse, she'd say,

"You have to eat. Come and lie down on the couch. You're not going anywhere. Give me your keys." She would cook me a healthy meal, and I'd cry and apologize. I'm not saying it was a healthy relationship, but it was different. God bless her for having that kind of unconditional love and compassion toward her junkie-ass, selfish bastard boyfriend.

I was on my way home and stopped a few blocks from the house to call her from a pay phone. I couldn't just go there and face her, I had to apologize first on the phone. Actually, I didn't even know if I was going to come home, because I was still on a run. When she answered, I said, "Ione, I'm so fucking sorry that this is what I'm doing." She was wailing and sobbing. I was thinking, "This is weird. This is a bigger reaction than I've ever gotten from calling." She was screaming, "Come home right now. Something terrible has happened." I don't think she told me the details, but Hillel's name came up, at which point part of me knew that he might be dead. But I went quickly into a rock-hard state of denial: "She's confused. Maybe he just OD'ed and she thought that must mean he's dead."

It was enough to get my attention. I drove home, got out of my car in a chemical fog, and Ione came running out into the street, half dressed, her face all puffy and red and splotchy and wet. She was screaming, "Your friend Hillel is dead." And she lost it. You would have thought he was her best friend. But she felt all of this pain immediately, whereas I refused to accept it. "There must be some mistake." Deep inside my core, I knew he was gone, but I would not allow myself to accept that then.

The rest is a real blur, because I think I turned off my brain. I know I didn't stop using the rest of that night. I woke up the next day in a state of shock and denial. Everyone was dealing with this huge upheaval, death and aftermath and funerals and people laying blame, and I knew there was never anyone to blame when people get into drugs. They're always responsible for their own behavior, and it's not the dealer, and it's not the friend, it's not the bad influence, it's not the childhood. For some sad and disgusting reason, people associated me with being responsible for Hillel's demise at age twenty-five because my own addiction had started so much younger. His family tried to say I was the bad influence. It was kind of ironic, because I never blamed anyone for my own drug use. And I had tried to introduce Hillel to the idea of getting well.

Meanwhile, I continued to get loaded. It's a myth that something like that scares you into going straight. Even when your close friend dies, you maintain a false sense of invincibility. You don't want to deal with your own wreckage, you just want to keep getting high. I heard from Ione that they were planning the funeral, but I was in no shape to attend. I couldn't stop using, for one thing. I was at my wits' end. I couldn't quit, but I couldn't keep using; nothing was working, and my friend was dead, and I didn't want to look at that. Ione's mom had once mentioned that her friend owned a house in a tiny fishing village in Mexico, and we could use it anytime we wanted. So that's what we did.

People thought it was in poor taste that I didn't go to the funeral. Hillel was my guy, my best friend, but I was dying of the same thing that killed him. And it wasn't about taste. It was about insanity and unmanageability. Ione and I flew to Puerto Vallarta, and from there we took a small outboard motorboat to a place called Yelapa, a small fishing village of about a hundred people. We stayed in a nice house with a bed and a mosquito net, but there was hardly any electricity in the town. I lay there and went through another fucked-up, nasty, cold-turkey heroin kick, while I was light-years away from what was happening in Hollywood. I turned off that station in my mind. Ione was incredibly supportive, and after a few days I started feeling better. I began to exercise, and we went back to having sex and sharing this love. We caught fish in the ocean and cooked on the beach, and I developed a false sense of wellness. After ten days, my hiding had to end, and we went back to L.A.

The minute I got back, I couldn't get high quick enough. I didn't know what the fuck else to do. By now I was down to about ten grand to my name, and I was out of game. I went out and bought a bunch of heroin and coke. While Ione was asleep in bed, I was on the floor shooting up and doing some inane art project all night long. But something had gone drastically wrong with my chemistry, because I was putting these drugs in me and wasn't getting high, I wasn't disappearing, wasn't escaping, not feeling euphoric, not blocking out the pain, not blocking out the reality. I kept doing more and more and more, but I was right there. I couldn't escape myself.

Right around then, Jack Irons called a band meeting. He'd never done anything like that before. We met on Lindy's modest sailboat, and Jack sat us down and said, "This is not where I want to be. I do not want to be part of something where my fucking friends are dying." He quit the band. And we understood.

Lindy was probably thinking, "What's going to happen here? The guitar player's dead, the drummer's quitting, the singer's hanging by a fucking thread. What happens now?" But Flea and I did not plan on stopping playing music together. It wasn't out of lack of respect; it was out of respect. This was something that Hillel had helped build, and we were going to keep on building it, which was weird, because I was in no great mental shape. But I knew that it was what I wanted to do, and Flea knew that it was what he wanted to do. And Jack knew that it was what he didn't want to do.

Even though I was a mess, Flea and I hunkered down. We hired D. H. Peligro to play drums and Blackbird McKnight to play guitar. We had known D.H. for years, and at one point Flea, D.H., and I had a joke band called the Three Little Butt Hairs. We had played with Blackbird when Hillel was temporarily fired, so we were comfortable with him. But before we could even think about playing, I had to do something about my drug problem.

When I was going to meetings that spring, I'd met a guy named Chris who was a young and crazy, skirt-chasing, mischief-making, sensible, funny guy. He had introduced me to a guy named Bob Timmons and said, "This guy could be your sponsor." Timmons was a bearded guy with tattoos who had a pretty hard-core past, but I immediately trusted him. He was quiet and not pushy, and he didn't seem to want anything from me.

After one of those drug runs when I couldn't get loaded, I called up Bob Timmons. "I don't know what to do. My friend is dead. I can't stop using, and it's not even getting me high. I'm fucking going crazy."

"Why don't you go into rehab?" he suggested.

"That sounds horrible. What is it?"

"For one thing, it's ten thousand dollars."

"Ten grand! That's all I have," I said.

"I think it would be a good investment," Bob said. "I think your life is at stake, and maybe one day you'll be able to make another ten grand if you spend ten grand now. If you don't, that might be the last ten grand you ever know."

I didn't know what else to do, so I agreed. The rehab was a place in Van Nuys called ASAP. I got in the car with Ione to drive out there, and I was so infuriated that I was trying to drive the car into the tarmac. I zigzagged all the way down Van Nuys, into oncoming traffic, and Ione was cowering in the passenger seat. I was mad that I had to check in to rehab, I was mad that I couldn't get loaded anymore, I was mad that my friend had died. We got there, and I checked in, and they took a Polaroid of me. I was not looking real good. My skin was green and orangey yellow, my eyes were dead, and my hair had a life of its own.

Then I was assigned a room. And a roommate. I was sharing a damn room with some other crazy bastard. He turned out to be this kid from Palm Springs who became my first sober rehab buddy. When you go to rehab, you end up meeting people from dozens of walks of life, all races, different financial realities, different religious backgrounds, but you end up loving all of them and seeing yourself in all of them. There was a female basketball player who couldn't stop smoking crack, a Brazilian businessman, a doctor, and a black SWAT team cop who busted people to get their drugs.

I settled in, and it wasn't that bad. I stopped hating and started just being. My whole life, I had been the most defensive person you'd meet, unable to tolerate any criticism. But now I started listening and being. Ione came to visit, and we broke the rules and had conjugal visits in the bathroom, which meant the world to me. I was so in need of some love and affection.

From time to time, Bob Timmons would send different random sober people to visit me. I didn't know any of them, but I'd sit down to talk to them, and therein lay the magic of recovery. No one will ever really understand your predicament better than another addict. This stranger came and talked with me, and the next thing I knew, the process of recovery was happening whether I liked it or not.

About two weeks into my time there, Bob Timmons came to visit. He'd seen that I had avoided going through the grief of Hillel's death, so he told me that he was going to take me out on a day pass. We drove to the Jewish section of Forest Lawn Cemetery and wandered around until we found Hillel's gravesite. There was a humble plaque in the grass, not even a tombstone. The inscription was something simple like "Hillel Slovak. Devoted son, brother, friend, musician."

I was sitting there with Bob, saying, "Yep, okay, there he is. I guess we did that. Can we get out of here now?"

"No, I don't think we should leave quite yet," Bob said. "I'm going to take a walk. Why don't you do me a favor and talk to Hillel and tell him how you feel about him dying? And why don't you also make him a promise right now that you're not going to put another needle in your arm and that you're not going to drink and use?"

"Talk to what? It's a plot of grass with a rock on it," I said.

"Just act as if Hillel is here listening and have that conversation," he said, and walked away.

I was sitting there feeling really awkward about talking to

no one. But then I said, "Yo, Slim," which was the way I'd always greet Hillel. And it was like this wall came down in a second. I started weeping like I'd never wept before. From that point on, I was a waterfall of blabbering and blubbering and crying and coughing. I had this talk with Hillel and told him how much I loved him and how much I missed him. And then I made him the promise. "I'm clean. I'm in this rehab. I promise you I'm not going to put a needle in my arm again. I'm going to stay clean." I cried all the way out of that cemetery.

Early on in my stay at rehab, we had a group meeting, run by a counselor who was this big semi-biker-looking dude. He'd been clean for five years. He got thirty patients into the room, everyone who was part of the class that month. Everybody was listening intently, because we were all giving it our best shot. He said, "I've got some pretty unfortunate news for you people right now. Statistically speaking, only one person in this room is going to stay clean for any length of time after you get out of here. That's just usually what it boils down to." I looked around that room and saw the basketball player, and the cop, and the businessman, and the doctor, and the criminal, and all these people, and I was like "They can all go home right now, because I'm taking that slot. So you guys can save your money and your time, because I'm the one who's going to be sober from now on."

No fifty-day celebrations, no wiggle room, I just vowed to give everything up. There wasn't any single moment of bedazzling revelation, it was more of an educational process. The more I learned about the nature of addiction, the more I was willing to look at my own behavior and history. And the more I was able to help the people I was in there with, the more it all made sense. A lot of this process came through witnessing the sickness of these people I was in rehab with, for me to see these people and care about them, and to know how slim their chances were of ever changing the demonic possession they had been living with. I realized this was not the jail I wanted to live my life in.

When I made the decision that no matter what happened in

my life, I was not drinking or using, this gorilla that had been beating me down for years evaporated. By the time I walked out of rehab, I didn't even want to get high. I turned off that voice in my head, which was wonderful, except it was almost too wonderful. I wasn't compelled by that pain anymore to keep working toward getting better and putting myself in a position where I could help someone else get better. I was so relieved of the pain of wanting to get high that I was able to coast and skate a little bit. I still went to meetings, and I showed up on panels and went to hospitals and talked to other alcoholics, but I didn't dive into this incredible opportunity of instigating a true psychic change. I went halfway and then started backing off.

When I checked into ASAP, I wanted to die. Thirty days later, it was "Let's rock. Let's go write songs. Let's go be a band." And we did. Flea was excited and supportive when I got out of rehab. We went right into rehearsals with D.H. and Blackbird. D.H. seemed to fit right in—he was fun-loving and absolutely lived to play music. Blackbird had a harder time fitting in. He was a uniquely talented guitar player, but he'd never been in a band where everyone rocked together. He was used to George Clinton giving him some tape and then going into a studio by himself and working for days on his parts.

We had been friends with D.H. for years, but Blackbird was harder to get close to. He was a little older and a little kookier. The more we played together, the more obvious it became that it was not clickety-click-clicking. Our idea of working on new material was always the jam, and it wasn't happening.

Around that time, D.H. introduced Flea to a young guitar phenom named John Frusciante. John was a Chili Peppers fanatic who had been going to our concerts since he was sixteen. In fact, I had met John before Flea did. Around the time *Uplift* came out, we were playing a big show at Perkins Palace in Pasadena. I was still struggling with my addiction, and I had to do a little bit of smack before the show, to get right. I drove to the gig and parked a few blocks away and walked through a park adjacent to the venue to find a place to shoot up. Just then, two fresh-faced kids walked up to me and gushed, "Oh my God. Anthony. We just want to say hi. We're huge fans of the band."

I chatted with them for a while, and then I walked across the park and sat down on the first staircase I could find and cooked up some dope. Then I looked up and saw that I was shooting up on the steps of the Pasadena police department.

After John had impressed Flea so much, I started hanging out with him. At the same time, Bob Forrest was all over John to play guitar in his group, Thelonious Monster. John told me he was going over to Bob's garage to audition, so I drove him there. In my mind, he was auditioning for the Red Hot Chili Peppers. One song into his performance, I knew this was our guy.

Now it was my turn to do the firing. Blackbird lived in South Central L.A., so I decided to do it on the phone. "Blackbird, this is Anthony. I've got bad news. I'm really sorry, but it's not working out, and we can't be in a band with you. We're going to go in a different direction. Thank you very much for everything."

"You motherfucker," Blackbird said.

"What?"

"You motherfucker."

"C'mon, Blackbird, it's not me. It's the situation. I'm just the messenger here," I said.

"You motherfucker. I am going to burn down your house."

"Blackbird, don't burn down my house," I said. "It's a band decision. It didn't work out. It's not us or you. It's just the situation."

"All right, all right. I accept," Blackbird said. "Just so long as you can accept that I'm going to burn down your house."

That was the end of our conversation. I was a motherfucker, and he was going to burn down my house.

Not everything made perfect sense for us the minute John joined the band. But what did instantly change was the chemistry. There was a wholeness to the love of being in the Red Hot Chili Peppers, which we hadn't felt for a long time. Here was this young man who had dedicated every waking moment in his young life to music, and you could feel that. As inexperienced as John was, we were getting everything he had to offer. It was just better chemistry. D.H. and John were friends. We now had a group in which we were coming from the same place and wanted to go to the same place. It was pretty exciting, but it would still take a long time to gel.

Instead of trying to make a record immediately, we decided we should just play for a while, write some songs and rehearse some old ones, take time to become a real band. We ran into some obstacles. D.H. was an unbridled wild mustang of enthusiasm, but Flea was a perfectionist for accuracy and diligence when it came to learning songs. D.H.'s forte was not necessarily that. Flea was riding D.H. pretty hard, being sort of a dictator when it came to that, which he was no stranger to because he had been the dictator in other configurations of the band. It was "Come on, let's make sure we get this done. Don't be lazy, and don't forget to do your homework, and make sure you learn your parts."

Some tensions developed between D.H. and me as well. Once I got sober, I had the audacity to think that everyone else should follow my lead. "Okay, world, the party's over. I don't know if you noticed, but I'm sober now, so close up Bolivia, and everyone put down their drugs and alcohol." My controlling nature and my insecurities continued, so my ability to make other people feel bad in order to deal with my own not feeling good continued. On some level, D.H. must have realized that his drinking and using could become an issue. He started showing up late, and not always in the clearest frame of mind. My level of tolerance and patience and acceptance of another man's difficulties was not a flourishing element in my own personality then, unfortunately. I wasn't exactly clashing with D.H., but I was brooding that now I had somebody else's unmanageable behavior in my band.

While we were rehearsing, I started a cautionary song

called "Knock Me Down." It was a song that described what it was like to be a drug addict, to have that ego and to think you were impenetrable and impervious to the forces of nature and life. But it also was a love song for Hillel. I had pages and pages of verses but no melody or organization. John had come to me right after he joined the band and told me that I could show him anything and we could write together. One of the first things I showed John was "Knock Me Down." I warned him that it was very verbose.

"Oh, that's okay. I've been working on this really verbose melody, and I can see how it's going to apply exactly to these words," he said. He sat there, studied the lyrics, and started smushing them into his melody. It was uncanny. In a few minutes, he had a complete verse melody. This was a real epiphany: "Okay, here's another way songs can be written." Even when Hillel was there, everything we wrote was in a group context. Flea and I had written songs together, but it was different on the bass. Now I felt that I could write anything—a melody, a rhythm, a lyric—and go to this new friend of mine and sit down, and when we left that session, we'd have a song. I felt like anything was possible with this kid. I could show him my most sentimental writings, and he didn't stop to judge them once. There was no moment when he read the lyrics to see if he liked them or if they were something he wanted to do. Whatever I'd written had to be a song. Now I didn't have to second-guess myself or be afraid to show something or try something new, which opened up the avenue for writing songs and making cool music.

John and I started to slowly but surely become the kind of friends who would spend every single day together and then go home and call each other to say good night before going to bed. When we woke up, it was "Good morning, what are we doing today?" After a while we didn't go anywhere or do anything without doing it together, which is a rare and valuable but sometimes too intense experience. Though John had gone through a period of cocaine and alcohol abuse, he was clearly willing to sacrifice getting loaded to focus on being in the band.

He was living near Canter's with his girlfriend, but when we went out to parties and clubs, she started resenting that this guy in the new band was whisking him away from the routine of their relationship. Ione had no problem with that, she was doing great, working a lot. But John ended up breaking up with his girlfriend shortly after he joined the band.

We decided that it would be a good idea to break in the new band at obscure, off-the-beaten-path venues, so Lindy booked a tour that we called the Turd Town Tour. It was a disaster. We played holes in the wall in cow towns in Wyoming and northern Colorado and Utah. Nobody in these Turd Towns cared enough about us to show up, and when they did, it was a real rodeo crowd. Unfortunately, D.H., bless his heart—sweetest guy in the universe—was drinking quite heavily, and he wasn't at his sharpest for these shows.

One night on that tour, D.H. was dropping the beat, forgetting parts, not so clear on the songs. After the show, he and I had a huge confrontation.

"Look, if you want to be in this band, you're going to have to do something about your condition. It's either do something or bow out," I told him. Flea and John were both backing off, going, "We're not sure what to do here. Anthony's being kind of a jerk, but the fact is, D.H. *is* fucked up, and he isn't really carrying his weight in the band." They didn't want to side with me because I was being such a teetotaling killjoy, but they knew it wasn't working out with D.H., either.

When we got home, it went from bad to worse. He started to miss rehearsals, and his addiction started consuming him. Every other time we'd fired someone, with the exception of that bizarre Hillel thing, it had always been obvious and necessary, and without a doubt for the betterment of the band. But D.H. was our friend whom we loved and cared about and didn't want to see anything bad happen to. Still, it wasn't salvageable. Unluckily for Flea, it was his turn to do the firing. It was worse than we could have imagined. Flea had to stay in bed for days after firing D.H. The only beautiful thing about it was, years later, I got to be a huge part of D.H.'s sobriety and his rebirth into the universe as a human, because from the moment he was fired, he went on a crash course of deceleration into a whole other level of unbelievable abuse.

By now we had moved into a rehearsal space in Glendale. It was there that we began the process of auditioning drummers. We assumed that all of the greatest drummers in the land would come marching in from near and far to have this opportunity. Looking back, it wasn't as brilliant an opportunity as we saw it. Everybody and his grandmother did start coming through that door with a set of drums, but not too many of them were any good. During the process, a friend of ours, Denise Zoom, called up Flea and told him that she had a drummer for us. According to her, this guy Chad Smith was the best drummer she'd ever heard, and he ate drums for breakfast. Anytime someone calls you up out of the blue talking about some dildo from the Midwest who eats drums for breakfast, you're like "Save me the time, please."

But we let this guy come down and audition. We were waiting and waiting for him to show up, and he was late. I went outside to see if anyone was there, and I spied this big lummox walking down the street with a really bad Guns N' Roses hairdo and some clothes that were not screaming "I've got style." I had already decided against the guy, based on how he looked, but he came in and we were all business. "There are the drums. Get ready to play. You've got ten minutes. We're going to jam for five, and then we're going to try a song or two for five." Chad was not in the least bit intimidated by all this attitude we were giving him. Every other poor bastard who had sat down at the drums would look over at Flea, who would launch into an aggressive, hard-core, slapping funk-rock bass line, and the drummer would fall over himself trying to follow. Flea would wash them away with his intensity.

Flea started playing something hard, complicated, fast, and awkward to see if the guy could follow. Chad instantly not only matched him but started leading him and taking him for a ride. He overaggressed Flea, and did it with finesse, and did it some more and some more and some more. We couldn't believe what was happening. I was so turned around from my initial impression of this guy that I started laughing hysterically. Now Flea was looking at him like "Whoa, what do I do? Where do I go? What the hell's happening here?" Chad wasn't stopping for a second to let Flea catch up and figure it out. He was screaming like Art Blakey did behind the drums, when you're getting your gusto up for the moment, because there was a lot of energy being released at that moment between Flea and him.

It was a big eruption of sound and energy, and all I could do was laugh hysterically, howling at this fucking guy with the bandanna and the puffy hair-spray hair and the bad Venice Beach muscleman shorts, thinking how funny was this that the goofiest guy we'd ever seen blew all of us away right in our own rehearsal studio. It was genius, and everyone loved it.

We all knew that Chad was the guy, and now we wanted to see what his level of commitment was. We also wanted him to change his look. We said to him, "Okay, you're good. You can be in the band if you shave your head today. Show up later at Canter's with your head shaved, and you have the job." Chad said, "Whoa, whoa, a shaved head. I don't know."

"The choice is yours. Shave your head and be in the band. Don't shave your head and don't be in the band." And we went to Canter's and waited for him. He showed up with the same bandanna and stupid hair.

"Dude, do you want this job or not?" we asked.

"Yeah, I'm going to play in the band, but I'm keeping the hair," he insisted, and we conceded. We realized that anybody who was bold enough to stand his ground in the face of all that pressure was not going to be a bitch. Later on, we found out that the real reason he didn't want to shave his head was because his hair was receding and he was hiding that behind the bandanna. Either way, it was another important day in our history, because now we had a drummer who was reliable and an awesome person to jam with. Now we could get down to work.

9.

Refourming

Because John was so young and inexperienced, he came in for a lot of good-natured ribbing. He was a kid who'd spent most of his young life holed away in his room, practicing his guitar, so everything about being in a rock band was new to him. Flea and I used to continually tease him, calling him "Greenie" or "The Green Man" or "The Green Hornet." Years later, John confessed to me that all this ribbing made him incredibly self-conscious, but at the time, we had no idea of the effect we were having on him.

Flea and I didn't consciously want to make him feel bummed out or insecure; that was just the playing ground of our comedy. The litany of green names spoke of something else—a huge sign of affection. You're in our graces and in our hearts if you have more than one nickname. All that Green stuff was because we loved this kid and we were so happy to have his creative energy in our lives. If we did it with a smirk and a poke, maybe it was just to *not* show how much we cared about him. If you look at it like "Whose phone number are you dialing the most and whose house are you going over to the most and who are you sharing the most experiences with," it was clear I was completely in admiration of this young man.

John and I recently talked about the fact that when things wouldn't go my way, I'd ignore him. "Okay, this guy's acting in a way that I can't appreciate and, without him having any idea, affecting my sense of well-being, so I'll ignore him until the feeling goes away." It wasn't a healthy or communicative way of dealing with stuff, but you have to remember that John went from being a seventeen-year-old unrecognizable kid to being in the Red Hot Chili Peppers. He was equally, if not more, abusive to the people around him. He was a pretty crass fellow for about a year there. I had people coming to me constantly, going, "Your guitar player is a fucking dick. He fucked this girl and then threw her out in the street in the middle of the night and told her to never come back." I never saw him acting like that, so I defended him. I was willing to accept the fucked-up aspects of his personality because he was young and going through a rough transition.

Chad wasn't getting renamed every day because we weren't as close to him. He stayed very much a man unto himself within this band. He had a whole different way of dealing with being the new guy, and that was "I don't need them, I don't want them, I've got my own life." He never showed any signs of needing to be in our inner circle. He would rather run with his own kind, which was a different breed of person than either Flea or me. Chad showed us very little of who he was and where he was coming from and what he was thinking. Just to give an example, he's been in this band since 1988, and it wasn't until the end of 2003 that I found out when Chad left Michigan to come to L.A., he was heading to Hollywood to become a handsome leading man. We never sat down and had the heart-to-heart of what his hopes or dreams or fantasies were. Chad shows up to do his job, he's friendly and personable. I considered him one of the weird pillars that held up our fortress when times got rough.

When it came to clothes, his sensibilities were way different from ours, and I used to tease him about it all the time. He'd show up in '80s-looking purple double-breasted suits, and I'd say, "Did you raid Arsenio's closet for that?" He thankfully stopped teasing his hair when he joined the band, but instead of hanging out at a punk-rock dive like Small's with Flea and me, he'd go to the Mötley Crüe bar and wear funny jeans with belts and cowboy boots and play pool and go after rock chicks. People would see him and report to me that he had his hair teased up higher than a girl's, but the next day he'd come to rehearsal wearing a baseball cap. It wasn't that he was a chameleon by nature, he just wouldn't show off all his colors around us.

We found common ground in the music. Even there, his musical sensibility was different, but his energy and passion and the power he had for creating rhythm were unsurpassed. Just about every time we had a rehearsal or a show and he was practicing by himself, I'd rock the mike and sing along, and it always felt exciting and fresh, even when he was playing simple, basic "You've heard that beat before" beats. He wasn't experimental or avant-garde, and he didn't listen to a super-different variety of music, staying pretty much in the rock and pop genre, but what he did was fulfilling nonetheless. We'd never had a drummer who had a supercharged angst battery that never seemed to run low. I shudder to think that we ever would have made him feel unwelcome or unwanted by giving him the same tough-love, boot-camp-style introduction into the band that we gave John, but we did it because we cared about him, we wanted him to be close to us.

We had our new guys and started working. It was weird and difficult at first to develop songs, more so than ever before. Flea was showing up with parts, and John and Chad were trying to find themselves. Michael Beinhorn was throwing in another wrench. There were a lot of days when we had a lot of good ideas, but we didn't know how to craft a song out of all this music that was coming up. It was a lot to expect to pick up where *Uplift Mofo Party Plan* had left off. I think John felt a big responsibility to follow in Hillel's footsteps, though he wasn't trying to replicate Hillel's sound. He had a cleaner, more modern sound. We just needed new songs. When Cliff and Jack Sherman came into the band, we had already written a body of work. Now we had to write an album's worth of new songs.

Slowly but surely, some pretty different-sounding grooves started to develop. The drums had a new über-intensity. Cliff was artistic and creative and intricate, Jack Irons was very much the metronome, but Chad was moving more air than had ever been moved by a drummer, so that was giving us a new vibe. I'd listen to the jams and go home and sit in the kitchen with piles and piles of papers. It never dawned on me that you could write a song with five sentences of lyrics and a chorus. I thought because Flea was busy and the drums were busy and these textures were complicated, I had to do the same thing. When I sat down to write, I wasn't looking for one or two interesting ideas, I wanted a five-page poem to rap. I'd sit there for eight hours at a time, writing songs like "Good Time Boys" and "Subway to Venus" and "Johnny, Kick a Hole in the Sky," where the lyrics go on and on and on. Even my tribute to Magic Johnson was constant wordology. Anything that was hard to say, I was happy to write it.

When it came time to record, we began butting heads with Michael Beinhorn. He had an agenda that, unlike Andy Gill's, had more to do with sound. Michael had a lot of smarts and musical savvy in the studio, but he was also domineering. He wanted John to have a big, crunching, almost metal-sounding guitar tone, whereas before we always had some interesting acid-rock guitar tones, as well as a lot of slinky, sexy, funk guitar tones. John wasn't into it at the time, so there was a lot of fighting between them over tone and guitar layering. It was not a good time for John; he was wrestling with a lot of different behaviors that were making him tense, and Beinhorn was pushy and manipulative. If it wasn't for the Traci Lords porn tapes that were constantly on rotation in the lounge, I don't know if John would have made it through the sessions.

We worked hard on all the songs, but Beinhorn put an extra amount of focus on our cover of Stevie Wonder's "Higher Ground." Flea had been playing that bass line for years, and John and Chad came up with monster parts for the song. Beinhorn went through hell and high water to get John to play the layered sound on that cut. For me, doing the vocals was totally daunting and frustrating and challenging. A song like that was not my forte, but Beinhorn was sure I could sing it, so he kept pushing and pushing me. I know it sounds like a bullshit whine, but when you're in front of that damn vocal mike and you're having a hard time, your insides start to hurt. It took me forever to get that song. But it was well worth it. When we got to the choruses, we called all our friends to come down and had a roomful of twenty-five people singing together. Half of them were competent singers, and the other half weren't, but it didn't matter, it still sounded surprisingly good.

I had a great time up until the last few weeks of recording. I was just loving life and feeling so happy to be sober, to be making a record and to have these songs. But Beinhorn and I came to a relationship-ending moment of tension at the end of the recording process, when he wanted me to do ad-libs at the end of "Higher Ground." I couldn't tolerate his direction any longer. He was trying to squeeze something out of me that I wasn't feeling, and we got in a fight and I knew that I was done with him.

We didn't finish that record and say, "This is our best record ever," but I didn't feel bad about *Mother's Milk*. I did feel bad about the album cover. Flea had come up with the title of the album as an homage to Loesha's bodily fluids, which were sustaining their young daughter, Clara. (We can put to rest the rumors that "mother's milk" was a slang reference to heroin.) We went back to our good friend Nels Israelson, who had done the photos on our second and third album covers. I had an old poster from the '60s of Sly and the Family Stone where Sly was holding out his hand and his band was congregated in his palm, and I thought it would be great to be a little person held by a giant. Only in my vision, the giant would be a naked female, and we'd be held near her chest. I brought this concept to the band, and they weren't 100 percent enthusiastic, but I was, so they agreed to humor me. Nels started to audition models for the cover, and because they were taking off their shirts, it had to be a closed set. Unfortunately, I showed up late and he had already decided on a girl. EMI planned to cover up her nipples with some lettering and a flower, but they were definitely part of the featured package. Then we found out that the model was up-tight about the whole concept. I couldn't understand why we couldn't have found a model who was happy to have her tits on a cover.

I started to choose the photos of us that she'd be holding in her hands, and John despised every last photo of himself. He finally let me use one, and I think the cover came out great—it was like four Tom Sawyers being held by this giant naked lady.

The album cover was printed, and her nipples were contrac-tually covered, but EMI printed up a couple hundred posters of her with her nipples exposed. These were for record stores and friends, whatever, and the poster-signing machinery went into ac-tion. This was a period in the life of the band when we were all still pigs and heathens, brash and obnoxiously sexual. I think it was Chad and Flea who wrote some stupid, sophomoric, perverted things on one of the posters, and lo and behold, the model caught wind of the poster and sued the piss out of us. She won fifty thou-sand dollars, which was a huge settlement back then.

Despite the cover tempest, EMI must have heard something in the grooves, because they gave us a budget to make two videos before the album was released. It was odd; we weren't coming off a successful record. *Uplift* had sold about seventy thousand copies, maybe making its money back. But we were happy for the new level of interest and commitment, so we made the videos back to back to accompany the singles from the album. The first was for "Knock Me Down," and Alex Winter played a Chaplinesque vagabond who's paranoid and wanders around a house of horrors, shocked by the psychedelic, morbid images of dead rock stars on the walls. He comes to an all-white room where Flea, John, Chad, and I are rocking out and bouncing off the walls, playing the song.

We shot the "Higher Ground" video on one of the famous old SIR soundstages where the Three Stooges made their movies. We had a full makeup and art department and separate wardrobe people and a huge, huge stage, which was quite a departure. When we shot our "Catholic School Girls Rule" video, Dick Rude's mom catered the shoot. But now we got to dance around and outdo one another jumping off things, so it was a fun video to shoot.

From "Knock Me Down"

I'm tired of being untouchable
I'm not above the love
I'm part of you and you're part of me
Why did you go away?
Too late to tell you how I feel
I want you back but I get real
Can you hear my falling tears
Making rain where you lay
Finding what you're looking for
Can end up being such a bore
I pray for you most every day
My love's with you now fly away
If you see me getting mighty
If you see me getting high
Knock me down
I'm not bigger than life
It's so lonely when you don't even know yourself

That ending is lonely, sad, but true. Those are the feelings you feel when you're out there and enough dark energy possesses you and you think, "Who the fuck am I? What happened to me?" I'm sure that was where Hillel ended up. He so clearly knew who he was and what he wanted early in his life, and he was a determined and hardworking, creative, life-loving guy. By the end, he forgot who he was, which I've seen happen to many people.

"Knock Me Down" was the first single off *Mother's Milk,* and it actually got on the radio. Every now and then Lindy would tell us that a station had added the song, but that didn't really compute. A few months later, on a weekend tour to Washington, D.C., Flea and John and I flagged down a cab in the middle of the nation's capital. We got in and the driver looked at us and said, "Hey, aren't you those guys? What is it, 'Beat Me Up,' 'Slap Me Around,' 'Kick My Ass'? I love that song. You're those guys, right?" That was the first time somebody other than the musical underground had arbitrarily become aware of us.

In September '89, we started a yearlong cycle of touring behind *Mother's Milk.* Another indication of our escalating level of success was our upgrade to a full-fledged tour bus. But we needed the room, because we had so many people on the road. We hired Tree to play horn, but he came up with this cockamamy notion to play an electric hybrid synthesizer that you blew into and produced several different horn sounds. Then we hired Kristin Vygard and Vicky Calhoun as backup singers. Kristin was a full-on character who had been a successful child actor. She was a five-foot-nothing redheaded freckled-faced madwoman who had been a jazz singer on the Hollywood scene. Vicky was a large black woman who had sung backup on "Knock Me Down" and been featured in that video. Besides the band, we had Chris Grayson, our soundman; Mark Johnson, our tour manager; and a new face in the organization, a roadie named Robbie Allen. When we got to England later in the tour, Robbie developed an alter ego, Robbie Rule, who opened our shows for us. With the help of Flea and John, Robbie developed a musical comedy act where he would go onstage and pretend to cut off his dick. It was a sleight-of-hand magic trick; he'd go out with a proper butcher knife that was sharp on one side and extremely dull on the other. Then he'd stretch his dick out, put the knife to it, and subtly turn the knife over so the dull side would be doing no damage to his private parts. Like Bob Forest, Robbie was a tortured musician working as a roadie, so we gave him his moment on the stage. It was a crazy play within a play, and Flea played comedy drums during the act. All the kids in the countryside of England had to endure this dick-slashing before we came on.

Since I was no longer chasing cocaine or alcohol, new entertainments had to be created. Something called The Job spiced up the tedium of being on the road. Since we were playing a lot of college dates, we'd routinely get fed meals at the venues, which consisted of reheated cafeteria food that had been topped with industrial-strength salad dressing. It was hard to tell if that mystery liquid was for garnishing your food or cleaning the floor.

The first job we created was in Canada, where we encountered a super-sized bowl of bacon bits on our dining table. We came up with the idea of collecting some money and challenging Mark Johnson with the job of eating that entire bowl. It turned out Johnson was capable of eating some shit, and he successfully completed his job.

My first job was to eat what appeared to be half a pound of butter brought to our table at a gig. I had three minutes to finish it off and $120 bucks to gain, but I got only halfway through before I had to quit. I thought I could mind-power the job, but my body rejected that much butter. Eventually, Flea, John, Chad, and I realized it was silly to torture ourselves with these jobs when we could torture those around us. Besides, we weren't as much in need of the money as the soundman or a backup singer or the roadie. One night we were backstage at some college in the middle of Pennsylvania, and our hosts brought us some inedible food. The girls had been bugging us for a job, so we took an empty wine carafe and started mixing up various salad dressings and condiments and wound up with a bottle full of green stuff that wouldn't have been out of place in *The Fifty Foot Bug That Ate St. Louis*. Then we selected tiny Kristin, who needed the money, and we all chipped in $180 if she'd drink the entire carafe and keep it down for five minutes. She was such a firecracker times ten about everything that she not only accepted that job but offered to eat some various other foodstuffs if we threw in fifty bucks more. Accepted.

We didn't want to leave Vicki out of this, so we raised some money and gave her the job of eating an entire huge metal container of butterballs. She agreed and sat down and ate that whole bucket like it was whipped cream. Then we all watched Kristin. I would have been projectile-vomiting at the smell of that sludge, but Kristin Zenned out, took the liter of goo, drank it, and then ate the bonus bogus food. Then I got out the old watch and sat with her as she began to sweat, cry, and turn fifteen different colors. But she made it to five minutes, and when that time was up, she calmly got up, turned around, and went into the toilet and it all came flying out of her. At the sound of Kristin's first heave, Vicki lost it and ran to the bathroom, and like two dragsters side by side, they egged each other on. When they returned, the whole meal degenerated into a food fight until a stern matronly cleaning lady came back and chastised us and ordered us to clean up after ourselves, which we did very sheepishly.

The road food was execrable, but a few months into the tour, sex had been added to the menu. That was possible only because I had broken up with Ione in December. I had managed to stay sober by not ingesting drugs, so my body had pretty much healed from all that torturous activity, but my mind still wasn't healthy enough to work out the problems that come up in a relationship. Neither of us adapted after I got sober. I had been the needy, groveling fuckup, and she had been the caretaker who, for whatever reason, loved me and nursed me back to health. When that changed, instead of us both finding a workable, healthier, more sustainable dynamic, we just didn't. I didn't have anybody in my life for whom I was willing to listen to "Dude, you're sober now, but you're acting like a fucking asshole. Work through your steps and take an inventory and see who you are and get better." I was still the jealous, raging, controlling, selfish, bratty kid that I had been, only drug-free.

We became another typical fighting couple, and I knew that our relationship was doomed. There wasn't anything horrible going on between us, but we weren't making each other happy, and we weren't giving ourselves completely to each other. We were fading and fighting, and I think we were both over it, but we were afraid to give each other up, because we were at times tighter than I'd ever been with anybody.

At the end, it was my house, and I said, rather crassly, "Please take your stuff and just get out of here." She argued, "No, no, I don't want to leave. I want to be here with you." That happened over and over again, and on the tenth time, I did the big "Take your stuff and get the hell out of here." She looked at me and said, "I think I will." "Well, do it then. Just take your stuff and keep on walking, little lady," I said. She left the house and never came back.

She moved back in with her mom, and I kept waiting for the pattern to play itself out, when she would come right back a day or so later, but she didn't. I was desperate and lonely and confused, and I wondered why I had told her to leave when I really wanted her to stay. About three days later, I called her up and said, "Isn't this where you come back to the house like all those other times?" She said, "No, no, no, in fact, nope. Actually, I'm never coming back again. I finally agree with you. It's over."

This was right before Christmas. Before I went home to Michigan, I bought Ione an art deco statuette and delivered it to her house. Her mom answered the door. "I've got this gift for Ione," I said. And she said, "You're going to have to leave it on the porch." I thought, "Wow." So I left her gift, and bummed out on the plane ride, and wrote a sad and lonely heartbreak song about it, which never became a full-fledged song, just something to sing to myself. I used to write song mantras to sing to myself and deal with whatever it was I was going through at the moment.

At my mom's house, I was alone for the first Christmas in years. I realized it was over with Ione and that she already had somebody else in her life, so I'd better accept that this was all part of the beauty and the flow and it was time to move on to a new chapter of life and love and adventure. Even still, there was a lot of unfinished business from the relationship. It would take years and years and years before I was even able to understand and cop to all of my lying and insanity and emotional terrorism. I'm glad that I was ultimately able to express that to her and try to make amends for it.

When I got back from Michigan, the band played a big show at the Long Beach Arena, which was filmed for a documentary. In the middle of a backstage interview, the interviewer started asking me about Ione, and I told him we'd had a rough breakup. Just then, John peeked into the camera frame and said, "That's right, ladies and gentlemen. Anthony's a free man, and you know what that means: It's time to fuck." It was John's way of bringing me out of my doldrums, and it was a tactic that we'd both use on the rest of the *Mother's Milk* tour. I might still have had reservations about the easy availability of girls on the road, but they remained theoretical reservations. Sex was once again on the menu.

Once again, it was freely available. In Houston, we were coming off the stage on the way to the bus when I ran into another Marilyn Monroe look-alike. Unlike her New Orleans counterpart, this little Marilyn never broke character. She became my Houston girlfriend, and every time we'd play there, I'd wind up going back to her apartment and having sex, and she'd be in her own private Marilyn movie.

Not all of my road affairs were consummated. We were playing a college show in Kentucky, and I was backstage getting ready to go on when Robbie, our roadie, made a surprise visit to the dressing room.

"Swan, I thought you might like this girl. From what I can tell, this is what you're into," he said. I looked up and saw an absolute princess of a college student, with white skin and black hair. A princess who'd been handcuffed, her hands behind her back, with gaffer's tape.

"Thank you, Robbie, now go away," I said, and proceeded to provide this delightful young girl with explicit directions to my nearby motel for an aftershow rendezvous.

"Oh, no, I was just having fun. I just wanted to say hi," she said in her adorable thick Kentucky accent. "I'm out there with my girlfriend, and I have a boyfriend at home."

"Let's at least hang out. I'm not saying anything has to happen," I countered.

"I don't know if that's possible," she said. "I'd like to be friends with you, but I don't know if he would like that, and I'm loyal to him."

I was looking at her thinking that I would die if I didn't have this girl. There was no way I could continue to tour if I didn't get to know her. She told me she lived with her mom and dad, and somehow I finagled her address out of her.

It was time to go onstage, and we played the show, and as soon as I got backstage, I searched out Robbie. "Where's the girl?" I implored him.

"Brother, I've been looking for her for the past half hour. She's disappeared," he said.

There was no way I was going to let that girl disappear into the Kentucky night. I grabbed a pen and some paper and sat down and wrote her a poetic letter, and then I got some college kid to drive me to her house. It was around midnight, and I found the house and went around the back and started calling her name, but there was no answer. I left the note, along with contact numbers for the next hotels we'd be at, in her mailbox.

A few days later, we were in Chicago, where I met a girl who looked like a '70s starlet with her kinky chestnut-colored full head of hair. She was very free and easy and sweet and obviously sexually enthusiastic, so I took her back to the hotel. I was rooming with John, and I could tell just by kissing and touching this girl that she was one of those hypersensitive live wires who become super-intensified when you touch them anywhere. I told John that I needed to be alone with this girl, and he said that Chad happened to have an extra bed in his room and he was out drinking. John also happened to have an extra key, so I grabbed it and shifted over to Chad's room.

We lay down on the extra bed and took off our shirts and were kissing and touching, and she was unusually responsive. It was all getting ready to go on when I heard what sounded like Clydesdales stomping down the hallway. Before I could react, the door flew open and it was Chad, except it didn't look like Chad, something had come over him. He had some little heavy-metal tramp in tow, and he saw me and screamed, "What are you doing in here, you motherfucker? I'll fucking tear your head off!"

"Whoa, Chad, come on, hey, whoa," I said, but Chad was out of control. He charged me and I jumped over a bed and he followed, knocking over lamps, banging into walls, taking huge swings at me. I told the girl to grab her shirt, but Chad was still diving for me and I was still eluding him.

"What is your problem? Chill out," I said.

"Who let you in my room? I'll kill you," he slurred, and kept taking full haymaker swings at me with hate and vengeance in his eyes, as if I had done something horrible to him, but if you knew the history of our behavior on the road, there was always that give and take with rooms if you ended up with a girl. Finally, the girl and I made a break for the door. It turned out that Chad had drunk a whole bottle of tequila and was in a blackout rage. To this day he has only vague recollections of seeing me in his room.

The girl was very understanding of the whole matter. "Your drummer drank a little too much, I guess," she said. "Let's go somewhere else to be together." We were staying in a lightly traveled, quiet old brick hotel with lots of hallway space, so we curled up next to a radiator in a stairwell and had relations right there. What I didn't know about this girl was that she was not only hypersensitive but also a world-class screamer. At first I thought she was kidding, because I touched her pussy and she started bellowing at the top of her lungs. Every single person in that hotel could hear her clearly, but at that point, there was no stopping.

This went on for some time, and when I got back to my room, John was wide awake. "Jesus Christ, do you realize that every single person in this hotel listened to everything that just happened?" I was touting the virtues of a girl who couldn't control herself on any level when John cut me off.

"If there's ever a time when you're feeling like it would be permissible for all parties involved, I have to experience that," John said.

"Hold your horses there," I said. "We'll see. One never knows."

She wound up coming with me to the next few cities. We parted company in Milwaukee, her hometown.

The next stop on the tour was Cincinnati. Against every odd in the universe, both the Screaming Girl and the Kentucky Girl of My Dreams showed up at the show. At that moment, I had to make a decision, and it's not something I'm terribly proud of, but I called John over and said, "John, can you please take the screaming sensation, because I have to pursue Kentucky." I had no choice. I couldn't imagine having a better sexual partner than the screamer, but as great as the sex was, I had to have Kentucky.

The poor screaming sensation saw what was happening and looked at me like "You motherfucker," but at the same time, she conveyed that she was willing to accept the affection of John, and they went off. We played the show, and then I begged the Kentucky girl to come back to my room to be with me. Luckily, I had my own big room, and we sat there and talked for a couple of hours. I just wanted to be around her and smell her and look at her and touch her hand. She told me she was about to go to graduate school in Massachusetts, and I was making all these mental notes, because I was ready to follow this girl anywhere. Slowly but surely, I got closer to her, and she let me hold her and kiss her. Finally, she allowed us to get into the bed together, but she drew a line in the sand at intercourse.

"Listen, I'll be happy to lie there naked with you, believe me, this is wonderful, I'm just happy to be with you," I gushed. I was thinking that she wanted to cuddle naked, and I felt the hand of God brushing me one more time. We lay there in that bed, in that high-ceilinged old room, and we kissed and touched, and her purring, revving, undulating spiritual motor started humming, and she allowed me to engage her in a very long and wonderful exchange of oral sex. I was stone-cold sober and lying on my back and she was giving me head and there was so much love being exchanged, and she was pouring so much of her heart into that physical expression, that I started to leave my body and was able to look down and see myself lying on a bed with this girl, with her flowing chestnut locks and her beautiful white skin, making love to me. I just watched for a while and then came back down and everything went on and I had the realization that that was the single most beautiful sexual moment of my life to date.

She disappeared after that, and the next time out, when we hit the Massachusetts area, I looked in the phone book and called every school, to no avail. Every time we came anywhere near Boston, I'd be out on the pavement—"Do you know a girl named blah, blah, blah. She looks . . ." Nothing. I called up Kentucky and found people with her last name. "Did you have a daughter who blah, blah, blah . . ." Years later, I found someone who remembered her and told me she had mentioned me once. I never could get with her again, and she meant everything to me. I'm sure she's married with ten kids by now, but you never know. Maybe she'll read this book.

If you are reading this, my Kentucky dream, please skip the next story. Later in the tour, we were playing a gig at a restaurant/disco club in Baltimore. It was a couple of hours before the show, and I was hanging out in my room with John in another old crazy weird classic hotel, when the phone rang. It was Flea, who was rooming with Chad.

"Guys! Guys! You gotta get up to my room right away," he said. "There's some craziness going on up here with some girls. Gotta go. Bye." John and I went running up the stairs and bounded into Chad and Flea's room and were struck by one of the most bizarre sights I'd ever seen.

Chad Smith was sitting on a couch, fully clothed and calm and relaxed. In one hand he had a cooking spatula, and in the other he had a big wooden spoon. There were three girls in the room, two of whom were topless and ample of bosom, dancing on top of a table. One girl actually had one of Chad's shoes tucked under her breast, and the massive weight of her mammary was holding it in place. The other topless girl had a pile of coins that she was balancing on top of her grandiose globes. Chad was sitting there like some weird impresario, alternately spanking the girls with the spatula and tossing coins on top of their chests.

"We want to dance, play us a song," the girls were pleading. There was no stereo in the room, so we broke into a cappella renditions of some of our songs and some Led Zeppelin covers. We were running around the room singing songs to two girls whose asses were pinkened by the marks of a spatula. One thing led to another, and John and I both wound up in the bathroom with the two topless girls, who had become naked girls. John was standing in the bathtub, and I was sitting in the sink, and we had a fevered little sex party. What's amazing was that the girls were so nonchalant about it, making small talk while they blew both of us. John and I looked at each other and shrugged. "Whoooaa, Baltimore. Who knew?"

By the time we got to Japan in January, not only were we all getting along, we were also starting to feel like a real band. We played a warm-up gig in Nagoya, then picked up momentum in Osaka. After the show, the promoter took us all out to a Japanese sushi feast, where Mark Johnson won a job by downing the largest ball of leftover wasabe. By now I had made the observation that Japanese girls were much more reserved and not as overtly sexual as their American or European counterparts. Normally, we'd all be carousing or at least trying to hang out with some girls, but their quietness and shyness seemed off-putting. You can't entirely be fooled by appearances, because in the end, we're all biologically driven creatures, and if you get your foot in the door, the biology can take over and the culture can lose its power.

On the way out of the restaurant, I persuaded a gorgeous Japanese girl and her fairly homely friend to accompany John and me back to the hotel. After about five hours of nonstop subtle loving coercion, at the break of dawn, the gorgeous girl was so turned on and so unable to repeat that she couldn't possibly have sex that she gave in and gave up the whole enchilada of love. It was an incredible experience to see her go from "No, no, I'm not that kind of girl" to "Please fuck me more." It was all good, and she slept over and we spent the morning together.

Now it was time to take the train to Tokyo, and she was a bit weepy. She insisted on meeting us at the train station to say goodbye. When I checked in to my hotel in Tokyo, there was a demanding message waiting for me. "You must send for me now," she wrote sternly. Must send for her now? Maybe there was some Japanese etiquette that if you have sex with a girl, you must send for her now. I didn't know, but I didn't send for her. That night we played to another polite and restrained audience. After the show, I was sitting backstage when I looked up and saw the cutest girl I'd even seen in my life walk into the dressing room. She was a five-foot-nine, nineteen-year-old blond Nordic goddess with big blue eyes, a boyish bowl-cut hairdo, and an unbelievable smile. Plus, she was wearing a T-shirt with a huge face of Woody Allen on it, and her tits were poking out of each of Woody's eyeglasses so that his eyes seemed to be going in different directions. I couldn't have put in an order with God for a more perfect physical specimen.

At that very moment, my destiny became clear to me. She was my new girlfriend. As she walked into the room, I whispered to every dude who was near, "Back off. That's my girl." Then I walked straight over to her.

"Hi, my name's Carmen," she said. "I'm visiting from San Diego."

I introduced myself and told her that we'd be hanging out for the next year or so, and she seemed amenable.

I swooped Carmen up, and she joined us for dinner. Then she came back to my hotel room. Unlike the girl from Osaka, we didn't have to wait till daybreak to get in bed together. She was so beautiful, and I was so attracted to her, that I got nervous about having this sexual moment. Carmen sensed my uneasiness and, with a calm and loving grace, said, "This is such a perfect moment. No matter what happens, there is no place in the world that I'd rather be than lying with you right here."

Whatever wave of insecurity that I was feeling got washed away under the tsunami of her love. That night became one of the most powerful and magical coming-togethers I'd ever experienced. I felt like I had ended up in the lap of true love, with this girl who was different from anyone else I'd ever met. There was a certain whimsy about her; she was smart and she knew good music. She seemed relaxed and loving, and we were pure magic together, and I was completely and utterly prepared to be her man from that point forth.

Carmen was an Elite model working in Japan, and the next night I went and stayed with her in her little model's apartment in Tokyo. We started sharing our stories that night, and hers was rife with dysfunction. Her father had abandoned her when she was still a baby, and she never was able to connect with him. She told me she had relatives back in Missouri who were full-out white trash living in makeshift lean-tos along the river and eating squirrel for dinner. It was all pretty intriguing. Without realizing it, I reversed the roles of my former relationships and began becoming a caretaker for her.

I would be delinquent if I didn't mention that, sexually speaking, Carmen was from a different planet. She was the most sexually magnified person I'd ever been with, and in retrospect, I think it was a compulsion. She lived through sex, and whatever pain she was experiencing, it was nothing that sex couldn't fix. I was all for it, because I had a lot of pain and troubles of my own, so as our relationship developed, whenever we had a problem, we'd just have sex. She would say things like "I can come twenty times in a row without a problem. I could come for an entire hour straight," and she could! Nothing could ever prepare you for meeting a girl who's built like that, psychologically and physiologically.

God bless Carmen Jeanette Hawk for being my first girlfriend at a new time in my life when I was vulnerable and needing to locate my confidence. Of course, we were in a faraway land, and as much passion as I was feeling for her, I was going to England, and who knew if I'd ever see her again. I desperately wanted to, but time and distance have a way of playing tricks with your best intentions.

After Tokyo, I had every intention of not being a single person anymore. I wasn't out there on the hunt in England, but when we stopped in New York on the way back, I met a model named Karen who was a big, sturdy, muscle-toned goddess from South Africa. It was confusing, because I had fallen head over heels for Carmen, but she was still in Japan, and Karen was warm and friendly and interested in hanging out. She was a picture of health, full of cheek, full of breast, and full of heart.

We had a break in touring, so I went back to L.A. and moved back into my apartment on Orange Drive, which was now devoid of Ione's stuff. A few days later, I got a great package from Karen. It was filled with professionally shot beautiful nude photos of her. By then Carmen had returned from Japan and moved in with her mom in San Diego. We made plans for her to come up and spend a weekend with me, and it was a portentous experience. We spent the first few wonderful days in bed together, just getting really close. Then I had to go do some errands, and I left my little sex kitten purring contentedly under the covers. When I returned to the bedroom, there was confetti all over the room. I had no idea what had happened until I picked up one of the pieces of confetti.

"Oh, shit. That's a nipple. She must have found the pictures," I thought.

I was right. And Carmen was not having any of it.

"If you're seeing me, why is this girl sending you photos of herself?" she raged. "That fucked-up hussy slut can just go ahead and lose your address." This was a mild outburst compared to what was to come.

But I adored her and she was so much fun and she had the greatest laugh and she was always smiling. I don't want to gush on about the sex things, but she was the most sexual person I had ever found myself in love with. She was starting to pick up some steam as a fashion model, so she decided she was going to move to L.A. Because I had recently gotten out of that long-lasting situation with Ione, I was gun-shy about her moving right into my house, so we went apartment-hunting and found her a cute one about two miles away. After spending about a week there, she ended up living with me. Thus began a topsy-turvy, whoopsie-daisy relationship, which was sometimes fun and always exciting.

I won't say she was manic-depressive, but she was manic something. She would go from bam, through-the-roof happy, excited, grab-kiss sex to ready to sock me straight in the face because she was convinced I was looking across the street, down and around the driveway, and trying to memorize the house number where a beautiful girl had just entered. Half the time I had no idea what she was even talking about; her imagination was running wild. But those times were always balanced by the ones when she would let me tie her up and blindfold her in bed and take Polaroid pictures.

In April 1990, Lindy held a band meeting to tell us that by the end of the week, we'd have our first gold record. *Mother's Milk* was about to go over five hundred thousand units sold. It was no thanks to EMI, who were the most backward people ever, except for Kim White, who always believed in us and who fought to get our record played on college radio and helped it cross over to the alternative charts and then mainstream radio.

EMI flew us to New York to have a party celebrating our first gold record, but none of it meant anything to us. It seemed awkward and disingenuous that EMI was trying to create this celebratory ambience of record-sales success. Still, in the midst of that hurricane of weird record-company energy, I looked at Flea, and we hugged and embraced and felt that we'd really accomplished something that we'd never done before, even if it took us four albums and countless ups and downs.

Suddenly, other record companies started paying attention to us, especially after our lawyer, Eric Greenspan, pored over our

EMI contract. Even though we were due to deliver three more albums to them, Eric noticed that there was a personal-services clause that made the contract invalid after seven years. We were fast approaching that anniversary. So nearly every bigwig in the industry began putting on a dog-and-pony show for us. Chris Blackwell, the founder of Island Records, invited us to his house in the Hollywood Hills and talked to us about Bob Marley and the history of his label's involvement in reggae. It was fun, but even he admitted he didn't have the money to match what the other major labels could offer us.

David Geffen did. He made a serious pitch for us, even flying us home from our concert in Oakland in his company jet. The funny thing was that Warner Bros. had flown us to the concert in their corporate jet. Mo Ostin of Warner's was the coolest of all the record-company executives we met during this process. He had founded Warner's, and when Flea and I went to his office, we sat and listened to Mo's stories about Frank Sinatra, Jimi Hendrix, and Neil Young, who were all on his label. Later in the negotiations, Mo invited us out to his house in Brentwood. If you put a roof over the better part of Disneyland, that's how big this house was. After giving us a tour of his home, he took us outside. His compound was set on top of a mountain that looked all the way from the ocean to downtown L.A. His pool was the size of a small lake, and when he invited us to have a dip, Flea and I stripped down to our underwear and dove in. When we got out of the pool, there was a butler with hot towels waiting for us. Despite all the opulence, Mo was a real human being with a huge spirit and a palpable love for and connection with music.

While this courtship was going on, we decided to move on and begin work on our next album. We weren't going to work with Michael Beinhorn again, so we started talking to other producers, one of whom was Rick Rubin, who was famous for his work with the Beastie Boys. We had considered Rick as a producer around the time of *Freaky Styley,* and he came to visit us with the Beasties at our EMI rehearsal space. Later on, he told me that the whole time he was there, he sensed the darkest, most oppressed energy in that room, and he couldn't get out soon enough. But now we were all in a different place, and we talked to Rick and really liked him. Rick had transformed himself from a brash, aggressive, obnoxious caffeine-saturated carnivore New Yorker into a mellower, kinder, gentler, spiritually minded, incredibly giving vegetarian Californian.

So Rick came on board, and we began preproduction in this rehearsal space out in a quiet section of the Valley on Lankershim called the Alleyway. The facility was a big, high-ceilinged space with couches and a loft and a great stage, just fifteen minutes away from where we all lived. As soon as we got into the place, we become the most prolific we had ever been. We just couldn't stop writing music. We'd jam all day, get super ideas, and then Rick would come and lie on the couch for hours at a time, taking notes, taking naps, and taking in all the music by osmosis. He wasn't in our face, he was real laid-back, but soon we realized that he didn't miss a beat. He gave us wonderful ideas for arrangements, and then he worked with Chad on drum patterns and beats.

On Halloween we took a break from working to attend a costume party thrown by an enigmatic filthy-rich guy who lived in a Bel Air mansion. He had built a huge outdoor stage and hired Jane's Addiction to play his party. All of us agreed that we would attend the party in matching costumes, which consisted of a huge rubber strap-on dildo and nothing else. I dutifully put mine on and went to the party with Carmen, who was appropriately costumed. We got there, and lo and behold, there was my good buddy Flea, totally naked except for his dildo. Then I saw John sporting his fake hard-on. Chad also didn't chicken out, even though it was the end of October, and it was pretty chilly. So we were four naked guys with hard-ons trying to act like nothing was wrong.

Jane's Addiction started playing, and everyone started singing along. At one point, Stephen Perkins from Jane's Addiction asked us if we wanted to play, so we decided to play the

Stooges' "Search and Destroy," something we'd been rehearsing at the Alleyway. There were literally hundreds of people at this party, and we got up on that huge stage naked as motherfuckers but with giant hard-ons. It was like walking on the moon, we were extra-amped because of the nakedness and the coldness and the gesture of camaraderie from Jane's Addiction, who had always been in a little bit of competition with us over the years.

The record-company negotiations ultimately came down to two companies, Warner's and Sony. We went to see Tommy Mottola of Sony/Epic in New York; he was currently riding a wave of success with Mariah Carey and Michael Jackson. Tommy was pushing the hardest to get us, and he made that clear by telling us he knew we were talking to all these other labels, but in the end, we'd sign with Epic.

Our thinking was that we had been mistreated at EMI. We'd had seven A&R guys in seven years, no stability at all. We were looking for a good home. When Eric convened a lunch meeting and told us that Epic had upped their offer by a million, the four of us got up and started doing a conga line around the restaurant chanting "Epic! Epic! Epic!" We had gone from being the earnest "Let's have a family situation" to "A million more? Let's go with the corporate monsters from New York."

Eric dropped a bombshell on us at that meeting. He sat us down and said, "I've got news for you guys. Each of you will be getting a check for a million dollars." We each had a few thousand dollars to our names, and we were instant millionaires. It felt like we'd won the lottery. We were screaming and hugging one another when we realized that for the first time, we wouldn't have to scrape and scratch and live from week to week. Each of us decided on the spot to buy a house. Within two weeks' time, we all had new homes.

My house was a brand-new construction on the top of Beachwood Canyon on Hollyridge. It was a blank palette that I'd end up redoing in a very nouveau-riche way. I took out all the carpeting and had antique teak hardwood from Thailand put down.

In my bedroom, I painted each wall a different color. I had a crazy mosaic installed on the staircase so it looked like a river was coming down the stairs. But the pièce de résistance was my living room fireplace. I took out the standard-issue one and had a stoneworker bring river rocks from Ojai. Then I had a fireplace fashioned into the shape of a giant nude woman. You'd load the logs into her vagina, and she had fourteen-inch-across purple glass nipples. But the nicest thing about the house was my backyard, which backed up to the west ridge of Griffith Park, a large nature preserve. If you were lounging in the pool, all you had to do was look up to see the famous Hollywood sign above your head.

We decided to go with Sony, with the proviso that they buy us out of the last album due to EMI. The entire brass of Epic/Sony records flew out to the Four Seasons in L.A. for a lavish brunch to celebrate the decision and do some photo ops. We were ready to go to work as soon as they could extricate us from the EMI contract. But even though they told us it would be only a matter of days, the days dragged on and on and turned into months.

Meanwhile, my relationship with Carmen was tumultuous. She was off her rocker. I got her to go to therapy so she didn't kill herself. One time we were in the car, and she started screaming and pounding on her face, giving herself a black eye. Then she tried to jump out of the car while I was driving full speed. I wasn't trying to force therapy on her; I was offering to pay for her to get help, because she was clearly in pain. If I was looking through a magazine, she'd come over, grab it out of my hands, go back a few pages, and say, "Why'd you stop on this page so long? Who is this girl?" We'd go to the movies, and we'd be walking out in the middle of this packed-sardine crowd of people. I'd have my head bowed down, inching along, and she'd sock me and say, "Why are you looking at that girl?"

By now we were verbal battlers, so when she'd beat herself up and then show up in front of my friends with a black eye, everyone would look at me like "Dude, are you beating her?" Who would believe she was giving herself the black eyes? I kept trying unsuccessfully to end the relationship, but after I bought my house, she simply would not leave. She locked herself in the bathroom with a knife. She had gone in there to cut her wrists, and I had to knock down the door to get to her. She was standing there holding the knife, but she hadn't cut herself, thank God.

The jealousy factor and the insecurity factor and the sex-as-medicine factor just got worse and worse. I think the minute she realized she was losing her hold on me, she felt she would perish. Anytime I suggested that we might not stay together, she would have a meltdown and start tantruming like an autistic child. The band had set a date to start working on our next album, and I had to become free of this crazed relationship so I could have the focus to work, because the record meant more to me than anything. I offered to get her an apartment, because she didn't have the funds, but she wouldn't accept that. I told her a hundred times that it was over and that she had to leave and we couldn't be together, and she would come over and scream and shout and bang, and I would go down to the gate and say, "Carmen, you don't live here. You can't be here. We are not together, this is finished." She would stay out there screaming and yelling and trying to force her way into the house.

I finally bought her a plane ticket so she could go model in Italy, and that was the end of our relationship. I was thanking my lucky stars that it was over. Maybe she had no idea how much hellish drama she was creating, because at the end of most of these episodes, we would end up having sex; maybe in her mind, that indicated that everything was fine.

Shortly after that, I got a phone call from Mo Ostin at Warner's. "I heard about the deal you made with Sony," he began. "Congratulations, it sounds like a fantastic deal, and Sony's not a bad record company, so just go out and make the greatest record you can make. Go get 'em." I hung up the phone, genuinely touched. The coolest, most real person we had met during all these negotiations had just personally called to encourage me to make a great record for a rival company. That was the kind of guy I'd want to be working for. I called up Flea, and he had gotten the same call. He felt the same way.

We called Lindy and asked for an update on the Sony/EMI situation. Apparently, Sony was hitting a wall with EMI. That was all we had to hear. We begged him to get us out of the Sony deal and go with Warner's. We let Mo step up to the plate, and in one phone call to his old friend who ran EMI, we were off that label and signed with Mo. And we were ready to record the greatest record we could make.

10.

Funky Monks

We were all elated with our relationship with Warner's. Mo Ostin and his associates Lenny Warnoker and Steve Baker were all such soulful and musical people. Even though Mo was the corporate executive officer of Warner Bros., he rocked our world on a daily basis the entire time we were making our first album for him. He'd come down and hang out with us in the recording studio, happy to listen to anything we played. We'd never had a record-company relationship like that before.

Even though John and I had grown apart, the band was in the best space we'd been in for years. Chad and John no longer felt like the new guys, they were the guy guys. Flea and John had grown close both musically and as friends, and Chad was playing better than ever. We all trusted one another, and it showed when we'd get together for hours and hours and jam out songs. We were really in the pocket. When we were working on *Mother's Milk,* it was squeezing blood out of a rock to get a song done, but every day now there was new music for me to lyricize.

Meanwhile, I began to bond with Rick Rubin. He was a fun-loving guy in a much different way from anyone I'd ever met. He loved to talk about girls, and he loved to ride around and listen to music ad infinitum. He started coming to my house. We talked about my lyrics and went through all of the different things that I was thinking of singing over this great music being produced, whether it was "Mellowship Slinky," "Apache Rose Peacock," or "Funky Monks." I showed him the lyrics for "Power of Equality," and even though he thought the music lent itself to that treatment, he made it clear that he wasn't into sociopolitical lyrics.

"I like songs about girls and cars and stuff like that," Rick told me.

"Girls and cars? I can't write about girls and cars. That's already been done. I want to write about some weird shit that no one's been writing about," I protested.

"I understand," Rick said. "But if you want to write one song about girls and cars, I'd be happy to hear it."

I did try to scribe one song following Rick's outline, "The Greeting Song." To this day, I hate that song. I hate the lyrics, I hate the vocals. It was a lively rock tune in the Led Zep tradition, but I never found my place in it. Ironically, years later, General Motors called us up and wanted to create an advertising campaign for Chevy by printing the words to "Greeting Song" on a blank page. I couldn't let them do it; I didn't believe in those lyrics.

Even though things were going well creatively, I began to feel like the outsider in the band, because part of Flea and John's new bond was their mutual appreciation for pot. Maybe Flea felt that this was his chance to show me what it felt like not to be included in a three-point triangle of friendship with John. I'm sure John was probably resenting the fact that I always wanted everything to be clean around me and that he never got to do his own partying and drug experimentation. Plus, he felt that his creativity and songwriting ability were enhanced by smoking pot. It's ironic, because by then I'd shed my militant cleanster feelings and was getting better about accepting the drug use of people around me, but there was still a sense of "here comes the narc" when I'd intrude on a pot-smoking scenario.

One day I showed up to rehearsal, and Flea and John were blazing on pot and in a "Let's ignore Anthony" state of mind, and I experienced this melancholy sense of loss that John was no longer in my world. I could tell from the way he was looking at me that we weren't really friends anymore, other than the fact that we were in a band together and respected each other on that level. I rode home from rehearsal that day on the 101 Freeway, and my sense of loss about John and the loneliness that I was feeling triggered memories of my time with Ione and how I'd had this beautiful angel of a girl who was willing to give me all of her love, and instead of embracing that, I was downtown with fucking gangsters shooting speedballs under a bridge. I felt I had thrown away so much in my life, but I also felt an unspoken bond between me and my city. I'd spent so much time wandering the streets of L.A. and hiking through the Hollywood Hills that I sensed there was a nonhuman entity, maybe the spirit of the hills and the city, who had me in her sights and was looking after me. Even if I was a loner in my own band, at least I still felt the presence of the city I lived in.

I started freestyling some poetry in my car and putting the words to a melody and sang all the way down the freeway. When I got home, I got out my notebook and wrote the whole thing down in a song structure, even though it was meant to be a poem to deal with my own anguish.

"Under the Bridge"

Sometimes I feel like I don't have a partner
Sometimes I feel like my only friend
Is the city I live in, the city of angels
Lonely as I am, together we cry.

I drive on her streets 'cause she's my companion
I walk through her hills 'cause she knows who I am
She sees my good deeds and she kisses me windy
I never worry, now that is a lie.

I don't ever want to feel like I did that day
Take me to the place I love, take me all the way
It's hard to believe that there's nobody out there
It's hard to believe that I'm all alone
At least I have her love, the city she loves me
Lonely as I am, together we cry.

I don't ever want to feel like I did that day
Take me to the place I love, take me all the way

Under the bridge downtown
Is where I drew some blood
Under the bridge downtown
I could not get enough
Under the bridge downtown
Forgot about my love
Under the bridge downtown
I gave my life away

A month later, Rick was over my house one day, flipping through my notebook, which demonstrates how comfortable I felt around him then.

"What's this?" he said, and handed me the notebook. He had stumbled upon "Under the Bridge."

"Oh, that's just a poem," I said.

"That's dope. You should do something with that," he said.

"It's not really our style," I explained. "It's slow and melodic and dramatic."

"But it's good. You should show this to the guys and see if they want to do something with it."

I was touched that he liked the poem, but I still had doubts that it was a song for us. A few days later, I was at rehearsal and had some time to kill, because Flea hadn't arrived yet.

"Why don't you show John and Chad that thing I saw up at your house the other night," Rick suggested.

"No, no, Flea's not even here," I said. But John and Chad were both paying way too close attention. They both sat down and said, "Hey, let's see that little gentle number you have in there." I sang it to them in probably three different keys from beginning to end, not knowing where to go with it, but after I had finished, they got up and walked over to their instruments and started finding the beat and the guitar chords for it.

The next day John came over my house to polish the song. He brought a miniature Fender amp and plugged in. "Okay, sing it again. How do you want it to sound? What do you want it to feel like? Where do you want it to go?"

I sang it to him, and he came up with three or four different chord options. We picked and chose until we came up with the perfect, most inventive chord progression for the melody. And that was the birth of one song on the album.

John was instrumental in realizing another song that would end up on the album. It was a song inspired by my short and curious relationship with Sinéad O'Connor. I met Sinéad at a festival we were playing in Europe in August 1989. Flea and I were big fans of her *The Lion and the Cobra,* and I liked bald girls to begin with, because I knew that someone who would shave her head was tough and real and didn't give a fuck. Here was this super-ridiculously hot bald Irish girl with a magical voice and great lyrics and a crazy presence. We were playing first, so during our set, I was retarded enough to dedicate "Party on Your Pussy" to this morally ethical, politically correct fighter for the rights of the underdog.

When we finished our set, Flea and I stood by the side of the stage and watched Sinéad. This was before she became famous, so she wasn't self-conscious; she was just bold. She came onstage in a dress and combat boots and hit her first note. Like a crazy little

Irish princess warrior, she started belting out these amazing songs. I was dying a million deaths of desire watching all this, and then she made a reference to my mention of her, and it was positive. Okay, now she was aware of me, so that was a good thing.

After the show, we sought her out and told her how much we appreciated her music. Instead of saying a cursory thank-you, Sinéad invited us to hang out. She was shy and demure, and we talked until her road manager stormed in and rounded her up for the ride to the next venue. Fearful that I was never going to see her again, I ran back to the dressing room and wrote her a pretty meaningful letter, letting her know that I had some feelings for her. I rushed back and caught her just as she was about to board her bus and gave her the letter. She accepted it and smiled and waved good-bye.

And nothing ever happened. Not a word back. She disappeared into the giant cloud of a different world, and we went on our way, and that was it, adios. Life goes on, we toured Japan, and I met Carmen and had a yearlong relationship with her. By then Sinéad had released another album and overnight became the most popular female vocalist in the world. One day Bob Forrest told me she had moved to L.A., and there'd been a sighting of her at Victor's Deli, one of our favorite breakfast spots.

A few weeks later, I was doing errands and ran into Sinéad. One look at her, and I just melted. I would have married her on the spot. We struck up a conversation, and I reminded her that we had met back at the festival and that I'd given her a note.

"Oh yeah, I know you gave me a note," Sinéad said. "I have it. It's in my kitchen drawer at home."

"That note I gave you is in your kitchen drawer?" I was incredulous.

"What did you think?" She smiled. "You'd write a note like that and I'd throw it away?"

The next thing I knew, she was inviting me over for dinner. Soon I began regularly hanging out with her and her son, Jake. I can't say that it was a typical dating scenario, because it was a strange time for her—she was gun-shy from everything that had happened to her—but we started going to movies and museums, and I gave her driving lessons in my '67 convertible matte-black Camaro. We'd drive around and listen to music and kiss and whatnot, but she wasn't exactly letting me all the way in her door, so to speak. And I don't mean just vaginally. This went on for weeks, and it became the most wonderful, nonsexual relationship I'd ever had. I adored her, and every day I'd wake up and write her a little poem and fax it to her.

Our relationship was progressing, she was showing me a little more love and affection, emotionally and physically, and then suddenly, it all came to an inexplicable halt. I had made a bit of an ass of myself when she told me that she was going to the Academy Awards. I suggested we go together, and at first she agreed, then she called back to tell me she was going with her friend Daniel Day-Lewis. I felt slighted, not so much because she was hanging out with someone else, but because it wasn't me, and I wanted to be with her so much at that point.

Even after that incident, she never gave me any indication that she was anything other than absolutely enamored with the time we were spending together. Whenever our time together came to an end, I looked in her eyes, and she was as happy as a blossoming flower. I was excited and probably a little heavy-handed and overbearing, but she had a soothing and subtle way of bringing me back down to a more reasonable state of mind. She was calm and laid-back and not buying into the heaviness of my approach. It was good, we were finding a balance.

One day I called and left a message on her answering machine, then went off. When I came back, there was a response on my machine.

"Hey, Anthony, this is Sinéad. I'm moving out of Los Angeles tomorrow, and I don't want you to call me or come by before I leave. Good-bye."

I was shattered. It had gone overnight from "Can't wait to see you again" to "Don't call and don't come by." I didn't know who to turn to, so I called up John. He was irate that she could treat me like that, and he suggested that I write about it and we'd get together later that night and create a song. It had been raining for two days straight when I sat down at my dining room table, put Jimi Hendrix's version of "All Along the Watchtower" on continual rotation for inspiration, and started writing some lyrics about what had just happened to me.

From "I Could Have Lied"

I could have lied, I'm such a fool
My eyes could never never never keep their cool
Showed her and I told her how
She struck me but I'm fucked up now
But now she's gone, yes she's gone away
A soulful song that would not stay
You see she hides 'cause she is scared
But I don't care, I won't be spared

I drove over to John's house around midnight. He was like a mad scientist, empathizing with me, but absolutely possessed with the idea of finishing this song. So we worked and worked and stayed up all night, listening to that pouring rain. We finally finished the song at five in the morning and, cassette in hand, rushed out to drive through this rainstorm of rainstorms, straight to Sinéad's house. It was her last night there, and I didn't knock, I just bundled up the tape and shoved it through her mail slot. She left town the next day. The years went by, and our record came out, and life moved on. There were tragedies and triumphs and successes and failures and people died and people had babies and I always wondered what it would be like if I ever saw that girl again.

Years and years later, I was at the Universal Amphitheatre for some stupid MTV awards show where Flea and I were presenting with Tony Bennett, of all people. After the show, I was in the back parking lot, hanging out and schmoozing, when a limousine pulled up. I looked in and saw Sinéad and Peter Gabriel in the car. I walked over, and she poked her head out of the window, and we both said hi, and then nothing came out of me and she gave me a really fake smile. There was nothing to say. I can't even remember if I asked her whether she had gotten the tape. The whole encounter was the most horrible, awkward, poisonous, communicationless exchange. Maybe she did me a favor in the end. Who needs that kind of trouble?

We really expanded our musical palette with this album. One day John approached me with some interesting music that was very melodic and in a unique time signature. John hummed a verse and a chorus, and the emotion of the chords he was playing seemed to correspond to my breakup with Carmen. Even in the heat of our turbulent battles, I never considered her an evil person or hated her. I just saw her as a girl who never got a chance to grow up and deal with all her pain. I wasn't hurt by our breakup, I was relieved; I wanted her to feel the same and find her way in life.

At the same time, I began to question myself and wonder if I was stuck in repeating my father's pattern of hopping from flower to flower, the girl-of-the-day thing. I certainly didn't want to end up like Blackie, because as exciting and temporarily fulfilling as this constant influx of interesting and beautiful girls can be, at the end of the day, that shit is lonely and you're left with nothing. The lyrics reflect both those points of view.

From "Breaking the Girl"

Raised by my dad, girl of the day
He was my man, that was the way
She was the girl, left alone
Feeling the need to make me her home
I don't know what, when, or why
The twilight of love had arrived

Twisting and turning, your feelings are burning
You're breaking the girl

She meant you no harm
Think you're so clever but now you must sever
You're breaking the girl
He loves no one else

Recording the song was tremendous fun, because there was this big industrial bridge, so we went out and got all these scraps of metal, and the four of us donned protective eye gear and smashed the shit out of the metal with hammers and sticks and came up with a beautiful orchestration of scrap-metal percussion.

When we started figuring out which songs would ultimately make it to the recording stage, it turned out that the delay with Epic and Mo's last-minute stepping up to the plate had enabled us to write almost two albums' worth of new material. Working with Rick had changed the way we thought about songwriting. In the past, we were coming from a groove place, as opposed to a song place, which was where Rick's heart lay. This album would become the best of both of those worlds. We never tipped over to the conventional notion of songwriting, which would have mitigated against our stirring the pot of Africa. But you need to get into jamming to do that, so taking Rick's advice and focusing on song crafting were hugely important. Yet we never turned our back on being a funk band, based in grooves and improvised jams.

One of those jams would lead to the breakout song on the album. I was off on one side of the rehearsal studio, working on lyrics, while the band was jamming as a trio. Sometimes they'd be serious intellectual craftsmen, trying to intertwine their minds and come up with specific parts, but other times they'd rock out in a very joyful manner. On one of those latter days, Flea started playing this insane bass line, and Chad cracked up and played along. I was so struck by Flea's bass part, which covered the whole length of the instrument's neck, that I jumped up and marched over to the mike, my notebook in tow. I always had fragments of song ideas or even specific isolated phrases in mind. I took the mike and belted out, "Give it away, give it away, give it away, give it away now."

That line had come from a series of conversations I'd had years earlier with Nina Hagen. Nina was a wise soul, and she realized how young and inexperienced I was then, so she was always passing on gems to me, not in a preachy way, just by seizing on opportunities. I was going through her closet one day, looking at all her crazy clothes, when I came upon a valuable exotic jacket. "This is really cool," I said.

"Take it. You can have it," she said.

"Whoa, I can't take this. This is the nicest jacket you have in there," I said.

"That's why I gave it to you," she explained. "It's always important to give things away; it creates good energy. If you have a closet full of clothes, and you try to keep them all, your life will get very small. But if you have a full closet and someone sees something they like, if you give it to them, the world is a better place."

I had come from such a school of hard knocks that my philosophy was you don't give things away, you take whatever you want. It was such an epiphany that someone would want to give me her favorite thing. That stuck with me forever. Every time I'd be thinking, "I have to keep," I'd remember, "No, you gotta give away instead." When I started going regularly to meetings, one of the principles I learned was that the way to maintain your own sobriety is to give it to another suffering alcoholic. Every time you empty your vessel of that energy, fresh new energy comes flooding in.

I was busting out on that mike, going, "Give it away, give it away," and Flea was flying down the length of his bass, and Chad was laughing hysterically, and John was searching for his spot on the canvas to put his guitar part, and we just didn't stop. We all came away from the jam convinced we had the makings of a great song.

Rick's emphasis on the mechanics of songwriting led to a tradition that we still use to this day, called "face-offs." Let's say we're working on a song, and we have the verse and the chorus, but we need a bridge, and there's no piece of music we have that works there. John and Flea will unplug their guitars, run up to each other in the rehearsal space, and get in each other's faces. Then one of them will go into the parking lot, and the other will go out into a hallway, and they'll each have five minutes to come up with an idea. They'll both come back, and we'll all listen fairly and objectively and decide which part serves the song best. We've never had a major disagreement with one of the guys holding out for his idea. Face-offs are a fantastic tool for developing a part, because they're spontaneous and creative. The idea appears competitive on the surface, but it's all playful and very much in the spirit of serving the song rather than an individual. By the time that part gets put through the process of Chad doing his thing to it, and either John or Flea putting his part to it, we all own that little piece of music equally.

After that long, long period of rehearsal and songwriting and incubating ideas, we were ready to record the album. Rick suggested that we consider recording in an unorthodox setting. He turned up this amazing, huge, empty, historically landmarked Mediterranean haunted mansion a stone's throw from where we all lived. Then he hired some guys from Canada to come down and set up a studio in the rambling house. There was a beautiful wood-paneled library in the house that connected by a window to the giant Mediterranean living room, which worked out great for us, because they built the control room in the library and set up the drums and the guitars in the huge living room, putting the bass amps and the guitar amps in separate rooms to get all the sounds just so. As we walked around the house, we spontaneously decided to live there for the duration of the recording, so we all chose our bedrooms in different wings of the house.

John had his own stairway that went up to one single room, which was quite modest. That was where he would dwell in his own soup of weirdness for months on end, painting and recording and reading and listening to music. Flea's little daughter, Clara, had done some nice drawings for him on the wall of his bedroom. I was on the far and opposite side of the house, with a lot more space, and I'd end up recording all of my vocals from my bedroom. We set up a microphone with a cord that wound through the house and down into the control studio, and I'd stand at the window that overlooked a hill and the moon, and sing. Flea went all the way up to the third floor and occupied a room that was tiled as if it were a steam room. Chad bowed out. We had heard that the property was haunted by a woman who was murdered there in the '30s, and that didn't set well with him, so he opted to ride his motorcycle home each night.

We hired Brendan O'Brian to engineer the record, which was a coup, because he was the best engineer around. He'd go on to produce many, many important multiplatinum albums. Brendan was a whiz at getting the right drum sounds; plus, he was a great musician in his own right. He wound up playing on the album and was a big part of both the sound of that album and creating a fun-loving atmosphere every day.

We decided to document the recording process, so we hired Gavin Bowden, whom we had met in England when Flea and I went on our trip to Europe before our first record. Gavin had emigrated to America, and ironically, he wound up marrying Flea's sister. One of the requirements for the cameraman of the film was that he be completely invisible during this process, and Gavin was just the guy to do that, because he was mild-mannered and English. He could blend in, and he was someone you felt comfortable performing around. He was a one-man band, crawling on the floor, hunched over backward, working his ass off to document everything from the basic tracks to the control room to me singing up in my bedroom. He also interviewed all of us and put together a nice piece that was released as *Funky Monks*.

Soon we realized that we needed someone to answer the phone, because we'd be trying to record, and the phone kept ringing off the hook. We also needed someone to get us whatever we needed, as soon as we needed it, so we wound up hiring a kid named Louis Mathieu who used to work for our friends Bob and Pete with Thelonious Monster. Louie came over at a moment's notice and assumed his duties, and that would be the beginning of a long road with him. He went from secretary to drum tech to assistant road manager to caretaker/personal assistant to John and ultimately tour manager.

So we moved into the house and made the record. Flea and John and I stayed in the house for over thirty days without even leaving to go to a restaurant. While we were cloistered, there were rumors that John had an experience with a succubus up in his room, but in reality, we were getting nocturnal visits from a more tangible entity. We all knew this girl who worked on Melrose Avenue and was a supporter of the band. While we were in the house, she'd come over and visit. At night it was just the three of us, there was no security in the house at all. And like in some weird scene out of a movie set in a castle in the countryside of England, this very young, very self-assured girl would come and spend time with each of us, one by one. She was getting sexed in every room she visited, but it wasn't purely sexual; she'd hang out and talk and spend time with each of us.

She'd visit me, then Flea, and then John last, because they were better friends. It was nice to put in a full day's work on the album and then have this girl come and be so loving and so unaffected by the experience of having three different men in one night. It didn't seem that she was engaging in this activity because she had low self-esteem or she just wanted to fuck. At that point, John had become a much different person sexually, not at all interested in abusing resources that were available to him because of his status, so I don't think he would have done it if he thought it was causing her any pain or discomfort. It all worked out for everybody. It was nice and cozy and warm, and we even had a name for her visits, depending on the day of the week. If it was a Wednesday and we were feeling randy, someone would say, "Hey, isn't it wacky Wednesday?" Or "By George, this is freaky Friday. Get her on the phone."

Being confined to the house was good for me, because I had a lot of lyrics to finish during the basic recording process, and there were few distractions. But then it was time for me to step up to the

Maybe you can see from these pictures why I fell like a ton of bricks for Carmen Jeanette Hawk. This was somewhere between 1989 and 1990, and we would run like rabbits in love until around '91. God bless this incredible pixie.

I'm a lucky guy. Jaime Rishar loved me with all her heart, and I loved her right back. Here we are reflecting some sunlight in Papa's backyard garden. What a blessed feeling to be held by such an angel. Damn. Somewhere in the mid '90s.

Back in the early years we would come up with absurd and unthinkable concepts for our live performances. On this day for a show at the Whiskey, we dressed and went in character as rabbis. Cliff, our drummer, who is not pictured here, thought that was cool, but chose instead to dress as a top-hatted piece of poop. What a genius. Oh yeah, the guy on the left is legendary musician and producer Al Kooper. *Freaky Styley* era.

Beneath our kayaks here are the brackish waters of an Alaskan fjord called Endicott Arm. Historically my friends and I would drop whatever nonsense we had going on in the city and head for the great outdoors. This particular trip to Alaska was called the "Kevin Seven." Three of the fabled seven are pictured here, left to right—Marty Goldberg aka Hal Negro, Michael Peter Balzary aka Mike B. aka Flea, and me.

Two club-kid lovebirds in profile. I imagine this was at a club called Power Tools in downtown L.A. Jennifer Bruce was the hottest go-go dancer this side of the East River. She out–Gwen Stefanied Gwen Stefani before there even was a Gwen Stefani. That's a compliment to both girls. Circa 1985.

My first roommate, Donde Bastone, had a pretty cool little Hollywood bungalow backhouse. I moved in when I was sixteen and made good use of his record collection, his weed supply, his refrigerator, but maybe not his full-length mirror. Can somebody please undo the top button? Wilcox Avenue. 1979.

This is the rare Siamese ostrich plant that can be found posing amongst the shrubs of the Hollywood Hills. Jennifer was really on a no-holds-barred roll when she dressed me up on this night. Not exactly the Ramones uniform. 1987.

(Photo credit: Gary Leonard)

I met Ione on her sixteenth birthday. We fell in love and stayed together for about three years. This was taken about a year and a half into it, and I often think I would have died without her care. We did have lots of fun playing house together.

The Dalai Lama was unbelievably sweet and down to earth when I met him in Dharamsala, India. Notice how he's holding my hand, which he did for the entire length of our chat (about ten minutes). The guy's not a bad dresser either.

HAIGHT-ASHBURY 1972

Here's the old man on a dope-dealing weekend in San Francisco. Could be the height of his outlaw lifestyle, as I was about to move in with him a year later and put just a hint of a crimp into his gangster way of livin'. Notice his perfectly adjusted nutsack trouser package. Very '70s.

Not sure who the little three-year-old monkey is on the left, but that's my mom at age twenty-three looking like she's thirteen. We lived in California then and apparently I rather enjoyed her company.

For me, this group of four black-and-white snapshots is nothing short of monumental in my tiny life. It's me smoking pot for the first time. My dad was taking the picture and I was handing the joint to a pretty girl who was about to take her top off. I had only been in L.A. for a day or two and was on my way to doing almost everything imaginable in that kitchen. Palm Avenue, West Hollywood. 1973.

plate and do my vocals. I still wasn't comfortable singing. I was comfortable making noise with my mouth, I was comfortable writing songs and knowing in my head how they were supposed to be sung, but the actual execution seemed like this out-of-control animal that sometimes I could rein in and find a way to tame, and sometimes I couldn't. One of the reasons I set up my room so far away from everyone was so I didn't have to feel the eyes on me, I could be by myself when I was recording.

My level of discomfort depended on the song. I remember going up to sing "Under the Bridge" and just feeling "Oh my God, I can't believe I have to sing this." But Brendan made it as comfortable as humanly possible. I would be all serious and on edge and insecure, trying to let the spirits flow through me, and I had Brendan on the other end of the headphones busting jokes, laughing at me, laughing at himself, laughing about the song. He was remarkable, the perfect voice to have in your ear, reminding you not to take yourself too seriously and also knowing that you would get it when you got it. He'd say things like "I've heard you sing it, I know it's there, we'll find it. Don't worry about it, take your time."

Even still, three days before it was my turn to be the focus of recording, my lower back flew the coop. I'm sure it was all emotional, but my formerly broken back went kablooey, and Flea turned me on to an old Chinese acupuncturist named Zion. He not only fixed my back, he gave me a new exercise regimen—swimming—that I'd stick with up to the present day.

I don't want to give the impression that we were monks the whole time we recorded. We'd often invite friends up to the house and have these elaborate dinner parties. One of the people who was around then was the actor River Phoenix. I met River through Ione, who'd done a film with him. John and River had jammed at a party that we all attended, and they got close. I don't want to go off on River's trip, because his family is excruciatingly sensitive about it, but since I'd known him, he had drunk heavily and used cocaine heavily, and it was no secret to me or anybody who knew him that he was quite out of control with this stuff and it would be just a matter of time before bad things started to add up. River was around a lot during the writing and recording of our album. He was a big supporter of our band, and I even wrote a whole verse about him in "Give It Away": "There's a river, born to be a giver, keep you warm, won't let you shiver/His heart is never going to wither, come on everybody, time to deliver."

After two months, we were finished with the recording. Flea and John had managed to stay cloistered the entire time, but after six weeks, Rick and I started making some forays into the outside world. It was a strange feeling to reenter the atmosphere of Hollywood after being so completely single-minded and focused for so long. But the whole time we were in that house, we all knew we were doing our best work yet, and that we had created something that was real and strong and beautiful, something I couldn't wait to share with everyone around me. This album was a real step forward for everybody. John defined his playing for the first time and created a whole new approach for the guitar that became his signature. From that point on, guitar players around the world would look at him as a major player.

Flea also went in a completely new direction. Everything up to that point had been based on slapping and plucking and popping, and he abandoned that. There were only a couple of songs on the album based on the popping format; everything else was finger-plucked, which was a big departure for a guy who had became known as the crazy popping bass player. Chad also stepped up and made his mark as one of the premier rock drummers. It was also a new thing for Rick; he had never made a record like ours. He'd made hip-hop records, hard-core metal records, but never a record that had so many varied styles going on. He and Brendan actually did, in some ways for the first time, capture the essence of the Red Hot Chili Peppers. Part of our live energy and our individual personalities were captured and allowed to breathe and exist on the album, and that was something we had struggled to do in the past. Rick found a way to let that happen in unconventional surroundings.

Now that the recording was finished, it was time to come up with a name. One day I was in Rick's car, and we started throwing out titles, but whenever you do that, you're going to come up with shit. Conversely, whenever a title just comes to you, it's going to be great. Finally, Rick said, "I don't know why we're even having this conversation. Clearly the best title we have now is 'Blood Sugar Sex Magik'" (which was a song that was partly an homage to my incredible sexual encounters with Carmen). I couldn't argue with him, and that was when we realized that even though it wasn't necessarily the featured song or the single song or the song we wanted people to pay more attention to, it did somehow encompass the record's entire vibe.

With the album in the can, it was time to shoot a video for the first single, which was "Give It Away." I knew we'd have the support of our record company, so I started viewing reels and reels and reels of video directors, but nothing looked good to me. Everything was the same, boring, homogenized, contrived shit. Finally, I came across a video for a French band made by a director named Stephane Sednaoui. I was blown away by this video, which looked like nothing else. It was slower and poetic, shot in black and white. It seemed like authentic art, not something done for MTV. But when Warner's followed up, they told me to forget it, this guy was 100 percent booked up. I couldn't accept that, so I called him up and cajoled him to come out for a meeting.

He agreed, and we met at Flea's house and spoke for hours about our favorite photographers and our favorite colors and we all concurred on a silver theme. We set up a video shoot out in the desert, where all good videos are made. Stephane brought an entire crew of French people: designers, stylists, makeup people, hair people, caterers, AD's, all French. We spent two solid days out in the desert, and we were all on a creative roll, everyone stepping up to the plate and feeling great about the song. Chad was glad to dress up in his red devil horns. I was worried that when Stephane told John he was going to cavort with a dancing ribbon, he'd say, "Fuck you and take that dancing ribbon and shove it up your French ass, buddy," but he gladly went off and made love to the air with this dancing ribbon. He would have danced around for hours with that thing.

Blood Sugar Sex Magik was released on September 24, 1991. "Give It Away" was the first single, but the number one radio station that Warner's wanted to break the song on, a station out of Texas, told them to "come back to us when you have a melody in your song." That was bad news, since the conventional wisdom was that this station dictated what America was going to hear. Of course, "Give It Away" was never about melody. It was a party song.

When the album was about to be released, John and I made a trip to Europe to promote it. Flea decided against making the trip. I was surprised that John was willing to take one for the team and go on this torturous trip where you march around from city to city and talk for hours and hours to every silly publication imaginable, which is enough to drive anybody crazy. Well, it did John.

Of all of us, I think John had the hardest time readjusting to life outside of the *Blood Sugar* house. He had such an outpouring of creativity while we were making that album that I think he really didn't know how to live life in tandem with that creativity. It got to a point where he wouldn't want to see a billboard for, say, *The Arsenio Hall Show,* or an advertisement for lipstick. He wanted to be in a world that was a beautiful manifestation of his own creation. You're not going to find that on a promo tour. All of the interviewers' questions seemed to be coming from the wrong angle for John, so he became a dark, angry, resentful "I'm too cool for this school" guy. The only thing that I imagine could have made him comfortable was to be back in L.A. with his new girlfriend, Toni.

John started to dabble in using heroin. When you first start doing it and then you walk away from it and you're not feeling great, it's something that weighs heavy on your mind, like "Whoa, there's a girl and a fucking dope dealer waiting for me at home. I could live without the German weather and the food." John may have acted like a prick, but it's not difficult to imagine why someone gets that way in the middle of twelve interviews, because sometimes the interviewers are decent and thoughtful and considerate and interested in music, but sometimes they're abominable, and you want to slap them and tell them to leave because they're so thoughtless and small-minded and the things they want to talk about are rude.

I remember being in Belgium with John at a really cool old boutique-style hotel. We were checking out in the morning, but he didn't look so good. Then the guy at the front desk told him, "And that's two thousand dollars for the phone bill." He had been on the phone with Toni in L.A. for six hours. By the time we got to London, he came to me and apologized: "I'm sorry to do this, but I really want to leave badly. Can you finish this by yourself?" and frantically rushed to get the next plane back home.

In France we met with record-company people, and Lindy and I got to see the "Give It Away" video for the first time. I was more hysterically ecstatic about that piece of visual footage than any we've ever done. But the record execs had reservations about it, worried that it was too weird to get played on television. The first two salvos from "Give It Away" had now been met with reactions that didn't suggest we'd be getting much radio or TV play. But the tide turned around when K-Rock in L.A. started playing "Give It Away" all the time. That was the beginning of the infusion of those songs into mass consciousness.

The *Blood Sugar Sex Magik* tour seemed to augur a changing of the musical guard. There was definitely a sense at that time that the whole late '80s musical mentality was dying out. Cheesy pop-metal bands like Warrant and Poison and Skid Row were finished; cheesy family sitcoms like *The Cosby Show* were on their way out. There was something new in the air. I remember getting a tape of a new album by a band called Nirvana and driving around the valley in my Camaro with the top down and marveling about where these guys had come from, the songs were so out of this world. We were getting ready for our tour, and one night I saw a video on MTV from a band called the Smashing Pumpkins. The song was "Gish," and it was a really beautiful song, with a different texture and energy from the usual trash on MTV. So I called Lindy and told him to get the Pumpkins for our tour.

Then Jack Irons called us up out of the blue while we were at Lindy's office, listening to tapes of bands to figure out who else to take out on tour with us. Jack asked that, as a favor, we listen to a tape by a new band, whose singer, Eddie Vedder, was a friend of Jack's. Jack had met Eddie when Eddie was in a Chili Peppers cover band, basically doing an imitation of me. Apparently, Eddie had also worked as tech for us when we played the San Diego area. Eddie's new group was called Pearl Jam. We listened to the tape, and it wasn't our cup of tea, we were such musical snobs at that point. But these kids sounded real and genuine, and we were happy to do Jack a solid, so Pearl Jam was booked as the opening band.

We began the tour at the Oscar Meyer Theatre in Madison, Wisconsin. Pearl Jam opened, and when they played their first single, "Alive," at the end of their set, I realized that Vedder had an incredible voice and they had a pop smash on their hands. Backstage, we made friends with the Smashing Pumpkins, and it turned out they were way weirder than we could have imagined. I met D'Arcy, their bass player, and thought she was cute in a weird Gothy way. James, the guitar player, was super-shy and mellow, and Billy Corgan, the leader of the band, was jovial and approachable. But after their set, D'Arcy got hammered on vodka and whippets. She was high as a kite. If this was the way she was starting out a tour, imagine what she'd be like by the end of it. Finally, we went out and played a lot of songs off of *Blood Sugar*. We tried to play "Breaking the Girl," and it fell apart, but the rest of the show went well.

As the tour progressed, we got closer with both of the opening bands. Most people will tell you that Billy Corgan is the most difficult and unhappy human in the world, but my experience with him was completely different. I found him very intelligent and sensitive, with a keen sense of irony. His e-mail address used to be "blackcloud @ blah, blah, blah." He was also a remarkably talented basketball player. We were playing backstage at a Shriner's Club gig in Milwaukee during a sound check, and my immediate read on Billy was "tall, gangly, musical, nerdy intellectual," not "ball-player." But we started shooting around, and Billy stepped up and started draining outside shots.

We went on a lot of multiband outings that tour, going to movies, and I always found Billy supportive and never competitive or weirdly jealous. But he clearly was the boss of Smashing Pumpkins, and the rest of them were pretty much under his thumb. D'Arcy was really sweet, but she seemed to be an accident waiting to happen. James wasn't as much a loose wire as D'Arcy, but their drummer, Jimmy Chamberlain, was a monster. Thank God I was sober that tour, because if I hadn't been, he would have been my running partner, and we both would have been dead. He drank and used and caroused like a fucking gorilla with a huge heart. I remember going out to clubs after these shows, especially in New York, and he'd be at the bar in a trench coat, feeling the joy of his own success in this band, touring the world for the first time and drinking with a pocketful of this and a pocketful of that and some girls nearby. He was a real Chicago Polack with a lot of musical talent and no rules whatsoever. He's doing all right now, but he had his escapades with the dark side.

We hung out with Eddie and Jeff Ament and Stone Gossard from Pearl Jam quite a bit. Stone was cool; he was the shy distant fellow. Eddie and I became equal friends, there was never any of that saccharine idolatry of "Oh, I've been into you guys for so long." We were on an even playing field from day one, and there was no ego interfering with our friendship.

By the time we got to Boston, the buzz and the hype and the attention Pearl Jam were getting was phenomenal. Normally, a small arena show is empty when the first act goes on, but our audiences were filling up for Pearl Jam, and it was exciting. At that time in his life, Eddie was so happy to be playing music, and he was humble and loving and went out of his way to make friends with everyone. He went and told my mom what a great kid she had, and he bonded with Blackie.

Meanwhile, our record started taking off. For the first time, we were getting heavy radio play and regular rotation on MTV. So both Pearl Jam and our band were skyrocketing to a new stratosphere at the same time. All of this was making John miserable. He began to lose all of the manic, happy-go-lucky, fun aspects of his personality. Even onstage, there was a much more serious energy around him. It was disconcerting to see how sullen his approach to being an artist was getting. What I didn't know till later was that John was ambivalent about even being in the band then.

In his interior dialogue, John figured that quitting the band right after completing a successful album would put him in a mysterious place where he'd have the opportunity to do other projects and not be part of the star-making machinery. John felt that touring would sap the amazing creativity that he was experiencing. Of course, we didn't know any of this, because John was rapidly pulling away from the rest of the band. He brought Toni on tour with him, and they cocooned all the time.

Warner's was thrilled with the initial reaction to the album, and they immediately began discussing a second single and video. We were about halfway through our U.S. tour, playing in the Midwest, and some record-company people came to the show to discuss the possibility of releasing "Under the Bridge" as our next single. That was a song that had been hit or miss for me as a vocalist; sometimes I could get through it, and other times I couldn't sing it in tune. That night we had a huge audience, and it came time for "Under the Bridge," and John started the opening chords, but I missed my cue. Suddenly, the entire audience started singing the song at the spot where I was supposed to have come in. At first I was mortified that I had fucked up in front of the Warner's people, who were there to hear me sing that song, but it turned out that they were way more impressed with the audience singing it than they ever would have been if I was singing it. I apologized for fucking up, but they said, "Fucking up? Are you kidding me? When every single kid at the show sings a song, that's our next single."

I saw our newfound success as a monumental blessing. It wasn't that I thought we were greater than we used to be—it was more that we were the same guys, but we were singing to a lot more ears and a lot more eyes and a lot more hearts. I felt we should be respectful of this gift, this incredible stroke of good fortune. We didn't sell out, we didn't change what we believed in to reach more people, we just did it. John, however, saw our newfound popularity as a bad thing. We used to have these raging backstage discussions.

"We're too popular. I don't need to be at this level of success. I would just be proud to be playing this music in clubs like you guys were doing two years ago," John would say.

"It is not a bad thing that these kids showed up," I'd argue. "Let's fucking be there for them. We don't have to hate ourselves and be mad at them because this is what happened."

He'd be all pissed off and hide and pout and not do what I wanted him to do, which was my huge mistake, wanting everyone to react to this new situation the same way I had. John had made up his mind about what was credible and what was cool, and playing for an arena full of kids stopped being cool for him. He would rather be home listening to Captain Beefheart and painting. John was reading a lot of William Burroughs then, and his view, from Burroughs, was that every true artist is at war with the world.

Ironically, the more disdain he developed for our success, the more popular we became. The more he would stomp his feet, the more records we would sell; the more disenchanted he became with the number of people who walked through the door, the more people *would* walk through the door. I thought it was the most beautiful thing that we had created something special, put it out to the world, and this was how the world was responding.

My ongoing problems with John were creating huge tensions in the band, which were causing additional anguish for Flea. Flea was in the process of breaking up with his wife, so all this stress led him to take something to go to bed, something to get up, and something for the middle of the day. His brain chemistry was getting perforated by doctors' prescriptions. What could have been the most exciting time of our career ended up being very strange. John was being dark and withdrawn, Flea was under the influence of all kinds of prescribed medications, and I was this high-strung but still-clean weirdo. And Chad was Chad.

My tensions with John came to a boiling point at a show we did in New Orleans. We had a sold-out house and John just stood in the corner, barely playing his guitar. We came offstage, and John and I got into it.

"John, I don't care what you're thinking or where your head's at or where you'd rather be, but when we come to a show and there are this many people who are paying money to see us and care about us and they want to experience these songs with us, the least you can do is fucking show up and play for them," I yelled.

"That's not how I see it. I'd rather be playing for ten people, and blah, blah, blah." The argument just went on and on. Flea was watching us, thinking, "Oh no, this was bound to happen: Control Freak Anthony against Hater of This Experience John, and they're finally having it out." John and I went from fighting to going into a bathroom and trying to get to the bottom of it so we could understand each other. Ultimately, we didn't see eye to eye, but we did come to an understanding and agreed to disagree and accept each other's differing perception of reality.

The longer we toured, the larger the crowds got. By the time we were scheduled to play the West Coast, we had jumped from theaters to full-fledged arenas, so the promoters felt we needed to add another band that was bigger than Pearl Jam. Nirvana's second album, *Nevermind,* had just exploded, and I was crazy about that record, so I suggested we get Nirvana to take Pearl Jam's place. Eddie and the guys were understanding about it, so Lindy called Nirvana, but their managers told him that they were unavailable. I picked up the phone and called Nirvana's drummer, Dave Grohl, myself.

"Anthony Kiedis! Wow, we love you guys. We grew up

listening to you in Seattle," Dave said. He told me they had just come off a huge tour, and Kurt Cobain was pretty worn out, but he'd try to talk him into doing the West Coast shows. And he did. Nirvana joined the bill, but then Billy Corgan pulled the Smashing Pumpkins off the bill. Apparently, he used to go out with Courtney Love, who was then Kurt's girlfriend, so he refused to be on the same bill with Nirvana, let alone open for them. So Pearl Jam was back aboard.

Our first show was at the L.A. Sports Arena, and I was desperately trying to get John excited, telling him what a trip it would be to play with Nirvana, but he was just like "Nirvana, Shirvana, who cares?" Eventually, he would discover Nirvana on his own and became a live concert/obscure B-side devotee, but this time he didn't care—although his ears pricked up when Nirvana opened their show with a cover of a Who song. This was a big deal for us to be back home playing our biggest show ever. Perry Farrell from Jane's Addiction came to the show dressed up like a handsome prince, and to me that was a sign of our newfound status.

That night was the first time I met Kurt Cobain. Before the show, I went back to Kurt's dressing room to say hello, and he was back there with Courtney. He looked torn up, like he had just come off a hard bender. He was wearing a ripped dress, and his skin was bad, and he looked like he hadn't slept for a few days, but he was just so beautiful in a different way. I was blown away by his presence and his aura. He seemed really kind. We had a nice chat, and I thanked him for playing these shows, even if going back on tour again was the furthest thing from his mind.

I kept looking over at Courtney, convinced I knew her from somewhere. Then she started yelling at me, "Anthony, don't you remember me? I used to pick you up hitchhiking down Melrose in the middle of the night, when you and Kim Jones were all strung out. I was a dancer back then, and I lent you twenty bucks, and you never paid me back." It was time for Nirvana to play, and Kurt dragged himself up and out of that dressing room, but this guy who looked like death warmed over got onstage and slayed the entire audience, putting on as good a show as you could ever want to see. Their raw energy, their musicality, their song selection, they were like a chain saw cutting through the night.

We'd saved a couple of tricks for our hometown audience. Our show opened with Flea's thunderous bass, but he wasn't on-stage, he was attached to a special harness that was propelling him down to the stage from the roof of the arena, upside down, while playing. John was in one of his moods. I don't know if he was secretly terrified to go out there and have that kind of responsibility, or if there was just so much energy going on that maybe it was too much for him to be comfortable facing, but he was very moody and very distant. He played well, but there wasn't a lot of interconnectedness happening among us. For the finale, we donned the socks, an event that was becoming rarer and rarer.

The next show was in Del Mar, a town just north of San Diego. We played a giant airplane hangar of a room, and once again Nirvana went out and destroyed with their set, and the kids went insane. It was so packed in there by the time we came onstage that steam had risen off the audience and formed a discernible cloud. We played better that night. There was less pressure, for one, and John felt like rocking a bit more. Maybe Nirvana was pushing him. That night was the beginning of my ongoing battle with tinnitus. Chad and I both came offstage and hugged backstage and realized that our ears were perceptibly ringing. By the end of that tour, I'd have permanent ear damage, which, unfortunately, is one of the hardest things to cure.

Our next gig was in San Francisco at the Cow Palace for a big New Year's Eve bash. We stayed at the Phoenix Hotel, which was a glorified motel in a scurvy neighborhood. After the show, I rang in the New Year by sitting poolside with Kurt and Courtney. We sat there for about an hour under the stars, just talking, having a bonding session. Kurt was the most relaxed I'd ever see him, and probably the straightest, too.

By the time we hit Salem, Oregon, my vocal cords were shot. They were like two fat sausages smooshed into each other, and I couldn't make a sound, so we had to reschedule the last few dates of the West Coast tour. After a short break, it was time to tour Europe. John was not only continuing to distance himself from the joy of being in the band, he had started losing the battle of psychic wellness. He went through a period when he was convinced that someone—our driver, the hotel bellman, whoever—was trying to kill him every day. I'm pretty sure he believed it, so we had this constant struggle of having to convince him that no one was trying to kill him. "Well, I don't know," he'd say. "I saw our driver talking to someone on the street, and I think that someone is connected with the people who want me dead." I think John was experiencing good old-fashioned weed paranoia taken to an extreme. He was smoking shitloads of weed and drinking gallons of wine, not wanting to be on tour but finding himself there.

Traveling was no longer jovial. We wouldn't get on the bus and sing and listen to music together and talk about the day's events and have little competitions. The bus became a dark and unwelcoming place, because we had divided into camps. John had broken our unwritten rule of no spouses or girlfriends on the road. It wasn't a great thing for us that Toni was on tour, because it allowed John to further insulate himself. A lot of people compared their relationship to John and Yoko, but that wasn't accurate. Toni would never think of speaking for John; she was there to coddle him and support his decisions. Even in the face of tension, she would smile placidly. So I never thought she was coming between John and the band. It was clearly John's doing, and she was tagging along.

Things deteriorated to the point where John and I didn't talk on the bus, and if we ran into each other in passing, we wouldn't even acknowledge each other. That was a pretty unbearable place to be, and I didn't have a palette of spiritual principles to choose from to help me deal with all the madness. I became sad and angry and resentful and poisoned by the whole experience. I was being an asshole, John was being an asshole, and poor Flea was hiding under the covers, unable to deal with it at all. Even Lindy, who had always been the mediator, was at a total loss. He had been getting frantic calls from John's mom and dad, begging him to help John, because he seemed to be in so much trouble. But Lindy was as stupefied and paralyzed by the situation as anyone else. No one was being proactive. We didn't stop to assess the whole situation, we just tried to get through it from week to week, which didn't create a healing environment. Considering the severity of the dysfunction being displayed, it's strange for me to look back and think that we didn't realize things couldn't go on like this.

It got worse before it got better. We interrupted our European tour to fly into New York City near the end of February to do *Saturday Night Live,* which was a disaster from beginning to end. We weren't there for five minutes before John started fighting with the staff. The music supervisor, a guy who'd been up there for years, came over and made an innocuous remark to John, and John turned his back on him and told Louie, "This guy says another word to me, I'm not doing the fucking show." I was already apprehensive, because we were planning to do "Under the Bridge" as our second number, and that song always was a challenge for me to sing. I was entirely dependent on John for the musical cue into the song, and when we did the dress rehearsal, he was playing something in a different key, out of tune, in a different timing, basically reinventing the song for himself and nobody else. I was flummoxed. We retreated into our dressing room and tried to hash it out, but there was no talking to him. He'd find Toni and go into another room.

But he was in the dressing room long enough to feel dissed when Madonna came by to visit. She was going to be in one of the skits that night, so she came by to say hello. I had known her for years and years, going back to her "Holiday" video, when she wanted to cast me if I would agree to change my hairstyle (which I didn't). The whole time she was back there, she inadvertently ignored John, and he stormed out, irate that she had given him no love and no props.

The show began, and we did our first number, "Stone Cold

Bush," an uptempo rocker. It went well. Then we came back to do "Under the Bridge." I've since heard that John was on heroin during this show, but he might as well have been on another planet, because he started playing some shit I'd never heard before. I had no idea what song he was playing or what key he was in. He looked like he was in a different world. To this day, John denies that he was playing off-key. According to him, he was experimenting the way he would have if we'd been rehearsing the tune. Well, we weren't, we were on live TV in front of millions of people, and it was torture. I started to sing in what I thought was the key, even if it wasn't the key he was playing in. I felt like I was getting stabbed in the back and hung out to dry in front of all of America while this guy was off in a corner in the shadow, playing some dissonant out-of-tune experiment. I thought he was doing that on purpose, just to fuck with me.

We got through the song, and it sounded like four different people playing four different songs. At the time I was dating Sofia Coppola, another one of my unfulfilled attempts at a relationship during this period of my life. She was by far the coolest girl I had gone out with, especially in that period after Carmen, and I told her to make sure to watch the show, and now I was just fucking dying. When something happens like that, it's like the kicker who misses a field goal as the clock is running out: The only thing that's going to take away that pain is playing another game and getting another chance to kick the field goal.

That pain was there for a long time, because we went back to Europe, and John's behavior got even more erratic. When it came time for him to solo, he would pull the cord out of his guitar and create a jarring noise and then plug it back in and, if he felt like it, play the chorus. The ironic part about *Saturday Night Live* was, the week after our performance, our record went through the roof. Maybe it was a coincidence, but maybe people heard something in that chaotic performance that touched them.

After we finished the European leg of the tour, we went back home and had a couple of weeks off before going to Hawaii, Japan, and Australia. When we came home between legs of tours, I saw less of Flea, and I never saw much of Chad. John disappeared and started pursuing his drug use. So I'd hang out with whatever girl I was seeing at the time, although I was mainly doing the random dating thing, and nothing was sticking. Since my split with John, I had room in my life for a new running partner, and I found one in Jimmy Boyle. He was a friend of Rick Rubin who looked exactly like Rasputin, with a full beard and mustache and long Jesus hair and crazy-psycho blue eyes, and he dressed like an elegant ragman. The more we saw each other, the more we realized the many things we had in common. He was a recovering drug addict who had just gotten divorced from a tragic young beautiful dope fiend whom I'd dated as well. He was also a vegetarian (a practice I had picked up from Ione), he loved music, and he loved chasing girls. Every day I was in town, we'd meet for a ritualistic breakfast of blueberry pancakes at A Votre Sante on La Brea.

I invited Jimmy to come to Hawaii with us. He loved it because he loved to be around the excitement of music, not to mention the girls. Plus, we were going to Hawaii, for Christ's sake. John was still being distant while we were in Hawaii. Our record had been doing okay, better than any of our previous ones, though still only okay, barely in the Top 40. Once we were in Hawaii, we got a call from Lindy. "Guys, I don't know what to tell you, but this record is going through the roof. It's charting next week at number eight," he told us. For me, that was cause for celebration. Flea was feeling the same way, but John was staying removed from the whole thing.

That whole trip was teeming with hot young Hawaiian girls, and it was a fun time for all, because everyone was feeling full of life in the sunshine and the ocean. Boyle and I were sharing a room, and at four in the morning, we were asleep when there was a knock on the door. I went to answer, and it was this young Hawaiian maiden.

"Can I come in?" she asked.

"Well, my friend's sleeping. It's not really a good idea, it's four in the morning," I reminded her.

"Really, I can't come in?" she pressed.

"Uh, it's kind of an uncomfortable situation." Right there, in the hallway of this hotel, she dropped to her knees and gave me a blow job. Jimmy was so jealous. "I can't believe this. You fucking hear a knock in the middle of the night, you go to the doorway, and the most beautiful girl on the island gets down on her knees and gives you a blow job. What is that? What have I done wrong in my lifetime not to deserve this kind of treatment?"

I wasn't overjoyed about all this new adulation I was getting. I wasn't having the same reaction John was, but on a personal level, I wasn't letting it all go to my head. I think I didn't feel entitled now that I was becoming famous, and I stayed relatively humble. That was my perception, and I'm sure somebody else had a different take. I recognize when I feel a sense of entitlement—you get used to having things your way—but I also recognize the absurdity of that, and I'm willing to laugh at myself and to acknowledge when I'm being a spoiled brat and when I'm not. I found it fascinating and peculiar, more than suddenly thinking I was better than or holier than.

It's ironic, because on most days, Flea is the biggest spoiled brat in the band, but he and I had this talk in Santa Monica, and he said, "You know, Anthony, this record is doing so good, I think you're becoming a bit of an egomaniac."

"Me? Me? You're the egomaniac. Take a look at your own ego," I proposed.

I'm sure there was some bloated-ego thing happening that I wasn't able to recognize, but I didn't feel like it would last for long. The weird thing is that long before we ever had success on a commercial level, I had already developed a sense of entitlement. I had an unnecessary, unwarranted, unfounded, self-centered sense of entitlement from childhood. In elementary school, I always felt like I should be the president of the school and that I was somehow above the law of the school and I could break the rules. When I moved in with my father, he was arrogant and full of himself, and that carried on to me, so I always had this sense of entitlement and a semi-false sense of self. I would steal because I had that sense, whether it was houses or cars or furniture or cactuses, whatever. I understand how people can be cold and ruthless criminals, because I remember at that point in my life, I did not think of the consequences for anybody else involved except me. And the consequences for me were that I got what I wanted.

The richer and more famous I got, the less I'd behave in that manner. Sure, the ego does get inflated and retarded and grotesque in some ways, but that's a chance to learn, a chance to go, "Okay, what do I have to do to deal with this weirdness, and how do I diminish the ego to a point where it's not interfering with my relating to the rest of the universe?" If anything, everything was making me less selfish and less self-centered, and more interested in getting out of myself and being in a place where I could share. A lot of times people will judge you on their perceived idea of how you're acting. If you're in a room and you're feeling shy and you don't want a certain amount of attention, you're not going out of your way to make friends with everybody. Then someone's going to walk away going, "That arrogant motherfucker, he didn't even try to talk to me." You're trying to lay low and not make a big deal about yourself, but they're seeing you as this guy who's all that and a bag of fucking chips.

I don't feel like I started thinking of myself any differently while this was happening; if anything, I was thinking of myself in a worse light, because I'd lost an important connection in my life with John. I began realizing that I'd been carrying on as a control freak, wanting to have everything go according to my plans, which turned out to be the biggest pain in the ass ever. I used to think that everything would be great if Flea just behaved this way and John did what I wanted him to do, and that was probably the biggest mistake I made during that time, thinking that I knew better or had a plan, and if everyone followed it, things would be peachy. That was a recipe for misery and ruin. Once I recognized all that, the brotherhood of our band had once more been compromised beyond repair.

We hit Japan in early May 1992. It's strange, because John thought that we had worked out our differences by then, but I still felt that we weren't close. He was still in his cocoon with Toni. And he was again exhibiting some strange behavior. The night before our Tokyo gig, John was in the lobby of our hotel with Louie, and he became convinced that he had exposed himself to some female autograph seekers and that he was in imminent danger of getting arrested and deported.

There was a distinctly erratic, unpredictable vibe happening around John. He was smoked out of his mind, and also hitting the wine in such a way that he didn't strike me as being typically drunk. I don't know if it was a combination of the wine and the pot, but it seemed like he was drinking psycho juice rather than just wine. There was the typical dopey, daffy, wobbly, slurry normal drunk behavior, but there was also this weird PCP-like drunk going on, like he was in a different space.

The next morning John traveled to the venue with the crew. Lindy and Flea and Chad and I came on a later train, and when we got to the arena, Mark Johnson told us that John had quit the band and he wanted to go home immediately. Mind you, we were slated to go to Australia after Japan, and it would be our first Australian tour ever. This was incredibly important to us, because it was a land that we loved, it was the birthplace of Flea, it was the new land of milk and honey and sunshine and girls, just a magical place. So there was panic in Lindy's eyes and in Flea's and my hearts. We had to talk to John right away, even though the final die had been cast.

We went back into the room where John was holed up.

"I have to leave the band, I have to quit. I have to go home right away, I can't do this anymore," he told me. "I will die if I don't get out of this band right away."

I saw the look in his eyes, and I knew there was no other

choice. There was no point in even trying to talk him into staying. A huge sense of relief came over me. The last thing in the world that I ever would want to happen was happening, but thank God he was walking away, because as much as this was going to hurt, the relief of not having to deal with the drama on a day-to-day basis would be greater than the self-imposed pain and suffering.

Lindy was concerned with the sold-out venue. Finally, we got John to agree to play the show before he got on a plane to go home. It was the most horrible show ever. Every single note, every single word, hurt, knowing that we were no longer a band. I kept looking over at John and seeing this dead statue of disdain. In some ways, I wish we would have canceled the show and returned everyone's money rather than have them witness this display of twisted energy. And that night John disappeared from the topsy-turvy world of the Red Hot Chili Peppers.

11.

Warped

While we were still in Japan, we came up with a plan. We would go on to Australia, where we'd meet up with our friend Zander Schloss, who was going to take John's place. Zander was a talented guitar player who could read and write music, a quick study with a zany, soulful, comic sensibility. We had seven days to teach him enough songs to rock out Australia.

Zander met us in Sydney, and we started intensive two-a-day rehearsals. But after four days, it was clear to Flea and me that this wasn't happening. Zander was playing the songs, but it didn't feel like the Red Hot Chili Peppers. At that point, we decided we'd rather cancel the dates than present a half-assed version of ourselves.

When we told Zander, he was devastated. You'd have thought he was in the band for four years instead of four days. "Oh my God, I just went from having the richest, most incredible future to not only being where I started from but being eight thousand miles from home," Zander said. "Am I going to get a ticket back?"

We assured him we weren't going to strand him, and we all stayed in Australia for a few more days and enjoyed the gorgeous weather and the beautiful girls.

I was friendly with Greer Gavorko, a New Zealander who was one of our crew members. When he showed me pictures from a recent trip he'd taken to Thailand, I thought, "I'm in Australia, which is nowhere near Hollywood. I have no idea what's going to happen with my future, because we're now limping through life as a band. My left nut, in the person of John Frusciante, has just departed my testicle sack. So why don't I just go to Thailand by myself?"

Greer recommended some islands in the Gulf of Siam. So I flew to Bangkok, stayed the night in a hotel airport, and then flew to the south and got on a boat to Ko Samui. It was a beautiful island, and the weather was incredible, but the place was teeming with Eurotrash party animals. It was coke, bad music, and half-naked beautiful women all high on Ecstasy. I hadn't come to Thailand to immerse myself in a techno-fantasy world, so I traveled to the next island, Ko Pha Ngan. It was a little more laid-back and beautiful, but I was still discontented, so I got a recommendation from some Thai natives to go to Ko Tao, a small island with no hotels.

Ko Tao was exactly what I had been dreaming of. I rented a little house from a Thai family and stayed for a week, going scuba diving every day. I left the island feeling recharged and cleansed, and more prepared to deal with John being gone. As soon as I got back, Flea and I went to the drawing board. We were familiar with an L.A. band called Marshall Law, which consisted of two brothers, Lonnie Marshall on bass and Arik Marshall on guitar. Both of these guys were funky, freaky oddball prodigies on their instruments. They were from South Central, and they were half black and half

Jewish, the old Blewish thing. I had seen them a number of times, and Arik's guitar playing, especially, had blown me away. It was funky but also hard-rocking and inventive.

We auditioned a few other people, including this guy called Buckethead, who would play his whole set with a Kentucky Fried Chicken bucket on his head while encased in a chicken coop. When Arik jammed with us, it was fun and inspiring, so we ended up hiring him, and he was thrust into the insanity of our world. Even though we had just lost John, who was such a fundamental element of our huge success with *Blood Sugar*, the promoters and MTV and the whole music industry didn't perceive us as being finished, because nothing was stopping. We were offered to headline Lollapalooza, the biggest tour in America that summer. Lindy had booked some huge European festivals for us in June as well.

Luckily for us, Arik was an incredibly fast study. He could hear a song on the radio and, within sixty seconds, play it with the same vibe and spirit of the original. But going to Belgium a few weeks into his tenure in the Chili Peppers before seventy thousand people was truly a baptism by fire. He was petrified. Arik had hardly ever left L.A. County, and now he was in an exotic country in Northern Europe where they speak three languages.

Arik was extremely introverted, so he dealt with all this pressure by sleeping. The motherfucker would sleep all day and all night, then get in the van on the way to the show and sleep some more. But he never let us down in concert. He just stood up there and played his ass off.

Headlining Lollapalooza was a pretty big-ass deal for us. It was the second year of that festival, and the idea of traveling across the country with a bunch of like-minded maniacs appealed to us. Anytime you're part of a festival, the pressure is cut in half. Even if you're the headliner, you don't have to carry the weight of the whole show. Since this was a tough time in the life of our band, thank God the shows were not all about us. Plus, you get to meet some interesting performers whom you might never encounter if not for this. I was never a fan of Ministry, but they wound up blowing me away every night. I didn't know how they could be so fucked up on booze and heroin and coke and whippets and go out there and crush it.

After a few shows into the tour, everybody started jamming with everybody else. Ice Cube was rocking the house, and Flea and I used to go onstage for a song. We danced, happy to be part of his flag-waving posse. Then he joined us on "Higher Ground." Eddie Vedder, who was there with Pearl Jam, would sing backup for Soundgarden, but in keeping with his humble-servant-of-music attitude, he'd stand way off by the back of the stage. Chad played drums on one of Ministry's songs. The whole show was a lovefest except for the Jesus and Mary Chain, this British group, who were just bitter. They'd polish off a giant bottle of booze by two in the afternoon and curse and put everyone down. One time they went too far with the guys from Ice Cube's band, and they got themselves a beating.

I bonded with these giant gangster Samoans called the Boo-Yaa Tribe, who were playing on the secondary stage. I was enthralled, listening to their stories of gang warfare in East L.A. They told me that their friends would get shot and not even know it because they were so big, so they'd walk around for a couple of days with bullets in them. By the end of the tour, I got one of the Boo-Yaa guys to come onstage during "Higher Ground," and he put out his arm, picked me up, and perched me on his forearm. I rocked the whole song sitting like a puppet on his arm.

We added some special elements for our Lollapalooza shows. We built a giant psychedelic *Twilight Zone*–looking spiraling wheel that we placed in the center of the stage for hypnotic purposes. But the ultimate touch was the fire helmets that we wore for our encore. Whenever I think of performing, fire comes to my mind—it's such a visual thing, and it goes so well with music. I wasn't thinking in the grand pyrotechnical arena of bands like Kiss or the Who. I just thought it would be great if we wore helmets that belched fire. So we went to a prop designer Lindy knew, and he came up with a silver construction helmet that had a spigot sticking out of the top and a tube that ran from the spigot to a can of propane housed on a waist belt. We each had a valve at our side so we could control the intensity of the flame.

But when you're dealing with fire and a delivery system, there are bound to be some screwups. We'd be able to spew out a good three-foot plume of fire, but on some nights, someone wouldn't hit the valve right, or the propane can would be nearly empty, and there'd be three guys with raging volcano heads and one guy with a three-inch Bic lighter coming out of his head, only he had no idea his flame was so small. It was very emasculating. Flame envy.

At several venues, fire marshals tried to stop the show. Lindy used to have to carry extra cash, and when the marshal told him that we could be fined if we lit up those helmets, Lindy pulled out his wad and asked, "How much?" In another city, the fire marshals required our roadies to wear firemen's outfits, complete with helmets, when they lit us up. Mark Johnson, our tour manager, was, in some ways, the original Homer Simpson, so just imagine Homer with a full fire-retardant outfit trying to get it together to turn the right knobs and light the fire. It's amazing we got through that tour alive.

In September 1992 we played the MTV awards show and picked up two awards for the "Give It Away" video and the viewer's choice award for "Under the Bridge." It must have been awkward for Arik to be onstage accepting awards for work that John had done. We were full of ourselves and obnoxious and loud that night. When we went up to get the breakthrough video award for "Give It Away," Flea simulated masturbation. I had a list of thirty people I wanted to thank: artists, musicians, filmmakers, scholars—and Satan. Back in Florida, my grandmother, who was a devout Christian, didn't realize I was joking around and disowned me. A little while later, I asked my mom why I never got any letters anymore from Grandma Kiedis, and she said, "She thinks you're in league with Satan." I had to write Granny a postcard on her eightieth birthday, explaining that I wasn't really a Satanist.

That fall we traveled to Australia and New Zealand to make up the dates we had canceled. Even though we weren't on an arena level yet, since this was the first time we'd ever played there, the audiences were amazingly responsive. As soon as we set foot in New Zealand, I fell in love with the place. It seemed like a home away from home. There was more plant life than I'd ever seen, and towering majestic mountains and very few people. After our shows, everyone raced back home, but I decided to stay and explore the country.

I got a room in a cool art deco hotel in downtown Auckland and hung out with Greer, who was a native Kiwi. One night we were playing pool when a longhaired brunette goddess out of a Kiwi fairy tale walked into the room. She stood at the bar and watched me, and I got up the courage to approach her.

"What are you doing here?" I said, since she was out of place in the seedy bar.

"I came to find you," she explained. "I heard you were in town, and I've come to get you."

Julie got me, all right. We spent the rest of my stay together. We took a trip to the Rotorua, and checked out the giant hot mineral lakes and the mud pits. We broke into a national park and made love at the edge of a mud pit that was a big bubbling cauldron of steam and mud. On November 1, we celebrated my thirtieth birthday at the seaside home of Mr. and Mrs. Murdoch, who owned Warner Bros. records in New Zealand. They organized a beautiful picnic on the beach for me. It was a bittersweet milestone. I was far from home, surrounded by relative strangers. The band was doing great, but it also was not right. Ever since John left, we had kept forging on without stopping to look at the lack of perfection, just moving forward to try to keep it alive.

I was also lonely without a true love in my life. A lot of my close friendships had unraveled. John was out of the picture. Flea and I had been growing apart. Bob Forrest was deep into the exploration of his own drug abuse. I felt like a man alone.

With nothing compelling me to return home, I decided to

go on an adventure to Borneo. Even as a kid, I was always reading about the most remote tropical jungle locations in the world, and of all the places I'd ever read about, from Mongolia to Papua New Guinea to Tuva, Borneo always struck me as the most remote, the least Westernized: a place where you could go back in time and see what life was like before industry and creature comforts.

On our visits to Amsterdam, I had befriended an amazing tattoo artist named Hank Schiffmacher. Hank, also known as Henky Penky, was an icon of his country—an underground philosopher, artist, Hell's Angels associate, booze hound, drug hound, girl hound, an absolute rapscallion of Dutch proportions. Over the years, Hank had injected much ink into my skin, and in the process, we'd become close. So when Hank suggested that we travel to Borneo to search out primitive tattooing techniques and replicate the crossing of the Borneo rain forest by a nineteenth-century Dutch explorer, I was all for it. I had visions of being Mowgli from *The Jungle Book,* hanging out with orangutans and swinging from vines over rivers and eating berries and meeting naked native girls and being a tough nature fella. It didn't turn out quite that way.

We put aside a month for the trip. At first I thought it would be Hank and me traveling to the land of the Punandaya tribe, who had practiced cannibalism, according to some reports, as late as the 1960s. But Hank brought a photojournalist who thought getting his pictures was more important than the humanity or the dignity of the foreign culture. Hank also brought a Caspar Milquetoast of a kid who had wandered into his tattoo shop, a bank employee who'd never been outside of Holland.

So we were a motley crew when we met up in Jakarta, Indonesia, to plan out our journey. I didn't like Jakarta, a third-world megalopolis saturated with trash and pollution and teeming with a fundamentalist energy that didn't make us the most welcome guys in town. We were a long way from Kansas, but every time we went to a bazaar or a marketplace, in every shantytown, I'd be surrounded by giggling Indonesian girls. They were selling bootleg Red Hot Chili Peppers T-shirts in every stall. It was surreal.

From Jakarta, we took a series of small planes to Pontianak, a town on the west coast of Borneo. That was where we'd start our adventure. We planned to cross central Borneo from Pontianak to Samarinda, the trans-Kalimantan tour. It had taken the Dutch ethnographer Nieuwenhuis fifteen months to make this trip in 1894. We gave ourselves four weeks.

We stayed in Pontianak for a day, stocking up on supplies and cigarettes. Then we got on a ferry barge and made our way up the river toward the center of the island. The river started off huge, like the Mississippi, and then kept getting smaller and smaller as we went deeper into the jungle, until it became these raging rapids-type rivers that were capable of quadrupling in size in about ten minutes during flash floods.

Everyone was in fantastic spirits, viewing this beautiful confluence of two rivers, until we saw miles and miles of decimated jungle. The logging industries had infiltrated this ancient civilization and raped the forest. It was as if an area the size of Rhode Island had been shaved clean off the map. After changing to a smaller boat, we reached the fishing village of Putussibau, the last outpost before we were confronted with true wilderness. Putussibau consisted of two main streets, one transvestite, and a Dutch missionary priest who almost gleefully warned us of the dangers that lay ahead, things like malaria and poisonous snakes. According to him, all the anti-malaria pills we'd been taking were completely useless, and if we ended up catching malaria, we were dead meat. Nice.

The next day we set off in our own boat. We stopped after a few hours to explore an authentic longhouse, which was a jungle version of an apartment complex, except it was a commune where everybody lived together, sharing one common porch. Then we went on and on and on, deeper into the jungle. The farther up we got, the faster the water moved, the fewer the villages, and the more difficult passage became in general. Then the rains came. After changing to smaller and smaller boats, we made it to Tong Jang

Lokam, the last village before the terrain became too mountainous and too perilous to travel by boat. It was a serene setting before the maze of the jungle, where there was no river or even a path to follow, just an overlap of mountains, forests, and streams.

It was here that we'd hire our guides from the Punans, a nomadic tribe considered the masters of the forest. The local Punans could probably cross the mountains in five days, but there was no telling how long it would take when they were bogged down with four slow white guys. I was uneasy with the guides they were choosing for us, because one was the grandpa of the village, a guy in his seventies, and the others were barely teenagers. I couldn't figure out if we were getting worthy guides or whichever nomads happened to be in town.

We had a nice day or two of rest in the village, and then we set off on foot. It was a wild landscape, like nothing I'd ever marched through. The density, the heat, the wetness, the noises, all of it evoked a prehistoric feeling, especially when we spotted the giant hornbilled birds flying overhead. This was a different reality. After a day of hiking, we had to come to terms with the fact that there were no paths to follow. It was just wet and mucky terrain.

When nightfall came, we needed to find a dry, level space protected from the inevitable rains. We stumbled upon an old decrepit outpost shack, so instead of building a lean-to out of huge leaves, our guides told us to stay in the shack. It didn't look inviting—the structure was teeming with insects and covered in spiderwebs, but we lay down in there like sardines, crawled into our sleeping bags, and tried to sleep. I was starting to doze off, half conscious of the spiders dangling over me, when, all of a sudden, my entire skull started to vibrate. It felt like a woodpecker practicing on my skull. I was terrified that I had been bitten by something poisonous and the toxic venom was going to work on my nervous system, so I bolted up and screamed for Hank to help me.

The horrible vibrating noise in my skull was intensifying, and I couldn't bear one more minute of this agony, so I begged Hank to take out his flashlight and look inside my ear.

"No, I don't see anything. Everything looks—ARRGGGHH," he screamed, and dropped the flashlight.

A huge sense of relief came over me, and my head stopped vibrating.

"Oh my God," Hank said. "Some little animal came scurrying out of your head, man."

It turned out that a cockroach had somehow squeezed into my ear canal and gotten lodged there. It took the light to get it to depart my head. I was glad to be rid of the roach, but then I started worrying that the monster had laid eggs inside my head and my brain would become dinner for a family of insects. But after a while, that obsession left me, probably because I was too busy dealing with the leeches that had begun to burrow into my body. Because the jungle was so dense, we sought out the rivers, which were anywhere from knee- to waist-deep. While you were in the water, these leeches would swim up and attach themselves to your skin. They'd suck your blood and become enormous, and every day we'd have to burn them off with a lit Marlboro. Then we'd be left with gaping open wounds, which could get infected. If you didn't pick up leeches in the river, they'd also be in the trees, waiting for you to walk under, so they were coming at us from all angles.

About five days into the trek, we had our first major crisis. Our guides realized that we were totally lost, and they began to have powwows to figure out what to do. No one had any idea which direction to go. Our food was running out, and I got the distinct impression that they were looking at us like "Let's ditch them or kill them or just eat them." But I think the grandpa nixed those stirrings, and we all set out to try to find our bearings.

Then the sickness began. I started having severe nausea and diarrhea and vomiting, though I had no choice but to march tens of miles every day, straight up mountains and cliffs, carrying this heavy backpack. I couldn't sleep; all night long, I'd flame diarrhea and simultaneously vomit. I began to hallucinate from dehydration and lack of food and sleep, but I became fixated on survival and willed my body onward.

We started splitting up, sending out groups to climb to the tops of the mountains and figure out where the mighty Mahakam River began. Once we found that, we would be home free. One day I went off with a guide and climbed to the top of the nearby mountain. The only way back down was a sheer vertical drop, which was, thankfully, covered with vines. I followed him step by step down the cliff, holding on to the vines. We came to a spot where there were no footholds, so now we were dependent on vine power alone to get us down. He scaled this ten-foot traverse clinging to the vines, but when it was my turn, I questioned whether the vines would hold my weight. He assured me it was okay; I was still dubious. The minute I let go of the cliff and put my weight on the vines, the vine ripped loose from the cliff, and I went falling over backward. Now there was nothing to save me from plummeting to a certain death on the ragged rocks hundreds of feet below, except for the fact that on the way down, my foot had gotten tangled up in another series of vines. I was dangling upside down off of this cliff. My guide was safe above me, laughing hysterically. I had to claw myself to an upright position and untangle myself before I could reach a safe spot.

Days later, we came upon the Mahakam, this fat mountainous river with deep, blue, fast, treacherous water. We were still a few hundred miles from the ocean, but now it was a doable trip by boat, which we could hire at the first village, about twenty miles downriver. We were celebrating on that bank, kissing the ground, when we spied some locals in a boat. They had a whole deer, and our guides cajoled them into giving us a leg of the deer and a turtle. I had been a vegetarian for years, but I had no compunction about tearing into that poorly cooked venison. Before the natives departed, our guides ordered a boat to come get us the next day.

Then the dreaded rains came. We were in a canyon, and there was no shoreline, just sheer rocks, and the river rose and spilled over our campsite. We were forced up this steep slope that had some vegetation and a few trees, and we had to spend the night standing up against the mountain, resting our feet on some tree stumps below. The next day the boat showed up, we made a deal for passage to the ocean, and said good-bye to our guides, who turned around and scurried back over the mountains to their village. That night we stopped at a village and managed to rent a room, but my fever returned with a vengeance. Again I was up all night spewing out of both ends, feeling weaker than I ever had in my entire life. My condition wasn't helped when we got the news that a few days earlier, a team of Australians doing the same trek had died in a flash flood.

The next day I was so sick and so desperate to get back to civilization that I went to the local communications base, got on the shortwave, and ordered a helicopter to come get us. Hank and I were choppered to Balik, where I found a doctor who prescribed some antibiotics, which seemed to take the edge off my illness without curing it. Then I hugged Hank good-bye. Our bond had been strengthened by our conquest over death by making it through that damn jungle.

On the way back to L.A., I stopped in New Zealand, but I still wasn't feeling normal. A few days later, when I got on the flight to L.A., I sat down and nearly passed out. Buckets of sweat started pouring out of me, my fever escalated, and I started hallucinating again. When we landed, I could barely get off the plane. After spending a day on my couch, I checked in to the UCLA medical center, where they were baffled by my condition. They gave me some painkillers, which I was willing to take even though I was sober. I went back home, but now I was going into feverish, painkiller sweat baths. I checked in to Cedars-Sinai, where, after days and days of testing, they determined that I had a rare tropical disease called dengue fever. At least now I knew what I had, and the treatment course was the same potent antibiotics. I recovered, although we did have to cancel our New Year's Eve show in San Francisco.

I was fine when we flew down to Brazil to perform some big shows in January. It was a four-night festival, and we were alternating nights with Nirvana, each band doing shows in Rio and

São Paolo. We all flew down together in a big 747, and it was a real festive situation, but nothing could have prepared me for the reception we got in Brazil. Even though Nina Hagen had told me that after the rest of the world had forgotten her, she could go to Brazil and get a welcome like she was one of the Beatles, I still couldn't believe the fervor of the Brazilian fans. We needed members of the armed services to help us leave the hotel. The fans had an exuberance that bordered on being dangerous.

The day before we were scheduled to play Rio, we got a police escort and were ferried deep into a favela—a slum neighborhood that even the police were afraid to enter—to see an authentic Mardi Gras Samba troupe practice. We were so knocked out by this South American Mother Earth soul music and pageantry that we invited the whole troupe to come onstage and jam with us the next night. And they did. At least twice as many members poured onstage as were at rehearsal, all decked out in their best costumes.

Chad didn't know what to do, so he started to beat on his drums, and they started playing along, shaking their percussive sticks and dancing and singing. Flea found his groove and got in there, and Arik started playing something funky that worked. I had a hard time finding a place in that arrangement until two Samba girls came over and started dancing with me, and then we all danced and percussed and had a rad psychedelic jam.

Nirvana was headlining the next night, and we were all excited about their show. Meanwhile, Courtney Love was making an unbelievable spectacle of herself every chance she possibly could. I had never seen anyone so designed for attention and spotlight and drama. She was out of control. Whenever a photographer aimed his camera at a group of people, Courtney flew into the frame, grabbing everyone like she was their best friend.

We didn't see much of Kurt, who was very reclusive. I spent some time with him backstage before his second show. He was high on pills, which somehow never affected his performance, and he was quiet and withdrawn. But he had such mad style, wearing the best combination of colors and sweaters and mismatched stuff.

Nirvana just killed both nights. They played a lot of new songs that would turn up on *In Utero,* and then they all switched instruments and went into some '70s pop songs like "Seasons in the Sun." During one of the two shows, Kurt took this insane guitar solo that lasted ten minutes. He took off his guitar and started playing it while it was on the ground, and then he bashed it into his amp. He wound up in the audience playing the destroyed guitar. When he went back onstage and the crowd started fighting over the guitar, Courtney came flying out of the wings, dove into the audience, and beat up a few Brazilian kids to take possession of the guitar.

She climbed back onstage and proudly held up the mangled guitar, strutting around and milking every minute. She finally went offstage, and somehow Louie, our crew member, wound up with the neck of that guitar, which he still has to this day.

We flew back home, happy to have shared those experiences with Nirvana. Everybody loved that band. Meanwhile, the *Blood Sugar* album was still rolling along. I still wasn't used to any of the extra public awareness. I remember going to a party for Lisa Marie Presley in an airplane hangar in Santa Monica around this time. I went to the bathroom to take a piss, and this normal-looking businessman in a suit walked up to the urinal next to me, looked over, and recognized me.

"Oh my God, you're that guy," he said, and started howling a version of "Under the Bridge."

Another time I was riding my mountain bike by my house, and a random car drove by, and I heard "Under the Bridge" blaring out the window. I realized that our music was now in the public domain and no longer some underground phenomenon. Which made me a bit more shy and reclusive. Ironically, Flea and I had spent most of our lives craving attention and trying to create a spectacle, doing outlandish things to be seen and heard and felt. One time back at Fairfax High, we found out that the corner of Westwood and Wilshire Boulevard was the busiest intersection in the world. So we drank a bit and split a quaalude and went down to that corner, shimmied up a pole, and climbed onto an enormous billboard that looked down on that busy intersection. We stripped naked and danced around, swinging our dicks for every passerby to see. It felt like the whole world was watching, and that felt good, a memorable moment when we could be exhibitionists and performers and daredevils and junior lawbreakers, all at the same time. Now we were on those billboards instead of dancing naked in front of them. So I didn't feel the compulsion to fight for attention or brag about how amazing our music was anymore.

Now it was time to create more of it. Flea and I had both started to write, and we were looking forward to bonding with Arik and exploring his mind and musical talents. After we finished touring, Arik rented a nice apartment close to my house. But every time I tried to get together to work with him, he wasn't available. I wound up going over to his house and dropping off some lyrics and a half-baked tape because he didn't seem comfortable getting out the guitar at that moment, but again, there was no response. No callback, no "I've got some ideas." It wasn't long after that we decided he might not be the writing partner we were looking for.

That was when we got the most god-awful idea, which was to advertise and audition guitar players. We thought we could audition every guitar player in the world and find the most perfect, talented, soulful, and fun player around, but it doesn't work that way. It's like finding a wife, you have to hope she crosses your path. We put an ad in the *L.A. Weekly* and held auditions. It was a circus, and it went nowhere. Some people could play, but some kids came by hoping to meet the band. Around that time, I had seen a band called Mother Tongue at the Club Lingerie, and I liked their guitar player, a kid named Jesse Tobias. I told Flea about him, and we decided to bring him in. We jammed, and it was very raw and energetic. He definitely had the most exciting chemistry of anyone we had played with, but Flea was mildly concerned that he might not have the technical range required to play our music. In the end, we hired him, and he quit his band, and we began to play and write music.

After a couple of weeks, something wasn't right. We jammed and jammed with Jesse, but no one was satisfied, particularly Flea. I was still holding out hope that it could work when Chad came to me and said, "I have a feeling that Dave Navarro is ready to play with us." Dave had always been our first choice after John left. We had approached him early on, but he'd been too busy with his side project after Jane's Addiction broke up. Lately, Chad had been hanging around with him, and he was sure Dave would love to come over. It was the ideal situation, because when Dave was in Jane's Addiction, they had virtually invented a sound and shared a spirit of music that was unique and enormously emotional and was the voice of L.A. for a long time. It was passionate, original art coming from all the right places, with all the right insanity and love.

So we fired Jesse and hired Dave. Navarro had the best line. He told us, "I heard a rumor out on the street that the reason you fired Jesse was 'cause he was too cute and was stealing some of the female attention away from you. And then you hire me. What does that say for me?" He had the most sardonic sense of humor. When he first joined the band, he made up guitar picks that listed each guitarist we'd ever had in the band. After his name, there was a question mark.

With Dave in the band, it was inevitable that our sound would change. He had a different style of playing than anyone we'd had before, but he was very competent and quick to learn our songs. He didn't carry with him the mysterious essence of funk, but we weren't stressed about that; we were prepared to explore other territory. I couldn't have predicted his incredible kindness. He was a very sensitive, tender, there-for-you person right off the bat, which was wonderful in combination with his sardonic wit.

Despite all this, we got off to a strange beginning, because not everyone adjusted right away to our dynamic. John had been a true anomaly when it came to that. He made it even easier than Hillel, in some ways, to create music, even though I'd known Hillel for years. I just figured that was how all guitar players were, that you showed them your lyrics and sang a little bit, and the next thing you knew, you had a song. That didn't happen right off the bat with Dave. I remember going over to Dave's house, and he and I wanted to learn a Beatles song together, and it was a much slower, more difficult process than in the past.

We all liked Dave, but unbeknownst to me, he was feeling like an outsider. I don't think he knew how open we were to making him an equal partner. He had been through a lot of battles with Perry Farrell in Jane's Addiction, and their writing styles were independent, so he wasn't used to our collaborative style. It wasn't until years later that he told me he was concerned he would get fired any minute.

At the end of October 1993, I decided to take a short trip to New York to both celebrate my birthday and accompany my good friend Guy Oseary of Maverick Records to all the festivities surrounding Fashion Week. Guy was hot on the trail of Kate Moss, and I had no aversion to hanging out with him and going to runway shows. We stayed at the Royalton and got in late from a Halloween party. A few hours into my sleep, the phone started ringing off the hook. I picked up the receiver, and it was my dad. He was in a frenzied state, babbling, "Did you hear what happened? River's dead." I was half awake at the time, so it took a few seconds for me to process the information. After I did, I called him right back, and he told me that River Phoenix had died the previous night outside a club in L.A. of a drug overdose. Once again, I felt an unbelievable sense of loss. I called up Flea, who had accompanied River in the ambulance from the Viper Room to the hospital, and we both sobbed for quite some time. River wasn't my best friend, but he was a completely enchanted spirit of a human, living every day in a very free way.

It was my birthday, but I didn't feel like celebrating. I spent some of the day with my friend Acacia, who had been the girlfriend of both Flea and Joaquin, River's brother. I went to her apartment in Chinatown, and we lay in her bunk bed together, sobbing. I was feeling gutted and hollowed out. I made my way back to the

Royalton, and Guy O forced me to let him take me out for a birthday dinner. As is Guy O's wont, we went to the trendy, goofy restaurant of the moment. We ate and played some pool, and then Guy dragged me to a place called the Soul Kitchen. There was a great DJ that night, and at one point I got up and tried to dance my blues away.

When I got back to our table, there was a cluster of humans around Guy, including two hot, model-looking girls who were doing the typical things young model girls do, drinking alcohol and smoking Marlboros. I couldn't take my eyes off one of them, this glowing pixie with a butch haircut, especially when she started making out with her girlfriend. I could tell that they weren't *girlfriend* girlfriends, they were just kissing for entertainment purposes. We didn't have much of an exchange that night, but she did tell me she would be in the Calvin Klein show the next day.

By now my crosshairs were fixed on this girl. I'd been touched by something about her, and it wasn't simply a random biological reaction to a gorgeous girl I wanted to sleep with. There was a more metaphysical feeling about her and our possibilities. I told Guy O about my attraction, and he pooh-poohed it, telling me to keep my options open. Then we went to the Klein show the next day, and there was that hot blonde's picture on the cover of the daily *W* newspaper for the fashion show. All at once Guy O took a lot more interest in her. We watched her walk, and I was smitten by Cupid's arrow. I have an overwhelming tendency to get ahead of myself in these matters, so if I see a girl I like, even if I've never talked to her, I'll sit there and look at her and go, "I could marry that girl. She looks like she'd be a good mom and a good sex partner." I was convinced that the young Jaime Rishar would be thinking the same way, and she'd be my girl.

That night we all met at Indochine, a trendy downtown restaurant, but the interaction was nothing like I had imagined. She was sitting there with a table full of hens, quacking away, all models, all drinking way too much, smoking way too much, and taking what they do way too seriously. I showed up with Guy O, expecting her to make herself perfectly available to me, but she was being aloof, intentionally distant and intentionally shitfaced. I was patient and tolerant. Christy Turlington started talking to Jaime and filling her head with negative information about me: "Stay away from that guy, he's a womanizer, he's a slut, he'll love you and leave you, blah blah blah."

I started to lose some of my interest in Jaime, thinking she was too young and too wrapped up in the nonsense of her micro-community. But something in me wasn't going to give up all the way, and at a certain point I could see that she needed to go home and be in bed. So I put her in a cab, and she asked me to go home with her, so I went and we slept together that night but nothing happened because she was too full of booze to start our romance off. The next night we had an out-of-control, over-the-top sexual encounter. She rocked me in a way I hadn't thought was possible by a person of her age—seventeen. There was some very adult behavior taking place, and I remember going, "Wow! What fucking porno has this girl been watching?"

I went back to L.A., and we were on the phone every night. The first night we were talking, she said, "I have a small problem. I'm seeing this guy, and I have to let him know that it's over between us." Turned out he was a trust-fund baby whose dad was a Wall Street gazillionaire. She said the other problem was that her parents had gotten wind of our relationship, and they weren't having any of it.

Her dad started leaving threatening messages on my answering machine, especially after her jilted boyfriend told him that I had AIDS. But Jaime was undaunted, and we started plotting and scheming to get her out to L.A. for a visit. I called her dad and convinced him that 1) I didn't have AIDS, and 2) I wasn't an ogre. I also sweet-talked her mom, and they let her come out for a visit.

I don't remember too much about her first trip, other than going to pick her up and watching her walk out of her hotel room, wearing some go-go boots. I thought, "Whoa, this is definitely where I want to be." We had a lot of fun and were at ease with each other right away. That Christmas we made the obligatory trip to Michigan, and she bonded with my mom right away. To this day, they speak to each other every day. Then we flew to Pennsylvania, and I met her parents. I was nervous, but it was actually pretty mellow. I got along with her mom right away; she was sweet and loving, the classic mom. I didn't have any real problems with Dad. It turned out that he was the true music lover in the household. He had these stacks and stacks of doo-wop stuff and R&B 45s, and he would start playing them, and Jaime and he would sing along and do dances in the kitchen.

In January 1994, I was five and a half years sober, with no intention or desire to ever take drugs again. Then I went to a Beverly Hills dentist to have a wisdom tooth removed. I had been to see many doctors and many dentists during that five and a half years, and I had this canned speech that I gave them: "I'm allergic to narcotics. Whatever you have to do to me, you'll have to do with local anesthetics or some non-narcotic substance."

The dentist thought he could do the operation with a local, so I got in the chair and got jacked up on Novocain. He started to extract the tooth, but in the middle of the process, he told me it was so badly impacted that he'd have to cut it out of my mouth. In order to do that, he'd have to put me under. I'd already been in the chair for an hour, so I agreed. So he stuck an IV in my arm and shot me up with liquid Valium. That stuff ran up my arm, up my throat, and into my head, and a golden cloud of euphoria came over me. It was the first time I'd felt that loaded in five and a half years. It felt so good, and I was so under the influence, that I was no longer me, I was now the stoned, under-the-influence guy.

The dentist got the tooth out, and I was feeling warm and cozy and fine, floating on this cloud, and also becoming aware of this new voice in my head that said, "We've got to keep this up, right away. We're not letting this feeling go away." And I was like "Don't worry. We're on the same team here, brother." As soon the dentist was finished, he asked me if I was in pain, and I told him I was hurting so bad, I needed some Percodan. He looked confused, but I insisted that all that previous allergic talk was nonsense, and I needed those Percodans right away.

I ate a handful of the twenty-five pills before I even left the building, and shortly after I got home, there were only two left in the bottle. Now I had a proper opium buzz going. Right at that moment, I decided it would be a good idea to drive to downtown L.A. and buy some heroin and cocaine. I didn't think twice about it, I didn't think about my sobriety or where I'd come from, I was strictly in the moment of being high and wanting to get higher, no consciousness of any consequences, nothing, zilch. So I drove to my old spot, Bonnie Brae and Sixth, and I found out that those packages of nice cocaine had been supplanted by the crack-cocaine trade. All I could get was rocks. But the good old-fashioned Black Tar heroin was exactly the same, and I knew what to do with that. I went into a drugstore to get some needles and pulled my usual diabetic scam, but I forgot that now I was recognizable. The pharmacist looked at me and said, "Oh, Mr. Kiedis, I didn't know you were a diabetic." I said, "Yup. Diabetic. That's me." On the way back home, I stopped at a pipe shop on Sunset Boulevard and bought this big goofy pipe for freebasing. They recognized me there, too, but I pretended it was a gag gift for a party.

I went home, and I didn't have a lighter, so I tried to light the crack with matches, which was a horrible idea, because the match doesn't stay lit long enough to get the rock going. This went on for a couple of days, and then I made another trip downtown and found some powdered cocaine. I did the heroin and got completely anesthetized and passed out in my bed, the bed that I'd always been sober in up until that point.

Now my house was full of that dark energy, especially the bathroom, which was trashed. When I woke up, my first thought was "Please God, tell me that this was a nightmare." I figured there was a 2 percent chance that it hadn't happened. I was holding on to that, saying, "Come on, two percent, tell me that was a dream, tell me none of that happened." I got up and I was shaky and I peeked into the bathroom and it hit me. How did that happen? That was not in my script. Now the guy who was going to live and die sober had fucked up the track record. I didn't know what to do; I was dumbfounded.

Now that the beast within had awoken, it wasn't done. Part of me wanted to go with it, but part of me was so ashamed about having done that to myself that I cleaned up the mess and pretended it hadn't happened. But I felt empty and hollow, like I was made out of Styrofoam. All my strength was gone, and my brain felt empty. Looking back, it would have been an opportunity to go straight to somebody and say, "This is what happened. Let me start Day One right now." I should have gotten rid of the secret and gotten some help, but I couldn't do that.

I certainly didn't tell anyone in the band. We were still feeling our way, rehearsing and trying to write new material. One of the ways we bonded was by each buying a new Harley-Davidson. We even started a mock motorcycle gang that we called "The Sensitives."

Now that we were coming off a huge hit and we had a supportive record company that was prepared to spend money, we decided that a change of scenery might help in the creative process. Chad and I took a reconnaissance mission to Hawaii and found a beautiful farm on the south side of the Big Island. It was on acres and acres of land and complete with white horses in a corral. The main house had a nice kitchen and a big living room to rehearse in. There were two or three guest houses scattered across the property, along with a pool and a tennis court, all of this overlooking the magnificent Pacific Ocean and about a three-minute ride to some of the best snorkeling in all of Hawaii. We rented it for a month and shipped our motorcycles out. Extravagant stuff for guys who'd been living in small apartment buildings a couple of years previous.

The problem was the spot was so beautiful, it was difficult to start playing music, because we just wanted to swim in the ocean and have luxurious lunches and find some cliffs to jump off of. Finally, we started jamming. It was a slower, different flow than we'd ever had before. Good sounds were being created, but there wasn't any effortless telepathic transmission happening, where we were all instantly in one river going in one direction. I think I must have been lost in my own mental space, because I didn't go in there with an unquestioning sense of confidence. I wasn't sure what to make of the new sound that we were creating; I didn't know exactly how I fit into it. But I was willing to keep putting one foot in front of the other and keep on with my weird, bizarre style of writing, which seemed interesting to me, even though I wasn't getting much feedback from anybody else.

Some very nice things did get planted during those rehearsals, things that would later turn into songs. Flea wanted to reassert himself as a force in the creation of our sound and the direction of our songs, which was fine, because he'd always been an essential contributor, but I think he felt like it was now his turn to dominate in that respect, and it was different. I could tell that Dave was perplexed by our methods; he was looking around, going, "Is this how it's supposed to unfold? Anthony goes over there and writes in a corner all day while we jam? Are we getting anywhere?" Chad and I were like "Yeah, that's how we do it."

In retrospect, there was pressure because we were following up such a massive hit album. I don't think it was conscious pressure, where we talked about it, "Okay, it's time to do better than we did last . . ." It was more low-grade, subconscious pressure, a sense that we were under a microscope, that there was a built-in number of people who were looking at what we were doing. We had removed ourselves from mainland America, which gave a further bizarre flavor to everything.

While we were there, I would write lyrics for hours every day, but sometimes there were periods when new music would accumulate and I wouldn't have ideas for all of it. To get a change of atmosphere, I'd get on my motorcycle, drive to a corner of the island, find a bed-and-breakfast, and hole up with my tapes and write lyrics. I remember coming back once and Chad saying out of nowhere, "What's the matter, are you having writer's block?" I had to educate him that there was no such thing as writer's block, that writers write when they write, and when they don't, they don't.

But he was convinced that I had it, and he actually gave an interview to *Rolling Stone* in which he told the guy that the sessions were going well except I had writer's block. That was a bone of contention for a while, coming from him, of all people.

Back at the ranch, we'd work in the morning, then we'd go snorkeling and have lunch. We'd work for a few more hours and usually spend our nights playing poker and Screw Your Neighbor. It was fun to sit outside, drinking beverages, after a long day of playing and writing, and just joke and shoot the shit and play cards. When we got ambitious, we'd take a day off and explore some of the places I'd found on my outings. We went scuba diving and volcano hiking, everywhere, on our four choppers.

All this time in Hawaii, I'd talk on the phone to Jaime for hours every night. After a month of work, our lease ran out on the house, and everyone went home for a week. But I stayed in Hawaii, and Jaime came out to visit. I picked her up and brought her back to the house, where we spent a very nice first night together. We had an arrangement: I was to do no ejaculating of any kind in her absence, no masturbation, no wet dreams, no other girls; I had to save every last ounce of my chi. Jaime was quite a sexual young girl, and she needed repeat performances, so she didn't want me having a shortage of juice. After that, we rented a tree house in the magnificent Waipio Valley, which was an enormous Garden of Eden. Then we spent a few days in Maui before it was time to reconvene the band and work again.

When we came back, we rented an old tropical mansion on the north side of the Big Island, which was a vastly different environment. It was a large bed-and-breakfast, and we rented the entire place for a month. By then we had about half of the album written. We worked but played, too, taking two scuba-diving trips, including one where we saw an amazing school of melon head whales pass right by us.

One day we were working and got a call from Lindy, who informed us that Kurt Cobain had killed himself. The news sucked the air out of the entire house. I didn't feel like I felt when Hillel died; it was more like "Jesus Christ, the world just suffered a great loss." Kurt's death was unexpected, because even if I see somebody who's on a mission to hurt himself, I always hold out hope that he can recover. Some of the worst junkies I've ever known in my life have gotten sober.

It was an emotional blow, and we all felt it. I don't know why everyone on earth felt so close to that guy; he was beloved and endearing and inoffensive in some weird way. For all of his screaming and all of his darkness, he was just lovable. So his death hit us hard, and it changed our whole experience out there. It did wake up a thing inside of me that wanted to express my love for him, in a particular way, without having it be an obvious "ode to." That day, I retreated to a back house on the property and started writing the lyrics to "Tearjerker."

Tearjerker

My mouth fell open hoping that the truth would not be true, refuse the news
I'm feeling sick now, what the fuck am I supposed to do, just lose and lose
First time I saw you, you were sitting backstage in a dress, a perfect mess
You never knew this but I wanted badly for you to requite my love
Left on the floor leaving your body
When highs are the lows and lows are the way
So hard to stay, guess now you know
I love you so
I liked your whiskers and I liked the dimple in your chin, your pale blue eyes
You painted pictures 'cause the one who hurts can give so much, you gave me such

We finished the rough outlines for probably ten songs in Hawaii. Now it was time to go back and finish the lyrics and begin work with Rick Rubin in the studio. Then I got derailed again. Someone had given me a coffee-table book about drug use in the New York projects. The book was rife with incredible tales of drug street life and resplendent with amazing photos depicting that world. I was sitting at home alone one night, and that book was on the coffee table looking at me. So I picked it up and started reading it, and a lightbulb went off in my head, and the little horns came out. I checked my pockets to see how much money I had, and I checked my schedule to see if I was free for the next few days. I realized it had been a few months since my last slip, and I could get away with this. My intention was always to go out just for the night and sleep it off, and then I'd go back to being a normal guy.

The drive downtown is an experience unto itself. You're controlled by this dark energy that's about to take you to a place where you know you don't belong at this stage in your life. You get on the 101 Freeway and it's night and it's cool outside. It's a pretty drive, and your heart is racing, your blood is flowing through your veins, and it's kind of dangerous, because the people dealing are cutthroat, and there are cops everywhere. It's not your neck of the woods anymore, now you're coming from a nice house in the hills, driving a convertible Camaro.

So you get off at Alvarado and make the right. Now your senses go into this hyper-alert radar situation. Your mission is to buy these drugs, and you don't want anything interfering with that, it's like being in a battle where your life is going to depend on seeing everything around you, the guy on the corner, the undercover cops, the black-and-whites. You don't want to commit any obvious traffic infractions, so you signal and make your left onto Third Street, cognizant the whole time of any cars behind you. Then you go two blocks and you're passing Mexican families and a couple of motels and a corner store and there's a grocery store on the left, which was the scene of many incidents in your life with Jennifer when you used to shoot up in the car and start throwing up out the window. All these memories are flooding back at you, and the minute you make the right onto Bonnie Brae, half a block up on the left, you see groupings of dealers. They're incredibly aggressive, and they watch every car that comes around that corner to see if it's a car there to buy stuff. You either pull straight up on Bonnie Brae or you make a left onto the next side street, and they come swamping down upon you. They're in your passenger window, they're in your back window, and you have to choose which madman you're going to buy from.

The dealers are used to people buying twenty dollars' worth, or forty or maybe sixty, but you pull out a wad of hundreds and tell them you want five hundred dollars' worth. They can't even keep five hundred dollars' worth of crack in their mouths, which is where they store it, just like the balloons of heroin, under their tongues, so they start hustling and pooling their resources and come to you with a handful of saliva-covered crack. You make the deal and then you ask these guys, "Who's got the Chiva?," and they point. Chiva is the dope. Then you go to another block and buy three, four, or five balloons, the whole while trying to make it happen quick, because the cops could be there any second. By now you know where to get pipes, and you're buying the little Brillo pads to use as screens in the pipe, all the techniques that you picked up from the street dealers. Then you go home and get high.

As soon as you hit the pipe, boom, there's that familiar instantaneous release of serotonin in the brain, a feeling that's almost too good. You instantly start short-circuiting in your brain, because to get all that serotonin at once is so crazy and so intense that you're liable to stand up and take off your clothes and go walking into the neighbor's house because you feel that good. And on one occasion I almost did do that. I came back to my beautiful, sweet, blessing-from-God home, up against this park, and I walked into the kitchen and took that first hit—and it's always about the first hit; the other hits are all in vain, trying to recapture that first one—and I stuffed as much rock as I could in the pipe and as much smoke as I could in my lungs, and I held it for as long as possible and then I released the smoke, and all that manic, psychotic energy came swirling around me again and I instantly became a different person. I was no longer in control of this person. I threw off my shirt, and it made perfect sense to go next door to my neighbor's house with half of my clothes off and see what was going on. I knocked on the door, and she came out, and I said something like "Did I leave my keys in there?" And she said, "No, I don't think so, but let's have a look." I was ready to take off the rest of my clothes and see how things went, because I wasn't in control of my faculties. She was kind and sweet, and fortunately, I didn't make too much of a scene. Three minutes later, that feeling evaporated, and I realized I was over there half naked, looking for keys that didn't exist, so I mumbled an apology and went back home and hit the pipe again. Absolute madness.

I'd been struck with a couple of bolts of relapse lightning, and my thinking wasn't that great. I was carrying around this secret inside of me, and it was poisoning my entire thought process. I was pretending that everything was A-OK, but the integrity of my entire psychic structure was starting to collapse. I had a few more songs to write lyrics for, and when you're in that state of mind, it seems like a good idea to change your geography. The problem, obviously, was the town I was living in. So I decided to go to New York, which was always an inspiring town for me. Plus, Jaime was there. She had made many a sojourn to L.A. to visit me, so I decided to return the favor.

My plan was to check in to the Chelsea Hotel and write for a month. The Chelsea was an artists' compound, full of freaks and old-timers and misfits and drag queens and dope fiends and jilted harlots. It was the land of a thousand character ghosts. For the same price as a four-star hotel room, I was able to get a beautiful penthouse with a full kitchen and an incredible view looking south.

I moved in, but I wasn't feeling right inside my own skin. Here I have this wonderful space in which to write, I've got great tapes to work with, I've got tons of notes and ideas, my girl's a ten-minute cab ride away, I've got the city in my view, but I feel fucked up inside. I set up my workspace, and I went to work and wrote a little bit and ate a little bit, and Jaime came over and we watched movies, but I didn't feel like myself, which is a horrible feeling. I was edgy and uggghhh, in that limbo of not being on a run and not being sober.

One night a week after I'd checked in, Jaime must have been off doing her thing, and I was home alone and it was nighttime and this overwhelming notion came over me to go down to Washington Square Park and see what the action was with the drug dealers. I jumped in a cab, went down there, and started talking to some of the local scalawags. I scored a handful of rocks and couldn't find any dope, so on the way back, I bought a couple of bottles of red wine, thinking that would take the edge off the coke. I smoked the crack, and it wasn't even getting me high, but one more time I was on this ride. I wasn't digging it. I started hammering the wine back, and I just wasn't well. I was like a clock that had exploded— my springs were hanging out, my hands were cockeyed, and my numbers were falling off. Jaime showed up, so I hid the wine and told her some cockamamy line of excuses that I must have eaten something bad. In the end we had an argument, because I was out of my mind. That was the color of my experience during that whole month. I'd get it together for a few days, but it basically disintegrated into an unproductive and sad month, because I wasn't getting much done. I wasn't sober, but I wasn't using in the way that would have given me relief.

In July the band went into the studio to record the album. Even though I wasn't finished writing all the lyrics, we decided to start cutting the basic tracks. By then I had put down the getting-high thing and was white-knuckling the dryness of not using, but I was behind in my work and not well prepared emotionally or physically. I did have some lyrics that I believed in, but I hadn't trained my voice to go in there and be able to do my thing. However, Rick and Chad and Flea and Dave were all ready to fire away.

It's funny. No one suspected that I had slipped from my more than five years of sobriety, but if you look closely at the lyrics I was coming up with, there were clues galore. In "Warped,"

I wrote, "My tendency for dependency is offending me/It's upending me/I'm pretending see to be strong and free from my dependency/It's warping me." Later in that same song: "Night craving sends me crawling/Beg for mercy, does it show?/A vacancy that's full of holes/Hold me, please, I'm feeling cold." Even on an upbeat song like "Aeroplane," there were lyrics like "Looking in my own eyes/I can't find the love I want/Somebody'd better slap me before I start to rust, before I start to decompose." That's a cry for help. Later: "Sitting in my kitchen/I'm turning into dust again/My melancholy baby, the star of Mazzy must push a voice inside of me/I'm overcoming gravity, it's easy when you're sad to be." Even "Deep Kick," which was a historical account of our journeys, referenced "this giant gray monster" of drug addiction that had enveloped so many of our friends. At that point, John was getting into his sordid drug trip. Bob Forrest, Pete Weiss, and Dickie Rude were all in never-never land. And River and Hillel were dead.

We laid down the basic tracks, but I was still having trouble with the lyrics. A lot had to do with my state of mind. When you're at odds with yourself, it's hard to create. Sometimes the writing process is as easy as opening up the window and letting in the breeze. And sometimes it's like chiseling away at a block of granite with a pencil.

On August 1, I should have been celebrating my sixth anniversary of sobriety. To the outside world, I was. My dad hadn't acknowledged the first five years of my sobriety, but on that would-be sixth anniversary, he sent me a T-shirt that said SIX YEARS CLEAN. I had to accept it, but it was one more thing to feel horrible about.

The band took a break from recording to play the Woodstock festival. Judging from my love handles in the photos, I'd have to say I stayed sober for at least a month before Woodstock. Woodstock was our first show with Dave, even though he'd been in the band since the previous September. Lindy came to us and said, "Okay, you're headlining Woodstock. Anything special you want to do?" I sketched out a giant lightbulb on the floor, and Lindy thought I meant a cartoon lightbulb that went off over your head, but I meant lightbulbs that would encompass our whole heads. Dave was looking at us, going, "I'm going to be wearing a giant lightbulb?"

We got a Hollywood propmaster in the Valley to create the lightbulb costumes, and we hired this Russian Mongolian seamstress to make five identical Jimi Hendrix costumes, because our encore was going to be "Fire." The fifth costume was for Clara, Flea's daughter, who at times became an integral part of our show. The lightbulbs were a tough way to initiate Dave into our performing thing, because that wasn't his style. He was more into being cool and sexy and risqué, a naked muscle guy, and here we had him dressed up in a silver spaceman suit with an enormous lightbulb head. But he didn't complain at all.

We didn't know what to expect for our first show with Dave, but we played for more than two hundred thousand people, and it sounded pretty damn great. The lightbulb costumes turned out to be difficult, because we didn't rehearse with them and didn't realize that it was impossible to look laterally out of them and see your fingers on your instrument. But they were a striking, sensational look.

Now it was time to return home and finish my work and concentrate on my sobriety. Instead, I did the opposite. My house had been tainted, and it was the perfect little isolation castle at the top of the hill. I had a gate down below, so no one could get up to the door. I decided it would be a good bad idea to start getting into the cocaine and heroin zone again. I ended up finding this Mexican billiards place downtown that was a full-service stop. I didn't have to go up to the corners, I didn't have to buy stuff right on the street or go to different guys, I could just go in there and grab a beer, and when they finished their pool game, they'd come by with gumball-machine containers filled with rock cocaine and heroin balloons. Occasionally, I'd see somebody I didn't want to see, some young white males from Hollywood who might recognize me, but I had taken to pulling my hair up under a baseball cap and wearing glasses, and that was a pretty good disguise.

Then I'd hop onto my motorcycle and drive to a deserted, derelict area of downtown. I'd take out my pipe, pack it full of rock, and smoke it, and it would be like a steam engine exploding in my head. My eyes would fall out of my head, my heart would start racing, and there'd be this ringing in my ears. Then I'd fire up the bike and kick that thing into high gear and take off like a rocket for home.

I'd come home and close the front gate, lock the front door, and turn off the phone. I had two or three places in the house that I would spend my high time in. One of those was the kitchen, which was where all the implements of destruction were. But I'd end up on the third floor of the house. I had this weird old '50s couch, a television, and a boom box on the floor. I'd go up there and drag along my art supplies—drawing pads, glitter, markers, and pencils by the gazillion, inks, and other weird objects that I could cut up and paste around. I'd get into this fixated thing where I'd get high and go to work on these bizarre creations, meticulous and precise drawings of faces and nude women, bizarre bodies and breasts and mouths and eyes, and also scary Japanese demon faces. Days would go by and I'd just sit there, very comfortable, because my whole body was acclimated to these chemicals. I'd also get out random art books and books of nude models and lay them all around the house so I could see the images wherever I went.

Meanwhile, I'd make the occasional contact with either Lindy or Flea. They'd ask me when they could book the studio so I could do my vocals. My excuse for not working was that I had a weird stomach ailment, something that had to do with my experience in Borneo, so I'd constantly see this stomach doctor and buy more and more time. I was even taking walnut-shell medicine that was supposed to rid my body of its "parasites." It was such an obvious line of crap, but it worked. Nobody questioned why I wasn't coming to the studio.

I kept going deeper and deeper into this world of repetition. Jaime would come to visit, and it wasn't pretty, because I wasn't well and she didn't know what the situation was. The sad thing is, people don't want to believe that the person they're in love with is out of his mind, drinking and using, so if you give them even half an excuse, they're going to want to believe it. A girl with no prior exposure to the disease had to be blissfully unaware of the nefarious tricks of the dope fiend. That's how I was able to get high all late summer and autumn and pretend like it wasn't happening. I was saying, "I'm sick." I *was* deteriorating physically and emotionally. Jaime was tolerant, and it did speak well of her character, because she was not the type to abandon ship during a crisis. She didn't consider backing off or bowing out, she was just there, which I can't say about everybody. I don't know if I could say it even about myself.

I began to drop some pretty tantalizing clues. I drove to the studio one day, and Flea came by the car and saw a discarded Cheetos bag on the floor. That would be a huge tip-off, because if I was clean, I would never even think about eating junk food. But Flea wasn't sure it wasn't left over from Jaime, so he never put two and two together. Another time Jaime was at my house, and we ordered some food delivered. I collared the delivery boy on the front steps and offered to give him a hundred-dollar tip if he would give me all the cash he had on him; I'd put the tip and extra cash on my credit card. Jaime was eavesdropping on this whole negotiation from the landing at the top of the stairs. There I was, in total conniving-whisper mode, trying to do this dirty deal with the delivery guy, who by the way did come through for me. Jaime said, "What was that all about?," and I had to be the abominable lying machine.

In the middle of October, we played two dates with the Rolling Stones. It was an awkward time, because my father was in town to visit, and he was staying at my house. I came home after the first show and made some lame excuse to drive down the hill and came back with a small amount of narcotics. And I wasn't Jimi

Hendrix or Janis Joplin. I couldn't go trash myself and turn it into a soul stew onstage. I would trash myself and be half a man with half the joy in my step.

But opening for the Rolling Stones is a shite job anyway. I can't recommend it to anybody. You get the offer and you think, "Historically speaking, they're the second most important rock band in the history of music, after the Beatles. So we should have a brush with history." But the fact is, the Rolling Stones' audience today is lawyers and doctors and CPAs and contractors and real estate development people. This is a conservative, wealthy group. No one's rocking out. The ticket prices and merchandise costs are astronomical. It's more like "Let's go to the Rolling Stones mall and watch them play on the big screen."

The whole experience is horrible. First you get there, and they won't let you do a sound check. Then they give you an eightieth of the stage. They set apart this tiny area and say, "This is for you. You don't get the lights, and you're not allowed to use our sound system. And oh, by the way, you see that wooden floor? That's Mick's imported antique wood flooring from the Brazilian jungle, and that's what he dances on. If you so much as look at it, you won't get paid." You're basically like a little TV set on the stage, playing your show as eighty-five thousand wealthy, bored-out-of-their-minds fans are slowly finding their seats. They're all wearing their Rolling Stones letter jackets and leafing through their catalogs, deciding which Rolling Stones T-shirt and which pair of Rolling Stones slacks they're going to get. We were the music to be played for ushering, seating, snack-getting, and clothes-buying. It was a nightmare.

In November I tried to go back into the studio and do some singing, but I wasn't in any kind of shape to do it. I did a mediocre job. I was skinny and sucked up, bad color, bad skin, scraggly hair, droopy, dead-looking eyes. The cat wasn't out of the bag yet, and everyone thought I was run-down from being sick all summer. I was beginning to realize that drug addiction really was a progressive illness and, God forbid, if you should start using again, it would be worse than it was before.

When Jaime came to visit, I'd force myself to go without for a few days, then I'd take her to the airport and head straight downtown. I had a few close calls with the law. One time I was smoking coke in the car and was way too high to drive safely, and I had a bunch of paraphernalia and drugs right under the seat. I must have been driving erratically, because a cop pulled me over. I got the window halfway down, and this young, vicious-looking LAPD cop shone his flashlight on me and said, "Oh, Mr. Kiedis! My bad! I'm sorry, sir, excuse me for the interruption, but I really have to tell you that this is a pretty dangerous area, so you might want to exercise caution around here. You have a good night, now." That wasn't quite the reception I was expecting.

Another time I had purchased both of my products and peeled away, cutting through traffic, and a black-and-white pulled me over. I had stashed the coke under an ashtray, but I had the balloons of heroin right in my hand. I didn't want to get busted, so I quickly swallowed the three balloons, which weren't digestible, so I wasn't in any danger. When the cop came over and asked me why I was in that neighborhood, I made up some story about visiting a girl, and that mollified him, so he didn't search the car. Then I had to backtrack and buy some more heroin.

That was the beginning of what would be a marathon binge. Four days later, I wound up finishing everything, and it was daytime, and I was beat down and delirious. I'd spent all my cash, and the last thing in the world I felt like doing was driving downtown in the daytime heat and interacting with drug dealers. I was on my way into a liquor store to buy some paraphernalia, but I was so full of toxins that I had to casually stroll over and vomit into the gutter. As I vomited, I looked down and spotted those three intact balloons full of heroin. "Yeah! Free drugs. I hit the jackpot!" I thought, and fished out the balloons and saved myself a trip downtown.

Jaime came to visit in December, and by then I had an ugly heroin habit. I'd been smoking both crack and heroin for a couple of months straight. This was in anticipation of our Christmas trips home. We had decided over the phone that we would give our dads big cars. Jaime was on a roll with her modeling, and she wanted to give her pop a pickup truck, and I wanted to give Blackie a Bronco. By then he had moved back to Michigan. Right after we did so well with *Blood Sugar,* I'd visited him, and he was living in a tiny apartment in downtown Grand Rapids. I had an epiphany that I had just made a ton of money touring, so I should buy him a house. We found a nice house on a lake in Rockford, out in the country, and Pops was taken care of.

Jaime and I arranged for the truck to be shipped out to Pennsylvania. Our plan was to drive Blackie's brand-new, luxurious, spacious Bronco to Michigan. After the two holiday celebrations, Jaime and I would go to the Caribbean together, to a resort on Caneel Bay on the island of St. John. She still didn't know what the hell was going on with me, but since my clothes were hanging off my emaciated frame, she could see that I was sick. I was like "Oh, we're going to go away for Christmas, I'll get healthy, we'll go to the Caribbean, everything's going to get better from here on out." Unbeknownst to her, my foolish notion was that I'd buy a bunch of coke and a bunch of heroin and wean myself as we went across the country. This is never a good idea. But I'd convinced myself that the farther away from L.A. I got, the fewer drugs I'd do. I had to make a number of sojourns downtown, during which I bought out every dealer I encountered.

Jaime still had some last-minute Christmas shopping to do. By now I was taking a hit off the pipe every ten minutes, wherever I was—in a phone booth, a bathroom, behind a tree, wherever. Once I got high, I wasn't acting all spooked out, because I was so accustomed to it. So we started packing and gathering goods, and she was gleeful about this imminent departure for a cross-country trip, and I was going along with the glee, but really I was Spirograph Brain. I drove her to pick up some slippers at a fancy shoe store on Melrose, and as soon as she left the Bronco, I fired up the old pipester. I was sitting there smoking like a fiendish monkey when, all of a sudden, I heard a sharp rap on the window. It was Jaime. She had caught me red-handed. The whole masquerade that I'd been holding up was over. I was mortified, and she was shocked. She popped me the finger and tried to run off, but I grabbed her and talked her into coming back into the car.

I went through this psychedelic Rolodex of what page works for this problem. I had no choice but to tell her what had happened and how I'd ended up here and what I was prepared to do about it, as long as I didn't have to stop getting high at that moment. We drove to Waddle's Park, and I put it all on her, the whole sordid story. I told her that I loved her from the bottom of my heart, and I'd do anything for her, and this was a serious fucking problem that I'd been through before, and there was no easy solution. I told her my plan to drive across the country and wean myself off the cocaine and heroin, so by the time I got to Michigan, I'd be clean. It was a temporary solution to an enormous and life-threatening problem, like putting a Band-Aid onto a severed jugular.

She was not having it. "Fuck you, fuck you, you mother-fucker. Where's my plane ticket? I'm going home. You're an asshole, you're a liar, you're a scumbag."

"Yeah, I'm all that stuff, but I still think you should stay. I've got my stuff, and by the time we get to Michigan, I'll be done-zo," I said.

Jaime told me that she'd had suspicions all along and that she had been telling my mom and Flea that maybe I was doing drugs again. Of all the dreadful, self-deprecating, self-loathing, isolated, fucked-up feelings that you get as a drug user, one of the worst is having your girlfriend conspire with your best friends and your family on your behalf. It's the ultimate in humiliation, knowing that your best friend and your girlfriend are talking about you behind your back because you're using. Then your family's in on it, and you feel pathetic. You know they feel bad for you and want to help you, and it's just like agghhh, stay away, don't even bother.

I don't need your help, I don't want your help. Don't even talk to each other, please!

Finally, she agreed to take the trip with me. I don't think she realized how disconcerting it would be for her to be in a car with me getting loaded every ten minutes until the stuff ran out. We left California and got to the desert, and I was having to make all these stops, not sure if I should be getting high in front of her or if I should hide it. I was getting more comfortable with the idea of her watching me get loaded, but it was still not my favorite thing in the world, because the physical act of ingesting the drugs is so ghoulish.

We kept driving and driving, and at one point I was too high to drive, so she took the wheel. We were listening to *Nirvana Unplugged* and Mazzy Star, and she was crying her eyes out. Then it was nighttime and we were in the mountains of Arizona. The road was slick and icy and dangerous, and out of nowhere, what looked like a gigantic super-elk, bigger than the whole car, leaped across the road. Jaime swerved to avoid it and we were fine, but I looked at the road sign and realized that the town was where my grandmother had driven off the road to her death. I took it as an omen, as if the spirit of that elk was saying to me, "Wake up, motherfucker, because you're dying."

That wasn't the first time I had experienced interactions with spirits while I was doing drugs. One time during this era of relapsing, I came back to my house in the middle of the night, pockets full of drugs, ready to be the mad scientist. I was fiddling through my pockets to get my keys out when I heard this crazy scream. I figured it was somebody I knew who was on the balcony screaming at me like a crazy witch. But I didn't see anybody. I stepped back from the house and said, "Hello? Anybody there?" Again I heard that horrifying scream. I looked up on the gable above my bedroom and saw a giant hawk sitting there, staring right down at me, screaming his lungs out in this tortured human voice.

I thought that this guy did not want me to do what I was

doing. And if I didn't stop it, I would probably die. This would happen periodically, once a month or so: There'd be a bird, sometimes an owl, screaming at me at the top of its lungs when I came home on these furious misadventures of drug use. When you're using drugs, you're driven by this mystical black energy, a force inside you that just won't quit. And the weaker you get, the more you feed into that energy, and the more it fucks with you. When your spirit becomes dark and your lifestyle becomes dark, your existence is susceptible to infiltration by dark spirits. I've seen it so many times with addicts. You can see that they're controlled by dark energy, the way they look, their appearance, their voice, their behavior, it's not them.

I remember when Hillel died and I was just getting clean, I had a dream lying in my bed next to Ione. It was one of those horribly vivid half-awake, half-asleep dreams. All of this terrifying energy came flying into my bedroom along the top of my ceiling. There were demons and goblins and ghouls and creatures, a full-assortment platter of scary motherfuckers. I could tell that they were coming to fuck with me, to say, "Okay, we did our job on your friend, now we've come for you." At first I was like "I'm not having it, you guys, you came to the wrong house." As I was putting up this psychic fight, the granddaddy of all dark forces, this vast dark angel, came flying in and encompassed the entire ceiling of my room. But I wasn't open to them. "No, no, no. Be gone. Bye-bye." That was the beginning of my getting clean.

I noted the message from the elk, and we drove on and found a motel. I kept getting high in the room, and Jaime was beside herself. A lot of her pain and suffering were coming to the surface. She took a bath and locked herself in the bathroom and stayed in there for three hours. I was getting loaded and doing an art project with reflective letters I'd bought at some truck stop, and periodically knocking on the door, saying, "Jaime, are you all right?" After a while, I started to worry. When she finally opened the door, I saw that she had taken a razor blade and carved an "A" into her arm. That whole episode was scary, and even though I was loaded,

I was starting to come to grips with the fact that I had created a lot of pain and suffering around me, not just within me.

The next day we got up and drove into Flagstaff. Neither of us had really slept. I kept getting high. Jaime was sad and pissed off and confused and tortured by all of this, so I went into a Native American arts-and-crafts jewelry store and bought a couple of matching rings. In my mind, it was a promise-to-get-better-and-be-together ring. I think she may have taken it as an engagement ring, but I was desperate and lost and grasping for straws. Deep down inside, I loved this girl a lot, and I wanted nothing other than to be with her, but I couldn't stop using.

We got back in the car and drove to the end of New Mexico and checked in to a motel. I was down to my last balloon of heroin, and we'd been gone only two days. The coke had long since run out, but I was more concerned about having enough heroin to get through the next few days. Still, I announced, "This is it. This is the last time I'm going to be getting high." She was so sick of the whole drama. I got every last grain of that stuff into my body and didn't even get high. I tried to sleep that night, and the next day I awoke to the fucking hell that is heroin withdrawal. I was shaking and feverish, and we still had a long way to go. Jaime became the one and only driver, a tiny, beautiful blond princess behind the wheel of this huge truck. I pushed the seat back, got on the floor, crawled inside a sleeping bag, drank a whole bottle of NyQuil, and went into a raging dope kick, sweating and shaking and fainting, just out of it. And Jaime kept driving. She drove for hours and hours and hours while I was in this fever inside of this sleeping bag. She drove straight through to Michigan. Once again, I was home for the holidays with a raging heroin habit.

12.

Over the Wall

It was hard to hide my drug problem when I got to my mom's house. For one, I looked like a walking skeleton. Besides, Jaime had already voiced her suspicions about my drug use to my mom, who then had talked to my dad.

"Anthony was having stomach problems when I was out there for the Stones shows in October," Blackie told my mom. "He had to go out in the middle of the night and get Pepto-Bismol."

"Hello! What are you talking about?" Peggy said. "He's using."

Blackie always seemed to be in denial about my drug use. It was probably too painful for him to deal with, so he carried on as if everything was okay.

Now the cat was out of the bag. I settled into the comfort of being home. I knew I had to start going to meetings and eating lots and lots of food. I was okay with the idea of not getting high, but again I didn't recognize how serious my problem was. The measures I was taking to deal with it were light in the loafers. It's a good start to go to a meeting and get the truth on the table, but it's another thing to think that's going to work. You have to go back in full force and work the twelve steps and do the whole nine yards, you can't just show up and be a spectator and expect to receive recovery through osmosis. I was dabbling.

But we had a lovely Christmas. I tricked out my mom's house with a hot tub. My sister Julie had started dating a guy named Steve Simmons, and we were all so happy that she'd met a guy who dug her and treated her well that we spoiled them with lavish gifts. Especially when you're coming off a long drug run and you've been distant from your family, you feel obligated to make up for it with deluxe material goods.

Jaime was even able to relax a bit. The shock and horror started to subside, and I wasn't getting high, so I got a little bit of my sex drive back, and things got more joyful. She began to look ahead to a brighter future for us. When our relationship was working, it was tons of fun, because we were best friends and we laughed about everything. Jaime had a way of defusing my seriousness and was a great companion. How wonderful was it to be in love with a sexy, sweet girl who also loved basketball?

On Christmas Eve we drove the Bronco over to Blackie's. I had arranged for a giant ribbon to be placed over this rocking truck. Blackie answered the door, grumbling that we were late, and I told him to come out and see his present. He was befuddled, so I threw the keys in his hand and he got nervous. Then he stepped down the path from his front door to the driveway, and he saw that perfect Michigan winter car, and my poor dad seized up. He looked at the car and looked at the keys and said, "No! No! That can't be," trying to hold back the tears. It was really touching.

Christmas morning belonged to Mom. It was her time of the year; the whole house was done up in Christmas fashion. She had the old-school stockings hanging above the fireplace, with a stocking for Jaime, of course. There was the classic golden retriever, and the snow was falling outside, and my sister Jenny, the baby angel of the family, was into all of it. It was a magical time.

I came down at seven-thirty in the morning and started the fire. Under that towering tree, there were more presents than should be allowed by law. The first thing we did was go for the stockings, which had twenty individually wrapped gifts from my mother, things she had amassed all year long.

Then we opened the presents. My job was to deliver them, and people were getting jewelry and fine suits and sweaters and electronic stuff and blah, blah, blah. Steve Simmons had walked into an idyllic situation, because the love and generosity were flowing. The dog had a ribbon around his head, the fire was blazing, various delectable foodstuffs were constantly coming out of the oven, Johnny Mathis and Frank Sinatra and Bing Crosby were on the stereo. So this crazy guy Steve, who was the new love of my sister's life, stopped everything and said, "I just want to take a minute to say that this has been the best Christmas of my life. You've all been incredibly generous and given me so much . . ." We were thinking, "Yeah, he's right. I guess we really have lavished stuff on this guy." And he continued, "But I'm not quite done asking you for something."

The room got silent. "Geez, what more does this guy want?" He said, "I'm going to have to take this moment to ask for your daughter and sister's hand in marriage." He reached over to Julie and said, "Julie, with the support of this family in this room, will you marry me?" Everyone started crying. I couldn't believe this guy was busting this incredible proposal right there in front of the whole family. It was the ultimate capper to the morning, and Julie accepted.

After a few days, it was time to fly to Pennsylvania. Jaime was thrilled to give her dad the F-150 truck, which was a badge of honor in his community. Jaime's parents were liberal enough to let us sleep in her old bedroom, with them down the hall. I felt so awkward about having sex with her in that house. She was a go-getter fireplug, and she'd rip off my clothes and throw me down on the bed, and I'd be whispering, "I can hear them in the kitchen. We can't make too much noise." She didn't care, she just wanted to be loved.

From Pennsylvania we flew down to the Caribbean for some R&R. I had called my travel agent and asked her for the most pristine spot on the islands. It was an exorbitant amount of money per week, but with everything that I'd been through the past six months, I didn't care. I wanted to go to the warmest, most beautiful, most relaxing place I could find. Lying in the sun and swimming and eating and exploring and having sex were my idea of getting healthy, and it worked. We had a little house right on the beach, with no television or telephone to distract us, just hundreds of acres of tropical paradise. I needed that. Even after a week of gorging myself on lobsters and grilled fish and gobs of dessert and being Mr. Exercise Guy, my clothes were still falling off me. But eventually, I got my strength back.

Now it was time to face the music back in L.A. It was difficult coming face-to-face with Flea again, but I'd much rather see him knowing that I've changed the direction of my compass toward sobriety than to run into him when I'm loaded or when the compass is stuck on "Stupid." When push came to shove, Flea was incredibly supportive of me. I came back with some shame and embarrassment and regret for having disappointed the whole operation, but we'd been through it so many times that it had become customary. Flea is the type of friend who can be off doing his own thing, but when the shit hits the fan, he'll be there for me. At moments like this, he's nonjudgmental and accepting of the chaos. I don't feel like "Oh shit, now I have to go get an earful. This guy's gonna condemn me." He's like "Dude, I'm really sorry you had to go through that. I'm glad that you're alive, and let's go party," meaning let's go write music.

Dave stayed sober through all my troubles. He understood the mechanics of alcoholism, so he was incredibly supportive. He was probably hurting over the experience and bumming out on it, but he never once subjected me to any negativity because of my behavior. It was uncanny how loving and forgiving and tolerant they were all willing to be.

Now that I was back on my feet, our first priority was finishing the album. So we booked the studio for the end of January, and right before that, Flea and I took a trip to Taos, New Mexico, to write and play music and figure out the rest of the album. We rented an authentic adobe villa, and I holed up in my bedroom and wrote. Then Flea would take out his acoustic bass or a guitar, and we'd work on the song together. We were there only four or five days, but each day we finished a new song.

Flea had stepped up to the plate in my absence, even contributing lyrics to the album. He wrote the bulk of the lyrics to "Transcending," which was his tribute to River. "Pea" was his attempt at flying his humble flag. But he also wrote the intro to "Deep Kick" and the vocal melodies to the verses for "My Friends" and "Tearjerker." He was supplying me with a lot more information than I'd been used to receiving, but I was open to it, and it was a necessity, because I'd been so disengaged from the creative process.

Taos was productive and fun. We even went up to the mountain one day and skied through a blizzard. There's a peculiar thing that happens every time you get clean. You go through this sensation of rebirth. There's something intoxicating about the process of the comeback, and that becomes an element in the whole cycle of addiction. Once you've beaten yourself down with cocaine and heroin, and you manage to stop and walk out of the muck, you begin to get your mind and body strong and reconnect with your spirit. The oppressive feeling of being a slave to the drugs is still in your mind, so by comparison, you feel phenomenal. You're happy to be alive, smelling the air and seeing the beauty around you and being able to fuck again. You have a choice of what to do. So you experience this jolt of joy that you're not where you came from, and that in and of itself is a tricky thing to stop doing. Somewhere in the back of your mind, you know that every time you get clean, you'll have this great new feeling.

Cut to: a year later, when you've forgotten how bad it was and you don't have that pink-cloud sensation of being newly sober. When I look back, I see why these vicious cycles can develop in someone who's been sober for a long time and then relapses and doesn't want to stay out there using, doesn't want to die, but isn't taking the full measures to get well again. There's a concept in recovery that says "Half-measures avail us nothing." When you have a disease, you can't take half the process of getting well and think you're going to get half well; you do half the process of getting well, you're not going to get well at all, and you'll go back to where you came from. Without a thorough transformation, you're the same guy, and the same guy does the same shit. I kept half-measuring it, thinking I was going to at least get something out of this deal, and I kept getting nothing out of it.

We went back in the studio, and by the end of February, I had knocked out my vocals. We'd gone from getting nothing done for months to shazam! finishing the vocals. After I completed my last vocal, I was so jazzed about being done that I thought, "You might have to go get high." It was the same celebratory cognition that I'd had with Hillel after *Uplift Mofo*. I was a fucking broken tape. I had to rush into the bathroom at the recording studio right after this idea, because the thought of going downtown and copping was making my bowels churn in anticipation of getting high. Then I said good-bye, told everyone I'd see them in a week or so, and bolted for the darkness of downtown to start up the unstoppable chain of madness one more time.

Unfortunately, Jaime was coming to visit me in a few days. When she arrived at LAX, I was AWOL. She had to go right from the airport to a modeling job, and she kept calling me from the job, saying, "Where are you?" It takes away a lot of the thrill of killing yourself when people are looking for you and you're disappointing them, because it *is* a lot of fun when you're out there killing yourself. You're escaping from the cops. You're avoiding getting stabbed to death by dealers. You're running the risk of overdose. You're having escapades of delusion. It's exciting. But when it becomes "Oh shit, someone's looking for me," it puts a damper on the insanity party.

I hid out in a motel. This was the beginning of the great motel tour. I didn't check in to the Peninsula or the Four Seasons, places that I could have easily afforded. No, I opted for the Viking Motel or the Swashbuckler's Inn, shitty, torn-up, dirty-ass, dope-fiend motels that were for poor families who had no place else to go, or for prostitutes, dealers, pimps, hoodlums, and other scandalous motherfuckers. And a bunch of white drug addicts who were sneaking away from their real lives.

I started checking in to these places up and down Alvarado Street, because they were a few blocks away from where I bought my drugs. Maybe that's part of the thrill: You can make your score and then drive three blocks, check right in, and you're smack in the middle of this circle of hell. If you're in a reputable hotel, chances are that you'll run into somebody you know.

When Jaime was looking for me, my motel sophistication hadn't evolved that far yet. I had made it only to the Holiday Inn in Hollywood. That was where she and Dave Navarro tracked me down. Dave had the smarts to call up Bo, our accountant, and ask her where my last credit-card transaction had occurred. She called the company and told Dave that I was at the Holiday Inn.

I was in there trying to sleep off the heroin and escape from myself and this latest mess I'd made when I awoke to a crazy knock on the door. I went to the peephole and looked out and saw Dave and then Jaime lurking in the back of the hallway. It was that bad combination, your loved one and your friend conspiring together.

"Come on, dude, open the door," Dave said. "I love you and I want to help you get better. This isn't happening. Let's go to rehab right now. Throw away your junk and let's go."

I wouldn't open the door. "No, you don't understand,"

I called out. "I feel really bad. I need to sleep. I'll call you later and we'll go tonight."

"Nope. Nope. I got the car outside," Dave said. "I've already called Exodus. They've got a bed waiting for you. Open the door."

I opened the door. At that point, I couldn't fight or argue anymore. I had fucked up, and the only way I had to appease these people who were unhappy with my behavior was to acquiesce and go back to rehab. So I went.

By April 1995 the world of rehab had evolved into a much different animal than my first stay in 1988. Going to rehab had become commonplace. Among rehabs, Exodus was famous for two reasons. It was the place that Kurt Cobain had left right before he died. Kurt had climbed a four-foot fence to escape when all he had to do was walk out the front door. They can't keep you in Exodus against your will, but I guess if you don't want to see anybody on your way out, you bolt.

Exodus was also famed for the renowned doctor of rehabology who ran the place. Guys like him claim to know how drugs affect the body, but to me, all that information amounted to nothing. As long as a dope fiend is high, he's crazy. The minute he isn't high and he starts working the program, he'll start to get better. It's the simplest plan on earth, but they try to complicate it with psychiatric jargon and detoxology. Just get a junkie off the streets, get him three squares, and get him working on his steps, and he'll get better. I've seen it in thousands of drug addicts I've come across who have attempted to get well. It doesn't matter how wonderful their detox or therapist was.

Exodus was off the beaten path in a larger hospital in Marina del Rey. It wasn't connected to the prison system, so there were no end-of-the-liners there who chose rehab over prison. It was plusher than a Section 36 facility, but not as much so as Promises, a Malibu rehab that makes the Four Seasons look like the Holiday Inn. But again, the place doesn't make the difference. You're either going to do the work and figure out your problems, or you're not. You don't need Promises; you can get better at the Salvation Army on skid row. I've seen people get well in both, and I've seen them not get well in both.

Being there that time was actually a beautiful experience. I made ten of the most atypical friends I'd ever make in my life. There was a weird old lady from some town up north, a Brazilian doctor, and a pillhead from Texas. My first roommate was a gay kid from the heartland of America, Kentucky or Missouri or someplace. He had the classic story, young misunderstood kid grows up in a football town in the Midwest, doesn't get the whole macho deal that his whole world is revolving around, so he's alienated, isolated, and ostracized by his family. He moves to Hollywood, finds his gay brethren and the drug and alcohol world, and hits the downward spiral. He was so into Vicodin that he'd crush them up and sprinkle them on his cereal for breakfast.

He left, and my next roommate was a black anesthesiologist from Inglewood who came from a highly respectable family. Made his family proud by becoming a doctor, but then it turned out that he'd been abusing all the best medical drugs he could find for years. So he came in, like the rest of us, for thirty days. You could tell that he was keeping secrets and destroyed that he had let his family down. A couple of months after the rehab, I got a call. He had relapsed and couldn't bear the agony and the shame of facing his family, so he locked himself in a closet at the hospital where he worked and chose the most unpleasant drugs to overdose on. A few of us from Exodus went to his funeral, and it was really emotional. He had a big family, and one of his brothers was a preacher. There was a holy-roller vibe at the service, and everyone was crying their eyes out, including his rehab buddies, who were all in the back row.

There was an uncommon array of people in there with me, and I became friends with all of them. You recognize the possibility of your own demise in the lives of these other people. You're doing the same thing they are, but you can't see it in yourself. However, you start seeing all of these tragedies and potential miracles in other people. It's a real eye- and heart-opening situation.

Here you are in a fucking hospital in Marina del Rey, sleeping in a small bed, sharing your room, and having to go to the cafeteria for your breakfast. You're forced to think, "Where did I go wrong? I had a plan and was doing really well, but now I'm in here with a bunch of other crazy people, and nurses and doctors and wardens are telling me where to go and what to do, and I've gotta report to a group. Wow, I thought I was smarter than this."

At some point during my stay, I had a group meeting with friends and family, and Flea showed up. During the circle, the drug counselor turned to Flea and said, "Okay, Flea, tell us how it makes you feel deep inside when Anthony's out there using drugs and you have no idea where he is or if he's ever going to come back." I was waiting for Flea to say, "Ah, it pisses me off, that motherfucker. We were supposed to be rehearsing and writing. I was waiting for twelve hours, and that bastard never showed up. I'm ready to do something else altogether." Instead, Flea started sobbing, which caught me off guard. He said, "I'm afraid he's going to die on me. I don't want him to die, but I've kept thinking for years that he's going to die." I had no idea that was the way he felt.

I began a practice at Exodus that is a major part of my life to this day. During the five and a half years that I'd been sober, I never got into prayer or meditation. I wasn't clear on what it was to cultivate a conscious contact with a power greater than myself. At Exodus, someone who worked there suggested that I start each morning with a prayer. Now, to anyone in recovery that's Get Well 101, that's where you begin your program. I had never thought that it was what I had to do. But one morning I looked in the mirror and thought, "You're throwing your life away here, so maybe you're gonna have to try something that's not your idea, but an idea from someone who's actually doing well in life."

I started praying every morning. Once I opened my mind to the concept of a greater power, I never struggled with it. Everywhere I went, I felt and saw the existence of a creative intelligence in this universe, of a loving power larger than myself in nature, in people, everywhere. My prayers and meditations would gain steam and momentum over the years and become an important part of my recovery and daily experience.

I got through the thirty-day stay without even thinking about leaving. I accepted that I was there to do the work and get back on track. For the first few days, they give you a whole plethora of meds to detox on. You get chloral hydrate, which would put an elephant to sleep. They give you Darvocets and Colonodine patches to lower your blood pressure. When you see a guy shuffling down the hallway in his robe and slippers, that's the dude who's still on detox. The first few days off medication are rough: Your skin is crawling, and you're coming to grips with not being on anything. But then you pull out of it and start to feel better. They feed you all day long and you get to exercise and you go to meetings. They keep you pretty busy.

While I was there, Jaime came to visit. Bob Timmons brought Chris Farley in to see me, and it felt good to have his support. Kim Jones brought her two beautiful sons to see me. I was allowed a boom box, and I kept playing the first Elastica tape over and over again. I graduated from my thirty-day program and went back out and rejoined the world of the living. Thank God I was in that world when Jaime's dad left it. He died in June, and I was able to go out to Pennsylvania and be with Jaime and her family through this difficult period.

That summer the band put the finishing touches on the record and began to shoot the videos. We were getting tons of reels, but nothing was touching us, so we went back to Gavin Bowden, Flea's brother-in-law. He came up with an idea for "Warped," which would take place in a giant wooden cylinder. It was a two-day shoot and was our most expensive video to date. I still think it had elements of greatness.

The element that drew the most attention in that video was a scene in which Dave kissed me. Flea and Dave and I were supposed to come out from behind a wall and do a mysterious silhouetted shadow-dance thing. We shot the same scene about ten times in a row, and Gavin felt that we hadn't gotten it, so we went back to our places to try again. Dave turned to me and said, "This time when we walk out, I'm going to turn around and give you a kiss to spice it up." I said, "Okay, good idea," thinking that he would give me a friendly smooch. We walked out from behind that corner, and he went to give me what I thought would be a peck on the lips, which is already crazy enough for a rock video, but all of a sudden, Dave started giving me a wet, partially openmouthed, full-blown kiss. I wasn't upset or bothered, just surprised.

That was one of a thousand shots we did, and we moved on. Weeks later, we got the edited video, and there was the kiss, prominently featured. Minutes later, I got a call from Eric Greenspan, our lawyer.

"Warner Brothers saw the video, and they want to get rid of the kiss right away," he said.

"Why?"

"They don't think it's marketable," he said. "And I think you might want to get rid of the kiss, too. I think you're in danger of alienating a large segment of your fan base."

When I saw the kiss, I was thinking I could take it or leave it, but the minute the corporate suits started saying "No kiss" was the minute I started saying "Nope, the kiss stays." We had a band discussion and voted to keep the kiss. We did have a huge backlash from the college-frat-boy segment of our audience. We got letters denouncing us as "fags," and rumors started spreading, and we started to second-guess our decision. But then we figured, "Fuck it. Maybe it was time to thin out the yokels anyway." If they couldn't accept what we were doing, we didn't need them anymore.

We got in trouble with Warner's again when we used Gavin for our "Aeroplane" video. He came up with a super treatment: an expansive ode to Busby Berkeley, featuring a huge chorus line of half-naked, hot-costumed Mexican cholitas, tough gangster girls with heavy makeup and sweeping hair. We wanted lots of semi-nudity and sexy dancing and chewing of gum and blowing of bubbles. We shot the video in an old pool with trapeze artists and underwater ballet teams on a vintage MGM set that was about to be demolished. But a lady from Warner's was supervising the shoot, and it turned out that she was a PC feminist.

Gavin did the edit, and the video looked sumptuous. He captured the hot Mexican girls in close-ups and from wonderful angles, but this woman from Warner's got her knickers all in a knot about showing naked women in our video. Mind you, this would be tame today next to a Jay-Z video, but it was pretty strong for the time, so we were forced to end up somewhere in between our take and her aesthetic. We wound up not using the shots that were truly shocking and beautiful and eye-catching and disturbing all at the same time.

That summer I made the first of two open-sea kayaking trips to Alaska with Flea and our ex-drummer Cliff Martinez and our friend Marty Goldberg. We spent about a week kayaking into the deepest fjords of southern Alaska. It was an amazing trip, especially since both Cliff and Marty were gourmet chefs who were able to whip up three-star meals in the middle of the wilderness.

In September, *One Hot Minute* was released. We were proud of it, even if it wasn't as good a record as we could have made if we'd kept the band together after *Blood Sugar*. But for a brand-new band, it was a pretty good effort, along the lines of, say, *Mother's Milk,* the first album we made with John and Chad.

Before we began our touring, I was set to do some interviews to promote the album. Right about then, I started getting loaded again. I was holed up in my house on an absolute tear one day in September, and the phone wouldn't stop ringing. I finally answered it, and it was Louie. "Dude, MTV is outside your house. They're ready to shoot." I remembered that I was supposed to do an MTV shoot at my house with the VJ Kennedy. I dragged myself downstairs. I looked sick and lifeless, and I had to answer all these questions on camera in my living room from the bubbly, sweet Kennedy. "It's been a while since you had a record, blah, blah, blah . . ." What a disaster.

Now it was time to tour. Even though I'd been on a run beforehand, I never considered using on the road. I knew that would destroy everything overnight. We started in Europe. It was the first time we'd played before audiences since Woodstock, so we were like a car engine in need of a tune-up. I felt some responsibility for not allowing us to be as good as we could have been. I wasn't as focused on my musicianship as I should have been. We weren't bad, and there were some excellent moments, but overall I was feeling lackluster, and as a musician, I was experiencing a slightly broken reed.

The most memorable thing about that European tour was meeting Sherry Rogers, who would go on to become the wife of our road manager, Louis Mathieu, and the mother of his children. We met her in Amsterdam, where she was working for our old pal Hank Schiffenmacher. Whenever we passed through Amsterdam, we made a beeline to get some more tattoos from Henky Penky, and this trip we encountered a hot, lovely, full-of-spunk young lady named Sherry. She'd routinely dress up in a rubber maid's outfit, and the thought of having her come onstage in that getup was appealing. Our next gig was in Belgium, and she came along and blew everyone's mind when she took off all her clothes in front of everyone in the dressing room and donned the rubber costume. During the show, we had her come onstage periodically to wipe the sweat off our brows, serve us beverages, and light Dave's cigarettes.

Our U.S. tour, which was supposed to start in mid-November, got postponed—through no fault of mine for once—until the beginning of February. So I went straight from Barcelona, our last gig in Europe, to New York to be with Jaime. Jaime had left her dingy high-rise in Chinatown and moved into a charming, cozy, deluxe apartment overlooking the statue of La Guardia just south of Washington Square Park. It was a tranquil, gorgeous neighborhood. We had a nice autumn there, and then, as usual, we began early preparations for the annual Christmas trips. That was when I got the first inklings that all wasn't well on the domestic front. Christmas shopping started out well enough. We walked through the snow and enjoyed the pre-Christmas romance of buying nice presents for our family. I decided to buy Blackie some furniture for his house, so we went to ABC Carpet on lower Broadway and picked out a nice selection.

I went back to the store a couple of times to arrange the shipping and delivery, and one time I was there alone, standing near the elevator, when this elegantly dressed woman in her twenties walked in. She was beautiful and stylish, and I had a one-minute conversation with her while she was waiting for the elevator. This voice went off in my head: "You could marry this lady. Your wife is about to get in that elevator and disappear forever, so you might want to act on it right now." Just at that moment, the elevator came, and she got in and was whisked from my life forever. That was the first time while I'd been with Jaime that I had been open to that kind of idea. I couldn't tell if I was giving power to the fantasy or if there was a look in her eye or something in the way she carried herself, but it was a distinct foreshadowing of trouble.

Come Christmas, we made the usual trips. That year I gave my mom her first deluxe auto, a brand-new customized Ford Explorer that a western Michigan car dealer had specially painted and modified and tricked out for his wife before she divorced him. Blackie did all the research and development on that present. Then Jaime and I spent a few days in Pennsylvania to say hello to everybody, but with the recent loss of Jaime's dad, it obviously wasn't a very joyful time.

We returned to New York in time for New Year's. I was so fed up with the commercialism of New Year's Eve and the compulsion on everyone's part to have the best night of their lives that I decided we would go to sleep before midnight. We cuddled together on the couch and watched a movie, and about eleven-thirty we turned off the lights and went to sleep.

A few days after that, I got the epiphany that this period of my life had come to an end and that it was time to be single again, to be alone. I looked at Jaime one day and thought, "I'm not in love with her anymore." For no reason. It was nothing she did. It wasn't the way she talked or the way she walked or the things she said, because she never did anything that I found intolerable. Something just dawned on me. It was as if a fog had lifted. I was like "Jesus Christ, what have I been doing for the last two years? It's time to make some changes." But it was all about being sober. I had no intention of getting high.

I had probably done enough damage to myself that I was incapable of being in love with her. And that voice was so clear to me that to have ignored it would have meant faking my feelings from that point forward. I knew that I had to do the most undesirable thing of all. For me, it was much easier to stay in an uncomfortable relationship than to tell somebody, "I'm leaving." Historically speaking, I was terrible at it. I couldn't say, "I don't want to be with you anymore." I'd rather go hurt myself, which is part of my cycles.

I told Jaime, and she didn't accept it. She told me that she was planning on getting married to me and having kids, which was the saddest thing she said during all of our discussions. I went back to L.A., and she came out. There was a lot of crying and ranting, and then she packed up her stuff and got back on the red-eye and left.

Because I had caused somebody whom I truly cared about so much pain, it was the perfect emotional setup to go out on another binge. It started on a Friday afternoon. I drove my motorcycle down to Lindy's for a band business meeting. On my way there, I stopped downtown and filled up my pockets with drugs. Then Flea and Lindy and I had our meeting, and I left Lindy's house in the bright daylight, drove a few blocks, and started hitting that pipe right there in the street. The minute the drug hit my brain, I started the bike up and went. I ran for two or three days, smoking crack and putting the heroin on top of that, and all at once I was in another desperate predicament.

I figured I'd be in too much trouble if I stayed in L.A., so I got out the Yellow Pages and dialed up Aeromexico. I found the nicest hotel in Cabo San Lucas, a beautiful place where I had worked on songs with Flea a few years earlier. I was so high on heroin that I was a danger to myself, scratching holes in my body, and I certainly couldn't hide my condition from anyone, so I ordered a car to drive me to the airport. I had saved a handful of balloons that I was going to take with me for some weanage. There'd be no trouble getting on board with them, but I was wary of Mexican customs, so I decided to hide the balloons in the cassette area of my CD/cassette boom box.

When I landed in Mexico, I was still high, and my hair looked like a theremin. The airport had a customs system where you step up to the line, press a button, and get either a red or a green light. If I got a green light, I was home free. Of course, it came up red. I went to the table, and the customs guy was looking at me with great suspicion. He searched my bag and my pockets and then said, "Let me see the stereo." My heart started racing. The last thing I needed was to get busted bringing heroin *into* Mexico. He looked inside the battery compartment, which I'd considered as a stash place, and then he had trouble trying to operate it. He was hitting all the cassette buttons, just about to hit eject, when he looked at me and said, "Make it work." I clicked it right to CD, pushed play, and *The Jackson 5 Greatest Hits* started blasting. He passed me on.

I had booked a room at the Westin, a modern hotel that had been designed to look like a red-clay Mexican structure. I holed up in the bed, used the last of the heroin, and then cocooned, ordering room service and watching satellite TV and feeling lonely and depressed and remorseful. By the third day of lying in bed, eating, and trying to become human again, I forced myself to go down and jump in the ocean. I had to baptize my spirit. I went to the pool area and tried to swim, but I ran into people who wanted to talk to me, and I wasn't up for that at all. On that trip, I made friends with a pelican whose wing had been damaged in a fisherman's net. He had become the mascot of the pool area. I sat there and fed him and talked to him. We were two creatures nursing our wounds. I even wound up writing a song about that pelican.

At some point, I performed the selfish and errant act of calling

Jaime, even though I knew in my heart of hearts that our relationship was over. But she was still my best friend and a soothing entity in my life. "I'm down here and I'm lonely and I'm sick and I'm tired and I'm hurt and I'm fucked up and I'm sad. Do you want to come down?" She flew in the next day, and we had a decent couple of days together, staying in bed and eating and talking.

Cabo became my own personal rehab. I'd stay sober for a few weeks, relapse, make a mess of situations, then go back down and check in to the same hotel room, and do the exact same thing, which is one of the better definitions of insanity—doing the exact same thing over and over and expecting the result to be different. If you had to be sick somewhere, Mexico was the place. I did consider myself fortunate to have the luxury of going down there and lying out under those blue skies.

At the beginning of February 1996, we began a three-leg, two-month U.S. tour. We were opening the tour at the Nassau Coliseum on Long Island, but the day we got to town, the New York area was hit by an incredible blizzard and was under a monstrous blanket of snow. The subways and cabs weren't running, so Flea and I took a snowy walk from our midtown motel to the Lower East Side to eat at Angelica's Kitchen, a great vegetarian restaurant. Later that night, I met Guy O at the Spy Bar in SoHo. There were a lot of girls there, but most of them were too New York fabulous and difficult to deal with. Then we saw this girl who was a little tipsy, wearing a bright red dress with some weird '80s Zebra belt accoutrement. She was in her own world by the piano, doing a heartfelt pantomime to a Björk song. I thought that took a lot of chutzpah, so I went over and introduced myself. Her name was Christina, and she was a model who had grown up in Idaho but was now living in New York. She had natural orange-red hair and crazy-beautiful white skin and huge tits, way too big and pillowy for normal runway modeling.

I invited her to the show the next night, and she asked if she could bring her roommate, who, it turned out, was a huge Oasis fan. This was the moment that Oasis was the hottest band going, having permeated every nook and cranny of America. I had purposefully ignored this phenomenon, but on the ride out to the Coliseum, all Christina's roommate could talk about was Oasis and this brother or that brother. We plowed through the snow and got to the Coliseum, and I was relieved to see that the place was full and the audience was appreciative.

That night I began seeing Christina, which was a good thing, since it had been a while since I felt that connection with somebody. I wasn't falling in love, but she was a nice person, and we were definitely sexually compatible. I don't know if it was her smell or her energy, but we'd be in bed, and I'd feel like an opiated vampire from being with her.

Early on in that tour, I fell off the stage. We were playing these new *One Hot Minute* songs that hadn't seen too much stage time, and I was in the midst of my eyes-closed robotic dancing when I tripped over one of my monitors. I went plummeting right off the stage and dropped eight feet, hit my head on the concrete floor, and passed out. I came right to and was grateful to be conscious, but my head was the least of my problems. Before I tripped, my leg had gotten tangled up in my mike cord, so when I fell, the cord acted like a hangman's noose and ripped my calf muscle right off the bone. I was hanging upside down thinking I could deal with the head injury, but when I pushed myself back up onstage, my leg wouldn't work. I finished the show on one leg and went to the hospital. I got some stitches in my head, but my leg had become black and blue and green and wildly disfigured-looking. They rigged me up with a Frankenfoot-looking cast complete with a vast array of straps. I had to finish the rest of the tour with this Frankenfoot, which was not fun to perform in.

After the second leg of the tour, we had a two-week break. Prior to the tour, Sherry Rogers had moved up to San Francisco and begun a relationship with Louis Mathieu, who had moved up from L.A. to live with her. I used to visit them up there, and we'd go to meetings and haunt the tattoo parlors. I had begun to get close with Louie. Louie was half Mexican, half Jewish, and 100 percent

psychotic. He was crazy on the inside, but he put on this calm ex-
terior. He had started with us answering phones at the *Blood Sugar*
house, and then we took him out on tour as the drum tech, basically creating jobs for him because we liked him so much.

Louie had been a pot dealer in high school, and then he got
strung out on heroin. He went through years of back-and-forth
struggles to get sober, but he had been clean at this point for a lot
of years. Louie was kind and giving and would go out of his way to
be there for you, almost to the point where it became a defensive
mechanism so he wouldn't have to deal with what was going on in
his own life. But he was a great running partner, and we shared the
sobriety and a love for music.

The last thing Louie was, was an outdoorsman. When we
got the two-week break, I decided to facilitate a nice experience for
Louie and Sherry and take them on a trip to Hawaii, which they
couldn't have afforded then. Sherry was adventuresome and gung-
ho, but Louie agreed begrudgingly. We rented a house on the
sunny side of Maui. Every day Sherry and I would go out in front of
the house, dive into the ocean, and swim a mile out and a mile
back. Louie would sit on the beach, smoking cigarettes, drinking
coffee, and doing his crossword puzzles, naysaying all of nature's
beauty that was surrounding him.

At one point on that trip, Louie and I were having lunch at a
fancy hotel, and a thought popped into my head: "Louis, I hear
wedding bells for you in the near future." He confessed that he was
feeling the same thing. A few days later, near the end of our stay, I
had taken a nap in the middle of the day, and when I woke up, the
house seemed deserted. It was odd not to have Louie and Sherry
around, and I started going from room to room, calling out,
"Louis? Sherry?"

Finally, I cracked open the door to their bedroom to see if
they were napping. I saw Louie in full slow-jam love mode with
Sherry, naked man on top of naked woman. I closed the door right
up and felt terrible for walking in on them. Nine months to the

day later, their son, Cash, was born, which connected me further to the family. Most kids can't say, "Oh yeah, Uncle Tony was there when I was conceived."

We finished the U.S. tour with a West Coast leg. Considering that we had taken a four-year record hiatus and that the climate of pop music had changed so drastically, it was nice to see that people were still interested in coming out to see what we do. We were playing arenas, and it wasn't the every-date-sold-out tour of our career, but we were getting warm receptions to the new material everywhere we went.

In Seattle, I flew Christina out for a few days. The band had an off night, and Oasis was playing in town. Their management called up and invited us to the show, but no one wanted to go except Christina. By that point, Oasis was in disarray. The brothers were constantly fighting, and shows were being canceled right and left. But we went, and before the show started, we were backstage and I met the singer. He introduced himself to me, and I said, "Hello, Ian." "No, *Liam*." We went through a whole "Ian, Liam" *Spinal Tap* moment. Then we went out to watch the show. It would have been great, except it was obvious they hated each other. They were dead on the stage. The songs and the singing were good, though.

Halfway through the show, Christina had a couple of arena beers and got horny and decided she wanted to give me a blow job. So we wandered backstage. Most of the doors were locked, but I found one that was open. It was below the stage and opened into the electrical control room for the whole arena. There were all these levers and switches and buttons. So we got on the floor, took off our clothes, and started having sex. It was a nice atmosphere; we could hear the muffled sounds of the band playing above us. But somewhere along the way, we got too frisky and banged into a lever, and all of a sudden, the lights went out. I jumped up and rushed over to the board, convinced that we had cut the sound and lights to the entire arena. I frantically pushed a lever, and the lights came back on. I realized that we had cut off the power only in that room, but we were one lever away from bringing the concert to a grinding halt from having sex beneath the stage.

Christina was a lot of fun to be with, and our physical relationship was wonderful, but I wasn't falling in love with her to the point of her being my girlfriend. A few months later, right before we went back to Europe to tour, I told her I couldn't see her anymore. She was pretty upset, but Guy O was beside himself. "I can't believe you're walking away from this girl. She's the first girl you've been with in a long time who's totally considerate. She brings you flowers. She loves you. She's beautiful. She's sexy. She's smart." But when you're not feeling it, you're not feeling it. When I broke up with her, she said, "Ah, that really sucks. I was hoping that this relationship was gonna go somewhere, but I understand. At least we had a lot of great sex." I was like "That's the spirit!"

After the West Coast leg, we had a few weeks off before we set out to tour Australia and New Zealand again. We started off in New Zealand, and being back there made me realize that this was where I was going to make my home away from home. Somehow I hooked up with an ex–rugby player who had been a member of the all-black New Zealand rugby team in the '60s but now was an older, brutish, conniving, absolute shyster of a real estate agent. On a break from our shows, he took me out to look at this 169-acre farmhouse overlooking Kai Para Bay, which is an hour and fifteen minutes northwest of Auckland. We went out on the most gorgeous, sunny day. I fell in love with the place, even though Kai Para Harbor is an incredibly rough body of water where great white sharks go to breed. It's a furiously tidal, raging harbor.

My whole thrust of finding a home away from home was to buy a place near a clear, temperate, inviting body of water, one that I could swim in and play underwater. I have no idea why I chose this place, because none of that was there. But the view of the harbor was incredible, a kaleidoscopic, psychedelic patina of colors. And this agent had me all hyped up about an auction for the property, which was going to take place, coincidentally, while I was on tour in Australia. "This is your one and only chance to get this property. It's gonna go quick, there are a lot of people interested. I'll have you on the phone and I'll do the bidding for you. Blah blah blah blah."

I was on the phone from Australia, and he was at the auction. "It's at a million dollars. Going up. Going up. Someone here wants it for one point seven." I was like "Okay. Go two." The next thing you know, I'd bought this place for way more than it was worth. When I got back, people started telling me that they weren't even sure there was anyone else bidding. All these Kiwi businessmen were in bed with one another.

We finished the two-week tour cycle, and everyone went home to the U.S. except me. I went back to New Zealand, checked in to a bed-and-breakfast, and went through the process of closing this deal, which cost me about $1 million U.S. I was waiting for the farmer who had sold me the place to take his money and move to the Gold Coast of Australia, where it's always sunny. Meanwhile, I was thinking, "Why on earth would these farmers leave the most beautiful piece of paradise for the crowded-ass Gold Coast, which is like Miami Beach, only tackier?" I soon found out. It turned out that I saw that farmhouse on one of the few days of the year when it didn't rain. Three hundred days out of the year, that country just poured precipitation. It was cloudy, rainy, chilly, blustery, England-on-a-bad-day kind of weather.

Eventually, the farmer moved out, and I signed the papers and set up a bank account in Auckland. I got Greer's father to be the caretaker, because people in New Zealand were known to move in and occupy vacant country properties. There was this Wild West mentality out there. Greer's dad was going to check up on the property and make sure no one was squatting or stealing the fixtures.

It was time to go home and get ready for our European dates. Before we went to Europe, we played the first ever Tibetan Freedom Fest in San Francisco. It was a great lineup that included Smashing Pumpkins, the Beastie Boys, Foo Fighters, Beck, Björk, and Rage Against the Machine, but it wasn't a great show for us. We had problems with the sound, but it was for a good cause, so we didn't stress much. There was a party afterward, and I ran into Ione and attempted to make amends for being such a shite boyfriend when we lived together. It was the first amends I had ever attempted, and it was ill conceived to approach her in that environment, so she had every right to tell me that I was an asshole and that I should fuck off before she walked away.

When we got to Europe in late June, everyone was optimistic, partially because I had been staying sober for the tours. There was a distinct feeling of brotherhood among us. The only issue surfacing was the fact that Dave wasn't crazy about playing music for the sake of music, and Flea needed that kind of bond. He missed having someone who'd call him up and say, "Come over to my house and let's play guitars for a while." Dave wasn't that guy. He was like "Why would I come over and play guitar with you? Do we have to write a song for something?" There was a rift developing. But on the other hand, Dave and Chad were becoming quite close.

We started the tour off in Budapest. Everyone raved about Prague, but to me, Budapest was a much more interesting town, more exotic and wild and more recently detached from the Communist hold. In Prague, we performed in a small club. It was packed, and I went to do a flip onstage. I was a little bit out of control and landed on one of the monitors. When I went to stand up, there was no one home. We had to stop the set and wheel me off, because I was in such excruciating pain. The next day I couldn't move. I saw a few practitioners, but no one seemed able to diagnose what damage I had wrought upon my back. So they strapped me up in a back brace, and I did the next few shows standing in one spot, almost totally immobilized.

I had become totally constipated, and I couldn't even sit up straight, the pain was so intense. In every city we went, I begged our tour manager, Tony Selinger, to find somebody, an osteopath, a chiropractor, a voodoo practitioner, anyone who could help me.

I was bedridden until I had to go onstage. And that was when I remembered the advice that Carolee Brogue, my Fairfax drama teacher, had given me. She was on Broadway playing Peter Pan when she got a nasty stomach virus, but she strapped on a diaper and squirted out diarrhea the whole performance because, no matter what, *the show must go on*.

We were in Belgium when Tony showed up with a fat, sweaty, boisterous Belgian fellow who bounded through my door speaking Flemish. He was an osteopath. I was thinking, "Jeez, yet another quack who's not gonna be able to do anything." He examined me, had me stand and walk around, and then told me to get on the bed. This big bowling ball of a fellow went to work on me. He lifted my leg and put all his weight on it, and POP!, my whole back snapped into place in one fell swoop. It was like going from being a broken toy to being a brand-new one. It turned out I had dislocated my sacrum.

I was revitalized, and we began playing well. France was great, then we went to England, where we played Wembley. It was the single best show we played with Dave. Guy O was there, and he had taken it upon himself to become my matchmaker. Sometime during the spring, he had gone on a boat party in L.A. and met a girl who lived in London. He assured me she was just my type. So he beat away all the other guys on the boat and got her number for me. After the Wembley show, he introduced me to this girl named Rachel. He was right: I was immediately attracted to her. I decided to get a hotel room and stick around London, even though everyone else was heading home.

The next night Rachel and I went out to dinner and walked through the park. All of a sudden, we started making out, and it was all going on. We went back to her apartment, made love, and she was wonderful, everything Guy O promised and then some, a very special girl. We were in our postcoital glow when she said to me, "I have to tell you that this is so weird, because the very last person I had a sexual relationship with was your ex-girlfriend Ione. And by the way, I liked this experience much better." Out of the three billion girls in the world, I ended up being with one Ione had also been with. The ironic part of all of this was that when I first met Jaime, she was part of the Beastie Boy world through her trust-fund boyfriend. While she was hanging around them, she met Adam and Ione, who were married then. As soon as Adam walked out of the room, Ione went for Jaime with openmouthed kisses. It turned out that Adam and Ione were leading pretty separate lives by then, but I found it interesting that Ione and I had such similar tastes in women. I stayed with Rachel for a few days, but then it was time to go home.

It was also time to go on another drug binge. It was bound to happen sooner or later, because I wasn't taking care of myself. I think the fact that I'd spent all this intimate time with a girl I wasn't going to follow through on triggered this episode. Now I had some time on my hands, and I was home alone in what had become the palace of getting loaded. I did a two-week run, and then I went to Cabo San Lucas to do my routine of sleeping for three days, kicking, eating like a fiend, and swimming. Same hotel, same room, same *Northern Exposure* on satellite TV.

When I came back from Cabo, Louie was there for me, picking me up at the airport and hanging around with me. I was over at his house a few days after I'd gotten back when the phone rang. It was my beloved aunt Mickey, one of my favorite aunts, the second oldest of four sisters on my mother's side. She was hysterical, saying, "Steve died. Steve died," over and over again. I assumed it was her son, because she had both a son and a grandson named Steve. I asked her which Steve, and she sobbed, "Your mother's Steve." Suddenly, the heart and soul of my entire sense of well-being in Michigan was gone. He was the guy who brought my whole family together and gave us this loving homestead, the thoughtful, caring, hardworking, honest soul trooper of the bunch. He raised Julie and Jenny and the dogs and the cats and the horse, and my mom loved him, they were just so good together. I thought, "Oh shit. My fifty-one-year-old stepdad had to go and have a damn heart attack in the garden at two in the afternoon."

I thanked God that I wasn't in a motel room somewhere, smoking crack off a tinfoil pipe, when I got the news. I was newly clean with an extra launch in my stride. It turned out that I was the only one in a clear state of mind; everyone else was shattered and stunned and torn up. We had a huge funeral service, and the church was packed to the rafters with half of Grand Rapids to say good-bye to Steve and pay homage to this unique citizen. My family elected me to give the eulogy. It wasn't hard to write about a guy like him. For a kid like me, who had always been watching after his mother, Steve entering the picture was such a huge relief. It was like "Okay, now I can go be a boy again and not have to worry about my mom getting screwed over by a convict." It was a remarkable experience to look out at this church filled with hundreds and hundreds of people, all of us riding the same wave of love and gratitude and appreciation for this person.

Back in L.A., I was sitting at home one day when I got one of those periodic crazy calls from Lindy. He was in his apartment/office in Studio City, smoking his Merits and telling me that Molson Beer was offering us $1 million to fly up to the North Pole and do a show for the winners of a contest. They'd also get to use our name and our music to sell the hell out of their beer in Canada for a few months. This wasn't the first time we'd gotten an offer from a big corporation. A year after "Under the Bridge," McDonald's came up with a whole campaign to sell hamburgers using that song. They were offering $2 mil, but we didn't want our name to be associated with them.

The Molson offer was interesting because 1) they wouldn't use our image, and 2) it was just a radio campaign in Canada. Basically, our music would get heard many times per day. I guess this was a time in our operation when integrity wasn't as revered as it is now; plus, we all wanted to go to the North Pole. Molson made the whole thing sound appealing. We'd get private aircraft service to and fro, and accommodations. The show was for an audience of a hundred people, and we'd be in, out, and get to go to the end of the earth and see the Aurora Borealis. We weighed the good and the bad and agreed to do it.

We flew to Montreal and switched to a larger plane to fly north for eight hours. We got to the site, and there was only one place to stay, a run-down boot-camp barracks-type place called the Narwhal, named after the unicorn whale. There was no town, just a handful of native Indians who lived up there full-time. We were there a day before the show, so we did some snowmobiling, and they took us on a small-propeller flight tour of the North Pole. We marveled at the beautiful blue and white barren landscape. We were supposed to perform on the deck of a Russian icebreaker, but even though it was September 1, it was freezing outside, with gusts at fifty knots, so the concert was moved into a warehouse.

One thing we pride ourselves on is being professionals. When we play, we play all the fucking way. But there was something about the atmosphere that made it impossible to do a normal rock show where you go out there, and boom, you start getting into your shit. We stepped onto that stage, and I looked at the hundred people who had been flown up, and they all had their funny little clothes on and their Molsons in their hands, and the whole thing reminded me of a bad office party. I picked up the mike, and the music started, and it was time for me to sing, but I couldn't stop laughing. The preposterous nature of show business overwhelmed me, and I could not get it together. Eventually, I focused, but between songs I went back thirteen years and broke out some of our old comedy routines and started taking the piss out of people and having fun with the audience. There was at least as much comedic banter as there was music. I don't know how long we played, but I was happy when it was over. We flew home that night and saw the Aurora Borealis and the otherworldly colors and cloud formations, and it felt like we were on a mission to Mars.

When we got back to L.A., I began my own private mission to Mars, a furious round of benders that would consume my next few months. I would go out for a week at a time, and even though the whole idea of using had become repugnant to me and I wanted to stop, I couldn't, which is the textbook definition of active addiction. All this weird-ass shit would happen to me on my runs. On one of these benders, I ran out of drugs at four-thirty in the morning. At that point in time, I wasn't dialed in to ATM technology; when I needed money, I'd go to a bank and take out a chunk of money on a credit card, or I'd visit an American Express office, where I could take out as much as ten thousand dollars at a shot. But now I had no money, no stuff, and was in a frenzy to get high.

What I did have was a beautiful white Stratocaster guitar signed by all of the Rolling Stones. Tommy Mottola had given it to me when he was trying to sign the Chili Peppers to Sony/Epic. I figured I could go downtown and get a least a couple hundred dollars' worth of dope for that guitar. So I went down to those dimly lit back alleys where the men sell their wares, but there was only one guy working the street at that late hour.

"What can I get for this?" I asked him, proffering the guitar.

He shrugged. "Nothing."

"No, no, you don't understand," I pressed on. "This guitar is signed by the Rolling Stones."

"Dinero, señor, dinero," he kept repeating. He was fresh up over the border, and he obviously couldn't speak English and didn't give a rat's ass about the Rolling Stones.

"But this is valuable," I protested.

He finally offered me the tiniest amount of heroin I'd ever seen.

"No, more," I begged, but he indicated it was that or nothing. I was so desperate that I bartered the signed guitar for some drugs that would get me high for about ten minutes.

All during these runs, I had the support of Bob Timmons, who was constantly trying to get me to check in to Exodus again. I was also getting much love from a newer friend of mine, this wonderful white-haired hippie Communist from Venice Beach named Gloria Scott. I first encountered Gloria when she was speaking at a meeting in Hollywood during my first round of sobriety in the late '80s. She said she'd been a real-deal drugstore-cowboy junkie her whole life, knocking off pharmacies and running scams, but she also talked about the '60s and Allen Ginsberg.

By then she'd been sober for about ten years. I was thinking, "This lady is the coolest person I've ever seen. She's nasty and not trying to be all saccharine, saying stuff like 'Fuck you if you don't like what I'm saying, motherfucker, because I've been there.'" She said her higher power was Neil Young. Then she said, "I've lived in a one-room bungalow down in Venice since 1967. I was dealing to Jim Morrison before you were crapping in your pants. The only things I have up in my house are a poster of Che Guevara, a poster of Neil Young, and a poster of a bunch of Red Hot Chili Peppers with the socks on their dicks." I went up to her after the meeting and told her that I was honored to be on her wall along with Neil. We became fast friends, like Harold and Maude without the romance.

When I started going missing in action and becoming more desperate and isolated, I stopped answering my phone. Every now and then I'd check my mail, and there'd be a postcard of a Native American warrior. On the back, Gloria would write, "Don't ever give up your fight. You are a warrior and you will beat this thing that you're up against. I have faith in you. I never forget you, don't forget your own self." I'd read that in my kitchen and think, "There's a person out there who actually believes I can win this battle."

Around that time, I had a dream in which I was driving at about four-thirty in the morning, that darkest hour of the night before the sun even thinks about coming up. It was pitch black and raining, and I was going through the intersection of Melrose and San Vincente. The streets were dead, and I was driving fast and furious, screeching around corners, obviously going somewhere in a heated passion. I must have been going to cop drugs, because I was driving like my life depended on it. It was eerie and spooky and dark and rainy, and I was all alone in the car, driving and driving, and then out of nowhere, a hand came out and, whoosh, grabbed on to the steering wheel and started fighting me for control of the car.

I looked over to see who the person in the seat next to me was, but he was all slouched down with a hat covering his face, so I couldn't make out the demonic person. We kept driving, and I became terrified of what I was about to see. Then we drove under a streetlight, and the light illuminated the face of the intruder. And it was me. I had this horribly scary grin pasted on my face, and I was holding the wheel, saying, "I got ya. I got ya. I got ya."

Near the end of October, I checked in to Exodus again, this time resigned to being in there. That day I got a phone call from Bob Forrest.

"How are you doing?" he asked.

"I feel like a gangster in one of those old cops-and-robbers movies. I'm gonna have to shoot my way out of this place," I joked. I was teasing him, being a character, acting out a scene, trying to make light of the heavy and fucked-up place that I was occupying.

Bob said, "Oh, really? That sounds crazy. Are you sure you're all right?"

"Yeah, I'm gonna stay here and see what happens."

I stayed that night. The next day I woke up and got the call. And the call was to go out and get high again. So I gathered up my stuff and said good-bye to Nurse Kathy, who was the only sane person in that whole place. Everybody else was doing the rehab shuffle.

I walked into the corridor, and the woman who ran that wing of the hospital stepped into the hallway and confronted me. "Where do you think you're going?" she said.

"You know what, I'm just not ready to go through rehab right now, so I'm leaving," I said.

"You can't leave," she said with finality. "We're not going to let you leave."

"Let me see you try and stop me," I said. I took a few steps toward the exit, and she rushed up to me.

"No, really, we're locking the doors. We're going to have to put you in your room again," she threatened.

"Lock the doors? I'll fucking put my bed through the window and leave when I want to. You've got nothing to say about it, lady." What was she talking about? This wasn't a lockdown facility. I was there voluntarily, and I could leave whenever I felt like it. Or so I thought.

"I do have something to say about it this time," she said.

I was getting pissed off. I had a serious calling here. I had to go get some money, get a cab, and have it wait while I talked to Flaco on the corner. Then I had to find a motel room. I had a very important agenda. But all that went out the window when she pushed a button. Suddenly, there were some very large USC-football-linemen-sized fellows coming at me from every angle. They grabbed me like a little rag doll and started carrying me down the hallway.

"Hey, what's going on here? Let me go, buddy. I have things to do," I was ranting, but they ignored me and carried me past some electronically locked prison-style doors into a separate unit known as the mental ward. This was it. The lockdown. The no-escaping-you're-in-jail-now-insane-asylum-loony-bin ward.

I demanded an explanation: "What the fuck is going on?"

"You are now on a lockdown. You'll be here for the next seventy-two hours while we observe you," one of the behemoths said.

He may as well have said seventy-two years. Seventy-two hours was not acceptable to me. If he had said ten minutes, I could have worked with that. But I had pressing business outside.

"Oh no. No, no, no. Get my lawyer on the phone. I demand to talk to my lawyer," I screamed.

"Dude, shut up. Someone's gonna be in here to fill out a form, and you'll get a room and you can chill," my tormentor said.

I scanned the corridor. There was no getting out of here. The place was sealed tight as a drum. But as I stood there in the hallway, I saw a pack of loony birds being let into the facility from a smoking patio with sliding bulletproof glass doors. I looked out into the courtyard and saw an approximately eighteen-foot-high brick wall with nothing around it. There was no way I could get over that wall unless I had some rappelling equipment. Then I saw a basketball hoop about eight feet from the wall.

And I saw my opening. The goons had left me to wait for the admitting nurse, but just then a doctor walked by. He had the pens in the pocket and the stethoscope, and he was reading a chart. He also had a huge ring of keys dangling from his belt loop.

"Excuse me, Doctor. I was just outside, and I left my cigarettes. Could you let me out to the patio area to get them?"

"I'm not authorized to unlock the door. That's the policy here," he mumbled.

"I know. But if you open that door, I'll go out there for a minute in that secured compound and have a quick smoke." I was using every mind-control technique I could on this guy, and they worked. He unlocked the door, and I thanked him. The minute he turned around, I shimmied up to the top of that basketball hoop, stood on the backboard above it, leaned my body as far forward as I could, and jumped, just catching my fingers on the edge of the wall. Another inch and I would have done a face-plant into the wall and cracked my skull. I pulled myself up to the top of the wall and jumped down. I was free.

I started boogying down the sidewalk and got about two blocks before I stopped to figure out my next move. There was no one coming after me, so I figured they were happy to get rid of me because I was causing such a stink. Then I looked up and realized that I was right in front of a branch of my bank. What a stroke of luck. I could get some cash and begin my excellent adventure.

I never spotted the hospital employee who was in the bank depositing a check. But she was watching me as I marched over to the desk of the branch manager.

He looked up. "Anthony Kiedis! What a pleasure. How can we help you?"

"I happened to be in the neighborhood, and I need to withdraw some money. And perhaps you could call me a cab?"

"I'd be happy to," he said. "Come sit down."

He called a cab, and I told him I needed to withdraw a couple of thousand dollars, and it was all good. I was sitting there in the middle of the bank thinking, "Hallelujah, I'm gonna be high as a kite in about forty-five minutes," when all of a sudden, my radar sensors started beeping. I looked up and saw that the same big motherfuckers who had accosted me in the hallway of the hospital were advancing on me from every direction in the bank. Then I looked out the big glass windows and saw uniformed policemen surrounding the building, along with nurses, orderlies, and a friend of mine named Harold who worked as a rehab specialist in the hospital.

I vowed that these guys would have to chase me. Once I get into the open street, ain't none of these fuckers gonna catch me, including the cops. I will jump on the back of a bus. I will commandeer a car. I will get on a boat. I will disappear into the bushes. They aren't going to get me. So I jumped out of the chair and went running through the bank, hurtling over anything in my way. I got through a door that led into the office building housing the bank, but as soon as I entered the hall, a whole other contingent of security guards started running toward me.

"Whoop, can't go that way." I turned to run the other way, and there were more guys advancing on me from that direction. I had nowhere to go, so I just thought "Fuck it" and went head-to-head with these guys. I managed to knock down a few of the building guards and even made my way out into the street, but I was overpowered when one of those huge hospital guards tackled me and got me in such a strong body hold that I thought my liver was going to squeeze out of my ankle bone. I was a weakened little bitch at that point.

"Easy, pal, easy," I said. "Why do you fuckers care? Just let me go."

"No way. Once you escape from lockdown, we're responsible for anything you do," he told me. He also told me about the hospital employee who'd seen me in the bank and thought it was odd that I was sitting down with the branch manager when I should have been on the ward. When I turned up AWOL, it was the same as escaping a jail, and there was an all-points bulletin out for me, with every cop in the neighborhood searching.

They handcuffed me and threw me into a cop car and drove me back to the hospital, where I found out that I had been put into seventy-two-hour lockdown because Bob Forrest had been concerned about our conversation. He had called Lindy, and they got it in their heads that I was suicidal, so they tried to get me committed. The hospital could have ignored them, but they probably thought the last thing they needed was another Kurt Cobain situation on their hands. The whole thing was ludicrous. I never once verbalized anything about killing myself. I never once said I had a gun. All I said, in a Jimmy Cagney gangster voice, was "Ah, if I had a heater, I'd shoot my way out of this place right now." Lunatic Bob Forrest, the then–King of Exaggerations, Rumors, and Lies, had started the whole ball rolling.

And here I was in lockdown. When I got back in, I went straight for the phone and called Eric Greenspan. "I want a fucking lawyer to come down here and get me out. I am not suicidal. Get me out of this hospital."

Eric promised to help, but he said it might take a little while. In the meantime, I was assigned a room and a twenty-four-hour watchdog at my door. I was already checking out the ceiling ventilation shafts, trying to find a way out, because now my life was getting weirder and uglier by the second. The next day a nurse came in and told me I would be discharged as soon as the admitting doctor signed my papers. After a few hours, she came back in the room. I was already counting how many balloons of heroin I would cop when she said, "Before you go, there are some people here to see you."

"Uh, that doesn't sound possible. I'm supposed to be discharged—"

In through the door walked Bob Timmons, followed by a few of my friends and my poor mother, who had flown in from

Michigan. I was not at all happy that someone had called my mother and she had to fly out to deal with this mess. I had been ambushed with a full-fledged intervention. We all sat down, and they started to give me the intervention, and I was the sheer disease guy. Everything that came out of my mouth was a lie or a manipulation. Everything I said had an angle so I could position myself to psychologically dominate this scene and get free to go get loaded.

"Hey, everything's okay. I'm ready to get better, I just don't want to be in rehab. I've been through this. And of course I'm gonna go and get involved in my recovery and yada yada." I conned them into thinking that I was gonna get out of there and go to work on being a sober guy. I had no intention of it whatsoever, but I told them everything they wanted to hear just to get out of that hospital.

We left the hospital, and most of us went to break bread over my new beginning, which I knew was neither new nor a beginning. Everyone started eating, but I was nibbling and picking and pushing my food around.

"Okay, I'm going to leave now and go home and get my recovery notebooks, and then I'm going to meet up with Mom and fly home with her tomorrow and go back to the basics and work on my recovery."

"Really, you're going by yourself? Why don't I come with you?" my friend Chris said. I insisted on going alone.

I scrammed, got my motorcycle, got some money, picked up some drugs, and checked in to the Bonaventure Hotel, a big, modern, fancy hotel in downtown Los Angeles. It had been close to a week since I'd been loaded, so I was chomping at the bit. Right off the bat, I got crazy high, and a bad-idea lightbulb went off above my head. I got back on the bike and drove to the Chevy dealer by USC to buy a new car. My twisted logic was that even though I had just ditched my intervention posse, I was going to buy a car and then drive around with no destination in mind and get better.

Flea and I have always had a bizarre and sometimes dangerous bond. Like Cain and Abel without the bloodshed. Here we seem to be scowling at each other's very souls. We've probably played music together 10,000 times and I can't wait for the next. Circa 1990 or '91.

After we recorded *Freaky Styley* with George Clinton, he would periodically pop up at our club shows and make himself at home onstage. What a sensational stroke of good luck for us from my accidental mentor. If memory serves, this is us at Jack Spats in the Southbay, deep behind the orange curtain and on our way to a very long night.

I think I got these shorts from Bob Forrest's girlfriend Sabrina Judge. The knee pads? Well, I was still getting high during the tour for *Uplift Mofo* and I would get some wacky ideas. That's our old manager Mark Johnson in the background. Circa 1987.

Here we have the ultra New York East Village vixen, Yohanna Logan, punching the clock at Balthazar's about one month before I met her. I actually met her at her workplace in 1999. We toughed it out for almost four years after that, with a few breaks along the way. Her spell on me was beyond powerful and our time together was invaluable. Kiss.

After our first gold record with *Mother's Milk*, we got pretty cocky without even realizing it. This is us backstage at the Greek Theater with the actor Michael McKean in full character as David St. Hubbins from *Spinal Tap*. He did a five-minute introduction for us that we all watched from the wings. Needless to say, we were in stitches. Literally. 1989.

This is Yohanna and me messing around in a drugstore photo booth. The picture always made me think of some new-wave German techno duo called Wish You Were Here. We shared a lot of love, she and I.

Don't ask me where. It's backstage somewhere on tour for *Freaky Styley*. Flea, me, Slim, and Cliff. Come to think of it, it might be Dingwalls in London, England, because that's where Hillel wore the black leather Swedish military overalls. Skinny little tore-back road dogs. Gotta love it.

Professional photographers get some pretty bad ideas about what backdrops will look good for your band. This one is actually kind of attractive with its wannabe pink, alleyway chic. Back then Flea would let me draw all over him for photo shoots. It was a tradition. I think it was 1987. Left to right: Flea, me, Jackie I., and the golden ring–fingered Slim Bob Billy.

There were times when all Hillel and I had was each other. We were fucked up and understood what it was to be living in an out-of-control fog. We still had style and we still had funk. Looks like we're in the back of a car, but I have no clue when or where. Circa *Freaky Styley*.

Don't know what song we're playing,
but it must have been mere months after
John first joined the band. I remember
that is how J.F. was wearing his hair
when I met him, and that was the guitar
he was playing at that time. Safe to say,
he and I bonded right off the bat. Notice
the heavy-duty gloves I found it necessary to be wearing. 1988 or '89.

Flea and I had been up for a couple
of days when we wandered into this
San Francisco photo booth. As can be
seen by the unison of our expressions,
we had charted out a bit of a plan.
Somehow we made it back to L.A.
in two pieces and started a band a
few months later.

Ione's rare and soulful beauty really shows itself without any inhibitions as she holds her loving man against her naked body. I had come back from our first European tour with a rather large back piece at a time when they weren't a dime a dozen, and Ione was in shock. She got over it in time to make herself available for this photo. Oddly enough, the photographer, Patricia Steur, was the wife of the Dutch tattoo artist who had rendered the piece, Hank Schiffmacher. 1987 or '88. (Photo credit: Patricia Steur)

I got to the dealership just as they were closing. "Wait, wait. I need to buy a car. Give me the best big black Chevy you have."

They were all looking skeptically at this crazy-high guy who came off the street, but then I whipped out my Amex card, they checked it out, and they had a major attitude adjustment. They brought me a nice Chevy Tahoe and were more than happy to follow me back to the Bonaventure and deliver it.

The next morning I decided it was time to hit the road, so I left my motorcycle in the hotel parking lot, jumped into this brand-new Chevy SUV, and started heading east. I was thinking of driving to Colorado or the Dakotas, but I got only as far as East L.A. I just wasn't feeling right. So I checked in to a motel, got high, got high, got high, and realized that doing some long-distance driving might not be such a good idea.

I drove back to Beverly Hills and checked in to a hotel on Robertson and did all my drugs. I was at the point where I wasn't even getting high. I was just wide awake, raw, empty, lonely, tired, angry, confused, and terrified of having to deal with the latest mess I'd made. I decided that maybe I should go back to Michigan with my mom. I called her hotel, but she had left town that morning, furious that I had lied to her. I got in my new Tahoe and drove to the airport. I found a pay phone and called Lindy to apologize. When I was in Exodus, frantically trying to get out of the locked ward, I had called Lindy and trashed him.

I flew to Michigan and did the country-house Mom hang, trying to get it together one more time. This was a new bottom for me. I'd been institutionalized in a mental ward, escaped, gotten caught, had an intervention, escaped the interventionees, freaked out, bought a car thinking I'd go cross-country, pumped a bunch of drugs into my system and didn't even get high, and now I was back on my mother's couch, shivering through another withdrawal.

I felt so bad that my mom had to deal with one more emotional firestorm. Less than two months earlier, she had buried her soul mate, and now she had this weak little scarecrow to contend with. But moms are resilient, and she looked at the bright side: I was alive and prepared to go to battle for myself one more time. There was something to be grateful for when we went over to Steve's grandfather's house for a huge Thanksgiving dinner. I helped myself to some turkey, which was the first meat I'd eaten in a long time. Hey, if I can shoot dope and smoke crack and gobble pills, I can eat a damn plate of turkey and not worry about it.

13.

Nothing

Flea calls 1997 the Year of Nothing because the Red Hot Chili Peppers played only one concert that year, a festival in July, and even that show got derailed two thirds of the way through by a typhoon. But for me, 1997 was a year jammed full of adventure and misadventure, strides forward and many steps backward, another year in my topsy-turvy, Jekyll-and-Hyde existence.

The year began on a positive enough note. I was in New Zealand, setting up my new house. I remember being in Auckland on New Year's Eve and seeing amateur party people on the streets doing cocaine and champagne. It looked so appalling to me. I was glad I wasn't in that place. The truth of the matter was that there probably wasn't enough cocaine in a small country like that to keep me satisfied for any length of time.

I didn't have any band obligations at this point. *One Hot*

Minute hadn't sold well, especially compared to *Blood Sugar,* so we had cut back on the touring cycle. Since I already was in New Zealand, I had planned to take a month off and explore India. I went to Puttaparthi for a week, then to New Delhi. But the highlight of my whole trip was a spontaneous trek I made to Dharamsala to see the Dalai Lama.

I took a train to Rishikesh and then hired a driver to drive through the Himalayas. Dharamsala seemed to be in a different world, carved out of the mountains, with dirt roads and wooden sidewalks, like an old western town. I got a room and then walked into town. I ate at a delicious vegetarian restaurant and then browsed some shops and bought some tonkas. The town was filled with all these bald monks wearing saffron-colored robes.

The next morning I got up and walked over to the Dalai Lama's temple. I found the office and approached one of the monks who worked there.

"Could you please inform the Dalai Lama that Anthony Kiedis is here? I know he must be busy, but I'd like to say hi to him," I said.

All of the people in the office started laughing hysterically. "Sir, do you realize what you just said?" one of them replied. "Half of Planet Earth is in line to say hello to Dalai Lama. How do you think you can just come in here and see him? His schedule is booked for the next three years."

He went on and on, telling me all the pressing issues the Dalai Lama had to deal with and how he was the busiest man on the planet.

"Okay, I understand. Just leave him a note that Anthony Kiedis says hello. I just wanted to make some contact," I said.

They promised to tell him and then started laughing again. I walked away a little disheartened, thinking, "Oh well. I came a long way to meet the Wizard of Oz, but I guess I won't. Such is life." It was a five-minute walk to my hotel, and when I got back, the lady at the front desk seemed excited.

"Oh, Mr. Kiedis. Come here right away. You have a message

from the office of the Dalai Lama. This is amazing. They insist that you be there tomorrow morning at eight A.M."

I got up bright and early the next morning and made it over to the office.

"This is how things will go," they lectured me. "First of all, you go through the metal detector. Then you must leave your backpack behind. We have to have these security measures because we are constantly getting death threats from the Chinese. Then you will stand in the corner of the courtyard, where Dalai Lama will be walking down the path with his security en route to his class. Maybe as he is walking, he might wave to you, you never know. Don't expect him to, but maybe he will."

I dutifully went through the metal detector and handed over my backpack and my camera. I took my assigned spot in the corner, and lo and behold, here came the Dalai Lama over the crest, with his security posse surrounding him. He looked up and saw me, and his eyes lit up, and a big smile crossed his face. He veered off his path and came straight to me. I was shocked, hoping for a wink, and here he was jogging right over.

He cupped my hand in his hands and looked me in the eye. "Anthony. Welcome to India. What inspired you to come all the way over here?"

"I just wanted to see the country," I said.

"Isn't India an amazing place? Tell me about your journey. What have you been doing while you've been here?"

I gave him a rundown of my itinerary.

"Isn't it all amazing, the smells and the colors everywhere you go? Where's your camera? We have to get a picture of you and me."

"They took everything when I came in," I said.

"Go get his camera, for goodness' sake," he yelled to one of his aides. "What are you thinking? He needs the camera."

The aide came back with my shitty little disposable camera.

The Dalai Lama smiled. "Let's take a picture." The whole time we were talking, he hadn't let go of my hand. It was subtle, and I hadn't noticed it for a while, but he was definitely sending me some of his juice.

The aide snapped off a shot.

"Okay, now get a long one, a full-body one," he instructed.

We talked a little longer, and then he produced a signed copy of his latest book for me. He gave me the book, a few old Tibetan coins, and a white silk scarf, which he blessed.

"Thank you so much for the visit," I said. "If there's anything I can ever do to help your cause, let me know."

"There is something you can do. If Adam Yauch [of the Beastie Boys] ever calls you to play another festival for us, please make yourself available."

"If Adam calls, we'll rock the spot," I promised.

"You know I'd love to stay and chat, but all these Tibetan elders are waiting," he said. "I have to go teach an advanced course. Of course, you're invited to come. You won't understand a word anyone is saying, but I think just sitting there would be an enjoyable experience for you. I'll tell them to get you a seat right up in front so you can see what's going on in there." And then he was gone.

"This is so weird," one of the aides said. "I can't believe he invited you, of all people, to the advanced Tantric. You have to study for fifty years to get in there."

I made my way to the outdoor class, and they sat me down right in the front. The class was filled with these crazy-ass old monks wearing big Roman-looking headgear. They were all meditating and making noises. The Dalai Lama was sitting on an elevated platform, and an aide beside him was doing most of the talking and reading. They started passing around a silver goblet filled with rancid yak milk. All of the elder monks took a good hearty sip of the brew, so I thought, "Yeah baby, give me some of that rancid yak milk." A monk passed me the goblet, and I took a sip, but I was not prepared. I thought I could handle some weird-tasting shit, but this was not it. So that was why it took fifty years to be prepared for the course. I left at the first break, thoroughly impressed by the perseverance of the monks.

Before leaving for New Zealand and India, I had suggested to Louis that he and Sherry move in with me, because Sherry was expecting a child. I thought it would be nice to invite the energy and warmth and life of a family into my relatively unlived-in house. So I came home to them and baby Cash living under my roof. Cash was an amazing kid, and we had a nice family environment, making popcorn and watching movies together.

But it wasn't long before I started running again. When I started getting high, my friends didn't understand it. They all thought, "Oh, now he's met the Dalai Lama, he'll never get loaded again." That had nothing to do with drugs. I didn't have to go all the way to India for spiritual enlightenment. The blue-collar spirituality of everyday life was right in front of me, it was in every nook and cranny if I wanted to seek it, but I had chosen to ignore it.

I started doing the downtown motel circuit, staying out for six- or seven-day runs. The only inconvenience was now I had a whole family at home, waiting nervously for me to come back. On one of those trips, I sneaked home at five in the morning, trying not to wake Cash up. I wanted to slip into my bedroom and go to sleep for a couple of days and deal with the consequences of worried people as far into the future as possible, when I saw that Sherry had set up a little shrine for me. She had taken one of the pictures of the Dalai Lama and me and framed it in a sweet little tacky frame and set up a bowl of popcorn next to it. That almost broke my heart.

Another time I sneaked in late at night and opened the door to my room. A little guy sat up in the bed and said, "Oh God, please, oh, oh!" It was Louis's dad, sleeping in my bed in my absence. I had come back because I needed some more cash to continue my run. As I got some money and started to leave, Sherry was beside herself.

"That's it. Enough, motherfucker. You're gonna go into a rehab. This is crazy," she said.

I agreed to get on my motorcycle and go into Impact, an end-of-the-line rehab in Pasadena. The image of Pasadena is a safe, calm, residential paradise where the little old lady of Beach Boys fame comes from; but North Pasadena, where Impact was located, was a straight hard-core projects ghetto. Impact was known as the Last House on the Block. After you'd been to every rehab and every jail, that was where you ended up. It was the ultimate no-nonsense, get-sober-or-die place.

There I was at thirty-four, sharing a room with three other guys. I was determined to make it through the entire twenty-eight-day stay this time and begin to work through my demons. The problem was, despite all the work I did there, I never wanted to be sober the whole time I was there. I was inching my way forward and white-knuckling not getting high, but my desire to get loaded was still very much a part of my consciousness. Every day I'd spend at least a couple of hours thinking about going out and getting some money and getting high and doing it all over again.

It was worse when I went to outside meetings. Since Impact was run on a merit system, the more merits you got, the more perks you'd accumulate. One of the perks was going to meetings outside the facility. Whenever we'd pile into those short buses and drive to a meeting, I'd stare out the window at the seediest bars in the seediest neighborhoods and fantasize about going in there and drinking with other barflies. Anything to get me out and rolling again.

Once I got settled in, the daily routine wasn't so bad. You'd wake up, do your prayer and meditation, make your bed, and shower. Everyone in my bungalow was considerate and cleaned up so we wouldn't get negative write-ups and extra homework. My roommates fascinated me. I felt horrible for the white-trash kid from Florida: I could see that he was struggling and that his chances for recovery weren't so good, especially with a wife who shared the same obsession. A lot of the other people there were facing their third strike and looking at serious jail time if they didn't straighten out.

After tidying your room, you'd go down to the cafeteria, which was a fun place to hang out. The food was all fat, starch, and sugar, the worst imaginable, but it was intended to put some weight back on your frame. Everyone piled on the food. There was an enormous selection of desserts at every meal, including breakfast. I wasn't eating meat in there, but I was hitting the sweets big-time.

My typical day at Impact was different from most others'. For some reason, they didn't treat me like a normal person. Everyone got work assignments like mowing the lawn and mopping the floor, but I was assigned to an advanced relapse-prevention class, which was intense and time-consuming. During the course of this class, we all got a day or two to draw a big calendar of the last eight years of our lives on an enormous chalkboard. Then we entered the major events and dates when our relapses occurred and what preceded and followed them. I was in this class with twenty other chronic relapsers, and they started pointing out the obvious—that each time I ended a relationship with a woman, it precipitated a relapse. I realized I had an issue, that there was something in the dynamic of hurting somebody's feelings that always sent me out the door. That really manifested after I broke up with Jaime and started going out with a number of different girls for short amounts of time. It was go out with a girl for a month, break up, relapse.

I stayed at Impact my prescribed length of time and did all of the work in the relapse class, including filling out pages and pages of questionnaires, which was a psychologically productive thing to do. When you start putting pen to paper, you see a side of your personal truth that doesn't otherwise reveal itself in conversation or thought. I also liked these psychological exercises because there was a young hot shrink who had recently come to Impact. I spent a lot of time in her office. We'd break out the Rorschach tests and go out and sit in the shade of this compound, and I'd look at the inkblots and make some sexual innuendos, and we'd both flirt. There was no point in doing serious psychotherapy, since I was getting out in less than four weeks, so it was just nice to spend some time together.

I left Impact and got back on board with my recovery. I was

feeling pretty optimistic and healthy and happy about my life and the band. Lindy had booked a summer tour for us, so my intention was to start getting in shape for the road. One Sunday morning that spring, I was on my motorcycle, going to my favorite meeting, which was in a rec room in a park at Third and Gardner. I was moving at a good clip, as I was prone to do, but I'd never had any real mishaps on my bike. I'd studied the road conditions and exercised caution at intersections and assumed that cars would pull out at inopportune moments from driveways or parking spots. I was always alert and prepared to deal with those scenarios.

All this was going through my mind as I flew down Gardner, which was a narrow side street with cars parked on both sides. In a split hair of a moment, this car pulled out of a parking spot and started to make a U-turn, effectively cutting off the entire street. Normally, you'd have a back-door exit, even if it meant cutting onto the sidewalk, but now there was no way out; this idiot had blocked the whole street, and there were no driveways accessible. I used both my brakes, but the car was too close. There was an incredibly fast and violent collision, so strong that the bike pierced the vehicle. I flew off the bike and jackknifed right into the point where the driver's door met the engine compartment.

Amazingly enough, I hit the car and proceeded to somersault forward, landing square on my feet on the other side of the car. I kept my balance and started running, so I assumed that by some miracle, I was okay. Except when I looked down at my arm, it wasn't an arm anymore. My hand had been shoved up into my forearm, so I now had a double-decker, big, bulbous club of a forearm and no hand.

"Oh my God," I thought. "This is really, really wrong-looking."

Without stopping to consider how badly I was injured, I ran into the closest house without knocking. I took a few steps into the living room, thinking I'd grab the phone and call an ambulance, but then the initial shock wore off, and the worst pain of my life jolted my body. There was no time to call for help, so I turned around and ran back outside and flagged down a convertible that happened to be occupied by two women I knew who were on their way to the same meeting as I had been.

I ignored the driver of the car I had hit, who wanted to trade insurance information, and jumped into the backseat. We made a beeline for Cedars-Sinai. Later I would learn that the hand has more nerve cells than any other part of the body, which explained the intense pain, but at that point it just felt like my hand had been immersed in a hot bottle of lava. I was convinced I'd never have a hand again.

Within five minutes, I was at the hospital, being wheeled into emergency surgery. Just my luck, an amazing hand specialist, Dr. Kulber, was on duty. But first they had to prep me for surgery, which entailed giving me a healthy dose of morphine. I felt nothing. I turned to the nurse and said, "Unfortunately, over a lifetime of misbehavior, I've attained a rather enormous resistance to the opiate family of drugs. You're probably going to have to go ahead and double that dose right away." Another shot. Nothing. It wasn't even putting a dent in the pain. This process went on and on. They wound up giving me seven doses of morphine before I got some relief.

The pain was gone, and the nurses started looking mighty attractive, and the next thing I knew, I had my hand up the nurse's skirt and was flirting with a female doctor. I was the fucking patient from hell who had gotten the most morphine in Cedars-Sinai history.

It took Dr. Kulber five hours to reconstruct my hand from that pulverized mass of bone and matter. After a few days in the hospital, they fixed me up with a specialty cast that went all the way up to my shoulder. It wasn't until I got home that I recognized how dependent we are on our hands. Even something as mundane as wiping your ass became a big issue. I had to train my left hand to do things it had never done before. I couldn't write, I couldn't open a door or a window; getting dressed and tying my shoes were nearly impossible.

For some reason, all this didn't really bring me down. I hated not being able to sleep comfortably, and I didn't enjoy the excruciating pain, but I kept the outlook that I would find a way to use my hand again. And so began many, many months of hand therapy. I was lucky enough to find Dr. Dors, a Burbank physician whose practice revolved around rehabbing hands. He had a unique way of doing therapy: You were placed in a room with twenty other people who had severe hand injuries, all helping one another. When you see people with much worse injuries than your own, you thank God and decide you can deal with it. It took me nine months, but I got back most of the strength in that injured hand.

We had to cancel dates in Alaska and Hawaii because of my accident, but then Lindy called and asked if I could play the festival at Mount Fuji at the end of July. We were headlining and making a lot of money for that one show, and we hadn't worked that entire year. By that time, my cast was down to my elbow, so I figured if I just kept my arm in my sling, playing was doable.

There was only one catch. As we checked in to our hotel, we found out that there was a super-typhoon coming directly at us from the South. It was estimated to hit our area just when we were going to be onstage. The morning of our show, the rains began. But there were eighty thousand Japanese out on this mountainside, so not playing wasn't an option. The opening acts went on, and all the time, we were keeping an eye on the weather reports, which all said that the big one was getting closer and closer.

Finally, it was time to play. We looked out at the audience, and the kids were soaking wet and frozen to the bone. People were being taken away suffering from hypothermia. But no one was leaving voluntarily. So we hit the stage, and there was a little bit of a cover, though not enough to keep the windy rain from flying around. The energy from this storm was building everybody up, so we nailed the set. Chado was banging out the beat, and Dave was really going for it. It was the first time in a while that I'd been sober for a few months straight, so I was feeling great. The stronger we played, the stronger the wind got. At one point I remember being up at the front of the stage on the mike, and the wind was so robust that I leaned in to it and it held me up. Then the winds got even heavier, and shit started to blow off the stage. The equipment was still working, so we kept playing until the lighting rig blew away. We were about eight songs into the show, and we'd fulfilled our contractual and moral obligations by then, so we ran for our lives.

August 1997 was pretty uneventful. I was back in L.A., still living with my little extended family. But when September rolled around, I got the old familiar urgings and decided it was time to go get a bunch of drugs and do them for just one day. There was no downside, because Jane's Addiction were doing a comeback tour that fall, and Flea had decided to fill in as the bass player, which meant Flea and Dave had their own separate thing for a few months, and I had plenty of time on my hands.

Out of deference to little baby Cash, I decided to get high in my car and not bring that energy into the house. So I got my stuff and started driving back toward Hollywood, but I was too impatient, so I pulled over onto a side street and fired up my pipe. After a few hits, I got paranoid and decided to check in to a hotel to continue my bacchanal.

I found a nice fancy hotel down on Pico and Beverly and thought that would do for a night. I went up to the counter, and the desk person lit up. "Mr. Kiedis! It's an honor to have you in our hotel," he said. One night turned into two nights, which turned into three nights. At one point I had to drive downtown to replenish my supplies. I slept for a day and woke up and ordered plates and plates of quarter-pound burgers. Then the whole cycle began again.

Days went by, getting high, getting high, getting high. Each day I'd have to call the front desk and tell them my plans had changed and I was staying for yet another day. So it was drugs, drugs, drugs, sleep, sleep, sleep. Wake up emaciated, beat down, sad, depressed, demoralized, hurt, lonely, destroyed; order room service and watch a little TV. This went on for a few weeks. I woke up one night around eleven and discovered that I had copped a heroin habit. I ate some food and looked at myself in the mirror and said, "Jesus Christ, you're a wreck, brother. You better go hide under a mountain of cocaine and heroin right away."

I checked my pockets. I had some feeble amount of change, but I wasn't worried, because I knew I had about five grand in a suit pocket at my house. That would cover me for another week. In fact, my whole closet was filled with the accoutrements of serious damage-doing. I had jackets that had drugs, jackets that had pipes, jackets that had syringes, jackets that had money, jackets that had Polaroid sex photos, the whole gamut. I would have to scoot home, run up to my closet, grab the cash, and deal with Sherry and Louis. I was a possessed madman, so I planned to tell them to back off, mind their own business, and I'd get better when I got better. If I didn't, that was the price I had to pay.

I drove up to my house, pressed the garage-door opener, pulled in, and got a huge shock. The garage was empty. My bikes were gone, my surfboard was gone, the crazy mirror on the wall, the shelving unit, all gone. All the concrete was polished and impeccably clean. My heart started pounding as I tried to come up with an explanation. Maybe they wanted to have the place painted so they took everything out. Or maybe there was a spill of some kind. But it didn't look like somebody had cleaned up. Everything was gone.

I climbed up the stairs, slammed my key into the door, and prepared to do battle with Louis and Sherry. I opened the door and walked right into *The Twilight Zone,* except it was real. Nothing was in the house. No furniture, no paintings, no posters, no silverware, no pots and pans, no glasses, no plates, no cups, no trinkets, no doodads, no bric-a-brac, no television, no chandelier, no toilet paper, no toothbrush. It was like a vacuum from God had come down and sucked out my house.

I was thinking that if the bottom floor looked like this, what if I went to the next floor and there were no clothes in my closet and my jacket with the five grand was gone? I ran up the stairs to my bedroom. Empty! No bed. No curtains. No desk. No pillows. No nothing. Ran into the closet, just in case. Nothing. There was no one, nothing, in the house. I can't even stress the nothing enough. There wasn't a thimble.

What I didn't remember was that I'd had a casual conversation a few weeks earlier with a realtor and told him I was thinking of selling. I didn't tell him that I'd done so much heroin in the house that the couch was high. The realtor told me that it would probably take about a year to get my price. But he'd found a motivated buyer, so the motherfucker sold my house in one week and my possessions were packed up and put into storage.

I was in a panic. It was midnight, I had one bad jones and no money. My entire life depended on getting money, so I drove back to my hotel and remembered that somebody in our crew would routinely get money in Europe by asking the front desk to advance him cash and charge his room account. Back at the hotel, there was a new girl on the all-night desk. I asked her for five hundred dollars.

"Oh, I've only been working here two days. I'm not familiar with that procedure," she said. "Can you wait until tomorrow, when the manager gets in?"

"No, I can't," I said. "As a matter of fact, blah, blah, blah, lie, lie, lie, such and such and such. And I do it all the time." I put the Jedi mind whammy on her and got the money and was out the door, straight down Olympic to my one-stop pool hall.

My stay at the hotel continued. I went to an American Express office and got more money, which meant more drugs. By then I was a walking skeleton with muddy, dead, no-one's-at-home eyes. I was lying in bed, watching the local news, when I saw a report about the Jane's Addiction reunion tour. It made me feel horrible that my friends were out playing music and I was alone in a hotel room, wasting away.

But I couldn't stop. I changed hotels and kept the run going until the day of my thirty-fifth birthday, when I checked in to a re-hab in Ventura called Steps. They took one look at my arms and figured I'd been shooting heroin for a few years straight.

"Don't you worry about a thing. You're going on a four-day mega-detox. We'll wake you up for meals, but other than that, you're going to be out. By the time we see you in a week, you'll be detoxed, with no physical dependency on anything."

I was like "Great. Where do I sign?"

I started getting the biggest combination of detox medica-tion I'd ever been on: clonidine patches, chloral hydrate, Valiums, muscle relaxers. I was like rubber noodles the whole time, in bed with no arm or leg control, just goofazoid out. After three days of sleeping and eating, I woke up and thought, "I gotta go get high."

I was still wasted on the detox medications, and I was a good hundred-odd miles from downtown. My main problem was that I couldn't walk. They couldn't legally keep me there, but they would never give me my car keys. I stood up and could barely steady my-self in the room, but I was able to scheme and plot.

"All right, the office with the guy in it is down the hall," I thought. "If I hold on to the wall the entire way to the office and get in there and lean up against a doorjamb, maybe they'll think I'm okay." I walked down that hallway holding on to the wall, went into the office, puffed myself up, thanked them for every-thing, and demanded my keys. After a minor argument, they con-ceded, but then I had to wait until no one was watching me so I could incorporate the wall into my normal walking rhythm.

It all worked out. I stopped at a bank and got as much cash as I could, and I made record time downtown. I scored my drugs, checked in to a motel, and stayed up all night, trying to get as much heroin into my system as I could. I hatched a new brilliant plan. I would go to Big Sur, which was a lot farther away from L.A. than Ventura, find a hotel, and wean myself off heroin.

I flew up and checked in to the Ventura Inn. That first night I plowed through all of the heroin that I'd brought to gradually wean myself of, just gobbled it down like a pig. And so began the harrowing ordeal of kicking heroin once again. Luckily, I could eat when there were no drugs, but I started going through a horrible sleepless period of physical and emotional pain. I was experiencing a proper heroin withdrawal the likes of which I hadn't for quite a long time. I'd make fires in the fireplace and get too hot, so I'd open the window and freeze to death. I couldn't have a blanket over my legs, because it felt like pins and needles. Even the pillow hurt my neck.

After the first day, the hotel refused to send up room service, so I was forced to go down to the restaurant or walk a mile down a hill to a market. All that walking and fresh air started to bring me back to life. While I was there, I called up my boyhood pal Joseph Walters, who was living in Palo Alto and going through a catastrophe with his crazy-ass fiancée. He drove down, and we commiserated for a few days.

Somehow I found out that Jane's Addiction was playing San Francisco, so Joe drove me up there and then went back home. Guy O was in town for the shows, so we went together. I was excited because I was starting to feel human again; plus, I was going to see my brothers. I went backstage and saw Flea and was all happy to see him, but he didn't seem like himself. He was dressing differently and wearing eye makeup and changing his Fleaness to become Jane's Addictionness, which I didn't understand. I thought he'd be Flea in this other band, not a whole new persona. He seemed strangely distant. I don't know if he was angry with me for being a fuckup or if he was on his own weird trip, but I accepted that he was in that mode.

Then Dave walked in the room. I was always happy to see him. He greeted me, told me it was great to see me, and that he'd be right back to talk. But he was high and messing around with some girl, and they went off to do more drugs and never came back. It was fun to watch the show, even though it did seem weird to see Flea in that band. That night I walked home with Guy O, feeling detached from both Flea and Dave, which was ironic, since I just had detached from them for months on end. I accepted that this is what happens when you don't talk to anybody—you come back and it's a new ball game.

I was hoping it would be a new ball game for me. The fact that my circumstances had changed drastically but my behavior hadn't was beginning to wear on me. I remember one poignant moment when I still had the house in the hills. I was driving down Beechwood at night and getting high in my car. I came to a stop sign, and this car full of twenty-year-old boys pulled up next to me. They looked at me and said, "Hey, Anthony!" I was so torn up, the last thing I wanted to hear then was "Hey, Anthony" from some fans. I was trying to ignore them, but I sneaked a glance at their car. One of them stared at me and said, "Hey, it's not him," and they drove off. That couldn't be him, because Anthony didn't look like a fucking ghost.

It got worse. Another time on the motel tour, I pulled up to my downtown corner, and some desperado got in the car and told me he knew where to score some dope. He was doing this so he could get a taste for leading me to the prize, but I didn't care, so we took off. We ended up pulling into the parking lot of one of those cheap hooker motels on Sunset. He went off to find the dealer, and I was waiting in my truck, when this family got out of their car and headed for their room. They must have been a little down on their luck, because they were staying here. I looked over at their car and saw a Chili Peppers bumper sticker on it. Then I looked at the kids, and they both had on Chili Peppers T-shirts. I felt horribly ashamed and embarrassed. I slouched in my seat and pulled the visor down. Here was a family of fans proud to fly their Red Hot colors, and I was at the same motel but trying to score drugs from some insidious dope dealer. Ooofah.

I was really trying to stay sober, so I moved into Guy O's house at the end of 1997. That Christmas I went home, and Blackie introduced me to a beautiful, brilliant local girl. We spent a nice few weeks together, but by the time I had to leave Grand Rapids, I knew the interlude would end. Sure enough, true to my Impact relapse charts, a few weeks later—and two weeks before we were scheduled to leave for Hawaii to begin writing a new album—I went on another guns-blazing, full-speed-ahead run.

I came up with yet another ridiculous plan. I decided to use drugs like a maniac for days on end and then go to Hawaii a week before the band, so that by the time we started working, I'd have a week of rest and recuperation under my belt. I dragged myself to the airport and flew solo to Hawaii. I checked in to a luxury high-rise hotel in Waikiki, holding the last smidgen of dope that I had, telling myself, "Okay, I'm gonna finish this little amount of stuff and then call it quits, and whammo, I'll get better right here in Hawaii." But when the drugs were ingested, I was like "Ooh, not quite ready to come down and face reality." I went to some strip bars to find dealers.

When you're wrapped up in that kind of drug intake, you lose all sense of what's reasonable and what's not. Later that night, while I was injecting my drugs, I intentionally broke the needle off my only syringe because I thought that if I put any more drugs in my body, I would explode. Ten minutes later, when I was craving more coke, that seemed like an awful idea. In my delusional toxic state, I tried to reaffix the needle. By now it was bent, and it wasn't suctioning right, but a man needs his drugs in his veins, so I pushed the needle into a vein and hoped for the best. Well, I got the worst. The needle came off the syringe and lodged in the vein. I grabbed it and held it, paranoid that the needle would travel through my veins and pierce a valve in my heart.

I was high, and blood was leaking out of my arm, and now I had to grab the needle through my skin and pull it out from the inside lest it get released into my bloodstream. I managed to get it out, but my next dilemma was that I had no heroin to come down from this coke with. I ended up drinking the entire contents of my minibar. The whiskey, the vodka, the Scotch, the wine, one after another, I downed those little bottles and finally passed out. Always, you wake up to an unpleasant memory and an unpleasant body and your spirit is reduced to a pile of dirty ashes residing somewhere inside of your ass. You've gotta face the music, which is a beautiful island outside, but you can't even bear to look out the window. I kept those curtains drawn and stayed in that bed and ordered room service and hibernated, knowing that each day that clicked off the calendar was bringing me one day closer to when I had to get on a little plane and fly over to Kauai and see my friends, my bandmates, my compadres.

The day of reckoning arrived. I went right down to the wire and got up an hour and a half before the plane was scheduled to depart and showered and shaved. I went out into the world for the first time in a week, and it was all too bright and vivid, but I got on that plane. I got to our rented house, and everyone was there, but our spirits were dampened. Both Dave and I had gone off the deep end for the last few weeks. We were both dry, at least for the moment, so we spent most of our time running and eating tons of good food but unfortunately playing very little. I wasn't doing that well emotionally. I was dry, but my heart was broken, and I wasn't feeling like myself. Then we got the call that our old friend Bill Stobaugh, the Hallucinogenius, the man who was my mentor at the graphics houses and who had let me live with him, had died while undergoing a heart operation. Flea flew back for the funeral, but I begged off.

When we got back from our unproductive stay in Hawaii, we got another dose of bad news. Our manager, Lindy, decided to quit. His wife had recently died, but he'd met a new lady, and she convinced him that it was time for him to walk away from that dose of anarchy and retire to Ojai. We looked like we were going backward on the conveyor belt, and I don't think she saw much of a future in us; nor did he. Nor did anybody, really, including the people in the band.

Back in L.A., Dave started working on a solo record with Chad and went right back to getting loaded. I had stayed sober since Hawaii. When I went to a party at Dave's girlfriend's house and Dave picked up a beer, I was surprised. He was so nonchalant about it. He and I were both in the same place, where one is too many and a thousand is never enough. We couldn't use drugs moderately, and that would be proved to him in a short period of time.

We went back to rehearsing. We had downgraded into an abominable little studio in Hollywood, right near Transvestite Alley. Dave was getting high and I wasn't, so that was adding more tension to an already tense situation. Dave would come into rehearsals wearing oversize sunglasses and over-the-top large floppy Renaissance hats, which we called "coke hats" because you had to be on cocaine to even think of wearing a hat like that. Dave was coming in late, and it was impossible to communicate with him. The minute he was wearing that coke hat, he had his own agenda, and that was to get high.

We tried to play, but we weren't going anywhere. Flea's face was sunken with disillusionment, and Chad was like "This guy's off on his trip. What can you say?" I felt like we had to talk to Dave and get him some help. He used to come and pick me up at hotels to go into rehabs; it was my turn to talk to him about getting well so we could carry on.

We had a little talk. Dave was sitting on an amplifier, and the band discussion escalated into an argument between the two of us, which was bizarre, because all we were saying was "Hey, you're using drugs while we're rehearsing, and that's not working. How about if we talk about you getting sober again?" He didn't want to hear it, he had a real fuck-you attitude about the whole thing. When he came at me with the fuck-you attitude, I was like "Whoa, fuck me? Fuck you." Those weren't the exact words, but that was the energy that started to go around. Chad and Flea backed off, and Dave got up to get in my face, but as he tried to stand up, he went backward and fell behind the amp that he was sitting on. It was comical, but it was also sad.

With the band once again stagnant, I decided to take a trip to Thailand. I had been diagnosed with hepatitis C a few years earlier, and even though I wasn't symptomatic, it was a disease that could reappear if I wasn't vigilant. I brought along my liver-cleansing herbs and swam a lot, prayed, and meditated on the idea of my body getting healthy. It worked. Three weeks later, my hepatitis viral count came back undetectable.

By now it was April. Flea and I decided that it just wasn't working out—we had to fire Dave. Flea talked to him initially, but Dave was really upset, so I did the follow-up. It went horribly, because he was totally loaded, and even though he knew there was no way this band could work, the verbalization of the reality pissed him off to no end.

"Fuck you guys! How can you do this to me, you motherfuckers!"

"Dude, there's no band here," I said. "When was the last time you showed up? You're making a solo record, you're off getting loaded. You're not really into this anyway." Of course, Chad was staying totally Switzerland, because he was in the middle of making that record with Dave.

Meanwhile, Flea was going through his own health hell, fighting Epstein-Barr as well as girlfriend hell and band hell. He was like a general doing battle on too many fronts. He was really down, and on top of all this, he was trying to do a solo album. It came as no surprise when Flea decided he wanted out.

"I don't think I can do this anymore," he told me. I'd known that this was coming. It was so obvious; nothing was happening with the band.

"I know," I said. "I figured that's what you were going to say. I totally understand."

Then Flea dropped the bombshell. "The only way I could imagine carrying on is if we got John back in the band."

That threw me for a loop. "Why would John ever want to come back and play with us again?" I asked Flea. "He doesn't care for me and didn't really care for the experience."

"I have a funny feeling that he might be standing on the verge of making a comeback, a personal resurgence into the land of the living," Flea told me.

"That would be a wonderful miracle," I thought. And the second miracle would be if he'd even think of playing with us again.

"You've got to be crazy. John is not going to want to play in this band. It doesn't sound remotely possible, but if it is, I'm open to it," I told Flea.

John and I hadn't had much contact since he left the band, except for the odd and unplanned moments that we'd run into each other. Even then, you'd have thought there would be a lot of anger and resentment and dislike, bordering on hatred, but every time I saw him, there was no display of that.

The first time I saw him was a few years after he left the band. I had heard all these horror stories about John's descent into a drug hell, and I knew that Johnny Depp and Gibby Haynes, the lead singer of the Butthole Surfers, had even made a film documenting the squalid conditions that John was living in. If you saw that film, you knew that this was the home of a person who had absolutely no interests in life other than shooting drugs and painting.

I also heard about the interviews that John was giving journalists extolling heroin use. He'd even shoot up during interviews. I wasn't interested in reading that stuff or looking at the film. I didn't listen to his solo records at the time. I couldn't celebrate his lifestyle because it seemed like he was killing himself. There were a lot of people who were glorifying that and wanting to participate and wanting to get free drugs. Granted, his art, the songs he was writing, were great, but it didn't feel right for me to condone this eccentric person's demise. This guy used to be my best friend, and now his teeth were falling out, so I didn't look at it like other people might: "Oh, he's a genius, it's okay." I didn't care if he was a genius or a fucking idiot, he was rotting away, and it wasn't fun to watch.

I knew he'd been painting for years, inspired by Basquiat and da Vinci, so when I heard that he was going to have a show at the Zero Gallery on Melrose, I decided to pop in the day before the show opened and have a peek at the paintings. I dropped by, and lo and behold, John was there hanging the show himself. We were both a little startled. He was high on coke, and his hair was shorn, and he had big black circles under his eyes and was smoking

Gauloises. He was shockingly thin, a skeleton in a vest, this little bone man, but he had a lot of vigor because he had a lot of energy and chemicals in him, so it wasn't like he was passing out or looking weak.

Instead of being "Fuck you, I hate you, you suck," we were happy to see each other. His paintings were disturbing but beautiful. It was weird, because I think we wanted to dislike each other more than we were able to.

The next time I saw him, he had deteriorated quite a bit. Everyone was worried about his arms, which were all abscessed because he never did learn how to properly administer an injection; he would just go for the stab-and-poke mode and hope for the best. He wound up checking in to Exodus, my old haunt, in December 1995, more for his physical health than his mental health. The doctors there were seriously concerned that he was going to get gangrene and have to lose a limb unless he'd wash and take care of his arms, which he refused to do.

I called him up and asked whether it was okay if I came to visit him. He was fine with it and asked if I could bring him some cigarettes and a pastrami sandwich with a lot of mustard. So I showed up and he ate the sandwich and I tried to get him to wash his arms. Again, our exchange was kind and loving and caring, so different from what everyone around either of us thought our exchange would be like, based on our past turmoil. I still hadn't recognized how unhealthy my own dynamic of relating to him had been before he left the band. I never understood just how sensitive he was and how hurtful I was capable of being. I didn't know that all of the jokes and the jabs and the kidding and the goofing and the sarcasm had really hurt his feelings and had a long-lasting impact on him.

Long after John quit, Flea said to me, "Do you have any idea how much pain you caused John?"

"What are you talking about? He and I were best friends, we spent every waking moment together. We played pool together, we chased women together, we ate Lucky Charms together. We were two peas in a pod."

"No, you hurt John's feelings a lot of the time," Flea said, "because he looked up to you and you were so brutal to him." That was the first time I was even aware that my love for him had ended up being a difficult experience for him.

When John left the band, I resented him for not being my friend and for abandoning our musical comradeship. But all the time that he was out of the band and going through his anguish, I prayed for him constantly. From going to meetings I'd learned that one of the reasons that alcoholics get loaded is because they harbor resentments. One of the techniques they teach to get rid of a resentment toward somebody is to pray for him or her to get everything that you want for yourself in life—to be loved, to be successful, to be healthy, to be rich, to be wonderful, to be happy, to be alive with the light and the love of the universe. It's a paradox, but it works. You sit there and pray for the person you can't stand to get everything on earth that you would want for yourself, and one day you're like "I don't feel anything bad toward this person."

That was part of the reason I prayed for John. The other part was that I didn't want him to die a sad and miserable death, so I prayed for him almost every day. I would sit there and say, "Whoever's out there, whoever's getting this thought from my mind, could you please look after John Frusciante, because he needs it."

In January 1998, Bob Forest convinced John to check in to Los Encinos, the same old-school treatment facility that housed W. C. Fields, back in the day. John had already kicked heroin by then, but he had been smoking crack and drinking. I went to visit him there, and he seemed committed to being in there, but a little peculiar. Our conversations were sparse and unusual. Every now and then we'd talk about a Nirvana song or a da Vinci drawing.

During one of my visits, we were sitting there having one of these minimalist conversations when John jumped off the bed and went flying into a perfect James Brown split, circa 1968. Then he got up and sat back down. I don't know what his motivation was, but it seemed like he was feeling his oats and letting it be known that he still had the fire to fly into a James Brown split, if need be.

I was open to the possibility of John coming back to the band, even if it still seemed remote to me. After leaving Los Encinos at the beginning of February, John rented a small apartment in Silver Lake. One day in April, Flea went over there, and they sat together and listened to records. Then Flea popped the question: "What would you think about coming back and playing in the band?"

John started sobbing and said, "Nothing would make me happier in the world." They both cried and hugged each other for a long time. Then Flea took a trip to Cambodia, which gave John and me time to clear the air and talk about the problems we had in the past. We went to the Farmer's Market, one of my favorite places in all of L.A., and sat down and had some salmon tacos.

I broke the ice. "Do you have a problem with me at all about anything?"

"No, not really," he said. "What about you? Are you mad at me for anything?"

"I thought I was, but I don't feel mad right now. I thought we should probably go over all this stuff, but I don't feel bothered by any of it anymore," I confessed.

"Me, neither," John agreed.

Flea was expecting to get a report of some daylong deliberation deal, of all this animosity dredged up, but neither of us was feeling it. The major problem was John didn't even have a guitar to his name. So we went over to the Guitar Center, and I bought him a great old '62 Stratocaster.

John was thrilled by the idea of being back in the band, but he was also scared, because he hadn't played a guitar for a very long time. We decided to make his return low-key—nothing mattered other than playing music. We didn't give a fuck about record deals, or the fact that our manager had quit, or that our record company had lost interest in us. None of that mattered. We just wanted to get in a garage and rock out together.

Flea was living in an incredible Mediterranean superstructure in Los Feliz, a famous old house because tons of musicians like Bob Dylan and Lou Reed had lived there. We assembled in Flea's garage, a portion of which he had converted to a rehearsal space. Chad had set up his drums in the corner. Flea had this look on his face like "Okay, no great expectations. Let's just play music." We had some shitty little PA system set up. John wore a look of uncertainty, but he plugged in his guitar, and we started playing. And it was us again. I think I might be the only one who thought so, but the room filled up with heavenly music, made for no motive other than to see what it sounded like when we banged our instruments together.

For me, that was the defining moment of what would become the next six years of our lives together. That was when I knew that this was the real deal, that magic was about to happen again. Suddenly we could all hear, we could all listen, and instead of being caught up in our finite little balls of bullshit, we could all become players in that great universal orchestra again.

14.

Welcome to Californication

Despite my elation at our reunion, it took awhile for us to find the groove. John was rusty, both mentally and physically. I was a pile of rust dust, too, but slowly and surely, things started getting better. There was a lot of joy emanating from Flea's house. He had two dogs, a mastiff named Martian and a feisty boxer called Laker. Every day we'd make tea in the kitchen, play with the dogs, and then go out to the garage and work. Flea had set up the rehearsal space like a recording studio, so at the end of the session, I'd leave with tapes of the new music to lyricize.

Although he'll tell you it took years for him to get his chops back, I loved the way John was playing when he didn't have the technical capacity to do everything. He toned down and developed an incredible minimalist style. Every day he came up with something spectacular. I had a notebook filled with lyrics

400

that I was dying to turn into songs, so besides the rehearsals, I'd go hang out with John at his apartment in Silver Lake. In typical John fashion, there was no furniture at all, just records and a turntable and a bed and a blender. He was going through a smoothie phase, so there were smoothie materials on the walls and the refrigerator and the stove. It was like Jackson Pollock lived there. We'd sit and smoke and smoke and work. It was incredible to once again have one of the great musicians of our time so telepathically connected to me. He'd play me a complicated, weird instrumental piece of music that he had stayed up all night recording, and I'd be like "Oh yeah, I know exactly what I'm supposed to do with that."

John seemed truly humbled by life. He had been beaten down, and I think the clouds had lifted, and he saw what he had been through and felt like "Holy fuck. I can't believe I'm alive. I'm not going to blow it this time." He hadn't been back long enough for people to tell him how wonderful he was. It's always nice to be around someone who's that talented and that excited about life and music, and whose ego hasn't been inflated by other people yet.

Everyone was having fun. It was as if we had nothing to lose, nothing to gain. We didn't care; we were making music for the sake of making music. Compared to *Blood Sugar*, *One Hot Minute* wasn't nearly as successful, so people had lost faith in us. There was a feeling within the record industry that we'd had our day in the sun. But the more we played, the more we started creating stuff that we believed in and wanted people to hear.

It was really hot when we began rehearsing, so we would leave the garage door open. After a few weeks of work, I ran into Gwen Stefani of No Doubt. She was Flea's distant neighbor across the ravine on the opposite mountain. "I hear you guys play every day," she said. "My friends come over, and we sit around and listen. It sounds great!" It was nice to get the compliment, but it was a bit embarrassing, because we thought we were in this private world, working out our ugly spots.

At the beginning of June, we took a break from rehearsing

to play our first gig since John had rejoined the band. I had promised the Dalai Lama that we would be available if we got the call from Adam Yauch, and we did. The Tibetan Freedom Festival was a two-day event at JFK Stadium in Washington, D.C. The night before, we did a surprise gig at the 9:30 Club, just to get our sea legs. Come the day of the show, the area got drenched with a thunderstorm, and halfway through the concert, a girl got hit by a lightning bolt, forcing the evacuation of the entire stadium and the cancellation of the rest of the show.

That night there was a logistical meeting. The Beastie Boys camp obviously didn't have our back, because the organizers told us that due to the previous day's storm, some groups would have to be canceled. Since we were the last band booked, we wouldn't be able to play. I couldn't believe it. We'd come all the way from California and were pumped to play our first big show with John back in front of ninety thousand people. Thankfully, Pearl Jam was scheduled to close the show that day, and Eddie Vedder got wind of our dilemma and threatened to pull out unless we were given part of their allotted stage time. It was an amazing show of support from them, and we never forgot it.

It was still light out when we assembled backstage. We stood behind the backdrop, surrounded by amplifier cases, and got into a soul circle, bowed our heads, and did a collective group hug. Then we went out there and completely rocked out. The audience was 100 percent behind us, and it was such a joyful moment to be back onstage with John.

The next day I figured everybody had forgotten about the poor girl who'd been hit in the head by lightning, so I went to visit her in the hospital. She was in bed but awake, and she showed me all her burn marks. Her worst burns were where she had metal on her body—a bracelet, her underwire bra. But the really ironic thing was that she was talking on her cell phone when she got hit—that's probably why the lightning hit her—and her last name was Celfon.

Back in L.A., the songs were coming fast and furious. Except for one. The first song that John and I worked on, even before we convened in Flea's garage, was a song called "Californication." I'd written the lyrics when I was on that cleansing trip to Thailand, when the idea of John being back in the band was still inconceivable to me. While I was on a boat in the Andaman Sea, the melody had crept up on me, one of those simple melody structures that lends itself to flying words into. One of the things that struck me on my travels to exotic places, including the Sea Gypsy Village in Thailand and the bazaars of Indonesia, was the extent to which American culture had permeated all these places, even to the time of bootleg Red Hot Chili Peppers T-shirts. When I was in Auckland one time, I ran into a crazy lady on the street, and she was ranting about the fact that there were psychic spies in China. That phrase stuck in my mind, so when I was back home, I started writing and writing, and they became my favorite of all the lyrics that I'd collected over the last year.

I showed "Californication" to John, and he loved the lyrics and started writing some music. But for some reason, even though there was a perfect song in there, we couldn't find it. We tried ten different arrangements and ten different choruses, and nothing ever worked. All these other songs were pouring out of us. We'd been working for a few weeks when someone started playing an ultra-sparse riff that sounded like nothing we'd ever done before. As soon as I heard it, I knew it was our new song.

Around that time, I had met a young mother at a meeting. She was living in a YWCA with her baby girl, trying to get sober but failing miserably. The beauty and sadness and tragedy and glory, all wrapped into one, of this mother/daughter relationship was evoked by the vibe of that music.

From "Porcelain"

Porcelain
Do you carry the moon in your womb?
Someone said that you're fading too soon
Drifting and floating and fading away

Little lune
All day
Little lune

Porcelain
Are you wasting away in your skin?
Are you missing the love of your kin?
Nodding and melting and fading away

By late June, we had completed about twelve songs. "Scar Tissue" was another song where you open up the top of your head and it comes dusting down from outer space. Rick Rubin and I had been talking about sarcasm a lot. Rick had read a theory that it was an incredibly detrimental form of humor that depresses the spirit of its proponents. We had been such sarcastic dicks that we vowed to try to be funny without using sarcasm as a crutch. I guess I was also thinking of Dave Navarro, who was the King of Sarcasm, faster and sharper than the average bear.

All those ideas were in the air when John started playing this guitar riff, and I immediately knew what the song was about. It was a playful, happy-to-be-alive, phoenix-rising-from-the-ashes vibe. I ran outside with my handheld tape recorder and, with that music playing in the background, started singing the entire chorus to the song. I'll never forget looking up at the sky above that garage, out toward Griffith Park with the birds flying overhead, and getting a dose of Jonathan Livingston Seagull. I really did have the point of view of those birds, feeling like an eternal outsider.

From "Scar Tissue"

Scar tissue that I wish you saw
Sarcastic Mr. Know-it-all
Close your eyes and I'll kiss you 'cause
With the birds I'll share this lonely view
With the birds I'll share this lonely view

Push me up against the wall
Young Kentucky girl in a push-up bra
Fallin' all over myself
To lick your heart and taste your health 'cause
With the birds I'll share this lonely view

Blood loss in a bathroom stall
Southern girl with a scarlet drawl
Wave goodbye to Ma and Pa 'cause
With the birds I'll share this lonely view

We finished another song called "Emit Remmus," which had been inspired in part by my friendship with Melanie Chisholm of the Spice Girls. Around that time, the Spice Girls were a raging phenomenon, especially among young girls, like Flea's daughter, Clara. Even when I'd go to New Zealand, all the little girls there would know the Spice Girls' lyrics and their dance moves. The tunes were pretty good pop songs, especially when you had five different-colored crayons out there performing them.

That spring I got a call from Nancy Berry, who ran Virgin Records. She told me that the Spice Girls were coming to L.A., and both the Melanies wanted to go out and have some fun and get some tattoos. Being the resident fun- and tattoomeister, I was enlisted to show them the Hollywood ropes. I arranged to have my friend keep his tattoo parlor open after hours to accommodate them. I became friendly with Mel C (Sporty), and we stayed in touch for months and months. It was nice, because I got to take Clara to the show and bring her backstage so she could meet these incredible characters she'd been worshipping for the last year.

Fast-forward to September and Clara's tenth birthday. Flea had been arguing for months and months with Clara when it came to the background music in their house, because Flea wanted to hear Coltrane, and Clara had the Spice Girls on a nonstop loop. So Flea decided we were going to pull a stunt at her birthday party. He dropped the hint to Clara that the Spice Girls themselves might show up at her party. And, of course, we would be the Spice Girls.

The likenesses were obvious. Flea would be Baby Spice. John was Sporty Spice. Chris Warren, our drum technician, was enlisted to play Scary Spice, and I would be Posh Spice. Thank God Ginger Spice was already out of the band and we didn't have to fill her shoes. With the help of Flea's assistant, Sherry Westridge, we got the right clothes and the right wigs and wore the right makeup. We each studied the personality and the body language of our Spice Girl, and learned the dance moves. We even had some rehearsals.

Come the day of the party, Clara had her whole clan of ten-year-old friends over, all of whom lived and died for the Spice Girls. Everybody was whispering about the possibility that the Spice Girls were coming because Clara had actually met them at their show. So it came time for the surprise, and we were all up in Flea's bedroom, putting the final touches on our outfits, while the girls were in the living room one floor below. The music started, and the little girls all freaked out, screaming "Oh my God" as we walked down the giant staircase and they caught a glimpse of these fabulous costumes. Then something slowly started to filter into their little minds.

"Wait a second, these are not the Spice Girls. In fact, these are not even girls, these are men dressed like the Spice Girls. EEEEWWWWWWWWW!"

We sauntered down and never broke character and put on an immaculate performance. Scary Spice was phenomenal, Baby Spice was terrifying with her gap Flea tooth, and John absolutely nailed Sporty, working on it morning, noon, and night until his character was there. Posh was easy; she was just an aloof, uptight, narcissistic shopping girl. We took our little vocal solos and did our dances. I had on a really short skirt, because Posh wears her dresses too short, but I forgot to take into consideration that I was a man in front of kids. I don't think any of them have ever recovered, because we didn't shave our legs.

Now that it was clear our foursome was a viable configuration once again, it was time to get management. Two months earlier, we hadn't cared if we had a manager, because nothing was going on, but we were more passionate than ever about the music we were generating. A few years before, Rick Rubin had been extolling the virtues of Q-Prime Management. Q-Prime was run by a duo, Peter Mensch and Cliff Bernstein, and in Rick's mind, they were the brightest managers in the rock business, bar none.

These two guys flew in from New York to meet with us in Flea's living room. Cliff looked a lot older than he was, because his hair and his long Merlin-the-magician beard were all white. He was small and delicate and purposeful and mystical-looking. He wore glasses and looked super-intelligent. He was like a walking think tank, an organic computer man with a competitive nature that belied his appearance. Peter, on the other hand, was a gruff, loud, obnoxious bundle of muscles who alienated and was brash. He was also very smart and, in a bizarre way, very loving.

These guys were very New York. They'd been in the music business forever, having managed acts as diverse as Metallica—whom they raised from inception—AC/DC, Madonna, Courtney Love, the Smashing Pumpkins, Def Leppard, and Shania Twain. Cliff and Peter operated at a different level of professionalism than we'd ever dealt with. We were not exactly coming off a year of greatness, but we did feel that with John back in the band, we held a pretty good hand. Flea had a laundry list of concerns like "Are you going to get us on the radio?" Peter was countering that by barking, "And don't think we're the kind of managers who are going to take care of your little candy asses. If you're on tour and you're up in Alaska and you forgot your winter coat, don't call us to FedEx you a winter coat, because you're going to end up freezing to death."

I was like "Okay, make a mental note to bring my coat when we tour Alaska."

At the same time, I was sure they were wiping Madonna's ass if she was asking them to; maybe that was why he said that. But there was some chemistry in the room, and we were attracted to each other, so we signed with them.

With all this newness in place, we thought that maybe it was time to get a new producer. Every time you make a record, it doesn't matter how good it was working with a producer, and even if you know you're going to end up making a record with that same person again, there's always a day when someone says, "Do we want to get a new producer?" That was how we felt then about Rick Rubin. We considered our options. We had asked Brian Eno to produce us three times already, and he always said no, so we asked him again, even though that "no" was inevitable. We didn't know it, but he was doing us a favor by turning us down.

We even considered David Bowie, who wanted to work with us but finally sent a gracious note explaining that he had too many other commitments to take on another project. Another reason why we were reluctant to go back with Rick Rubin was that he was always working on six things at once, plus being CEO of his own record label, and we thought we should find someone who would work only on our project. While this process was going on, we contacted Daniel Lanois, who had converted an old movie theater in Oxnard, California, just up the coast, into a wonderful old-school recording studio. Lanois couldn't commit to producing us because he was on hold with U2, but he did graciously offer us the use of his studio to do a demo of the eleven songs we had finished. We went in and set up and recorded all of the songs in a row, all in one day. It was a soulful, smoking demo, not unlike the first demo we ever made.

A couple of weeks went by, and we talked to Rick. He cleared some space in his schedule, so we decided to work with him again. It was as if we had come to our senses and realized, "Why are we dicking around with all these other guys?" The next day I got a call from Daniel Lanois.

"I heard the demo tape you made at the studio," he said.

"I've reconsidered, and I'm interested in working with you guys. Those songs really caught my attention. I haven't heard anything like them in a long time."

I genuinely appreciated his kind words, though I told him we'd moved on. However, it was nice to have our own feelings validated by someone like him.

Before we started working with Rick, the guys at Q-Prime decided to send us on an under-the-radar mini-tour of out-of-the-way places in California, just to get the road rust off. We played on a makeshift stage behind some guy's house in Chino, in the old town hall in Fresno, and at some rodeo bar in Reno. We didn't even sell out the venues till we reached Santa Barbara. I remember thinking, "Sometimes you're riding high in April and shot down in June, but at least we have each other." We were full of enthusiasm and color, and you could sense that something was brewing that could be amazing, but we weren't quite there yet.

That summer I was still living under Guy Oseary's roof, commuting every day to Flea's garage. Sometime that August, out of the blue, I decided to go and get loaded again. I hadn't slipped since Hawaii, so I'd been clean for six months, but one day I just got on my motorcycle, headed downtown, and did the whole thing. It made no sense, and I didn't enjoy it, but I'd reawakened the eight-hundred-pound gorilla. I found myself in a hotel room, and when I woke up, I knew I couldn't mention this to anyone. It was a weekend, and I got my shit back together and went to rehearsal all the next week.

I went out again that weekend, only this time I couldn't turn it off so easily. I ended up in a hotel in San Diego, of all places, depressed again. I didn't know what to do—I didn't even have the strength to leave—when I heard a knock on the door. Who the fuck could that be? I went to the peephole and looked out, and there were John and Flea and Chad.

I opened the door, and they walked in.

"I'm really sorry," I said.

"Don't even worry about it," Flea said. "You fucked up. Let's just go home and get back to work." He was so matter-of-fact and nonjudgmental about it.

"Oh, man, I'm so sorry you had to experience that," John said. "It must have sucked. But you can't do this anymore."

We piled into Flea's multicolored Mercedes clown car, which exacerbated the absurdity of my surroundings, and drove north to L.A. They were telling me that we had a record to make, but they were really easygoing about it, so that took a lot of weight off my shoulders. We stopped to eat some Mexican food, and by then we were laughing and throwing food around and having a good time. When we got back to L.A., Flea offered to let me stay at his house, in this big octagonal-shaped downstairs bedroom suite with leopard-print carpeting. I moved in, and it was a really peaceful and productive two-month stay. All I did was read and write and go to band practice and hang out with Clara and Flea and the dogs. I got rid of all the extraneous complications of nightlife and girls and partying, and just stayed in the compound and got a lot of work done.

One day while I was at Flea's, on a whim, I decided to cut off all my hair. I'd had my tailbone-length hair for thirteen years, but I didn't think twice about going to my friend and getting that shit shorn. I did save the hair and send it off to my dad in Michigan. He and I had had a hair-solidarity thing since the early '70s. The night of my haircut, I got home late, and Flea was already asleep. The next morning I strolled into the kitchen in my PJs. Flea did the all-time eyes-bugged-out double take, then started laughing hysterically. "Oh my God, I'm back at Fairfax High again, and we're sixteen years old. Look at you!"

By this point, we'd made the transition from Flea's garage to a rehearsal studio named the Swing House, on Cahuenga. Rick Rubin started coming by and lying on the couch and listening to us play, taking a few notes here and there. We started amassing a rather enormous quantity of raw material in terms of pieces and parts and songs and half-songs and bridges and choruses and verses and intros and outros and breakdowns. Again we set up a chalk-board of these ideas.

Things were going so well with the album that in the mid-dle of October, Guy O and I decided to take a trip to New York. We went to lunch at Balthazar in SoHo with two other friends, and as we were being seated, I noticed that this girl who worked there shot me a glance. I was very single then, and very open to the uni-verse introducing me to a friend, and this girl zapped me with one look. We were sitting at the table, and the other guys were looking at every skirt that walked by, but I was still fixated on the blonde. The next thing I knew, this girl, who wasn't our waitress, came strutting by our table with a real Miss Sassy Pants attitude.

"That's the one I'm talking about," I told the others, but they couldn't have cared less. The food arrived, but I had to go talk to this girl. I sauntered over to the hostess podium, stepped in front of her, and said, "Hello, my name's Anthony." I was five sec-onds into the conversation when a guy from the next table, whom I'd met once in a rehab when he came to visit his brother, took the opportunity to hug me and tell me everything that he'd been up to in the last few years. Meanwhile, my gal was getting away.

"Dude, do me a favor. Be quiet and go sit down right now. I'll come over in a little bit," I said. Finally, he left. "What are you doing after work?" I asked this girl.

"Not coming to visit you," she said.

"How about tomorrow after work?" I countered.

She agreed. The rest of that day, I was very excited. I tuned the rest of the female race out of my consciousness; I was just smit-ten. That night Guy O wanted to go out to meet girls, but I shrugged. "Nope, can't do it. I met one," I said. So the rest of his trip was basically ruined, because now I was monogamous.

The bad news was that I was leaving in two days, so I had only one day to make something happen with this girl. I met her after work, and we walked over to have sushi at a nearby restaurant. I really liked Yohanna. She had crystal-blue eyes, looked like a magical fairy, was exactly my height, and had a real strong sense of self. Plus, she had mad style and was tough and a little crazy. When I looked in her eyes, I saw an invisible spirit of something that I already loved. This girl could be my girlfriend, I decided.

We had some sushi, and she drank some alcohol, and it didn't faze me. Then we smoked some cigarettes and walked around SoHo. I tried to subtly suggest that she might spend the night at my hotel room.

"Well, I might, but I'm not going to fuck you or anything like that," Yohanna said. That was fine with me, and we started heading back, but we stopped under a streetlight and started kissing. The kiss was definitely working. It wasn't a horny-lust kiss, it was a real human-connection kiss, and she was a good kisser.

In my room, we talked and talked for hours, getting to know each other. I read her some things from my book of lyrics, including a dense song called "Quixotic Elixir." We listened to music and had a lot of physical contact—there was nudity and touching—but she hadn't been kidding when she said she wouldn't fuck me. In fact, she made it clear that if we continued, she wanted to see an AIDS test from me. All of this was making me feel better, because who wanted to fall in love with a girl who was ready to sleep with anyone who came along? Another positive was that she wasn't a fan of my band. She was twenty-three years old from upstate New York and had been a straight upstate New York raver bitch on Ecstasy in her youth.

I went home the next morning. I'd moved back to Guy O's house and was talking to Yohanna on the phone at least three times a day. Guy started organizing my thirty-sixth-birthday party, and the day before, he asked me if I wanted any girls there. I told him that apart from Sherry and my friend Mary Forsberg, I just wanted my male friends and the guys in the band.

"Are you sure? I can invite a bunch of hot girls," he prodded.

"The only girl I'm interested in is Yohanna. I think I'd rather get on a plane and fly to New York for the day than have the party," I said. "Why did I have to meet a girl who's a million miles away?"

November 1 rolled around, and we convened at a fancy-pants

place down on Beverly. There was a bunch of tables pushed together, and it was a festive atmosphere. I was trying to make the best of a birthday occasion, feeling good because I had been back to being sober for a few months. The dinner was going on, and I was chatting and eating, and then I looked over at Guy, who had a really weird expression on his face. When I turned my head to the right, I saw Yohanna walking into the restaurant with Guy's assistant. Unbeknownst to me, Guy had flown her in for the weekend. Yohanna was all dressed up in a sharp outfit, with her New York fur jacket and her blond hair and her blue eyes and the lipstick and eye makeup and her big bright smile. And Chad, Mr. Class, turned to Guy and whispered, "What did you get him, a hooker?"

The first thing I did was grab her by the hand and take her to a table in the back. I felt that we needed a few minutes alone to make a connection without being scrutinized by everyone at the table. As soon as the dinner was over, I took her back to Guy O's house, packed a bag, and we got a room at the Chateau Marmont, where I'd live for the next few months while we were recording our album. We spent a really nice night. Yohanna drank a bottle of red wine and took a bath, and I snapped some pretty pictures of her in the tub, the pale green water contrasting nicely with her pale white skin. But we had no biblical relations. If I'd known Guy was flying her out, I would have had the results of that AIDS test right there on the dresser. She stayed for two days, and we were joined at the hip for the whole time, getting to know each other better.

She left, and I went back to work writing songs. I was absolutely into this girl, and a lot of my writing was beginning to get influenced by that fact. I had a whole new well of feelings to tap into. But the more I'd gotten to know her, the more I realized that she was a troubled girl herself, who was maintaining a calm, cool, and collected front around me.

It became evident when she came out in December to visit me. Even though I was still sober, I wasn't working at getting well. I wasn't working through the twelve steps or even going to many meetings. I was what they call a "dry drunk"—someone who's irritable and restless and discontented and, even though technically sober, is suffering from the same crippling character defects of an alcoholic. I was still an obsessive, self-centered, selfish control freak instead of living my life instinctively in the way of love and service. If I had been working on my sobriety, I would have been doing a lot of personal writing, which helps you recognize your behavior and start taking action so you don't repeat it. I was too busy writing songs and rehearsing and recording to put in that work, which was a cop-out. The only way the program will work is if you put your sobriety first, and then everything else in your life will fall into place.

I was a little rough around the edges, a little bit uncomfortable in my own skin, even though I was getting a lot of band work done. And here came this girl I liked a little bit too much, so I was a little overbearing and insecure about the relationship, instead of just letting it be. I was trying to manipulate it a little too much, and it started to get tense.

The first mistake I made on her visit was to drag her out to this Hollywood schmoozefest called the Fire and Ice Ball. It was a fashion show in a rented space filled with movie stars and fabulousness. Not the best place to take a girl you don't know that well. It was uncomfortable, it was awkward, it was Hollywood at its silliest, not a great date.

We double-dated with Guy O. The minute we got in the limo, Yohanna started rummaging through the booze collection and throwing back shots of vodka. "She's nervous," I thought. "She doesn't know these people, and she wants to loosen up." But I did notice that she wasn't sipping these drinks. We went into the party, and I was just not relaxed. Guys were flirting with her, and I was getting jealous and not feeling good about anything. So we started to drift apart, and we ended up leaving and going to a smaller party with Madonna and a bunch of actors on the top floor of a tall building on Sunset.

Now Yohanna started ordering triple Cosmopolitans, downing them one after another. By then she'd stopped talking to me, because she thought I was being an asshole. As she was guzzling these drinks, I thought this was definitely not going to work. I got up and started walking around the party. When I looked back at the table, she was gone. Then I looked across the room and there was Jack Nicholson sitting on a chair with Yohanna on his knee. They were passing a joint back and forth. That was not a pleasant sight at all.

Meanwhile, chaos had broken out around me, and I was summoned to help this girl who thought she was having a heart attack from doing too much coke. I told her to just go home and sleep it off and she'd be fine. Then I ran into the model who'd been making out with Jaime the night I met her in New York. The girl started rubbing up against me, and I thought, "Okay, this might work. Two can play this game." We got on the couch, and within minutes, the girl said, "Can I come back to your hotel, or do you want to come to my house?"

"Let's go to your house," I said. Even as the words came out of my mouth, my heart was dying a million deaths. I looked over and saw Yohanna sitting on the floor with a very drunk Joaquin Phoenix. This was going from bad to worse. Seconds later, Joaquin came over to me.

"I'm having a hard time getting a handle on what's up with this girl," he said. "I keep asking her if she wants to get out of here, and all she can say is 'I came here with Anthony.' Yet you're clearly on your way to another scenario. I just want to know where things are."

"She's a big girl, she can make her own decisions," I said. "Whatever she wants, welcome to it. I've got nothing to do with her anymore."

It turned into a Mexican standoff. I didn't want to leave with that other girl, and Yohanna didn't really want to leave with someone else. She'd also arrived at the point where she couldn't walk anymore. So I picked her up and threw her over my shoulder and got her in a car. I was ready to have this big talk with her, but I looked over and she had passed out cold.

I had to carry her into the hotel room. I laid her down on the couch and closed the curtains, and she passed out like a baby. Meanwhile, I had been through an emotional meat slicer. I lay down in my bed, but it was no rest for the tortured mind. I was up all night with visions of Jack Nicholson smoking a doobie with my girlfriend. Arrrrggghh.

She woke up feeling a lot more refreshed than I did. We had a talk and realized that we were both being idiots, that the night had been a mutual display of vulgar immaturity. That week showed me that nothing short of a small atomic blast could have derailed our relationship, because if we could get through that first night of her blacking out and me being a creep, we had proved our ability to weather a storm right off the bat.

The band began recording the album, and the sessions were going well when we took a Christmas break. I went home to Michigan and then back to L.A. On New Year's Eve 1999, Flea, John and I went to the Playboy mansion for their party. It wasn't really our scene. It was tacky being in the land of a million fake tits. We weren't into the Charlie Sheen/Fred Durst thing at that stage of our career. Plus, I was missing Yo. We had planned to be on the phone for the dawning of the New Year, but when I called, something in her voice sounded amiss. She was out on a ferryboat in New York Harbor. Here was this person who'd expressed her true love for me, and I'd done likewise, so there was an obvious heart connection between us, but she wasn't all there on the phone. It was disquieting.

Yohanna's birthday was early in January. Since everything was going well with the recording, I decided to take a weekend trip to New York to surprise her. She was living in Brooklyn with her sister and a guy who had enough piercings in his lips to make a zipper. I took the red-eye to New York and checked in to the Mercer Hotel. I was so excited about this surprise that I had to keep myself from going out to Brooklyn too early. To ensure that she'd be home, I'd told her that I was having an exotic plant delivered to her place that day.

Finally, I hopped in a cab and headed out to Brooklyn. The farther I went, the dingier the neighborhood became. When we got to the address, it turned out that she was living in a basement apartment in a very shady neighborhood. I knocked on the door, all excited, and she answered it and was just torn up and hungover. She was not looking good or feeling good, and certainly not blossoming with joy at my surprise appearance. She let me in, grunted, and got back in bed. I jumped into bed with her. We made love, but it was very uninspired.

Then we got into the shower together. I looked down and saw her arms, and my heart sank. She had crazy-assed black-and-blue track marks. I knew that she drank and I knew that she had been the X raver girl, but I had no idea that she was the coke-smoking, coke-shooting, occasional-heroin-chaser girl. I was devastated, not because I was upset with her, but because I realized that this person I was so in love with was a sick drug addict and that her poor little soul was probably doomed to a miserable life of chasing the drugs and feeling like crap. Yohanna saw the look in my eyes and was saddened because she'd been found out. She assumed that no guy in his right sober mind was going to hang out with a girl who was shooting coke.

I had to sit with my senses. This clear, beautiful intuition took over. I knew exactly how I felt, and I wasn't confused or clouded or compromised. I realized that none of my feelings had diminished, but I might have to lose someone I truly loved. I didn't want to run away from Yohanna, but I knew drug addiction was strong enough that I had to be willing, if need be, to let go of the person I'd just fallen in love with.

We went for a walk through Brooklyn and stopped to get some coffee. She was twenty-four years old that day, and she looked so unhealthy, with sunken bloodshot eyes and a sickly pallor.

"Does this mean it's over for us?" she asked me.

"I don't think so," I said. "I still love you. I don't know that it's possible for us to be together, but I'm not walking away from you because of this."

I think she was touched by that. Then we went into Manhattan, and I gave her some presents. The next night I had to fly back. When I left, I wished her luck and told her that I hoped she'd find a way to deal with her problem. I went back to work in Hollywood. Without telling me, Yohanna started going to meetings and got clean.

Back in the studio, things were going well, but the one song that was so important to me was less important to everybody else. That was "Californication." Every time I'd bring it up, everyone would go, "We've got twenty-five other songs recorded. We don't need another one."

"No, we have to have this," I urged. "This is the anchor of the whole record. It's as good a lyric as I've written in a long time. It has to be a song." I was not letting go. I kept telling John that we had to finish it. Meanwhile, the session was winding down, and we had only a few days of basic track recording left. In the last moments of recording, John came running into the studio with his new thirty-thousand-dollar White Falcon hollow-body guitar. He said, "I've got it! I've got 'Californication'!" He sat down and plucked this incredibly sparse yet haunting combination of notes. It was so different from any other approach that we'd taken for the song that I didn't quite hear it. Then he started singing it, and it was at the high end of my range, but it was doable.

He taught it to Flea and Chad, and we rehearsed it a couple of times and recorded it. It was such a sensation of relief and gratification, to know that the song didn't end up in the same trash bin as "Quixotic Elixir" and a number of other songs that I had high hopes for.

"Californication"

Psychic spies from China
Try to steal your mind's elation
Little girls from Sweden
Dream of silver screen quotations
And if you want these kind of dreams
It's Californication

It's the edge of the world
And all of Western civilization
The sun may rise in the East
At least it settles in the final location
It's understood that Hollywood
Sells Californication

Pay your surgeon very well
To break the spell of aging
Celebrity skin is this your chin
Or is that war you're waging

Firstborn unicorn
Hard core soft porn
Dream of Californication
Dream of Californication

Marry me girl be my fairy to the world
Be my very own constellation
A teenage bride with a baby inside
Getting high on information
And buy me a star on the boulevard
It's Californication

Space may be the final frontier
But it's made in a Hollywood basement
Cobain can you hear the spheres
Singing songs off station to station
And Alderon's not far away
It's Californication

Born and raised by those who praise
Control of population
Everybody's been there and
I don't mean on vacation

Firstborn unicorn
Hard core soft porn
Dream of Californication
Dream of Californication

Destruction leads to a very rough road
But it also breeds creation
And earthquakes are to a girl's guitar
They're just another good vibration
And tidal waves couldn't save the world
From Californication

Pay your surgeon very well
To break the spell of aging
Sicker than the rest
There is no test
But this is what you're craving

Firstborn unicorn
Hard core soft porn
Dream of Californication
Dream of Californication

One of the reasons I was able to sing "Californication" with little trouble was that I'd been taking vocal lessons with an amazing teacher named Ron Anderson. Over the years I'd tried a number of vocal coaches. Before *Mother's Milk,* I took lessons from a white-haired crazy lady from Austria, whose claim to fame was that she had worked with Axl Rose before *Appetite for Destruction.* Her whole thing was to stand in one place and press your belly a certain way, which didn't resonate with me, since I was ragdolling all over the stage.

Around *Blood Sugar,* I took some lessons with Michael Jackson's vocal coach, but I didn't like him much and bailed out after two sessions. For *One Hot Minute,* I took lessons with a pleasant fellow who played piano and sang in bars for tips. I don't know if

I improved my vocalizing abilities, but it was a lot of fun. Instead of doing scales, we'd get out one of his hundreds of songbooks and sing Beatles songs. Then I found Ron Anderson, who was a classical teacher possessed of an operatic voice. It wasn't fun to sit there and sing scales, but I could feel immediate results and had much more control over my voice. I worked with him every day during the recording of the album, which we ultimately called *Californication*. My biggest mistake was not to continue working in his style, so I'd lose my voice a lot when I was out on the road. It reached a breaking point while we were on tour in New York. Ron flew out and worked with me all day, and I was well enough to make the gig. He gave me a strict regimen of warming up my voice, which I do religiously to this day.

We were all thrilled when we finished work on the album. We felt like a forest that had burned to the ground and then new trees had sprouted from the ashes. Flea was still in his emotional wringer, but John and I and even Chad had been through our own wringers, so there was a real bond between us, and seeing this project through was a real unifying process. Having gone through it all had changed our outlooks. You can't be as much of a bitch as you were before, you can't be as much of an egomaniac, you can't feel as much like the world owed you something, you can't be the "where's mine?" guy. The "where's mine?" was that I was alive and getting the opportunity to play music with the people I most like to play music with. One of the most mystifying aspects of this era of our band was that we were as enthusiastic as we were when we started, if not more so. And when we started, we had cornered the market on enthusiasm.

We mixed the record, and people started coming by to hear it, and we were over the moon with the reactions. Things were going well on the home front, too. I was going back and forth to New York to visit Yohanna, who was now the Sober Girl. She wanted to go back to school, so I'd set her up at the Fashion Institute of Technology, and she was doing well. The light in her eyes was back, and we were getting along spectacularly.

The only snafu the band ran into was when we played the finished album for our new management team. Cliff and Peter flew to L.A., sat in the studio, listened, and were so unimpressed we couldn't believe it. We played them "Scar Tissue" and "Otherside" and "Californication," and they sat there saying, "Okay. We might be able to work with that one. I don't know about the other one. It's not a home run, but we might be able to get on base with that." They're still like that, they still underreact to things. We found it almost humorous that they were receiving the fruits of our labor with such a low-key reaction. We weren't worried about it. We believed in the record, and we loved it and wanted to share it, but we weren't anticipating its reception so much as we were just pleased with what we made.

Cliff decided that we should lead with "Scar Tissue" as the single and the first video. We decided to do a special small tour to unveil the album. Since it was being released in June, my friend Chris Rock suggested we play proms around the country to promote it. That got me thinking about my high school days and how exciting it was to turn out to see bands that came through, so we decided to do a bunch of free shows for high school students. Then Columbine happened, and a firestorm of fear swept over all these high schools. We felt it was more important than ever to do the shows, so we came up with the idea of having high school students write essays on how they could make their schools better, safer, happier, more rocking places, so that they didn't have to go to school afraid. If you wrote the essay, you got a free ticket to the show. We went out in May and played, and it was an absolutely magical grouping of shows, because they were small and for kids who clearly wanted to be there, who had taken the time to write the compositions. There was so much love coming off these kids, we couldn't have asked for a better reception.

We knew that the album was connecting with a lot of people when we went on a European press tour in June. We were in Italy, and John and I were riding in the back of a Mercedes with the window open. A scooter with two Italian guys on it pulled up next to us. They looked inside the car and started screaming, "Hey, Californication, Californication!" then started singing "Scar Tissue." The record had been out for five days. Everywhere we went, every shop was playing our record. Italy had caught fire. We went from selling a handful of records to selling more records than anyone that year in Italy. How does an entire country decide to start loving you in one day?

In July we began a series of huge shows. In the short amount of time since our record came out, there had been a huge buzz all over the world. The record was getting received in a much larger and warmer way than we ever expected. Somewhere along the way, we were asked to close Woodstock '99. That was perfect, because we had been asked to play an outdoor show on Younge Street in Toronto the day before. It was supposed to be a low-key show, but the whole town turned out. This massive expanse of humanity filled the street and every building and rooftop. It was another indicator that the world was with us and that we had reawakened the sleeping Red Hot fans from their Rip Van Winkleism. They all came out of the woodwork to rock with us for this record.

The next day we went to Woodstock. We planned to fly in, get on a bus, get to the venue an hour before our set, get focused, play, and get the hell out of Dodge before the mass exodus began. Before we got there, we'd heard reports that this event was less organized and the crowds were getting out of control. When we pulled onto this old military base way up in upstate New York, it was clear that this situation had nothing to do with Woodstock anymore. It wasn't symbolic of peace and love, but of greed and cashing in. The little dove with the flower in its mouth was saying, "How much can we overcharge the kids for this T-shirt and get away with it?"

We got backstage and were all hell-bent on getting straight into our rituals—the physical warm-ups, the stretching, the meditating, the finger exercises, the vocal warm-ups. It was about seven, so we would be taking the stage during an explosive and dramatic upstate New York sunset. We hadn't heard any reports about people getting abused or raped or anything like that. It just seemed to us like another big rock festival, with no particularly evil elements about it.

Our sacred hour of preparation was interrupted when Jimi Hendrix's sister came backstage and pleaded with us to do a song by her brother. It seemed that an all-star Hendrix tribute had fallen apart, and she was mortified that Woodstock would forget him. It had been a long time since we played a Hendrix song, so our first inclination was to say no. But she kept telling us how much it would mean to her, so ten minutes before we were to go onstage, we decided to do "Fire."

I reviewed the lyrics, and John reacquainted himself with the chords. Right before we were due onstage, Flea came to me and said, "I'm thinking of doing the show naked. What do you think?"

"If that's what you're thinking, then don't even question it. Go let your freak flag fly, brother," I said. In that setting, it seemed natural for him to be naked, and no one let it be a distraction. We played a fluid, dynamic show.

As night fell, we saw this giant column of fire far back in the audience. We'd been through tons of festivals where bonfires had been started, so this one didn't seem out of the ordinary. When it was time for our encore, we started into "Fire," not because there were fires raging, but as a palliative for poor Jimi's sister. And the old shoe fit. Then we ran offstage, drove to the plane, landed in Manhattan, and checked in to our home away from home, the Mercer Hotel. It was only midnight, but we started hearing this ruckus about the riots and the rapes and the fires raging at Woodstock. That was so weird, because to us, it had seemed like a normal rock-and-roll show.

But we woke up to papers and radio stations vilifying us for inciting the crowd by playing "Fire." We ignored these ridiculous charges, though it did turn out that the promoters were assholes and it had not been a user-friendly environment. We should have paid closer attention to that and not been so isolated from the fan's point of view. I guess it was irresponsible to just show up, play, and leave, without taking a closer look at some of the details surrounding the show.

Now it was time to go to Europe to play. Q-Prime was ideologically built on touring. Their basic philosophy was that after you put out a record, you had to crisscross the globe ten times if you wanted it to do well. We were used to touring, but not to that degree. The longer you've been in a band and the more times you've toured, the more difficult it becomes to say "I'm going on tour for two years and I'm going to sleep in a different bed every night and be in buses, trains, cars, taxis, shuttling and shifting and pushing and pulling and not eating normally and not sleeping normally and not being around loved ones." Flea had a young daughter, which made it even harder. But Q-Prime were very into it, and it had been a long time since we'd been there, so we were a bit more willing to hit the road incessantly than we would be in the future.

We started by doing a free show in Moscow on August 14, 1999. As part of Russia's glasnost awakening, they'd embraced MTV, and we were tapped to inaugurate MTV's Russian debut with a huge free concert in Red Square. The first problem was that John had to be talked down from his concern that we might be kidnap victims, because next to Colombia, Russia had become the kidnap capital of the world. After getting assurances for our personal safety, and getting assigned a contingent of security personnel, we agreed to do the show.

You'd expect that Moscow, Russia's biggest city, would be run efficiently, maybe even in a military fashion, but that wasn't the case. There was no order at all, and shakedowns were the norm. The cops, the military, the airport personnel, everybody wanted our rubles. It was the first time any of us had been to Russia, and we did feel a little unsafe there. We stayed at the Kempinski Hotel, a five-star gaudy, gilded, marbled oasis in the middle of a strikingly poor economy. Everything in Moscow was gray, gray, gray. The sky was gray, the buildings were gray, the streets were gray, the bushes were gray. There was this heavy cloud of Stalinesque gravity that suffocated the place.

We took a couple of days to decompress and tour the city. The day before the show, by some horrible stroke of fate, I wrecked, wracked, twisted, turned, sliced, and diced my back. I saw a physical therapist, but it did no good. I could see the enormous stage they had built from my hotel window, and I was bummed at the prospect of playing before all of Russia on MTV with a whack back.

The day of the show, Red Square was so filled with wall-to-wall Russians that we needed a police escort to get near the stage. By the time we went on, my back was still not happening, even though it was better than the day before. Still, I was able to stand up straight and present the songs. Nothing buck wild, no ability to do my song-and-dance thing, but we made the best of it. Then we hightailed it out of Russia, but we got pulled over and extorted by the police on the way to the airport. As a final indignity, Chad got shaken down for all the money he had on him right before boarding.

I'd never really liked Austria, mainly because the people I met there were so arrogant and pompous, but when we stepped off the plane in Vienna after a week in Russia, it was like going to Disneyland for the first time as a kid. The sun came out, the clouds opened, you could smell flowers, there was snow on the mountains, it was just heaven. However, the rest of this leg of the European tour was not my shining moment. It's difficult to keep a relationship prospering when you're in Europe and your girlfriend is in America and you're both relatively newly sober and you haven't worked through a lot of control issues and jealousy issues and insecurity issues and dependency issues. There was a lot of emotional frying going on.

It was hard being gone for months at a time, and so far away that the time difference became a huge obstacle. You want to communicate, but then you aren't able to, and days go by. You get mad and try to call her and you can't find her and then you finally do catch her and she's been out doing something stupid that she shouldn't have been doing, because she should've been there waiting for your phone call, but she blew you off and then she starts to get suspicious and "Who's that girl's voice in the background?" "Oh, that's my masseuse or my friend or whatever." I wasn't good at it, and Yohanna was no better, and together we equaled stubborn. These things always took a lot of repairing, and we'd have to wait until I got home.

The band worked our asses off touring that year. Yohanna finished school, and we decided that it would be a good idea for her to move to L.A., which meant I'd have to get a place to live. I'd always fancied a gorgeous old building in West Hollywood called the Colonial House, which was a stone's throw from the Chateau Marmont. When Jennifer Lopez moved out of the penthouse, I grabbed it. Yohanna moved to L.A. in September 1999. She had the use of my nice new Cadillac Esplanade and all her expenses paid, but she didn't have a job, and she didn't know that many people, and I was about to leave again for Europe.

On the way to Europe, the band stopped in New York and did a gig at Windows on the World in the World Trade Center for K-Rock radio contest winners. The show was lively and energetic, but the sound system was horrific: All I heard were drums and guitar and no vocals for the entire show. I ended up screaming my lungs out and losing my voice, which was a drag.

We flew to Finland and began crisscrossing Europe. When we got to Spain, Yohanna decided to come out for the last week of the tour. I loved the girl, I was happy to see her, happy to have my woman in my bed, in my arms, but she was hard to get along with on a daily basis, as was I. She never did come to a comfortable understanding that a lot of the people who were fans of the band happened to be girls, and for some reason, she held me responsible. There were times when we played shows and I'd be with her and we'd have to walk from the arena to wherever the car was, and frenzied people would charge me. A lot of times they were girls, and there were crazy screamings of "I love you, I love you, I want to be with you, please hug me." I have no reason to be mean to these people or to explain to them, "I have a girlfriend, you must not approach me with such sentiments." Their interaction with me is just an illusion. I'm like "Thank you very much, hello, good-bye, God bless, enjoy the night, carry on." If I was with Yohanna, she'd say, "No, you can't let those girls come up and say those things to you. They have to know that I'm your girlfriend."

Yo and I had this historical antagonism. When we were apart from each other on the road, we antagonized each other, and when we got together on the road, we antagonized each other. It was because all we wanted was each other's constant love and attention and for no one else to receive that love and attention, which is a selfish and difficult place to be in a relationship. We were emotionally retarded, and that was the best we could do at the time.

We played in Barcelona, and Chad had made friends with a Barcelonan sweet tart who was cute as a button. She came backstage, and when Chad introduced her, I stood up, gave her a European-kiss greeting, and welcomed her to sit down and grab a bite to eat. This, of course, infuriated Yohanna.

When the girl left, I looked up and said, "Bye-bye, sweetie."

" 'Sweetie'? Did you just call her 'sweetie'?" Yohanna fumed. "Oh, so now she's *your* sweetie?" Although she was making an ass out of herself, I was right there with her, because the next day it would be me saying, "Did you just say 'good-bye sweetie' to that guy?"

By the time we got to Madrid, the wheels had fallen off. We got into another unmemorable bickering match, like something off of *I Love Lucy* but without the happy ending. We were in this beautiful hotel suite in Madrid, madly in love, out there on a fun successful tour in the middle of Spain, and we started fighting about the dumbest thing on earth. And we brought it down the elevator, into the lobby, into the bus that was taking us to our plane.

Unfortunately, that carried on throughout Lisbon. Then we went home and fought there. I loved living in this cool penthouse apartment with her, but it was never smooth sailing. We'd both been such fucking dope fiends for so long that we never had a chance to grow out of our childish behavior. We must have loved the drama and the constant rush of fighting and making up and starting the whole cycle over again. It was just crazy.

I know that I had nothing but love for this girl. I had no interest in chasing any other girls. My only interests were in seeing her get well and in taking care of her, which turned out to be one of the problems. I took care of her so much that she just expected a constant "Oh well, Anthony will do it for me." I'd pay for everything she needed, I'd try to find her a job, I'd try to find her a friend, I'd try to find her a sponsor, always doing everything for her. Once she started expecting that response, I was like "Fuck that. Don't go expecting shit. Earn your place in life, earn your respect, just do your thing." So she was in a terrible place, because she probably felt resentful toward me for giving her stuff and then thinking that she should earn her own place in life. It was a lose-lose situation, and I wasn't very good at handling it.

Even when I financed her start-up fashion business, that became a troubled area of contention. As soon as I saw her stuff, I thought, "These clothes are so amazing. She's got mad style." I got on the phone with my managers in New York saying, "I need the names of all the major department-store buyers." But Yohanna was never satisfied, never grateful, and never comfortable with it. She was always on edge and discontented about something. I was equally maladjusted to life at that point. I had been off my gyroscope for so long that I didn't know how to handle any of life's basic scenarios with any clarity or intuition.

There were also some fun things happening at the time. Our sex life had started off pretty slowly, but it had developed over time into a spiritual attraction after we finally figured each other's bodies out. She had a depth to her sexuality that I had never experienced before. There was no question about our love, though we were both combustible personalities.

That year we visited both of our families at Christmas. It was the first time that my parents had met her. It's funny, my male friends were always terrified of Blackie. When they met him, they'd try to shake his hand, and he'd just look at their hands and walk away. But he was never like that with my girlfriends. He was always incredibly gracious and welcoming to whatever girl I happened to have in my life. He couldn't wait to hang out with Yohanna and go through the family photos with her. But Yo was not the warmest of people. Even though she might feel it on the inside, she didn't communicate any of it to anybody. That was how it was with her and my mom. My mom was very happy that I had this person I was in love with, but she could never tell if Yohanna had any love or compassion for her or the rest of our family, because Yo wouldn't wear her emotions on her sleeve.

I had a lot to be thankful for that Christmas. The album was continuing to sell phenomenally. Every so often I'd get a call from Gail at Q-Prime, and she'd tell me, "*Californication*'s number this in this country, and it's still in the top ten there." I'd jump around, skipping and hooting and hollering. It's a shame that my personal life wasn't flourishing in the same way my professional life was. Professionally, we were on fire. Besides the record sales, we were playing great. We had figured out how to breathe life into these new songs that had tapped into a deeper and more haunted emotional realm than we'd ever visited before.

Watching the constant evolution of John was also a movie unto itself. When we went out at the beginning of *Californication,* he was shy and withdrawn onstage, not going in for overt emoting. Over time, he developed into this hambone who just couldn't get enough. "Let's start the show with me soloing for ten minutes." He wasn't doing it out of narcissism, he was doing it out of his love for playing music and his desire to commune with the spirits, both invisible spirits and also the spirits of the people who were there to experience music and love. Watching him spread his wings was a delight.

We brought in the millennium at a concert at the Forum in our hometown. The Forum always had these great memories for us. Flea and I had sneaked into the Forum to see Queen back in the day, and more recently, when we came to Warners Bros., we hit the jackpot as Laker fans because Mo had four tickets at center court on the floor. After *Blood Sugar,* we were the number one perk-getters at Warner's. Flea and I and two of our friends were always sitting pretty at center court.

We'd played the Forum once with Dave Navarro, and it was one of our best American dates with him. It's always hard to do well when you're playing in your hometown. There are such high expectations, and then you have the added stress of arranging tickets for family and friends. So it can go two ways. Instead of doing what you do best, which is going out there and rocking, you might get too hung up on all these outside issues, and wanting the show to be the best ever, and end up sucking. Or you might hit the jackpot and rock your hometown like it's never been rocked before.

This show was somewhere in between. We were good, but we weren't unbelievable. The nice thing was that my sister Julie and her husband, Steve, flew out to spend New Year's Eve with me. That was also the memorable show when John Frusciante would get shot by Cupid's arrow and fall for Milla Jovovich, who had been rehearsing her band next door to us at Swing House. That night she came to the show wearing a wedding dress, and she put the whammy on John's flim-flammy.

We had a few days off after the New Year's show, and then we went from beautiful, sunny California to dismal, cold, gray Tokyo, Japan. It was the first time we'd played Japan since John was back in the band, and we wanted to leave a new taste in their psychic palates, since it was where John had played his last show before quitting the band. But the Japanese shows weren't much fun, and we weren't at our best. One of the problems was that by then, I had developed a chronic case of shin splints, and anytime I was out onstage, moving around would be "Ooh, ooh, ah, ah."

After Japan we had a week off before going to Australia and New Zealand. Everyone headed off for different holidays. I was going to meet Yohanna in Bali. I couldn't wait to see her, especially after being so bummed out in Japan. I'll never forget how happy

I was when I walked through that airport door and she greeted me. She had a big flower in her hair and had put on a few pounds, which I appreciated, because she looked good when her flesh was full and pushing out, rather than being sucked up.

We stayed at a fancy resort built into the side of a cliff overlooking the ocean. Each room was an individual unit with a stone pool. There were rose petals all over the bed and some more in the bathtub. That afternoon Yo and I enjoyed the best love-making we'd ever had. Then we snorkeled and drove into the interior, which was the most beautiful part of the island. You picture Bali as this pristine, remote location, but it's really an over-crowded cluster fuck of traffic with some air pollution thrown in. There had to be a few hundred thousand people jam-packed onto the island, but the interior was solid mountains and jungle. We went on an incredible rafting adventure on a river that cut through the middle of the island.

Then it was time to play Big Day Out, Australia's answer to Lollapalooza. January is the nicest time by far in Australia, because it's their summer and the whole country goes on joy time. We started our tour in Auckland, New Zealand, and we were especially excited because Nine Inch Nails were going to be on the bill with us, and we all just loved them. We were also playing with the Foo Fighters, and we would become incredibly close to them down the line.

The only downside to all of this was my shin splints. Even with the week off, the pain would not subside. My shinbones were getting hairline fractures because my muscles and tendons were so swollen, they were pulling off the bone mass. Walking was painful, jumping was even more painful, and I was going to have to go out there and give my best performances ever with these getaway sticks that were in maddening pain. Two days before the show, I saw a doctor.

"Doc, I got shin splints. Could you please give me a muscle relaxant, or something that's not going to affect me from the neck up, so I can go perform?" I asked.

He suggested Advil, but I told him I'd tried that and it hadn't worked.

"There's a new non-narcotic painkiller called Ultram," he said. "It really works on athletes who have to perform under similar conditions to you. Take one in the afternoon and one right before the show."

The day before the first show, I took the Ultram, and lo and behold, I started to feel pretty good. Not good enough to know for sure that I felt good, but I could swear I felt good in the subtlest possible way. It couldn't be the Ultram, because it was non-narcotic, so I decided that I just felt good. I took the other one before the show, and man, I felt no pain in my legs at all.

We played our show, and it was mad fun, fifty thousand Kiwis bouncing in unison. The kids knew every word to every song, even the new ones, and it was an unbelievable rush. John was blazing on his guitar, Chad was an orchestra of cannons blasting off, Flea was a ball of primal aborigine energy, and I felt totally in control of myself as a singer and performer. And there was no pain! I was ready to kiss the earth.

It was all good, and when we got back to the hotel, I had sex with Yohanna and something unusual happened. We were fucking and fucking, and I just was not coming. That had never been a problem. Later, it crossed my mind that it might have been due to the Ultram, but how could it make me not come? It was supposed to be a glorified Advil, a non-narcotic. It made no sense.

I thought it was amazing that I could be getting pain relief from a non-narcotic pill that was also making me feel pretty nice. There had to be part of me that recognized the voice in my head saying, "Okay, you're supposed to take your Ultram at three, and it's noon now, so maybe you should take it a little early." Halfway through the tour, I had to have my prescription refilled. But the doctor had told me it was not a narcotic, and I wasn't getting goofy high, just a foundation of artificial well-being, which I was loving.

So we rocked Auckland and went on to the Gold Coast of Australia. We were the inaugural event at the Olympic Stadium in

Sydney. Physically, I was in perfect health. My legs weren't bothering me, I was exercising every day, running and swimming and stretching. Yohanna and I were having fantastic sex. I was loving the whole experience. But then I started to become aware of the fact that Flea was not experiencing the same euphoric joy of life and touring and music and people and skies. He was not on the same heavenly ambient wavelength.

Flea had been going through a lot of personal shit with his girlfriend for this whole *Californication* time. I knew he was down and sick and depressed and anguished about everything, but I also knew the situation was of his own making. We create a horribly painful bouillabaisse to sit in for years on end, until we can't fucking sit there anymore; but it wasn't like some evil fate flew into his ass, he created it. He sat there and masterminded his own misery. So he was troubled, but he had to appreciate that the love he was experiencing from both John and me was immense. We were backing him, we weren't dissing him. It wasn't like during the *Mother's Milk* era, when John and I bonded up and left him unattached. And Flea can, at times, be a prima donna, especially earlier in the Dave era, when he was ready to quit the band at the drop of a hat.

Just for the record, anything negative that I ever say about Flea is only because he's my brother and I love him. The fact is, it's funny to take the piss out of ourselves. Each one of these guys, Flea, John, Chad, is individually a bridge to God for me, and there's nothing I would do to change any of these people or the experiences I've had with them. Every one of them has given me love and music and the best life I could ever hope to have. But at the same time, I feel compelled to laugh at all of our foibles. I'm not poking fun at the relationship to feel better about myself; it's just because we really are all such kooks.

Flea was suffering then, both emotionally and physically. He was feeling zapped and sapped and run-down and not centered. When we got to Melbourne, he called a band sit-down. Peter Mensch was there to tell us about our upcoming U.S. tour. And if we thought hitting Europe and the rest of the world was hard, Peter was about to tell us how many dates they were hoping to give us in the U.S.A. I was feeling gung-ho, let's go. But Flea basically broke down and explained that he wasn't able to enjoy this experience. You could tell by the look in his eyes that he was at his wits' end.

That was when he proposed the idea of touring in three-week segments, then taking ten-day breaks between segments. It was a fairly revolutionary idea, and it made it nearly impossible to generate any money, because you have to keep your crew on salary for those ten days. You have to keep your buses and your trucks, and it's the same amount of expenses, except for hotels, as being on tour, only you're not making a penny.

We realized that doing this tour was not about making the maximum amount of money; it was about having the maximum amount of fun and enjoyment and staying healthy. We implemented that schedule and, to Flea's credit, we stick to it religiously to this day.

Flea came up with another important idea. For a long time, we had both been charity-oriented and earlier, while we were on holiday at his house in Australia, he and I had talked about the idea of taking some of our profits and creating some sort of charitable organization. We decided to take 5 percent of our income from touring and give it away. Just give it to the best charities we could find, whether it was cancer research or children's hospitals or music programs, whatever. That's a pretty big percentage of income, because half always goes toward the expenses of touring, and then another 20 percent goes to the managers, and 5 percent to a lawyer, and another 5 percent to the accountants.

We went to John and Chad, and they both thought it was a great idea. It turned out to be an incredibly fun and positive change, because now we get the joy of helping all these people. It was shocking to the core how good it felt to be of service. Kids send us pictures of themselves and letters of gratitude and tell us how much it means to them to get some medical care or a playground or musical instruments. It was one of the best decisions we ever made as a team.

But that euphoria faded back to some fairly mundane realities. In Australia, Yohanna and I starting fighting again. There we were, walking down the great old section of Melbourne, and we got into a tiff. It wasn't a poisonous fight; we were yelling at each other and she was socking me and I was grabbing her and it was a good, healthy working-it-out kind of thing. But some people walked by and thought it was a spousal-abuse situation. I'm not sure who they thought was taking the worst of the abuse, but they stopped and asked if she needed help.

It was a testament to the potential of our volatility. There was no physical harm, but there was an intensity about us that would have made anyone stop and say, "Is everything all right here?" I remember thinking it was fun and playful, because I secretly liked it when she beat me up. She's a big strong girl, and heaven forbid she gets her legs in the party, because then you're going down.

After Big Day Out, Yohanna and I went back to L.A. and settled into our new digs together. We had been back for a week when I was invited to the NBA All-Star game, which was in San Francisco that year. The NBA was offering to provide us with a hotel, a car, tickets to the game, the works. Figuring we could spend a nice romantic weekend, we flew up. The hotel they put us in was not that nice a place, but it was free and in an interesting neighborhood. Unfortunately, the game wasn't exciting, so afterward we drove back to the city and found a restaurant. We were getting along fine, sitting at an upstairs table, holding hands, and enjoying each other's company. And then we made a huge mistake.

It's never a good idea for two addicts to reminisce about their old days of using drugs. When I'd met Yohanna, she was drinking, but I'd never seen her on drugs. And she knew me only in sobriety. Somehow the topic of drugs got placed on the table.

"God, I can't imagine you ever doing those things, it seems so out of character for you," Yohanna said. "You're so not into that self-destructive energy."

"Believe me, this is what I used to do," I said, and told her some of the war stories that I've recounted here. She told me some of hers, and we started realizing just what birds of a feather we were.

I don't remember who suggested it first, but someone said, "Can you imagine us getting high together?"

"It would be fun for a minute, and then it would be horrible," I said.

"Yeah, but it would be really fun for a minute," Yo said.

"It would be fun for a minute," I agreed.

"What if we did it?" she said. "What if we did it just this weekend and then went home?"

"That's crazy, but it sounds interesting," I said.

"Are you serious?" she asked.

"I'm not really serious, but now that you mention it, I'm a little serious," I admitted.

"I wasn't until you said that, and now I'm really serious," she said.

"Do you want to go get high?" I asked.

"Yeah, let's do it," she said.

"You're sure? Because once we do this, things will never be the same," I cautioned.

"Oh, we'll be all right. Let's go," she said. And we left that restaurant for our rendezvous with the eight-hundred-pound gorilla.

15.

A Moment of Clarity

Yohanna and I left the restaurant and went straight to Haight Street. I didn't even bother disguising myself; I just tried to stay out of the sight line of all the white kids on the street. We found a black dealer who had the coke but didn't have the heroin. We figured we'd deal with that problem later. On the way back to the hotel, we stopped in a liquor store, bought some pipes, and picked up a bottle of vodka and a bottle of cranberry juice. Yohanna insisted that she wanted alcohol. If she was going out, she was going all the way out. The poor kid had no idea what she was in for. All we knew was that we were salivating like Pavlov's dog at the prospect of getting high.

Probably part of the reason I had become so interested in getting high was that Ultram was actually a heavy-duty synthetic opiate. A few months later, Louie consulted the *Physicians Desk*

Reference and read that under no circumstances should Ultram be administered to ex–heroin addicts, because it induces a craving for opiates. I guess that idiot doctor in New Zealand didn't read his copy.

Yohanna and I got to the room and started smoking and smoking and drinking and drinking and, for the first time, saw each other in our getting-high mode, with all the quirky drugisms that go along with that. About five in the morning, we ran out of coke. We were both too annihilated to go back out on the streets, so I came up with a genius idea. I took out the Yellow Pages and called an escort service, knowing that the majority of those girls had drug connections. I'd pay one for her time, which would be spent in the pursuit of drugs. For once, Yohanna was easygoing about my talking to another woman. The girl went off to Berkeley, and it seemed like it took her forever, but she came back with twenty Valiums, some coke, some crystal methadrine, but no heroin. We did the coke and then took the Valiums and finally crashed.

Because we were in this together, it wasn't as horrible a wake-up as I'd had in the past. We were both feeling a little shaky, lying in bed, wondering, "What were we thinking? That was a really bad idea." So we ate and drank something, watched a movie in bed, and tried to forget about it. But then that voice came over us. "Hey, you've already fucked up. Ain't no sense stopping now." I went out and got some syringes, and we shot the speed. Of course, that wasn't enough, so Yohanna scoured the streets and found a one-eyed taxi driver who sold her some smack. How horrible was that to let my girlfriend go out into the streets of San Francisco to find stuff?

By now the hotel wanted us out of our room, but when I told them we needed to stay a few more days, they moved us to a bigger room. I got on the phone and did the escort-service trick again. This girl was dialed into the drug world, and she delivered everything we needed, including a bag of pure powder cocaine. My body was relatively resilient to shooting coke; it remembered stuff like "Oh yeah, this is where the heart goes into the fifth gear." I started injecting large quantities and doing okay.

Yohanna did up a smaller injection of coke, but something went drastically wrong. She'd done a million hits of cocaine in her life, but she was not doing well on this one. She lay down and got real pale and clammy, started shaking furiously, and began to have trouble breathing. She was convinced she was dying. That was the scariest moment of my drug-using career, even scarier than when I walked into Hillel's living room and saw Kim blue-faced and not breathing in his chair. I was so deeply in love with Yo that the idea of anything bad happening to her was terrifying.

Before I called 911, I prayed. "Okay, universe, we have a problem. The girl I'm in love with is possibly dying right here on the couch. I need a real big favor, and that is for her not to die." She had gone out like a frozen little fish Popsicle on the couch, but while I was on the phone with 911, she started to breathe again and then sat up and said she felt okay. I told 911 it was a false alarm and hung up.

Then the phone rang. It was the hotel operator. "Did you just call 911?" he asked.

"Me? 911? No. Wrong room. Wires must have crossed."

She was skeptical, but I wouldn't cop to making that call.

I hung up and went back to getting high. Because of her near-death experience, Yo put a moratorium on getting high and went to the bedroom, trying to collect herself. I was in the living room with a table full of cocaine and pills and heroin and syringes and pipes when, kabang, kabang, kabang, someone came to the door.

I threw a blanket over the entire table and opened the door. It was the San Francisco police department. Not an ambulance, not the rescue squad—the cops.

"Sir, we received a call from 911 that someone was overdosing in this room. The law mandates that we have to inspect the premises in that situation," the cop said. They were being pretty decent to not knock me down and barge into the room.

"I have no idea what that call was about," I said. "It's just me and my girlfriend, and we're both fine."

They could tell that I was lying. And stoned.

"Well, we need to see the girl," the cop said.

I called Yohanna into the room, and she looked good enough to satisfy them, so they left and she went back to bed and I started getting high again. Then again, bam, bam, bam, it was the door. Again I covered up the stuff. This time it was the damn sheriff's department.

"We got a report that a call was made to 911 concerning a possible drug overdose," the sheriff said.

"No, no, the police were just here. We handled this already," I said.

The sheriff recognized me and almost apologized for disturbing us, and left. But I was frazzled. Yohanna wasn't well, the cops kept coming, the hotel obviously was aware that two dope fiends were going for it on their top floor. The whole scenario was going from bad to worse.

In the morning we ate some food at a diner and then flew back to L.A. Both of us looked like wrecks. But I wasn't finished. On the plane ride down, I decided to drive downtown, buy a lot of drugs, and have Yohanna drop me off at a motel and then go home. She dropped me off at a sleazy motel on Alvarado.

"Be careful, don't hurt yourself. I'll be home when you're done," she said.

"I'm terribly sorry, Yo, but I gotta do what I gotta do," I said.

She left, and I started firing up and getting very, very out there. And bang, bang, bang. Again knocking at the door. It was already nerve-shattering to be smoking crack, so you don't want any intrusions into your psychotic little world. Then I heard a voice.

"A.K., it's me. Let me in."

It was Yohanna.

"I've changed my mind. I want to get high," she said.

She had gone a few blocks in the car and then decided to indulge, so she parked in this horribly scary neighborhood and, in her high heels and platinum-blond hair and vintage long jacket, walked all the way back to the motel.

That run went on for a few days. Eventually, we went home and brought the drugs into the house with us. Now our love nest had been soiled with the negative energy of crack and heroin. But we couldn't stop this demonic behavior. The only fun part of the whole experience was when we stopped smoking the coke and did heroin and lay in bed together, smoking cigarettes and watching movies till six in the morning.

Of course, we had these sweet heroin-induced conversations about how much we loved each other. I remember telling Yohanna on one such occasion that I not only wanted to be with her for the rest of our natural lives, I also wanted to make sure that after we were both dead, our spirits stayed together. That kind of craziness.

Most of the time, we'd watch a movie and she'd fall asleep in the middle of it, so I'd end up watching it by myself. One night *Less Than Zero* came on, a movie that the Chili Peppers were in for a snippet, playing "Fight Like a Brave." I'd never seen it before, and I was blown away by Robert Downey Jr.'s amazing performance, which absolutely mirrored his life. And spoke to my life, which had pathetically reverted back to the '80s. I'd gone back to less than zero. Was that what was waiting for me, dying in a convertible on the way to the desert?

I hatched a new plan. Yo and I would go to Hawaii and kick there. Who could do what we were doing here on the beautiful island of Oahu? We checked in to a hotel overlooking Waikiki Beach and ate some delicious ribs at the dusk barbecue. (I was back to eating meat.) But then we decided to keep the run rolling. There wasn't a street-dealing scene for heroin in Hawaii, so I dragged my lovely sweetheart to the strip bars of Waikiki to score. For backup, we ran a prescription scam and had Yohanna feign tooth pain to get a codeine supply.

We had no problem copping at the strip clubs. All the

strippers wanted to party and whoop it up with us, and the dealers were ecstatic to be dealing to me. "Dude, I've been listening to your music since I was in high school." Our routine was to go out to the clubs, buy the drugs, go back to the hotel, and do them until we couldn't do any more. Then we'd wake up and say, "Let's stop. Let's go swimming in the ocean and eat some good food and get our health back." By eleven that night, we'd be itching for more drugs. I was the sicker of the instigators. Yohanna would always beg to stop and go back to being clean.

After ten days of this cycle, we went back to L.A. The minute we were back, we got high at our place again. Yo's heart was into being clean, but I had a harder time surrendering. The sad thing is that all this using together had definitely affected our relationship. There had been an untroubled purity to our love that was tainted and never recovered from the bouts of using.

The only thing that stopped me from continuing the run was that I had to be on a plane on March 23, 2000, to start the first leg of our U.S. *Californication* tour. I had Louie hustle me up a bunch of detox medication—sleeping pills, muscle relaxants, the works. I was so weak, I don't know how I managed to play that first show in Minneapolis. I didn't really rise to the occasion, but I didn't collapse, either. This tour was the first time that we were using two tour buses for the band. John and Flea shared one, and Chad and I were in the other. We hit the highway, and in a few days I was feeling much better.

After about a week, Yohanna came out for a visit, which was good, because we probably needed each other to rebound onto getting sober again. But she seemed changed. Even though the drugs had been a consensual situation, she was extra pissed off at everything. One night we took a cab to a meeting on the outskirts of the town where we were staying, but when we tried to go back later, there was a thunderstorm and no cabs were available. Yohanna was furious, whining about the weather and the car service. She wound up storming off into the pouring rain by herself. It was as if she thought the weather was out to get her. Or it was my fault. She was hard to get along with, but she was obviously in pain and tortured by the setback.

By April 1, thanks to constant sweating and exercise, I was feeling like a million bucks again. On this tour we were really punching the clock and going to work, driving down the highway and not even knowing where we were. We rolled through Nebraska, Iowa, Missouri, Oklahoma, Arkansas, and Texas that spring. I was still rooming with Chad, so our tour bus wasn't particularly festive, but it was a great place for relaxing and reading and talking to Yohanna on the phone.

At that stage of my life, I was monogamous. I found out that being monogamous on the road was similar to being sober on the road. When you're sober, you're impervious to the drugs and the dealers and the people getting high and the parties. It's almost like there's a field of protection around you, and that scene doesn't even enter your radar. The same can be said of women. I was never tempted. When I look at it objectively, in hindsight, there were a lot of girls around, but I was detached from their sirenisms. I remember sitting on the crew bus with tons of girls who were clearly there to have fun. You can tell by the way they're dressed and the way their tits are hanging out and the way they're sitting next to you. They'd say, "Come on, you're in town. Let's go romp around," but I'd reply, "Okay, good night, everybody. Nice to see you. I'm off to call my girlfriend."

At the end of June, the band got an offer we couldn't refuse: to play for Paul Allen, the cocreator of Microsoft, at the opening of his Rock and Roll museum in Seattle. Allen had gotten Frank Gehry to design this incredible new building. To me, it looked as if Gehry had taken a hundred-foot-tall beer can and crushed it into the shape of a woman and then made a building out of it. It was sexy, flowing metal curves, more like a giant sculpture than a building.

We didn't play well that day, due to some technical snafus, so to save the experience, we broke out the socks for our encore. It was nostalgic to strip down with John. We hadn't done the socks with him since the *Mother's Milk* era. Afterward, there was a party in the museum. Chad was the first person to try one of the interactive exhibits, and it turned out that it was broken. But Chad was a little drunk at the time, and to this day, the curator of the museum is convinced that the Red Hot Chili Peppers got drunk and trashed his place, which, of course, we didn't.

We did another one-off, this time a charity concert for children, at the behest of Pearl Jam in Seattle late in June. I had a short break before the next leg of our tour, and I lost my mind and went out on a weeklong drug tear. There was no major event that precipitated it, other than I had time on my hands, but I hadn't started any real getting-well process for myself. I'd kept going out and coming back without addressing the issue of recovery. On June 27, it was time to report back for leg four of our tour, so there I was again, skinny and weak.

I got through the next three legs of the tour without slipping. We finished the U.S. tour, and my work was done, so it was time to start digging my grave again. The only commitment I had was to a VH1 awards show in November, so I started using until a few days before the show and then stopped, did a two-day detox using Ultram—the stuff that took me out in the first place—and Mickey Moused my way through the VH1 show.

Yohanna was understanding of my struggles, but thank God, she wasn't about to go down that road herself, which was a testament to her spiritual awakening and her commitment to sanity. It was a real blessing that she didn't follow me, because oftentimes, people go out together and one comes back and the other doesn't. Or both of them never do.

At the beginning of December, Yohanna had to go back to New York on business, which was a recipe for disaster. No work, no girlfriend, no commitments: I went hog wild. December was a pretty ugly month, because for twenty days in a row, I kept telling myself, "I'm going to do this just one more day, and tomorrow I'll definitely quit." Yohanna came home and had to deal with this maniac in her life. It was a hard ride; I just couldn't get back. At some point I left the house and found a new motel, the Paradise, downtown on Sunset. The front of the place was drenched in purple neon light, which made it incredibly attractive in the seediest possible way.

Once again the troops were mobilized. Louie and Bob Forest started scouring all my haunts. The ironic part was that Bob lived half a block from the Paradise, so on one of their reconnaissance missions, they drove past the motel and bingo! They spotted my motorcycle. It's funny how the mind of a dope fiend works. Later, Bob told me that when he saw my bike parked there, he was instantly jealous, because he had passed that motel a million times, thinking, "If only I could check in there and do speedballs for a couple of days." He'd been clean for years, he had a beautiful girl who loved him. He wasn't lying or stealing or being a miserable scourge, he was a productive, contributing, loving, giving member of society, but when he drove by, it was "If I could only check in there. That purple light looks so inviting."

When Louie knocked on my door, I knew I was busted again. I asked him for half an hour, and he said he'd wait in the parking lot, so I finished up the heroin and stepped out to face the music. I was taken aback to see John out there, sitting in his black Mercedes. He was so loving and concerned.

"We're going back to Louie's house to talk," he said. I got on my bike, and we caravaned over to Louie and Sherry's place. I had done my running by then and was ready to be intervened upon. I was so high that I wasn't that bummed out. I wanted to apologize to Yohanna, but she wasn't having any of it. It was one of the rare occasions when I deserved the trouble she was giving me.

I spent the night at Louie's, since they were afraid that I'd run off again. I wasn't much of a pill detoxer, but I asked Louie to call some doctors and line me up some pills. I didn't want to be the suffering, shivering, sleepless, muscle-aching guy. The plan was for me to go to Christmas at my mom's and head for Saint Bart's in the Caribbean and get healthy. Our next commitment was to play a huge festival in Rio, but that wasn't until January 21. It was the same old broken record, the pipe dream of going somewhere warm and getting straight and then going back out to work and fulfill my professional responsibilities. The fact was, if I didn't get better, I wouldn't have any professional responsibilities. You can't start and stop and expect everything to be okay, because there will be a day when you go to stop and you can't. Every relapse is the worst one, but this one was the longest of the bunch, and the idea that I was causing Yo so much emotional anguish was weighing heavily on me, even though I was trying to ignore it.

Our relationship was shaky to begin with. A certain amount of volatility and drama can be healthy and keep things fun and interesting if you're willing at any moment during a fight to say, "This means nothing. I love you, let's forget about it." We didn't have that ability. I eventually wanted us to go there, I wanted less drama, but we never evolved into that. Being with Yohanna was hard. She was probably the girl I loved the most of all my girlfriends, but also the toughest one to make things work out with. If I had put that much effort into any of my other relationships, I'd be married with five kids now.

Yohanna was too pissed off to go to Michigan with me, which was fine, because I was going to be a drooling Mongoloid for a couple of days, pill-detoxed out. But my mom was happy I was home, and it was nice to hang out with my sister Jenny and her boyfriend, Kevin. By the night of December 23, I had run out of my sleeping pills and muscle relaxants. It was pretty scary, because I had no buffers and couldn't get much sleep.

The next night was Christmas Eve. It may sound like something out of Dickens, but I had a moment of clarity about my using that night. It wasn't the first time. Years earlier, when I was still living at the Outpost office building on Hollywood Boulevard, I had been shooting coke for a couple of days and was in a bit of a cloud when I walked out of my room into the hallway. There was a huge floor-to-ceiling window in the hall, and I looked out of it and saw a sliver of the Hollywood sky. I stared at the sky, and for the first time in my life, a voice went off in my head: "You have no power over what happens in your life. Drugs dictate exactly what you're going to do. You've taken your hands off the steering wheel, and you're going wherever the drug world takes you."

That had never changed. The feeling would well up inside of me, and no matter how much I loved my girl or my band or my friends or my family, when that siren song "Go get high now" started playing in my head, I was off.

Now it was Christmas Eve and I was raw, without a single grain of medication in me. I drove over to a meeting in Grand Rapids. Before I entered the building, I paused and considered my choices. I could turn around and drive down to the ghetto. I knew the precise corner, I'd seen the dealers, so I could go cop some dope and get high in a matter of minutes. Or I could walk through those doors and turn my life over to a power higher than myself, and start walking out of the woods of my dependency.

I saw what I had been doing and where I'd been, and I didn't want to succumb to that kind of energy any longer. Giving myself up to a higher power was easy: I'd had so many experiences all over the world when I communed with a power greater than myself.

I walked into that meeting and announced myself as a newcomer and was welcomed with open arms. And I recommitted myself to recovery, just as I had done on August 1, 1988, when I went to my first rehab. I made the full-on commitment to getting better, no waiting for the right time, no "if I don't like the way things are going," no back doors. December 24, 2000, is my sobriety date, which is a festive holiday date, and very uncommon. Most dope fiends get loaded for the rest of the holidays and then get sober after New Year's.

I had called Yohanna the day before and asked her to come out for Christmas and then to Saint Bart's with me. She agreed, even though she was still mad at me. She flew into Grand Rapids, and I went to pick her up at the airport. Not only was I ashamed for having done what I'd done and what I'd put her through, but I was also terribly insecure about everything at this point, because I was torn up. She was plain pissed off. We hadn't even gotten out of the airport before we got into a Mexican standoff. We weren't fighting, but we were just so angry at each other. We ended up sitting on opposite benches in the waiting room.

"Are you sure you even wanted to come here?" I asked.

"No, I'd be happy to get right back on the next plane and go home," she said.

"Then you should."

"Then I will."

"Great, take your ticket and go talk to the lady, and adios."

We sat there for an hour, going back and forth. There was no way on earth I was going to let her get on a plane and fly away. I don't think she would have, but that was the way we were acting. To add to the general absurdity, I had accidentally taken a large dose of Niacin, thinking I was taking a different liver-cleansing herb, so my face was beet red. Finally, we stopped the foolishness and went home. We spent the next few days in Michigan, trying to become friends again, but it was rough. There was a lot of stuff that felt unresolved and strained between us. Though I'd been there with her when she was using and had to forgive her and go forward, she wasn't having an easy time saying, "Okay, you're a sick motherfucker, but you're willing to get sober now, so let's lighten up on each other." She was still holding it against me.

We flew to Saint Bart's, where we were going to share a boat with ten other people, an idea I would never recommend in retrospect, especially when you're not feeling your best. It didn't go that well down on the island. I'd had some shift of consciousness and was looking to move in a positive direction with respect to the energy I was putting out, but Yohanna was stuck on being pissed about everything. At one point, I'd either eaten some bad food or some residual toxins were coming out of me; I felt horrible and crawled into bed in our cabin. Everyone was going on a side trip for the day, but I couldn't get up and I couldn't eat, so I asked Yohanna if she could just hang out with me and be together and watch movies in bed.

"No, I want to go and do the activities with all the other people," she said, and left.

I had another moment of clarity when I thought, "I don't care how much weird stuff we've been through, I've been so good to her on so many levels. I've taken care of her to the best of my ability, but she doesn't have the capacity to take care of me when I need her. She's not a giving person, and she can't be my girlfriend." I made a decision in my mind to end it. But I didn't want to freak her out or ruin the vacation, so I didn't tell her, I just let her know that I wasn't happy. I was also willing to be proven wrong.

On New Year's Eve, we went to a party on a yacht, and Yohanna busted my balls all night. There was a Basquiat painting on this boat, and I was standing there admiring it when two nannies came up to me. They were frumpy and a bit homely, but they were acting flirty toward me. I was in no way interested, so I bantered with them for a minute, no fucking big deal. But Yohanna had been watching and swooped in as soon as they left. "Why were you flirting with those girls?"

"I was looking at a painting, and two wenches came up and interrupted me, so I made a few jokes and sent them on their way. That's not flirting," I explained.

That was it. She wouldn't talk to me for the rest of the night. There we were, under the stars on a beautiful island, and she would not give up this imaginary fight. That solidified my decision.

The next day we got on a plane to go home. It was hard, because I loved her like crazy, and the idea of being alone did not appeal to me. Plus, I didn't have the slightest interest in any other girls. But I didn't want to live with the constant discontentment. So I turned to her and said, "Yo, this is over between us. It's not working. I don't want to do this anymore, so you're going to have to move out."

She didn't try to discuss things in any depth. She just wanted to know where she was supposed to live. I suggested she move in with her sponsor, and when we got back to L.A., she did.

I was terrified to be starting afresh without this girl to whom I had dedicated my life. But it was also a relief that I didn't have to tiptoe around on eggshells and be afraid of a nanny coming up and talking to me. Little did Yohanna know, I was never unfaithful to her, but if I acted nice to a strange girl, I'd pay for days.

When I got back, I threw myself into recovery and started going to meetings and reaching out to people. I must have been sober for a week and a half when I got a call that a friend of mine who had been sober was back out on the streets, homeless, hopeless, helpless, hustling, and losing at every turn. Everyone had been trying to reach him, to no avail, so I called and left a message on his cell phone, saying, "Hey, there's a whole big life of fun and you're missing it all. Come on back and give me a call." He called the next day, and I took him to a meeting and we got sober together. He thought I sounded so happy and prosperous that I must have been sober for years, so he was shocked to learn I had about two weeks under me.

I had lent Yohanna our car, so I bought a new one. Then I moved out of my apartment. Any space that's been used repeatedly by you and your girlfriend doesn't have a nice collection of vibes. I was lucky to rent the coolest house of all time. It was Dick Van Patten's old house, high up in the Hollywood Hills, an old Craftsman house that was the first one built on the hill back in the roaring '20s. It had been occupied by the person who watched out for fires, because it had a vantage point that went from the Cahuenga Pass to the Valley, and all the way from downtown L.A. to the ocean. It was the insanest, most panoramic view of all time. And it was a beautiful, refreshing place to start a new life.

I had a new house, a new car, and no girlfriend. The week I moved in, a bunch of my sober friends started a Wednesday brunch gathering. We met first at Musso and Frank's, a terrific old-school restaurant on Hollywood Boulevard, but when the weather got nicer, we moved to Joseph's Café, where we sat outside and talked basketball, music, politics, girls, and sobriety. Then we'd all go to a nearby meeting. Pete Weiss and Dick Rude joined up. Flea came to the brunches but skipped the meetings. This Wednesday group was a significant part of my new sober thrust. When the weekend would roll around and I might be tempted to get high, I'd remember, "Nope, gotta be at Joseph's on Wednesday. The guys are counting on me."

The meeting we went to was on Yucca and Gower, a meeting where there was an eclectic mix of homeless people, transvestites, and Hollywood weirdos. I took a commitment to set up the chairs for the meeting, so I'd get there half an hour early. I did that for a year, and that also kept me sober, because if I went out and got high, who would set up for the meeting?

That first week in January 2001 was the occasion of another renewal of life for me. Back on my birthday in November, Guy O, who is one crafty gift giver, knew that I'd been talking about getting a dog for years. He also knew that I loved Rhodesian ridgebacks. I came home that day, and there was a little red wagon on my doorstep, with a stuffed animal inside it and a photograph of the most beautiful Rhodesian ridgeback ever. The attached note said, "Your puppy will be ready the first week in January."

Guy had found the best California breeders, in a little mountain town called Julian, about an hour inland from San Diego. Dick Rude and I drove down there to get my dog. I was the last person to pick up a puppy, but the owners had chosen the firstborn, biggest, strongest male and set him aside for me. He was also born the first week in November, so he'd been there for a couple of months and had gotten attached to the lady who ran the farm. My dog looked at me when I walked in, like "Oh no, what are you doing here? I live with this lady. I hope you don't think you're going to take me away."

He was so afraid to leave the safety of his home and this big, loving woman who cared for him that he looked destroyed. I picked him up and said, "Dude, we're moving to Hollywood. You're my guy." I had Dick drive home, and I sat him on my lap and held him the whole way back. I tried to tell him it would be okay, but he was so afraid of this big wide world he was facing, especially when we started hitting traffic on the 405.

He came up to that house with me, and I had to go through the massive ordeal of training him from scratch. Ridgebacks are the most willful of all breeds, and I was crate-training him. He went through diarrhea fits and barking fits and got skunked three times in the backyard. It was a constant job, raising this crazy puppy, but we were also having the time of our lives, playing in the backyard, with him smelling flowers and chasing insects and playing with sticks. I named him Buster, after Buster Keaton, one of my all-time favorite comedians.

Sometime in the middle of January, I met a new girl. I wasn't in the mood or the mode to go womanizing, but I went out with Guy one night to a club and saw this extra-fine girl from across the room. There was a line of guys waiting to talk to her, but I just cut the line, took her away, and sat her down on a couch. That line waited for the rest of the night, but they didn't get any face time with her, especially after she told me she'd had a dream that we would meet and spend time together. Her name was Cammie. She was an actress who lived in a Laurel Canyon house with a lesbian *Playboy* centerfold and Paris Hilton. She was wonderful and beautiful and smart and funny, and she started staying over at my house and became my girl.

About a month later, on a Sunday morning, I went to a meeting in West Hollywood. I was supposed to meet Cammie later that day for lunch. At the meeting, by sheer chance, I saw Yohanna. I hadn't seen her for about a month, and the last time we were together was not a pleasant time. I'd gone to visit her at her friend's house. I knew she didn't have a job, so as a friendly gesture, I offered her some money. A pretty damn friendly amount of money, an amount of money that no one has ever offered me for no reason. I figured she could use it to pay rent and expenses and maybe get a little car.

"I think I better see a lawyer," she said.

"About what?"

"I think I could get more money than that," she said.

"What are you talking about, 'get more money'? This is a gift. There was no marriage here. You haven't contributed anything. I've only ever helped you, you never helped me back," I said.

"A friend of mine said I could probably get some money if I got a lawyer," she explained.

I was mortified. I ended up dealing with some lawyer who proposed that I give her a certain amount of money, but I told him to forget it. It was a chump-assed, bullshit move to pull on someone who was trying to help you out. She came up with crazy stuff like "I moved out here and left my home for you."

"What? You were sleeping on a couch in a fucking ghetto. I put you through school, and then you left your couch to move into a penthouse." I wasn't buying any of it. But Yohanna seemed confused and scared, so I forgave her and went on with my life. There was no residual "Oh, I miss that girl." It was like a closed chapter, done, moved on.

Or so I thought. I was so happy to see her at the meeting that at the break, when everyone left the room, I rushed over to where she was sitting, sat down next to her, and started giving her kisses on the cheek. It was an impulsive reaction to seeing her and her smile and her eyes and her smooth white cheeks. We started kissing and cuddling and talking, and five minutes later, I was kissing her on the mouth.

The whole floodgates came rushing open out of nowhere. I had a new girlfriend, my life had changed, this girl was of the past. But here we were, making plans to see each other later that day.

I was so excited. I drove straight to Cammie's house, because I didn't want to lie to her or leave her hanging.

"I'm really, really sorry, but something fucking totally unexpected happened to me today, and it has to do with my ex-girlfriend. I think I'm going to be seeing her, so I can't see you," I said.

That night I met Yohanna at a one-year sober birthday celebration for a friend of hers at El Cholo, a Mexican restaurant on

Western. I felt like I had fallen in love and was on my first date with this girl. I was on my best behavior, and every glance she threw me made my heart flutter. Something weird had happened: Not only had I fallen back in love with this girl, it was like starting from the beginning. We ran with it, and she moved right into the house. My house had three stories, and I'd moved my stuff into the upstairs area, so I suggested that she move her things into the bottom story, which had a big bedroom and bathroom and huge closets with a dressing area. It was much nicer than the upstairs. Paradise didn't last long. Down the line, she started complaining, "Why do I have to have the downstairs dressing area? Why can't I have the upstairs?" It made no sense. Give her the continent and she wanted the hemisphere.

But at first our love was still in full bloom. The band started working on our next album in March 2001. That month I organized a family trip to Hawaii. I took my mom, both of my sisters, their husbands, and my adorable little nephew Jackson to Kauai. I wanted Yo to come, but she had a work commitment. My feelings for her inspired a song, "Body of Water," which was a tribute to her spirit and her inner energy, which always had me captivated.

In March we got some tragic news. One of my closest friends and mentors, Gloria Scott, was diagnosed with lung cancer. Her friends quickly rallied around her and tried to find her whatever treatments could help her, but there was a huge need for cash, because she had zero. So we played a benefit for her (and also for Huntington's disease, an affliction that had struck the family of Flea's longtime ex-girlfriend) and raised the needed cash. Since Gloria had always jokingly referred to Neil Young as her higher power, I put in a call to ask Neil if by any crazy chance he could perform.

"You tell me when, and I'll be there with Crazy Horse," he said.

By the night of the show, Gloria's condition had worsened, but she made it to the concert, and I was thrilled to introduce her to Neil. It was a magical moment to see these two people come together.

We got Gloria a little apartment on the water in Venice Beach, because she was always about the ocean, but she'd lived inland in Venice for thirty years. We hired a nurse and paid for her treatments, but the doctors had caught the cancer too late. I got to the hospital in time to say the painful "I know that you're dying, so you have to know that I love you." She didn't want to die in the hospital, so they brought her back home to the beach, and she faded away.

From "Venice Queen"

And now it's time for you to go
You taught me most of what I know
Where would I be without you Glo
G-L-O-R-I-A
Is love my friend, my friend, my friend

I see you standing by the sea
The waves you made will always be
A kiss goodbye before you leave
G-L-O-R-I-A
Is love my friend, my friend, my friend

Writing *By the Way,* our next album, was a whole different experience from *Californication.* John was back to himself and brimming with confidence. So we did the same thing we always did. Back to the Swing House, four guys holed up in a room with guitars and drums and mikes, playing every day for hours. We started finding some magic and some music and some riffs and some rhythms and some jams and some grooves, and we recorded it and added to it and subtracted from it and pushed it around and put melodies to it. I started collecting words by the score and listening and getting inspired by what the guys were playing.

All this time, I tried to make it work with Yohanna. She had started her own clothing line. She was productive and creative, but we weren't clicking as a two-person singular entity. We even went to a couples counselor, a practical, smart, unbiased woman who gave us some tools to work with, but nothing ever amounted from it; the changes that needed to happen didn't happen.

Sometime that summer, we half broke up. Yohanna moved into the downstairs bedroom, in theory, until she found her own place. I wasn't going to kick her out again. But of course, that led to late-night visits between floors. The forbidden fruit of liaisons in the downstairs bedroom on top of piles of her clothing did wonders for our sex life for a while. But eventually, we split up, and I rented a small bungalow for her in Beverly Hills. I let her keep the car until the lease expired, and she returned it to me without any door handles or stereo or carpeting. It was symbolic of our relationship. I tried to do her a favor, and she returned it destroyed and told me that the insurance would cover it.

Even after she left the house, our relationship continued off and on. Instead of relapsing with drugs, I'd relapse with Yohanna. We went back to Saint Bart's after Christmas in 2001 and rented a house on the beach. One day she wanted to learn how to surf, so we paddled out about a quarter of a mile until we got into the break, but the waves were big as houses, too big to learn on. We found ourselves in the crunch zone, where the waves were coming over us, so we held our breath and waited till the set went by. In the upheaval, the leash on Yohanna's surfboard had snapped, so I swam over and gave her my board. We finally made it back to shore. But in the confusion of the storm-swelled waves, we made the mistake of coming back in over a coral reef instead of going through the channel. The good news was that we were alive, but the bad news was that we had to walk over this coral reef, and the coral had barnacles and sea urchins. Even little waves were enough to push you around, so we were getting poked and sea urchined, the spines of which break off, are impossible to remove, and cause you much discomfort.

Yohanna started yelling hysterically at me, as if I wanted her to get urchined. I spent the next two days calling doctors and rushing to pharmacies to get her some relief, but she was crazed. She was so mean to me the whole trip that, once again, I realized she wasn't the girl for me.

While we were still in Saint Bart's, I reached a breaking point. "Yo, you've got to go home," I told her. "I won't sit here and be yelled at. I've done my best to make it a pleasant journey for you and to share my life with you, but you're impossible to be with." I sent her the hell home, and we broke up again. Sometime the next year, I relapsed. I'd keep getting back with her because I missed her friendship, but I always got the same result, never any progress. Four years into the relationship, she was as smolderingly distraught over the littlest things in life. She'd lie there steaming in bed over a fight the size of a ladybug. I would apologize and say, "Let's forget about it, my bad. I love you, I care about you, I want you to be happy, let's enjoy this love and this life." But she wouldn't let go, she wouldn't choose to be happy.

Even all my troubles with Yohanna couldn't derail my sobriety. My Wednesday breakfast meeting was grounding, and everyone got into the idea of being of service. We were picking people up and taking them to meetings and bringing new guys into that particular circle so they could see sobriety wasn't about giving up the party, it was just creating a new, saner party. Having a moment of clarity was one thing; I'd had moments like that before. It had to be followed with a dedicated push of daily exercise. It's a trite axiom, but practice *does* make perfect. If you want to be a strong swimmer or an accomplished musician, you have to practice. It's the same with sobriety, though the stakes are higher. If you don't practice your program every day, you're putting yourself in a position where you could fly out of the orbit one more time.

The good news is that being in recovery is a blast for me. I love going to meetings, I love hearing people speak. Some of the speakers are boring old twats with nothing to say, but some of them are truly angels. At one meeting I saw this big heavyset Mexican transsexual, in full woman's garb, tell her life story. She was up there cracking jokes and singing and talking and sharing the message of being of service, and she positively glowed. When she left, I knew that I'd seen an angel. I've seen the same thing with cowboys from Montana and preachers from down south, all types of people who used to be the walking dead and now are carrying this message of light and love and recovery. Meetings are a gas. It's like a combination of a free seminar and a lecture and a social. Sometimes there are even hot girls. And people are funny and creative and festive. As the book says, "We are not a glum lot."

All those years when I was going in and out, I'd lie to myself and say, "You're just relapsing, you're not going back to use for good. This is a temporary condition." It always went on longer than I planned, and I was able to come back, but now I knew that I had come back for a purpose—it wasn't because I outwitted drug addiction. It was because something, somewhere, wanted me alive so I could be a part of creating something beautiful and helping somebody else.

I'd made the decision to stop doing drugs many times before, but I never followed up with the daily maintenance, the cultivation of a path to a spiritual awakening. I think that anyone who comes in and works all of the steps and goes to meetings and is of constant love and service is guaranteed to stay sober. But anyone who comes in like I did in the past and picks and chooses and thinks, "I'll do it some days, I won't do it others. I'll work some steps, but I won't work the others. I'll take the call sometimes, but sometimes I'm too busy," is doomed to failure. You can't buy seven tenths of the way into the program and expect to get seven tenths back; you get nothing back unless you give yourself completely.

Another thing that I think is genius about the program is that they realize you can't preach sobriety or try to make converts out of alcoholics. What's crucial is that you take care of yourself and in doing so become a program of attraction, rather than promotion. The minute you say "Hey, *this* is what you should be doing" to an alcoholic or a drug addict, nothing will come of it. If you just do your thing, then someone will see it and think, "That guy used to throw up on his trousers, but he looks like he's enjoying himself now." There's no alcoholic in the world who wants to be told what to do. Alcoholics are sometimes described as egomaniacs with inferiority complexes. Or, to be cruder, a piece of shit that the universe revolves around.

Which is okay, because there's a way to deal with that. You're feeling like shit? Go get out of yourself and do something for someone else, voilà, you don't feel like shit anymore. You're confused and you're driving yourself crazy? Go call a guy who's got three days sober and has no clue what to do. The minute you get out of your self-centered mind-set, you're instantly freed of your own pain. The trick to staying sober is to constantly be of service to another alcoholic. It's like perpetual motion. All these people freely gave you what was given to them, and now you get to give it to someone else. It's a constant source of energy, like recharging a battery, only there's no pollution or toxic runoff.

The reason the program is so successful is because alcoholics help other alcoholics. I've never met a Normie (our lingo for a person who doesn't have a problem with drugs or alcohol) who could even conceive of what it's like to be an alcoholic. Normies are always going, "There's this new pill you can take and you won't want to shoot heroin anymore." That shows a fundamental misunderstanding of alcoholism and drug addiction. These aren't just physical allergies, they're obsessions of the mind and maladies of the spirit. It's a threefold disease. And if it's partly a spiritual malady, then there's a spiritual cure.

When I say spiritual, I'm not talking about chanting or reading Eastern philosophy. I'm talking about setting up the chairs at a meeting, picking up another alcoholic and driving him across town to a meeting. That's a spiritual lifestyle, being willing to admit that you don't know everything and that you were wrong about some things. It's about making a list of all the people you've harmed, either emotionally or physically or financially, and going back and making amends. That's a spiritual lifestyle. It's not a fluffy ethereal concept.

My friend Bob Forrest is a spiritual person. He doesn't go to church and he doesn't talk about God and he doesn't go do charity events on weekends, but he'll sit and talk for hours to a guy in jail who can't stop smoking crack. That's curing Bob of his spiritual malady, because he's willing to do something that's not really for him, it's for this other guy. He's not doing it with the expectation of getting anything out of it, but as a by-product, he is.

In the song "Otherside" on *Californication,* I wrote, "How long, how long will I slide/Separate my side/I don't, I don't believe it's bad." I don't believe that drug addiction is inherently bad. It's a really dark and heavy and destructive experience, but would I trade my experience for that of a normal person? Hell no. It was ugly, and there is nothing I know that hurts as bad, but I wouldn't trade it for a minute. It's that appreciation of every emotion in the spectrum that I live for. I don't go out of my way to create it, but I have found a way to embrace all of it. It's not about putting down any of these experiences, because now that I've had them, and now that I'm almost four years sober, I'm in a position to be of service to hundreds of other suffering people. All of those relapses, every one of those setbacks that would seem like unnecessary additions to an already tortured experience, are all going to be meaningful. I'm going to meet some other person along the way who was clean for some time and can't get clean again, and I'll be able to say, "I was there, I did that for years, I was going back and forth, and now . . ."

I went with Guy O to a kabbalah course the other night, and the lesson was about the four aspects of the human ego, which are symbolized by fire, water, air, and earth. Water represents the excessive desire for pleasure, and I'm a water sign, and that's been my whole life. I've wanted to feel pleasure to the point of insanity. They call it getting high, because it's wanting to know that higher level, that godlike level. You want to touch the heavens, you want to feel glory and euphoria, but the trick is that it takes work. You can't buy it, you can't get it on a street corner, you can't steal it or inject it or shove it up your ass, you have to earn it. When I was a teenager and shooting speedballs, I wasn't thinking, "I want to know God," but deep down inside, maybe I did. Maybe I wanted to know what that light was all about and was taking the shortcut. That was the story of my life, even going back to my childhood in Michigan, when I'd get home from school by going through a neighbor's backyard and jumping a fence. It didn't matter if I got bitten by a dog or I ripped my pants on the fence post or I poked myself in the eye with a tree branch that I was crawling over, it was all about the shortcut. My whole life I took the shortcut, and I ended up lost.

Things are good now. Buster and I share a nice house. I've got a terrific group of supportive friends. And when it's time to go out on the road, I'm surrounded by another group of supportive people. One of my main soul mates is Sat Hari. She came into our world in May 2000, when Flea brought her on tour to administer intravenous ozone therapy to him. Sat Hari is a nurse, an American Sikh, a sweet, incredibly sheltered, turban-wearing young lady. She looks like a female version of Flea, with the same gap-toothed smile, the same shape of face, the same color eyes, the same little pug nose. She's maternal and she's warm and she's loving and she's unassuming, a complete breath of fresh air and female energy, and I don't mean sexual energy, at least not for me. For me she's like a sister and mother and caretaker and nurse all in one.

Sat Hari endeared herself to everybody in the band and the crew, and she became the den mother to the entire organization. Everyone used her as their ultimate confidante, spilling their guts to her all day and all night about their deepest, darkest, most untellable secrets. We've all had an impact on her, too. She was a controlled, subservient Sikh who was told what she could and could not do, who she could and couldn't talk to. We showed her a new world of meeting all these freethinking people who were out dancing and loving life. She flourished as a person and came out of her shell. During the *By the Way* tour, Sat Hari and John and I shared a bus, and it was a cozy, moving cocoon of happiness.

We extended that vibe into the arenas that we played. It was clear after our first few tours that the backstage areas were always cold, stark, fluorescent-lit concrete tombs, places where you wouldn't want to spent two minutes. So for the *Californication* tour, we hired a woman named Lyssa Bloom who had a knack for beautifying these rooms. She laid down rugs, put up tapestries, covered the fluorescent lights, put in a portable stereo system, and set up a table of fresh fruits and vegetables and nuts and teas.

So now we hang out backstage before the show, and John, who became the official DJ of the area, programs the music. He and Flea get out their guitars and practice, and I do my vocal warm-ups. Then I make everyone tea and write out the set list. Sat Hari comes in and gives us ozone, and then we stretch on the floor and do a little meditation. We have all of these grounding rituals that keep growing and getting better and better.

Our final ritual before we go onstage is the soul circle. It's funny how that's evolved over the years. When we were this brash young band of Hollywood knuckleheads, we would get in a circle and slap one another in the face right before we went on. That got the juices flowing, for sure. Now we get in a circle and hold hands and do some meditation together, getting into why we're there and what we need to be together. Someone might chime in with "Let's do this one for the Gipper" or "There's a thunderstorm outside, let's tap into that." There are times when Flea's the one to give us little words of encouragement. Sometimes it's up to me to crack a joke or make up a rhyme. Lately, John has become the most vocal member of the soul circle. Chad doesn't usually instigate, but he's there with a "hear, hear" thing.

All of these rituals ground me. But ironically, what grounds me constantly is my obsession with drugs. It's funny—that first five-and-a-half-year period when I got sober, I never had any urgings to do drugs. The uncontrollable obsession that I'd experienced from the time I was eleven years old just vanished the first time I got clean. It was a true miracle. When I came out of my first rehab, the idea of getting high was a foreign concept to me. I could have sat there and stared a big mountain of cocaine in the face, and it would have meant nothing to me; a month before, I would have been shaking and sweating from the physical reaction alone. The way the sneaky motherfucker got his foot back in the door was through those experiences with prescribed painkillers.

Once I started relapsing, I would never get the gift of being relieved from the obsession of doing drugs again. This might seem like a tragic curse, but I look at the bright side of it: Now I have to work harder at my sobriety. When I was relieved of the obsession, I was doing very little work. Now I have no choice but to be more giving and more diligent and more committed, because a week doesn't go by when I'm not visited by the idea of getting loaded.

For the first year of my newfound sobriety, all of 2001, the feeling of wanting to get high came to me every day. Especially later in the year, after Yohanna moved out, it got so bad that I couldn't sleep. One night I got the closest I'd come to going back out there. I was home alone and there was a full moon out. I was writing the songs for *By the Way,* everything was going well, and I was feeling inspired. I took a stroll outside, and the night was clear, and I could see the alluring lights of downtown.

And I got ready to throw it all away one more time. I packed my little weekend backpack and left a note for my assistant to take care of Buster. I got my car keys and walked out of the house. I got as far as the porch and looked up at the moon, looked out at the city, then looked at my car and my backpack and thought, "I can't do it. I can't throw it away one more time," and I went back inside.

In the past, once those wheels were set in motion, forget about it—floods, earthquakes, famines, locusts, nothing would have stopped me from my abhorrent rounds. But now I'd proved to my-self that I could live with my obsession until it went away. I was willing to accept the fact that I thought about getting high on a regular basis, that I could watch a beer commercial and see that sweaty bottle with the cap popping off and actually want a beer (and still not drink one).

The good news is that by the second year, those cravings were about half as frequent, and by the third year, half as much again. I'm still a little bent, a little crooked, but all things considered, I can't complain. After all those years of all kinds of abuse and crashing into trees at eighty miles an hour and jumping off buildings and living through overdoses and liver disease, I feel better now than I did ten years ago. I might have some scar tissue, but that's all right, I'm still making progress. And when I do think, "Man, a fucking motel room with a couple of thousand dollars' worth of narcotics would do me right," I just look over at my dog and remember that Buster's never seen me high.